Governing California in the Twenty-First Century

SIXTH EDITION

THE POLITICAL DYNAMICS OF THE GOLDEN STATE

J. Theodore Anagnoson
California State University, Los Angeles

Gerald Bonetto
Vice President, Government Affairs, Printing Industries of California

J. Vincent Buck
California State University, Fullerton

Richard E. DeLeon
San Francisco State University

Jolly Emrey
University of Wisconsin–Whitewater

James J. Kelleher
California State University, Dominguez Hills

Nadine Koch
California State University, Los Angeles

W. W. NORTON & COMPANY
INDEPENDENT PUBLISHERS SINCE 1923

Copyright © 2017, 2015, 2013, 2011, 2009, 2008 by W. W. Norton & Company, Inc.

All rights reserved.

Printed in Canada.

The text of this book is composed in Berlin with the display set in Interstate.

Book design: Sandra Watanabe

Composition: Achorn International

Manufacturing: Marquis Book Printing

Editor: Ann Shin

Associate Editor: Emily Stuart

Editorial Assistant: Shannon Jilek

Project Editor: Tenyia Lee

Managing Editor, College: Marian Johnson

Production Manager, College: Ashley Horna

Marketing Manager, Political Science: Erin Brown

Permissions Manager: Megan Schindel

Permissions Specialist: Bethany Salminen

Photo Editor: Ted Szczepanski

ISBN 978-0-393-60369-9 (pbk.)

W. W. Norton & Company, Inc., 500 Fifth Avenue, New York, N.Y. 10110
www.wwnorton.com

W. W. Norton & Company Ltd., Castle House, 75/76 Wells Street, London W1T 3QT

1 2 3 4 5 6 7 8 9 0

Contents

PREFACE   viii

1 ● California Government: Promise and Practice   1

The California Dream?   2
Why Study California Politics?   2
What Determines the Content and Character of California's Politics?   4
    Who Are Californians?   5
WHO ARE CALIFORNIANS? How Is the California Population Changing?   6
The Crisis of California Politics   9
    The Ease of Passing Initiatives   11
    Term Limits   11
    The Two-Thirds Requirement for Raising Taxes   12
    Lack of Consensus on Fundamental Questions   13
    Reform Ideas   14
Conclusion   15
A Guide to This Book   15
Study Guide   16

2 ● The Constitution and the Progressive Legacy   19

The Rules of the Game: California's Constitution   21
    The 1849 Constitution   22
    The 1879 Constitution   23
    From 1900 to 1917: The Progressive Movement   26
    From 1960 to the Present: Late Revisions   27
WHO ARE CALIFORNIANS? Who Draws the Lines in California?   28
The Progressive Movement and Its Impact on California Politics   29
    Local Politics   29
    State Politics   30
Direct Democracy   32
    Initiative   32
    Referendum   37
    Recall   38
    Debating the Merit of Direct Democracy   39
California's Constitution: Where Are We Now?   40
Study Guide   42

3 ● Interest Groups and the Media in California   47

Character of Interest Groups   48
   Diversity of Interest Groups   49
   Proliferation of Interest Groups   51
Interest-Group Strategies   53
   Lobbyists   53
   Campaign Contributions to Candidates   55
WHO ARE CALIFORNIANS? Who Spends Money in California Politics?   57
   Grassroots Mobilization   58
The Legislature, Bribes, and Scandals   60
   Regulating Campaign Contributions   61
   Clean-Money Elections   64
   Contribution Limits   64
   Conflict-of-Interest Laws   64
The Media   65
   Television   65
   Newspapers   66
   The Internet   67
   Media and Political Campaigns   69
Interest-Group Politics in California: Where Are We Now?   70
Study Guide   71

4 ● Parties and Elections in California   75

Political Parties   76
   The Progressive Impact on Political Parties   76
   The Democratic and Republican Parties in California   77
   Third Parties in California   78
   Party Affiliation of California Voters   79
California's Local Political Cultures from Left to Right   84
Elections in California   87
   The Battle over the Primary   87
   Presidential Primaries: Maximizing California's Clout?   89
   Initiative Campaigns: Direct Democracy or Tool of Special Interests?   91
   The 2003 Gubernatorial Recall Election: A Perfect Political Storm   94
   The 2008 Election: Demographic and Ideological Shifts   94
   The 2010 General Election   95
   The 2012 Primary Election   96
   The 2012 General Election: More Demographic and Ideological Shifts   97
   The 2014 Election   99
   The 2016 Primary Election   100
   The 2016 General Election   100
Campaigning in California   103
   Money and Politics: California Style   104
   Campaign Finance Reform in California   106
Voting in California   107
   How You Can Register to Vote   107
   Who Votes in California?   108
WHO ARE CALIFORNIANS? Who Votes in California?   110
What Reforms Are Needed?   113
Study Guide   113

5 ● The California Legislature 119

Functions 121
  Representation 121
WHO ARE CALIFORNIANS? Who Represents Californians? 123
  Policy Making 124
Members and Districts 125
Elections 126
  Fund-raising 127
  Districting 127
Organization 129
  Leadership 129
  Committees 131
  Staff 131
Legislative Process 133
Differences from U.S. Congress 136
  Term Limits 136
  Item Veto 136
  Apportionment and District Size 137
  Media Visibility 137
  Court Appointments 137
  Filibusters 138
  Initiatives 138
  Seniority 138
Challenges Facing the California Legislature 138
  Money 139
  Term Limits Lead to a Lack of Knowledge and Experience 139
  Partisanship 141
  Gridlock, Minority Rule, and Lack of Accountability 141
  Initiatives 143
California Legislature: Where Are We Now? 144
Study Guide 145

6 ● The Governor and the Executive Branch 149

The Invisible Governor? 150
Formal Powers of the Governor 153
  Appointments 154
  Independent Executive Actions 155
  Commander in Chief 155
  Organizing and Managing the Executive Branch 155
  Budget 157
  Veto and Line-Item Veto 157
  Legislative Powers 158
  Legislative Recommendations 159
  Judicial Powers 159
  Public Roles of the Governor 159
Jerry Brown as Governor 160
WHO ARE CALIFORNIANS? How Does California's Governorship Compare? 163
Structure of the Executive Branch 164
  Personal Staff 164
  The Cabinet and Agency Heads 164

The Plural Elected Executive   166
Agencies and the Bureaucracy   168
California Executive Branch: Where Are We Now?   170
Study Guide   171

7 ● The California Judiciary   175

Structure of the California Judicial System   176
The Lower Courts   176
The Supreme Court   177
Jurisdiction   178
Access to the Court   178
Federalism and the California Courts: The Case of Medical Marijuana   179
Judicial Selection   181
WHO ARE CALIFORNIANS? Who Are California's Judges?   183
Judicial Elections   184
Removing Judges from the Bench   187
Contemporary Issues in the Judiciary   187
Change in the Court   187
Legislative Redistricting   187
Judicial Review and the Statewide Initiative   188
Caseload   189
California Courts: Where Are We Now?   190
Study Guide   192

8 ● The State Budget and Budgetary Limitations   195

How Is the Budget Formed?   197
Executive Proposal   197
Legislative Adoption   199
Gubernatorial Action   200
Implementation   200
Other Groups Involved in the Budget Process   200
What Is in the Budget?   201
Revenues   201
WHO ARE CALIFORNIANS? Where Does California Get Its Revenue?   203
Why Do Revenues Vary So Much?   207
How Well Does the Tax System Function?   207
Is California Overtaxed?   208
Expenditures   209
Budgetary Limitations   212
Recent California Budgets and the Budget Process   213
The California Budgetary Process: Where Are We Now?   214
Study Guide   215

9 ● Local Government   219

**The Legal Framework: Dillon's Rule, Home Rule, and
   Local Powers of Governance   220**
County Governments   222
Legal Framework   223
County Government Organization   224

WHO ARE CALIFORNIANS? Who Lives in California's Counties?   225

   County Government Functions and Responsibilities   226

   Local Agency Formation Commissions   228

City Governments   229

   Legal Framework   229

   Incorporation and Dissolution   229

   City Government Functions and Responsibilities   230

   City Government Revenues and Expenditures   230

   Forms of City Government and the Legacy of Progressive Structural Reforms   231

Special Districts   237

   School and Community College Districts   237

   Nonschool Special Districts   237

   Legal Framework   238

   How Special Districts Are Created   238

   The Advantages and Disadvantages of Special Districts   238

Regional Governments   239

   Regulatory Regional Governments   239

   Advisory Regional Governments   240

California's Community Redevelopment Agencies: The Old and New Models   241

Local Government: Where Are We Now?   242

Study Guide   245

10 ● Public Policy in California   249

Water Policy   252

WHO ARE CALIFORNIANS? Who Gets Water in California?   254

Health Insurance   255

   Employer-Sponsored Insurance   256

   Individual Health Insurance Marketplace   256

   Medi-Cal   256

   Medicare   257

   TRICARE   257

   The Uninsured   257

California's Infrastructure   258

   Highways   258

WHO ARE CALIFORNIANS? How Do Californians Get Around?   260

   Levees   261

   The Future of California's Infrastructure   262

Indian Gaming in California   262

Conclusion   264

Study Guide   265

ANSWER KEY   269

NOTES   270

PHOTO CREDITS   281

INDEX   282

Preface

We began this project over a decade ago with a working title asking whether California's political system and its politics were simply "broken." That is, politicians were caught within a system that was so contradictory in its rules, norms, and mores that budgets couldn't be passed on time or balanced, programs and departments couldn't be managed under the existing set of rules, and citizen expectations were so out of line with the ability of the political system to satisfy them that the level of negativism and cynicism was as bad as could be found anywhere in the nation.

We think after a decade of false and halting starts that the picture needs some modification. California has begun to repair its infrastructure. The state has new incentives for politicians to be less ideologically extreme on the right or the left, in particular the "top two" primary system and the commission that is now drawing new districts for the Assembly, the state Senate, and congressional districts every 10 years after the Census. Decision rules in Sacramento still leave much to be desired, but at least a budget can be passed with majority rule instead of having to obtain a two-thirds vote, a rule that necessitated some votes from the minority party and, unfortunately, some pork projects or other incentives to gain those votes. And the nation's strictest term-limit rules have been modified to allow members of the Assembly or state Senate to serve 12 years in a single house before being "termed out" and forced to seek another office outside the state legislature. Hopefully this will increase the level of expertise available among legislators.

At the same time, we have gone only part of the way toward a political system that would actually "function" and make efficient decisions. There still is no way to adjust the tax system without a two-thirds vote, and California's tax system badly needs modernization; its last overhaul was more than 50 years ago. While the economy has moved toward a services base, California's tax system remains centered on manufacturing, which was more common a half century ago. The income tax relies much too heavily on the capital gains tax, and that in turn creates revenue peaks and valleys that tempt Sacramento politicians to build the periodic surges of revenue into the base and to run deficits when times are tough.

Proposition 13, passed in 1978, caused a massive centralization of authority in Sacramento over the next decade at the expense of cities, counties, and school districts. As a result, local governments have little authority over their own revenue, while state government proved unable to provide local governments with the revenue and authority they needed to deal with the recent recession, financial collapse, and defaulted mortgages that still plague certain areas. This caused a number of local government to go bankrupt, and those that did not were unable to help people in a genuine time of need. In some dire cases, state government cutbacks combined with the revenue-depleting impacts of home mortgage foreclosures, high unemployment, business failures, and grossly overburdened public sector pension and benefit obligations created "perfect storms" of local economic and political conditions that bankrupted cities like Stockton and still threaten others. The state has been unable to help. The drought of 2013–14 exacerbated existing flaws in California's water policy, and while the state government has proposed several solutions, some controversial, the fact remains that the state's demand for water still drastically exceeds its supply.

In these circumstances, the Sixth Edition of *Governing California in the Twenty-First Century* offers a ray of hope but also the reality of a long distance to go. We hope you enjoy our analysis of California's politics as not quite "broken" but not as yet "fixed" either.

This edition continues the "Who Are Californians?" features, presenting visual snapshots of California's politics and people. These infographics, contributed by Melissa Michelson of Menlo College, shine a light on demographic diversity and political behavior in the state.

We divided the writing of this book as follows:

1. California Government: Promise and Practice—Anagnoson (tanagno@calstatela.edu)
2. The Constitution and the Progressive Legacy—Bonetto (gerry@piasc.org) and Anagnoson
3. Interest Groups and the Media in California—Bonetto
4. Parties and Elections in California—Koch (nkoch@calstatela.edu)
5. The California Legislature—Buck (vbuck@fullerton.edu)
6. The Governor and the Executive Branch—Buck
7. The California Judiciary—Emrey (emreyj@uww.edu)
8. The State Budget and Budgetary Limitations—Anagnoson
9. Local Government—DeLeon (rdeleon@sfsu.edu)
10. Public Policy in California—Emrey

There are websites for the fifth and sixth editions of this book. For the fifth edition, go to www.silcom.com/~anag999/g5.html. For the sixth edition site, substitute "g6" (without the quotes) for "g5." The sites contain:

- A link to the publisher's own site for this book.

- A list of *errata*. If you find any error in the book, please email the lead author, J. Theodore Anagnoson, at anag999@silcom.com or tanagno@calstatela.edu.

- Answers to the short answer questions at the end of each chapter.

We have constructed, in addition, a test bank for instructors. To gain access to the test bank, visit wwnorton.com/instructors.

W. W. Norton also offers a formative quizzing tool called InQuizitive for this and other titles. The system includes adaptive multiple choice questions with immediate responses and links to sections of the book online for reference and knowledge reinforcement. We tried several activities from the question bank and liked the feedback and the links. We recommend that you have a look also; you can try a demo at digital.wwnorton.com/govcali6.

We would like to acknowledge the helpful recommendations from professors who have reviewed the book; their comments have assisted us in updating events and materials. For the sixth edition, we thank the following reviewers:

Larry Bensky, California State University, East Bay
Joe Brookshire, College of the Redwoods
Pearl Galano, California State University, Channel Islands
Herbert Gooch, California Lutheran University
Sarah Hill, California State University, Fullerton
Wesley Hussey, Sacramento State University
Alison Keleher, University of California, Santa Barbara
Jamilya Ukudeeva, Cabrillo College
John Vento, Antelope Valley College
Joshua Pryor, California State University, Sacramento

We also thank the several students who have communicated their comments.
We would be glad to hear from you about the book. Please use the email addresses above to communicate with us.

J. Theodore Anagnoson
Professor of Political Science
California State University, Los Angeles

1

California Government: Promise and Practice

WHAT CALIFORNIA GOVERNMENT DOES AND WHY IT MATTERS

In the morning you drive to work on the freeway, stopping first at the gas station on the corner to fill up and to buy an apple from the corner grocery store for a mid-day snack. You then drive across a bridge to get to the university where you are currently taking general education courses. You are already considering what will follow after graduation. Perhaps you'll work for the California Highway Patrol (CHP), a private security guard service, or maybe even in the same grocery store where you stopped for your apple. In the evening, you are ready to relax after a full day of school, so you go out to a restaurant.

How is the government of California relevant to your day? Let's start at the beginning: your car is built to conform to government safety standards. The free-ways are built by the state government, with a mixture of federal and state money, to conform to federal and state standards; traffic is monitored by the CHP. The gas station has to meet local safety regulations, and it uses gasoline that conforms to federal standards for automobiles. The grocery store relies on scales that are certified by county government; both imported and domestic fruit must meet U.S. and state Department of Agriculture standards. The bridge is built by government and is maintained by government (although a large proportion of the bridges nationally and in California are behind on their scheduled maintenance). If you attend a K-12 school, the school must comply with state standards for curricu-lum at each grade level and administer tests to determine whether it is meeting those standards. If you are in higher education, the public university you attend must have a general education program that conforms to state regulations; if you are enrolled in a community college, California State University, or the University of California, the cost of your education is partially subsidized by state funds. (If you attend a private college, you might be receiving federal student aid.) If you eventually go to work for the CHP, you will work under state laws and regulations. The private security service is regulated by the state as well, and the grocery store must conform to state safety standards. The restaurant in which you enjoy your evening meal is inspected periodically by the local government health department, and in some locations, the department will post the summary score (A, B, or C).

The California Dream?

For almost 200 years, the **California dream** has attracted residents from other parts of the United States as well as immigrants from abroad. Governor Arnold Schwarzenegger, in one of his State of the State speeches (2004), said that California represents "an empire of hope and aspiration," a place where "Californians do great things." To some, the California dream is sun and surf; to others, the warm winter season; to still others, a house on the coast amid redwoods and acres of untrammeled wilderness; or to some it is the luxury of three or four cars per family. Many of these dreams can be summed up in the phrases "freedom from restraints" and "freedom from traditions." These are typical themes in statewide elections and gubernatorial State of the State speeches—evoking the image of an older, less crowded California.

A more modern conception of the California dream is finding a way to stick it out here. "California is a struggle, so we dream of the good struggle, of finding our footing, of figuring out some way to beat the statistics and buy a house and educate our kids."[1]

No matter what the conception, some of the dream is attainable for many—California's winter weather is the envy of most of the nation—but much of it is not. One of the themes of this book is the conflict between dreams and reality, between the ideals that we set for ourselves and the reality of our everyday lives. Particularly vivid for politicians is the conflict between our expectations of them and the constraints we place upon them.

Why Study California Politics?

The obvious answer is that you have to: your California history course meets some requirement for graduation or your major, since the state of California decided that every college student should know something about the California Constitution and California government and politics. But more important—why *care* about California politics?

- You are **the residents and voters of the present and future**. The policies and political trends occurring today will impact your lives, affecting everything from university tuition fees to the strength of the job market.

- California politics is plagued by **low levels of participation and turnout**, so much so that the electorate is older, more conservative, wealthier, more educated, and less ethnically diverse than would be the case if every eligible adult voted. So your vote and participation really can make a difference.

- California politics also suffers from **too much interest-group participation and not enough citizen participation**. The general interests of large groups of citizens need to be represented at the table.

That's the narrow answer. The broad answer is that California's government and politics are distinctive and worthy of study. How is California different from other states?

- We have much **more cultural diversity** than other states, including a much higher proportion of Latino and Asian residents. By some measures, we are the country's multicultural trendsetter. Our diversity affects our politics, and our solutions to multicultural issues become an example for other states.

- We are **one of the 10 largest economies in the world**. The California economy in 2015, according to the federal Bureau of Economic Analysis, is the sixth largest in the world, in the same ballpark as the economies of Russia, Italy, and Brazil. California's large and diverse economy means that we are able, in theory, to weather economic downturns more easily than other states. The fact that economic crises continue to plague California, then, indicates that our tax system is distinctive as well (see below and Chapter 8).

- We are **the most populous state, and we have grown more quickly than other states**. In 1960, New York had 41 members in the U.S. House of Representatives; California had 38. The 2010 census gave California 53 seats, followed by Texas with 36 and Florida and New York with 27 each. California has been forced to develop creative solutions to the problems engendered by high growth, such as uneven population distribution among various regions of the state and the need for housing and schools. California's growth puts pressure on many areas of infrastructure and public services.

- We are **more majoritarian than other states**, meaning that we rely more on the measures for direct democracy—the initiative, the referendum, and the recall—that were added to the state constitution by the Progressive movement in 1911. Every state uses majority rule for most decisions, but in a majoritarian state, the public is more likely than elected representatives to make policy decisions.

Consider the following continuum:

| majoritarian | republican |

A **majoritarian** government is one that is highly influenced by the public at large, through public-opinion polls and measures such as the initiative, the referendum, and the recall that enable voters to decide government policies directly.

A **republican** government is one in which we elect representatives to make our decisions for us, based on the Madisonian model for the federal government.

Advocates for November 2016's Proposition 66, which sought to accelerate the use of the death penalty on the 748 inmates on death row in California, make their case at a press conference. Proposition 62, which sought to abolish the death penalty, was on the same ballot. The November 2016 ballot thus confronted voters with two propositions on the death penalty—a not uncommon situation, where, some say, the real goal is to confuse voters.

California government has moved much more toward the majoritarian model than other states have. Initiatives to amend the constitution are routine, and interest groups often collect signatures for an initiative in order to pressure the legislature into voting in their favor. By voting directly on public policies and constitutional amendments that are placed on the ballot, California voters can influence policy in their state more than voters can in other states.

And Californians like being majoritarian: surveys show that most don't want to restrict use of the initiative in spite of its extensive use and manipulation by interest groups.[2] Ballotpedia lists 364 initiatives from 1912 through November 2014, and we had another 14 in November 2016, for a total of 378.[3] California's number of initiatives historically is second only to Oregon, with 384. Twenty-seven states do not have the initiative at all, and the top five states account for more than half of all initiatives considered from 1904 to 2012.[4]

What Determines the Content and Character of California's Politics?

Three factors shape the content and character of California's politics:

- the underlying demographic and sociopolitical trends that affect California and the other states;

- the rules of the game, as set out in the federal and state constitutions and in state laws;

- and the decisions of voters and politicians.

In Chapters 1 and 2 we will discuss the underlying demographic and socio-political trends and the rules of the game. The decisions of voters and politicians, and the way they shape California politics, will be discussed later in the text.

Who Are Californians?

The preamble to the California State Constitution begins, "We, the People of the State of California, . . ." This is fitting for a democratic form of government, which seeks to give voice to the people in the governing of their community affairs. So, who are Californians? Do the demographic characteristics of California differ from those of the United States as a whole? And how have changing demographic and socioeconomic trends contributed to the political challenges that face California voters and politicians? (See the "Who Are Californians?" feature on the next page.)

RACE AND ETHNICITY In many respects, California's population has a notable degree of **racial and ethnic diversity** compared with the U.S. population. **Latino or Hispanic** is not a racial category in the official census, but a separate census question asks about Hispanic or Latino origin. Answers to this question reveal that about 17 percent of the United States is Latino, but Latinos make up about 39 percent of California's population.[5] Almost 60 percent of that population is of Mexican heritage.

AGE California's population is relatively young, mostly because of immigration. Immigrants tend to be younger and to have larger families than those who have been residents for longer periods.

EDUCATION Californians are well educated. A greater proportion of Californians have gone to college or completed a bachelor's degree or higher than in the United States in general. Fewer, however, have graduated from high school (80.6 percent versus 85.3 percent for the United States as a whole in 2009).[6]

MOBILITY AND FOREIGN-BORN RESIDENTS About 60 percent of all Americans live in the state in which they were born, but only 50 percent of all Californians were born in California. In fact, 27.1 percent are **foreign-born**, more than twice the percentage of foreign-born residents in the United States as a whole (12 percent). Most are not U.S. citizens; only 46 percent of the foreign-born in both the United States and California are citizens. As one might expect with such a large foreign-born population, only 61 percent of those over age five speak English at home in California, as opposed to 82 percent nationwide. That is a substantial difference by the standards of social science. Many political issues have arisen from this, ranging from debates over whether local store signs should be written in foreign languages to the "English as the official state language" movement.

INCOME The U.S. Census Bureau has estimated California's median household income at $61,489 for 2010–14, $8,007 higher than the national figure of $53,482. The state poverty rate is almost the same as the national figure: 16.4 percent (California) for 2010–14 compared to 15.6 percent (United States).

Income inequality in California has increased in the last 35 years. A study by the respected Public Policy Institute of California (PPIC) found that pretax cash

How Is the California Population Changing?

California's demographics are changing rapidly. The state used to be dominated by non-Latino whites (Anglos), but since 2000 the state has had a majority minority population. Latinos in particular are a fast-growing population, while Anglos and blacks are an increasingly small proportion. The Asian population is also growing in size, albeit more slowly than the Latino population. If these trends continue, by 2060 less than 30 percent of Californians will be Anglo, while almost half (48 percent) will be Latino.

At the same time, the total size of the state's population is expected to continue to grow rapidly, from 39.1 million people in 2010 to 52.7 million in 2060. Population density will increase in the state's urban areas as well as in inland areas, particularly the San Joaquin and Sacramento valleys.

Projected Population Growth by Demographic Group

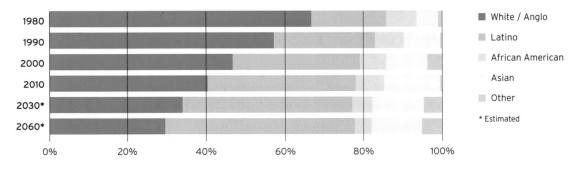

White / Anglo
Latino
African American
Asian
Other
* Estimated

Projected Population Growth between 2010 and 2060 by County

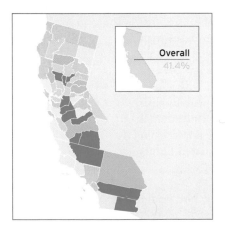

Less than 20% growth
20–39%
40–59%
60–79%
80% or more

Overall 41.4%

SOURCES: Frank Hobbs and Nicole Stoops, "Demographic Trends in the 20th Century," U.S. Census Bureau, www.census.gov/prod/2002pubs/censr-4.pdf (accessed 10/5/16); Sandra L. Colby and Jennifer M. Ortman, "Projections of the Size and Composition of the U.S. Population: 2014 to 2060," U.S. Census Bureau, www.census.gov/content/dam/Census/library/publications/2015/demo/p25-1143.pdf (accessed 10/5/16); and "Projections," State of California Department of Finance, www.dof.ca.gov/Forecasting/Demographics/projections/ (accessed 10/5/16).

forcriticalanalysis

1. What impact are these shifting demographics likely to have on California politics? Will they change the issues that the state government focuses on? Will they change the issues that are the subject of citizen-driven initiatives?

2. California's coastal regions have traditionally been more densely populated, but rapid population growth and rising housing costs are increasingly driving populations to settle further inland. How will this change California politics in the inland counties, particularly in areas traditionally dedicated to agriculture?

incomes of top earners in California are 40 percent higher than they were in 1980, but middle incomes are only 5 percent higher and low incomes 19 percent lower. Bay Area incomes are twice those in the Central Valley, on average. The report did find that California's safety net, including tax credits as well as nutrition, cash, and housing assistance, had played a significant role in lessening inequality in the state. When local, state, and federal safety net programs are included, the amount of inequality shrinks by about 40 percent.[7]

GEOGRAPHY AND POLITICS Over the last 40 years, the population of California has shifted so that the coastal regions have become significantly more liberal and aligned with the Democratic Party than the inland regions, which in turn have become more conservative and aligned with the Republican Party. These liberal coastal regions include every county on the coast, from Del Norte County near Oregon to Los Angeles County. The Central Valley and Inland Empire (Riverside and San Bernardino counties) are disproportionately Republican. Orange and San Diego counties have been very Republican in the past but less so in recent elections. Local politics, on the other hand, are quite different even among Democratic- or Republican-leaning cities (for example, San Francisco's local politics are very liberal compared with Los Angeles's more moderate politics).

POPULATION GROWTH Except for the four years from 1993 to 1996, California's population has grown by about 450,000 people per year for more than two decades. The 2010 census listed California's population as 37,691,912; at the end of 2015, the state Department of Finance estimated the population at 39.3 million. California's current rate of growth is approximately 350,000 people per year. This strong and consistent growth means that many of the problems that have plagued the state in the past will continue to do so in the future. The following are some of these issues:

- **Housing and Transportation** Even with the decline brought on by the recession of 2008–09, housing prices and rents in many areas have skyrocketed in recent years. Many lower- and middle-class people who work in San Francisco's Bay Area must live in the Central Valley, while many of those who work in the Los Angeles area must live in Riverside and San Bernardino counties. Commutes of one to two hours each way are common for residents of these areas. Our transportation systems, built for a much smaller population, have not kept pace with this growth.

- **Schools** Population growth means more schoolchildren and thus high demand for teachers across the state. In recent years, California has lacked enough fully qualified or credentialed teachers to meet this demand, particularly in many urban areas. Projections of the educational requirements of the future job market indicate that approximately 41 percent of jobs will require a college degree in 2025. The University of California, California State University, and community college systems do not produce sufficient numbers of graduates to meet this goal, which means that well-educated workers from other states will move in to fill these positions. The proportion of students who receive a college degree should be rising to meet future job requirements; instead, it is falling.

TABLE 1.1 ● Leading Countries of Origin of Immigrants in California, 2009

Country	Number of Immigrants in California	Percentage Naturalized (%)
Mexico	4,308,000	28%
Philippines	783,000	68
China (including Taiwan)	681,000	68
Vietnam	457,000	82
El Salvador	413,000	37
India	319,000	46
Korea	307,000	55
Guatemala	261,000	28
Iran	214,000	76
Canada	132,000	49
United Kingdom	125,000	40

SOURCE: Public Policy Institute of California, "Just the Facts: Immigrants in California" (April 2011), www.ppic.org (accessed 7/17/12).

● **Immigration**   California has experienced high levels of immigration since the 1950s—so high in some areas that candidates for Mexico's presidency have campaigned here. Between 1970 and 2011 the number of immigrants in California's population increased from 1.8 million to about 10.2 million; 27 percent of the state's population during that period was foreign-born, a much higher proportion than the 13 percent nationwide. Most immigrants in California are from Latin America or Asia; 4.3 million come from Mexico alone, composing some 43 percent of the total immigrant population in California. Immigrants live in all parts of the state, with those from Latin America more likely to live in Southern California and those from Asia in Northern California. Immigrants are younger than nonimmigrant Californians and are more likely to be poor, and although some have relatively high levels of education, most are less educated than the native population.[8] Table 1.1 shows the 11 largest countries of origin for immigrants in California in 2009.

As of 2013, there were approximately 2.67 million **undocumented immigrants** in California, according to the Urban Institute and the Public Policy Institute of California, which used the census figures on the foreign-born population and subtracted the numbers of people who are naturalized or here on legal visas and work permits.[9] Undocumented immigrants are a continuing political issue, with politicians arguing over the public services to which they should have access: Should they be treated in hospital emergency rooms? Should they be allowed to buy insurance on the state exchange under the federal Affordable Care Act? As of January 1, 2015, one issue was decided: California residents who cannot establish legal presence in the United States can apply for a California driver's license if they can establish proof of identification and state residency. Some 600,000 such licenses

TABLE 1.2 ● Undocumented Immigrants by State, 2012

State	Number of Undocumented Immigrants	Share of State's Total Population (%)
California	2,450,000	6.3%
Texas	1,650,000	6.0
New Jersey	525,000	5.9
Florida	925,000	4.6
Arizona	300,000	4.4
Georgia	400,000	3.9
New York	750,000	3.8
Illinois	475,000	3.7
North Carolina	350,000	3.5
Virginia	275,000	3.3
Other states	3,110,000	2.0
All states	11,210,000	3.5

SOURCE: *Washington Post*, www.washingtonpost.com/blogs/govbeat/wp/2014/11/21/the-undocumented-immigrant-population-explained-in-7-maps/ (accessed 7/6/16).

were issued in 2015, the first year they were available. Table 1.2 lists the number of undocumented immigrants by state, along with the share they compose of that state's total population. California and Texas have the highest proportion of undocumented immigrants, at 6.3 and 6.0 percent respectively.

Reflecting the controversies over immigration, both documented and undocumented, in recent years, a number of demonstrations have taken place in California on the immigration issue. These demonstrations have represented different views: against more immigration, in favor of closing the borders, in favor of a "path to citizenship," both for and against the Arizona immigration law of 2010, against housing undocumented children who have been taken into custody before their court hearings, and so forth. At least one of the demonstrations involved more than 1 million people, the largest ever seen in Southern California to date. But aside from the 2013 law that allowed undocumented immigrants to obtain driver's permits starting in 2015 (see above), little policy action has taken place at the state level.

The Crisis of California Politics

Is California government capable of making the decisions needed for the state to thrive and preserve its standard of living through the twenty-first century? The general sentiment among informed observers is that California is hamstrung by voter-approved rules and regulations, some of which are admirable on an individual level but make for a collective nightmare. However, some progress toward effective decision making began during the 2003–11 Schwarzenegger administration and has continued under present governor Jerry Brown:

- Proposition 11, approved in November 2008, took the power to apportion the districts of the Assembly and state Senate (**redistricting**) away from those bodies and gave it to a citizens' commission. Later, the voters added apportioning congressional districts to the duties of the new citizens' commission. In the first few years the new districts were used, they seemed to be fair (that is, not gerrymandered). Future years will establish whether unbiased districts will produce more moderate legislators who are willing to compromise for the good of the state as a whole, which was the goal of changing the reapportionment method. So far, elections have been more competitive.

- In 2010 the voters opted to change the state's party primary elections to a new **top-two primary** system, used for the first time in June 2012. Under the new system, there is no party primary. Instead, the election system is like a swim or track meet, in which there are preliminary heats and finals. Following the preliminary election, the top two candidates advance to the finals in November, even if they are from the same party or are not in a major party. Third parties such as the Green Party are strongly opposed to the new system, since they rarely finish in the top two candidates in the primary election and thus have no access to the general election ballot during the two months when voter attention is highest.

- In 2010 the voters also approved of a change in the legislative process for approving the state budget: the previous requirement was a **two-thirds vote** of the total number of legislators in each chamber, the Assembly and the state Senate, but it is now a simple majority (50 percent plus one). The budget approved in June 2011 was the first to use the new system. In order to raise or lower taxes, however, the state constitution still requires a two-thirds majority of both houses of the legislature, plus the governor's signature.

After the election of Governor Jerry Brown in November 2010, California's frustrating budget stalemate initially continued in spite of the new majority rule, largely because the taxation system had not changed. In June 2012, the budget gap was $16 billion—more than the total revenues received for the general fund in 40 of the 50 states. By mid-2014, however, the budget had a surplus almost as large as the deficit from two years before, and this surplus has lasted into the 2016–17 budget year. The California taxation system is dependent on income taxes paid on **capital gains** (funds received from selling stock); it produced a huge surplus in 2013 and 2014 when the stock market rose, inducing many investors to sell shares. The governor and legislature agreed to use the surplus to build up a "rainy day" fund and to pay off many old bonds issued when the budget was in deficit.

The first decade of the 2000s was one long downward trend, the result of difficult and tough decisions. Every college student in California knows some of them, having seen cut after cut to the budgets of the community colleges, the California State University system, and the University of California system. Tuition and fee increases have partially made up for these cuts. Other budget reductions have included Medi-Cal (California's medical program for the poor) rate and service reductions, many cost-containment measures in state programs for the developmentally disabled, and the elimination of local government redevelopment agencies and their state funding (see Chapter 9). Prisoners are being sent from the state prisons to local jails, and many state responsibilities are being passed to the local level of government. The fiscal years around 2014 show that California can have budget-surplus years as well as deficits, but no one should think that a permanent era of plenty has arrived. California's budget is unduly responsive to the economy and especially to capital gains. When the next recession arrives, and it *will* arrive, revenues will dive again.

California state government thus faces a series of paradoxes. On the one hand, we see progress in cutting the deficit and in making the hard decisions necessary to weather the national economic storm. On the other hand, the difficulty of those decisions and the fact that taxes can be raised only by a two-thirds majority has meant that a budget crisis occurred every year from 2000 to 2012 and to a lesser extent through 2016. Every decision in the state government became a budget decision—a decision made solely, or almost solely, on the basis of whether there is enough money and a budget source for the considered activity.

Let us take a closer look at some reasons for the recurring crises despite the promise of California state government.

The Ease of Passing Initiatives

One factor in these recurring crises is certainly the ease with which **special interests** collect signatures to propose, campaign for, and sometimes pass initiatives to help their own causes. The initiative was added to the California Constitution by the Progressive movement in 1911 as a way to promote the involvement of the people in public policy and affairs. One recent example of a special interest using the initiative for its own gain is Proposition 15 on the June 2010 ballot, which ostensibly allowed taxpayers to have more control over their government but was in fact designed to keep local public utilities from competing with PG&E. Proposition 33 on the November 2012 ballot ostensibly allowed insurance companies to give longevity discounts to drivers who had continuous insurance coverage from another insurance company; in fact, this initiative was designed to give one insurance company the ability to raise rates on drivers who had lapses in insurance coverage. Another example is the November 2016 referendum on the law banning single-use plastic bags statewide. The sponsors of the referendum, opposed to the law, make— you guessed it—plastic bags. In general, the initiative has ceased to promote direct democracy for at least the last two decades. Instead, it has mostly become just another method by which special interests convince voters who are paying little attention to government and politics to enact rules, laws, and constitutional amendments that benefit the particular interest at the expense of the public as a whole. While there are exceptions, far too many initiatives fall into this category.

Term Limits

The **term limit** movement found fertile ground in California in the 1980s and 1990s. Proposition 140 in 1990 imposed what were then the severest term limits in the nation on the legislature and the elected officials of the executive branch; the voters in many California cities instituted term limits on their local leaders as well. Part of the statewide anger and consequent push for term limit legislation was directed against Willie Brown, then speaker of the California Assembly, whose flamboyant lifestyle and prolific fund-raising provoked the ire of voters.

The theory of the term limits movement is that term limits will encourage members of the Assembly and state Senate to pay more attention to their jobs and spend less time raising money for future campaigns, and that the limits will make the legislative bodies more welcoming to minority and female candidates. Since term limits have been imposed, the proportion of Latino legislators has indeed risen; however, members now have much less expertise on the matters they vote on and, by the time they acquire this expertise, they are term-limited out. Additionally, many—perhaps most—members of the legislature spend a good deal of their time in office worrying about their next job and raising funds for future campaigns. Most observers believe that term limits have worsened the legislature, not bettered it.

While voters strongly support term limits, they recently took a step to address some of the institutional problems that have resulted from them. In June 2012 the voters approved Proposition 28, which allows legislators to serve as many as 12 years in the legislature, as long as those 12 years are served in one house. (The previous total service time was actually higher—14 years—but was capped at 6 years in the Assembly and 8 in the Senate.) Currently the term limits are 12 years (six terms) for the Assembly, 12 years (three terms) for the state Senate, and 8 years (two terms) for all statewide officials (governor, lieutenant governor, attorney general, controller, secretary of state, treasurer, superintendent of public instruction, insurance commissioner, and the four elected members of the Board of Equalization).

The Two-Thirds Requirement for Raising Taxes

As noted earlier, until the voters passed Proposition 25 in November 2010, California's constitution required a two-thirds vote of the total membership—not just those present and voting—in each house of the legislature to pass the budget. Only three states, Arkansas, California, and Rhode Island, required such a strong **supermajority** to pass the budget. Proposition 25 lowered the required vote to 50 percent plus one. It will take several years to see if this change makes a substantial difference. So far, the first six budgets passed under the new rules—which financially penalize legislators if the budget is not passed on time—have been passed around June 15, the constitutional deadline. Only those starting with the one passed in June 2014 were technically balanced, and only because of the surge in income tax revenues from individuals who had sold stock in previous years. A balanced budget clearly requires different procedural deadlines as well as improvements in the quality of the state's economy and tax system.

Herein lies the problem. A two-thirds vote of the absolute number of legislators in both houses of the state legislature is still necessary to raise or lower any tax level. With a Republican Party that refuses to countenance tax increases of any kind (plus the taxpayer groups that promise to sue the instant any tax increase is passed), the burden of balancing the state budget has fallen on low- and moderate-income state residents, who benefit disproportionately from the state programs that have been cut. For higher-income state residents, state services are at least partially irrelevant—their major "service" is a low tax rate, as well as exemptions and deductions that enable some of their income to be taxed at a lower rate.

This situation may change somewhat in the next few years. The 2012 elections saw the Democrats win a short-lived supermajority of seats in the legislature, which meant they had enough votes to raise taxes without any Republican support (see Chapter 5). Raising taxes, however, requires the approval of the governor, and Governor Jerry Brown has consistently wanted a balanced budget without additional tax increases beyond those instituted by Proposition 30, approved by voters in November 2012. This proposition enacted a four-year increase in the state sales tax and seven-year increases in the tax rates for citizens making over $250,000 in income (see Chapter 8). The supermajority lasted a little over a year, until early

2014 when three Democrats in the state Senate were suspended over corruption allegations. These developments have had a significant impact, but the two-thirds rule for raising taxes continues to hold sway. The structure of California's tax system has been frozen since the 1960s.

Lack of Consensus on Fundamental Questions

Another reason for California's perpetual state of crisis is the inability of legislators to unify on matters of policy and principle. In order to be effective, a political system must overcome the inertia generated by narrow interests to make decisions that benefit the broader public interest. This is a persistent issue in a large, complex state like California, but in the past, California politicians have been able to overcome the lack of **consensus** to make progress on significant questions. Has California changed? Why do interest groups cause impasse in the 2000s, when their influence was relatively minimal back in the 1970s and 1980s? After all, we have always had interest groups, and we had the two-thirds decision rule for adopting the budget or raising taxes in the legislature from 1935 until 2010.

Dan Walters suggests that the blame heaped on the legislature is inappropriate:

> In fact, California's governance maladies stem from the complex, often contradictory nature of the state itself. With its immense geographic, economic, and cultural diversity, California has myriad policy issues, but those same factors also have become an impediment to governance. The state lost its vital consensus on public policy issues, and without that civic compass, its politicians tend to ignore major issues and pursue trivial ones. . . . The real issue is whether the public's anger at Gray Davis will morph into a new sense of civic purpose or whether California is destined to be . . . ungovernable.[10]

If you combine the lack of consensus with the swift-moving news cycle typified by Twitter and other social media, you can get a sense of the problem. So far, the

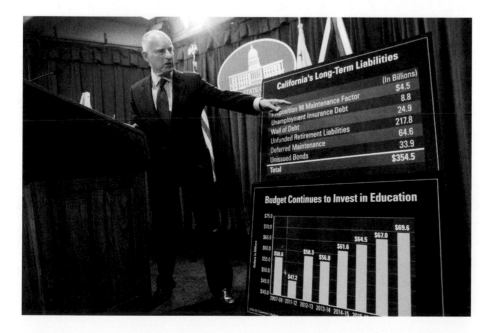

Passing a balanced state budget is a perennially contentious issue in California. However, the budget surplus in early 2014 allowed Governor Jerry Brown—shown here breaking down certain state expenditures—to propose budgets for 2014-17 that increased state funding for education and paid off some of the debt that the state had accrued over previous years.

events following the recall of Governor Gray Davis in 2003 have indicated very slow progress, with no "new sense of civic purpose." The same old problems seem to vex California's political class, over and over.

Reform Ideas

In addition to the steps already taken (as discussed earlier), numerous reforms have been suggested over the years to address the institutional hindrances to effective California governance. Some of the standard ones are listed below. See how many you agree with as you begin this book. You might check this section at the end of your course to see if you still have the same opinion; there's a significant probability that you won't!

On the liberal side:

- **Instituting public financing of election campaigns.** Public financing would reduce the impact of money on Assembly, state Senate, and congressional campaigns, because all or most campaign funding would come from the state, not from interests who want something in return for these donations. It would also lessen the impact of fund-raising on members of the legislature, some of whom spend up to half their time in Sacramento raising money. However, it would be difficult to devise a system that would not unduly benefit incumbents, who are typically better known than their challengers.

- **Lowering the required supermajority to raise taxes** from two-thirds to some lower, more achievable, percentage, such as 55 or 60 percent. This proposal would require an amendment to the state constitution, probably impossible on a tax issue like this unless it is proposed as part of a broad package of tax relief and reform.

- **Restricting the initiative process** to allow more citizen participation and lessen the need to hire professional firms to collect signatures and run initiative campaigns. This would require lengthening the time allowed to collect signatures. Changing an initiative process that California's citizens hold in high regard would be a tough sell, and the industry that sponsors initiatives and makes money from them might oppose it; this would make the campaign expensive.

- **Realigning the tax structure** to match the state's shift from a manufacturing economy to a service-based one (see Chapter 8). The most powerful method for doing this would be to change the sales tax to make it apply to services such as medical care and automobile repair. In order to pass, this would have to be sold as decreasing the sales-tax rate. Several recent commissions have indicated interest, but few politicians want to be associated with the cause.

On the conservative side:

- **Changing the legislature from full time to part time.** This idea is popular in Tea Party circles, reflecting their nostalgia for an earlier era and their desire for a less expensive government, not to mention the typical Californian's distrust of the legislature. However, it would weaken the legislature's level of expertise on the programs it is expected to enact and oversee.

- **Lowering California's tax rates**, making the system less progressive in the process. This is popular among conservatives but is a tough sell for liberals and Democrats.

- **Improving California's business climate** with lower taxes and fewer regulations. Almost everyone agrees that this goal is laudable, but there is little agreement on what taxes to lower (or how to make up the difference financially) and what regulations to simplify or abolish.

Most of these ideas involve so much controversy that they have little chance of being enacted, at least in the short run. Enacting major reforms such as those just listed is much easier through the ballot box (that is, via an initiative) than it is through the legislature, where constitutional changes require a two-thirds vote of the Assembly and the Senate before being placed on the ballot for ratification.

Conclusion

In this book we are going to consider the real world of California politics and the possibilities, both fascinating and frustrating, of the present, as well as changes that might make the future more positive for both politicians and the public. We will investigate what makes California different from other states and examine its unique political problems, which include the following:

- the inability to balance the budget, year after year (the most recent years under Governor Jerry Brown are an exception)

- the malapportioned districts for the California legislature that, in combination with the primary system, produce legislators who are more liberal than the public on the Democratic side and more conservative than the public on the Republican side (we shall see whether the new top-two primary system and the non-gerrymandered legislative districts make any difference in this area)

- the public's attachment to the strictest term limits in the nation

- the public's attachment to extreme majoritarianism, which produces the longest ballots in the nation as well as low turnout rates

Our coverage includes subjects that the newspapers and bloggers discuss in great detail as well as some subjects, such as the California tax system and the impact of Proposition 13, that receive little coverage in the media. Welcome to the journey.

A Guide to This Book

Chapter 2, "The Constitution and the Progressive Legacy," deals with California's state constitution and the Progressives, the two crucial factors that defined the shape and direction of today's California government.

Chapters 3 and 4 consider the bodies outside government that influence what government can accomplish. Chapter 3, "Interest Groups and the Media in

California," takes a look at the groups that are as prevalent and influential in California as they are in our nation's capital. Chapter 4, "Parties and Elections in California," examines how both parties and voters influence government through elections and campaigns.

Chapters 5, 6, and 7 cover the institutions of government. Chapter 5, "The California Legislature," discusses the legislature, the body we love to hate. We try in this book to understand the legislature and why it functions as it does rather than to simply condemn it. Chapter 6, "The Governor and the Executive Branch," asks whether California has become ungovernable. Chapter 7, "The California Judiciary," deals with judges and the criminal justice system.

Chapters 8, 9, and 10 provide an in-depth guide to policy problems and governmental structures that are particularly relevant today. Chapter 8, "The State Budget and Budgetary Limitations," addresses taxes, spending, and the California budget, asking whether the budget can be controlled in today's political and policy environment with the tools we have available to us. Chapter 9, "Local Government," considers local government and its dependency on the state, a dependency that localities are taking action to eliminate in part through the initiative process. Chapter 10, "Public Policy in California," delves into several contemporary public policy problems, illustrating how the institutions and voters have acted in these areas.

Study Guide

FOR FURTHER READING

Bonn, Sarah, and Caroline Danielson. *Income Inequality and the Safety Net in California*. Public Policy Institute of California, May 2016. http://ppic.org/main/publication.asp?i=1190. Accessed 7/18/16.

"California in Crisis." *California Journal* (August 2003): 18–27.

Davis, Mike. *City of Quartz: Excavating the Future in Los Angeles*. New York: Vintage, 1990.

Hill, Laura, and Joseph Hayes. "Just the Facts: Undocumented Immigrants." Public Policy Institute of California, June 2015. www.ppic.org. Accessed 7/8/16.

Horwitz, Sasha. *Termed Out: Reforming California's Term Limits*. Center for Governmental Studies, October 2007. www.policyarchive.org/handle/10207/2047. Accessed 9/20/16.

Lewis, Michael. "California *and* Bust." *Vanity Fair*, November 2011.

Mathews, Joe, and Mark Paul. *California Crackup: How Reform Broke the Golden State and How We Can Fix It*. Berkeley: University of California Press, 2010.

McGhee, Eric, and Daniel Krimm. *California's Political Geography*. Public Policy Institute of California, February 2012. www.ppic.org/main/publication_quick.asp?i=1007. Accessed 9/20/16.

Mejia, Marisol Cuellar, and Hans Johnson. "Just the Facts: Immigrants in California." Public Policy Institute of California, May 2013. www.ppic.org. Accessed 7/8/16.

Olin, Spencer C. *California's Prodigal Sons: Hiram Johnson and the Progressives, 1911–1917*. Berkeley: University of California Press, 1968.

Skelton, George. "California's Capitol—The Long View. A Columnist Looks Back on 50 Years Covering the Ups and Downs of Sacramento." *Los Angeles Times*, December 1, 2011.

Statewide Ballot Proposition Elections. Field Institute, California Opinion Index, October 2011. www.field.com/fieldpoll online/subscribers. Accessed 11/16/16.

Wilson, James Q. "A Guide to Schwarzenegger Country." *Commentary* (December 2003): 45–49.

ON THE WEB

California Choices. www.californiachoices.org. Accessed 11/16/16.

California Forward. "How to Fix CA's Government." www.cafwd-action.org/pages/how-to-fix-CA-government. Accessed 11/16/16.

The Field (California) Poll: Field Institute. www.field.com/fieldpollonline/subscribers/index.html. Accessed 11/16/16.

Los Angeles Times. www.latimes.com. Accessed 11/16/16.

Public Policy Institute of California. www.ppic.org. Accessed 11/16/16. A think tank devoted to nonpartisan research on how to improve California policy.

Sacramento Bee. www.sacbee.com. Accessed 11/16/16.

San Francisco Chronicle. www.sfgate.com. Accessed 11/16/16.

SUMMARY

I. California politics are important for several reasons.
   A. California is the most populous state, has an economy in the top 10 among nations of the world, and has a population more multicultural and diverse than the rest of the nation.
   B. California is strongly majoritarian, and its citizens like it that way.
   C. California is younger than many states, has a greater percentage of college-educated citizens, and is richer than most states.
   D. California has experienced some of the strongest population growth of any state, resulting in a number of political conflicts over the years.
   E. California has more immigrants, and more undocumented immigrants, than any other state, although Texas and New Jersey have almost the same proportion of undocumented immigrants.

II. Progress in dealing with California's problems has occurred in the last decade, in spite of the fact that the state is generally considered to be hamstrung by voter-approved rules and regulations.
   A. Redistricting, once the province of the legislature, is now done by a citizens' commission. The new districts (used from 2012 forward) seem to have considerably less gerrymandering than the old.
   B. The party primary election system has been changed to the new "top-two" system, in which the two top vote-getters from the primary election, regardless of party, move to the general election for a runoff.
      1. The new system is more like a swim meet or track meet, with a preliminary heat and final, than a party primary.
   C. In 2010 the voters approved a change to the state constitution so that the legislature could approve the state budget by a majority vote, instead of the prior rule of two-thirds of the total membership of each house of the legislature.

      1. The state constitution still requires any tax increase to be approved by a two-thirds vote of each house of the legislature, plus the governor's signature.
   D. These changes have not resolved the underlying problems with the state's taxation system, which result in soaring surpluses when the stock market is high and the opposite during recessions.

III. Some reasons for the continual crisis in California state government include the following:
   A. The ease of passing initiatives. Special interests find that the state has a congenial atmosphere in which they can spend several million dollars to collect signatures and fund a campaign to pass a law or change the state constitution in order to benefit the initiative's proposer.
   B. Term limits, in spite of the 2012 change that lengthened the maximum time to 12 years in either the Assembly or the state Senate, still hamper the legislature. By the time legislators learn their jobs, they are often looking for new ones.
   C. The two-thirds vote requirement in the Assembly and state Senate to raise taxes has meant that the only realistic way to balance declining budgets has been to cut services disproportionately used by the lower middle class and the poor.
   D. The lack of consensus on fundamental questions among both politicians and citizens has made it difficult to build the broad consensus that major change requires.

IV. Reform ideas are abundant, but few have the political support necessary for enactment in the short run. Several ideas from both sides of the political spectrum are listed in the text.

PRACTICE QUIZ

1. The budget must be passed by a majority of those present and voting in both chambers of the legislature.
   a) true
   b) false

2. Most states require a two-thirds majority to pass their budgets each year.
   a) true
   b) false

3. According to the text, California's total population, its foreign-born population, and the approximate number of undocumented immigrants living in the state are:
   a) 50 million, 5 million, and 2 million.
   b) 34 million, 8.8 million, and 2.4 million.
   c) 25 million, 20 million, and 18 million.
   d) 39.3 million, 10.2 million, and 2.67 million.

4. "Latino" or "Hispanic" is one of the racial categories in the U.S. census, which is taken every 10 years.
   a) true
   b) false

5. Compared to the proportion of immigrants who speak English at home in the U.S. population, the proportion of immigrants in California who speak English at home is
   a) greater.
   b) lesser.
   c) the same.

6. According to this book, the inability of the California legislature to make decisions that benefit the state as a whole is due to
   a) the influence of interest groups.
   b) the two-thirds requirement to raise taxes.
   c) California's size and diversity.
   d) all of the above

7. California's current term limits are
   a) 8 years for the governor, 4 years for the Assembly, and 6 years for the state Senate.
   b) 6 years for the governor, 6 years for the Assembly, and 8 years for the state Senate.

c) 8 years for the governor, 12 years for the Assembly, and 12 years for the state Senate.
d) 8 years for the governor, 8 years for the Assembly, and 12 years for the state Senate.

8. Undocumented immigrants were able to obtain a driver's permit in California as of 2015.
   a) true
   b) false

9. "Majoritarian" as applied to California government means that
   a) the state requires majority rule in all major decisions.
   b) the state does not have a "republican" form of government; it has a "majoritarian" form.
   c) the state makes many important decisions through direct democracy and the initiative process.
   d) the California legislature uses majority rule for all decisions.

10. California's institutions of higher education produce sufficient numbers of graduates to meet the the state's workforce needs in the foreseeable future.
    a) true
    b) false

CRITICAL-THINKING QUESTIONS

1. How distinctive is California compared with other states? Are we really that different from citizens in the rest of the country?
2. California's population differs from that of other states on several levels. What are the two or three that are most significant, and why are they significant?

3. What are the advantages and disadvantages of the "majoritarian" form of government? Of the "republican" form of government?

KEY TERMS

California dream (p. 2)
capital gains tax (p. 10)
consensus (p. 13)
cultural diversity (p. 3)
foreign-born (p. 5)
Latino or Hispanic (p. 5)

majoritarian (p. 3)
public financing (p. 14)
racial and ethnic diversity (p. 5)
redistricting (p. 10)
republican (p. 3)
special interests (p. 11)

supermajority (p. 12)
term limits (p. 11)
top-two primary (p. 10)
two-thirds vote (p. 10)
undocumented immigration (p. 8)

2

The Constitution and the Progressive Legacy

WHAT CALIFORNIA GOVERNMENT DOES AND WHY IT MATTERS

The purpose of a constitution is to define the rules under which political actors and citizens interact with each other to fulfill their goals as individuals, as members of a group, and as a population as a whole. The California Constitution is long and very detailed, with numerous amendments added over the years that deal with both the fundamental principles and power of government as well as commonplace issues such as the right to fish on government property, English as the state's official language, and grants for stem cell research. Today California has the second highest number of constitutional amendments (over 500 by some counts), behind Alabama, and the second longest state constitution, behind Louisiana.

One distinctive feature of the California Constitution is that it allows the people to enact both constitutional amendments and legislation through a majority vote without going through the legislature. The process through which citizens make legislation at the ballot box is called the initiative. The initiative developed out of a political movement called Progressivism, which opposed the influence of monied special interests in politics and called for political power to be returned to the people. Any individual or group can propose a statute or an amendment to the California Constitution.

However, the initiative process has not always lived up to its progressive ideals. Today, wealthy individuals and special interest groups spend hundreds of millions of dollars on campaigns for and against initiatives. In the November 2016 general election, more than $300 million was spent by both sides on 17 propositions. Although the initiative does put legislative power in the hands of the general public, it does not eliminate the influence of money in politics, and—ironically—it bypasses the more careful debate and compromise that might take place in the legislature.

For example, in 2006, California voters cast their ballots on Proposition 87, a high-profile initiative that was the most costly in history, with over $156 million spent advocating for and against the proposition. The goal of the proposition was to establish a $4 billion program, the primary goal of which was to reduce petroleum consumption by 25 percent. It included research and production incentives for alternative energy, alternative-energy vehicles, and energy-efficient technologies, as well as funding for education and training. The program would have been funded by a tax of 1.5 to 6.0 percent (depending on oil price per barrel) on California oil producers. The stakes were high because California is the third largest oil-producing state in the nation. At the time, roughly 37 percent of California's oil was pumped in the state, and another 21 percent came from Alaska. The rest was imported.

Supporters of the proposition contributed $61.9 million (with $49.6 million alone coming from film producer Stephen Bing), and opponents contributed $94.4 million (with Chevron Corporation, Aera Energy, and Occidental Oil and Gas contributing $38 million, $32.8 million, and $9.6 million, respectively).[1] The initiative brought out celebrities on both sides, including prominent individuals, companies, and organizations. These included former president Bill Clinton, actor Brad Pitt, and the Coalition for Clean Air in support of the measure, and Governor Arnold Schwarzenegger, Chevron Corporation, and the California Chamber of Commerce in opposition.

The campaign was bitter and acrimonious. Accusations of dirty tactics abounded, and both sides filed lawsuits. Supporters alleged that the opposition's print and television advertisements created the false impression that the opposition campaign was financed by a broad coalition, including educators and public-safety officials, when in fact it was subsidized by the oil industry. Opponents to the measure accused their adversaries of illegally registering several "no" web sites that, when accessed, redirected viewers to the "Yes-on-87" site. Although little came of either lawsuit, each helped sharpen and intensify feelings on both sides.

In the end, Proposition 87 failed to pass, getting 45.3 percent of the vote, as voters feared that passage of the initiative would raise gas prices, resulting in a greater demand for foreign oil. This proposition is a prime example of an issue that, rather than being debated by experts and elected officials in the legislature, was appropriated by wealthy individuals and interest groups in the name of direct democracy. In the November 2014 election, two high-profile initiatives pitted consumers against health insurance companies in one case and trial lawyers in another, but in neither case did the money spent approach the $156 million spent on Proposition 8 in 2006. Such examples abound in California politics.

In Chapter 1 we discussed some of the demographic differences between California and other states. We also mentioned that the institutional design of California's government prevents it from solving critical state issues. Here are some of the unique features of the state's political process:

- The **sheer size of the state** increases the cost of political campaigns and media outreach programs.

- The **competing networks of interest groups** cause groups to jockey for position and influence.

- The **increasing use of the initiative** significantly affects state and local governance and policy.

- The **divided executive branch**, composed of nine separately elected officials, each with his or her own area of authority and responsibility, leads to overlapping responsibilities and fragmentation in the execution of state policy.

- The **widespread, almost universal use of nonpartisan elections at the local level of government** eliminates a valuable clue that helps voters identify the policy positions of the candidates on the ballot.

Aside from the size of the state and its interest-group network, the other characteristics listed above are a result of the **Progressive movement**, which flourished in California from 1900 to 1917. The leaders of this movement focused on one goal: making government more responsive to the political, social, and economic concerns of the people. Their reforms continue to shape California's government and politics in ways that sharply differentiate it from other states. To some, these features hamper the political process and should be changed. To others, they form part of the essence of California—an essence that, were they to be changed, would be destroyed.

The Rules of the Game: California's Constitution

The California Constitution has a long and storied history that can be divided into four stages:

- **The 1849 Constitution**   Written by residents of the territory in anticipation of statehood, this constitution contains many of the basic ideas underlying California's government today.

- **The 1879 Constitution**   Written by a constitutional convention in 1878, this is the basic governing document, with amendments, that is in force today.

- **From 1900 to 1917**   During this period, the Progressives amended the constitution and passed laws to temper the power of special interests and make government responsive to the people's desires and needs. The most prominent reforms of this period are the initiative, referendum, and recall.

- **From 1918 to the present**   Amendment after amendment lengthened the state's constitution, resulting in a document that at one point was almost 100,000 words long. Several commissions proposed substantive changes, but only two commissions, one in the 1960s and the other in the 1990s, saw their proposals realized: the constitution's language was shortened and clarified, but no substantial changes were made to its provisions.

The 1849 Constitution

By 1849, 80,000 unruly gold miners had moved to California, inflating the state's population enough that the settlers could apply for territorial status and draft a constitution. Admitting California as a free state at that time, however, would have upset the balance between free and slave states that had existed in the Union since 1820. In 1849 newly elected president Zachary Taylor proposed that California draft a constitution and apply directly to Congress for admission as a state, rather than applying first as a territory and later shifting to state status. California citizens elected delegates to a constitutional convention; the delegates met in turn and drew up the proposed constitution in 43 days.

This constitutional convention of 48 elected men met in Monterey in September 1849 and relied heavily upon a book containing the constitutions of the federal government and some 30 states. Several of the provisions in California's constitution were taken directly from those of New York and Iowa. The basic provisions of the 1849 Constitution are still in force:

- The framework of the government rests on a separation of powers—executive, legislative, and judicial—interacting through a system of checks and balances, like the federal government.

- Executive power is divided, with the separate election and jurisdiction of the governor, lieutenant governor, comptroller, treasurer, attorney general, surveyor general, and superintendent of public instruction. This division weakens the governor, who cannot appoint—or remove—senior members of his or her own administration. Moreover, each of these statewide officials is a potential competitor for the governor's office, and each can release statements that contradict what the governor is saying.

- An extensive bill of rights begins the constitution.

- The legislature is elected and consists of two houses, one called the Senate, the other the Assembly.

However, there are notable differences between the 1849 Constitution and the framework that exists today:

- The right to vote at that time was limited to white males 21 years of age or older who had lived in California for at least six months. Another provision denied citizenship to African Americans, Chinese Americans, and Native Americans; they were also prohibited from testifying against whites in court. The legislature could, by a two-thirds vote, enfranchise Native Americans "in such special cases as such proportion of the legislative body may deem just and proper."

- The judiciary was elected, as judges are today, but they were organized into four levels—as Mexico's judiciary was at the time.

- All laws and other provisions were to be published in both English and Spanish, since California was a bilingual state.

In 1850 the federal government passed a series of bills that composed the Compromise of 1850. One bill admitted California to the Union as a free state. The Compromise also established Utah and New Mexico as territorial governments and allowed residents to decide whether or not to allow slavery in their state. It settled a dispute over the border between Texas and New Mexico and compensated Texas with $10 million to repay debts to Mexico. Finally, it abolished the slave trade in the District of Columbia and put the Fugitive Slave Act into effect.

California's 1849 Constitution quickly proved to be problematic. Its framers had written it so quickly that they had neglected to include provisions for the financial stability of the new government; within the first five years, California was in deficit. There were few provisions for taxation but no limits on spending, legislative salaries, or the governor's pardon power.[2] Four times between 1859 and 1873 the legislature called for a new constitutional convention to fix obvious defects; each time, too many voters left their ballots blank to achieve the necessary majority to approve the convention.

The 1879 Constitution

The call for a new constitutional convention finally succeeded in 1877, as California suffered from the worst recession in the brief history of the nation. In 1873 a Wall Street panic had spread into a full-fledged economic collapse, and thousands of businesses went bankrupt. Unfortunately, as Kevin Starr writes in *California: A History*, Chinese immigrants "became increasingly the scapegoats for collapsed expectations."[3] The situation had its origins in the expansion of the Central Pacific Railroad. A years-long project to extend the railroad over the Sierra Nevada mountain range began in 1863, when few California-born workers were willing to do the backbreaking work at the price that the railroad construction supervisor, Charles Crocker, was willing to pay. Starting in 1865, Crocker began to rely on Chinese workers, who lacked the bargaining power to campaign for higher wages; he eventually employed some 10,000. In 1869 the Union Pacific and Central Pacific railroads met in Utah, completing a track that would cut the journey across the nation to one week.

When the influx of Chinese workers resulted in unemployment for many non-immigrant workers, anti-Chinese sentiment began to grow. In 1871, Los Angeles witnessed a mass lynching of 18 Chinese men, including a boy of 14, after which an Anglo-American mob looted the Chinese section of town. By 1875 the state had seen an influx of over 150,000 migrants from other states, including many who had worked to build the Union Pacific Railroad, and by 1877 unemployment rates in San Francisco were high. On July 23 of that year, a group numbering about 8,000 assembled for a meeting of the Workingmen's Party, where speakers "denounced the capitalist system in general and the railroads in particular . . . , with emphasis on the Chinese labor the railroad had employed."[4]

Fifty-one of the delegates to the 1879 convention belonged to the Workingmen's Party; thus, it effectively enjoyed veto power over any of the decisions on both the convention rules and recommendations for the new constitution, for which a two-thirds majority was necessary. Joe Matthews and Mark Paul call the convention's recommendations "a demonstration of a difficult fact of California political life"—that "supermajorities are dangerous."[5] The Workingmen's Party supported restrictions on corporations and railroads and was strongly opposed to the presence of Chinese workers in California. One of its rallying cries was "The Chinese must go!"[6] The party also opposed the centralization of power for the government and the legislature. (It made an unsuccessful proposition to the convention that California collapse the two houses of the legislature into a unicameral one and abolish the lieutenant governor's office.)

The delegates at the convention adopted a large number of diverse provisions. Among these were the shifting of responsibility to stockholders for the debts of a corporation and various new rules regarding the railroads: the railroads could not give free passes to those holding political office, they could not raise rates on one line to compensate for reductions made to compete on alternative lines, and they would be regulated by a Railroad Commission.

These provisions added words—almost doubling the constitution's size—and policies that read very much like a series of laws rather than a fundamental framework within which laws could operate. In this way, the California Constitution differs greatly from the federal U.S. Constitution, whose articles and amendments deal strictly with institutional procedures and rules that construct a governmental framework. The Eighteenth Amendment stands as the only experiment in establishing a substantive policy in the U.S. Constitution; it prohibits the manufacture, sale, import, or export of alcohol and was repealed with the Twenty-First Amendment just 14 years later.

At the time, however, the many specific, substantive policies in the drafted California Constitution were viewed as beneficial, and it was approved by a vote of 54 to 46 percent in May 1879, with 90 percent of those eligible to vote participating. Most of the reform measures were not put into practice right away, as corporate and railroad power continued to dominate the state and sued to block their implementation. These setbacks were temporary, however. In a matter of three decades the broad reforms of the Progressive movement gained passage, weakening the grip of these special interests in the legislature and reshaping the landscape of California politics.

One notable feature of the 1879 Constitution is the procedures it established for amendment. The federal constitution and every state constitution in the United States include procedures for their own amendment, but these procedures vary considerably. The U.S. Constitution is one of the most difficult to amend in the world, requiring a two-thirds majority vote in the House and Senate followed by ratification by three-fourths of the states.[7] This very high hurdle explains in part why the U.S. Constitution has only been amended 27 times since 1789. In contrast, the California Constitution is much easier to amend. See Figure 2.1 for an overview of the different paths through which the constitution can be amended. Convening a constitutional convention is a more dramatic method of reform and has been used rarely. It is not particularly difficult, however, to get 8 percent of voters in the most recent gubernatorial election to sign a petition adding an amendment to the next ballot; the amendment then needs a simple majority vote to pass. This method has been used more than any other to amend the California Constitution.

You can get a sense of the California Constitution and how different it is from the U.S. Constitution by examining California's bill of rights, called the "Declara-

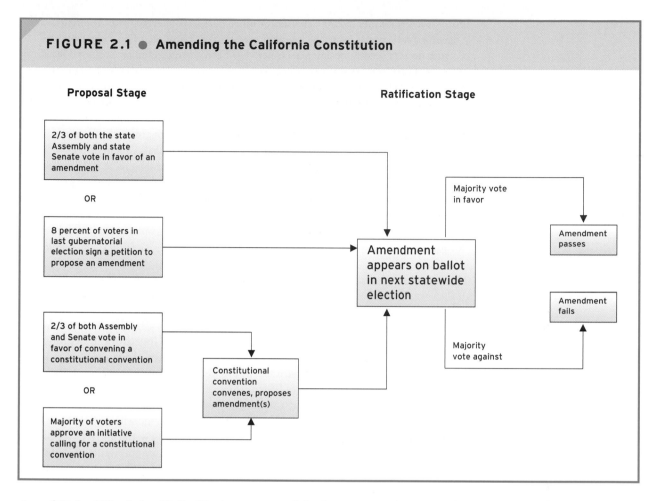

FIGURE 2.1 ● Amending the California Constitution

Proposal Stage

Ratification Stage

2/3 of both the state Assembly and state Senate vote in favor of an amendment

OR

8 percent of voters in last gubernatorial election sign a petition to propose an amendment

2/3 of both Assembly and Senate vote in favor of convening a constitutional convention

OR

Majority of voters approve an initiative calling for a constitutional convention

Constitutional convention convenes, proposes amendment(s)

Amendment appears on ballot in next statewide election

Majority vote in favor

Majority vote against

Amendment passes

Amendment fails

tion of Rights." The federal Bill of Rights consists of the first 10 amendments to the U.S. Constitution, and while other amendments may be passed, the first 10 will remain the Bill of Rights as they were written. California's bill of rights, meanwhile, can be expanded or rewritten as times change, and it therefore reflects the political changes and conflicts that have occurred over time, with some of the rights described in much greater specificity than the corresponding federal right. You can see an example of this specificity in the provisions for freedom of speech as they apply to a newspaper. The federal constitution has the familiar First Amendment:

> Congress shall make no law respecting an establishment of religion, or prohibiting the free exercise thereof; or abridging the freedom of speech, or of the press; or the right of the people peaceably to assemble, and to petition the Government for a redress of grievances.

California's corresponding section has both more detail and more specificity, since it has been amended over time.

> SEC. 2. (a) Every person may freely speak, write and publish his or her sentiments on all subjects, being responsible for the abuse of this right. A law may not restrain or abridge liberty of speech or press.

(b) A publisher, editor, reporter, or other person connected with or employed upon a newspaper, magazine, or other periodical publication, or by a press association or wire service, or any person who has been so connected or employed, shall not be adjudged in contempt by a judicial, legislative, or administrative body, or any other body having the power to issue subpoenas, for refusing to disclose the source of any information procured while so connected or employed for publication in a newspaper, magazine, or other periodical publication, or for refusing to disclose any unpublished information obtained or prepared in gathering, receiving, or processing of information for communication to the public. Nor shall a radio or television news reporter or other person connected with or employed by a radio or television station, or any person who has been so connected or employed, be so adjudged in contempt for refusing to disclose the source of any information procured while so connected or employed for news or news commentary purposes on radio or television, or for refusing to disclose any unpublished information obtained or prepared in gathering, receiving, or processing of information for communication to the public.

Note the use of modern language, such as *wire service* and *television*.

From 1900 to 1917: The Progressive Movement

Pressure for political reform did not end with the 1879 Constitution. Beginning at the turn of the twentieth century, the Progressives pursued three goals: attack corporate political influence, eliminate the political corruption that accompanied such influence, and democratize the political process.[8]

The Progressives understood that these goals had to be accomplished before they could address equally pressing but more mundane concerns of the time. They accomplished all of their goals—and much more. Beginning with the 1911 legislative session, these reformers passed dozens of constitutional amendments and statutes that changed the face of California government and politics.[9] The most prominent of the political reforms were the following:

- **Nonpartisanship**   This is the norm in local elections and means that no party label is affixed to the candidates' names on the ballot. Of the more than 19,000 elected public officials in California, fewer than 300 are elected in partisan races.

- **Primary elections**   Before the institution of primary elections, political parties chose their candidates in party conventions (the stereotypical smoky back room) or caucuses—meetings of party members at the local level. In a primary election, each prospective party nominee has to obtain more votes than any other prospective nominee in order to run as the party's candidate in the November general election. (This system was changed again in 2010; see next section.)

- **The office block ballot**   This is the ballot that we vote on today, with a "block" for each office and the candidates listed for that office. Before this reform, in some elections, voters cast ballots for their preferred party, not for individual candidates.

- **Direct democracy**   These grassroots processes—the initiative, referendum, and recall—give citizens the ability to exert some control over both the legislative and executive branches. In this way, citizens can rein in the abuse of power by elected officials or ignite officials who have become paralyzed by inaction and partisan bickering. These processes will be examined in detail later in the chapter.

- **The civil service**   An essential element of the Progressive reform movement was the implementation of a civil service in which government employees are selected on the basis of merit, replacing the spoils system in which employees are selected based on their personal connections to the party in power. In California, the 1913 Civil Service Act created a Civil Service Commission to eliminate politics and the spoils system among the state's public employees.

During this period, the California Constitution grew substantially as the legislature enacted dozens of constitutional amendments and statutes. In the first three months of 1911 alone, the legislature passed more than 800 statutes and 23 constitutional amendments.

From 1960 to the Present: Late Revisions

In 1963 the legislature created a constitution revision commission as a result of a 1962 initiative. The commission, composed of 50 citizens, 3 state senators, and 3 Assembly members, submitted two major reports containing recommended revisions to the state constitution. The legislature incorporated these into 14 constitutional amendments and submitted them to the voters for approval between 1966 and 1976; the voters approved 10. These amendments simplified, shortened, and reorganized the constitution but made few substantive changes to it.

In 1993 the legislature again established a constitution revision commission, which proposed a number of substantial changes, some of which reformers had discussed for generations. For a variety of reasons, including the difficulty of achieving the two-thirds vote in the Assembly and Senate required to place the proposed changes on the ballot, they were never submitted to the voters.

In 2010 the voters implemented a change to the primary election system that echoed the effort of many Progressive Era reforms to further democratize the political process. This change replaced the party primaries with a "top two" primary election, in which the top two candidates from a list of all candidates, regardless of party, proceed to the November runoff. The new system is no longer a party primary; instead it is like a swim meet or track meet, with preliminary and final races.

Despite its numerous amendments, the California Constitution is not well suited to a state that is 25 times larger than it was in 1900. The legislature is the same size, with 40 state senators and 80 Assembly members, but each state Senate district has grown from just over 60,000 persons to almost 1 million; legislators are able to offer far less individualized attention to their constituents than they could in an earlier era (see the "Who Are Californians?" feature on the next page). In the early twentieth century, small amateur groups could utilize the initiative, but well-funded interest groups are now uniquely able to take advantage of it. Unfortunately, serious efforts to modernize state government have been few and far between, and when they have occurred, as with the constitutional revision commission of the 1990s, the results have been subject to partisan voting and have not achieved the majorities necessary to send them to the people for a final decision.

Who Draws the Lines in California?

The Constitution of 1879 provided for 80 Assembly and 40 Senate districts based on population, and after each U.S. Census the lines were supposed to be redrawn by the state legislature (to account for births, deaths, and people moving). This procedure was followed until 1910, when conflict between urban and rural areas led to the Reapportionment Act of 1911, which shortchanged the growing urban areas of Los Angeles and San Francisco. In 1926 a constitutional amendment made representation in the California Senate even more unequal. In 1964 this unequal representation was declared unconstitutional by the U.S. Supreme Court (in *Reynolds v. Sims*), leading to new districts of roughly equivalent populations.

In 2008, California voters approved a constitutional amendment that placed redistricting in the hands of the new Citizens Redistricting Commission. The commission drew new districts that followed a set of nonpartisan rules, such as creating geographically compact districts that kept existing cities and communities intact.

State Senate Districts, 1883

Population per district

Approx. 29,000

State Senate Districts, 1961

Population per district

▫ 50,000 or less	▪ 200,000 – 499,999
▪ 50,001 – 99,999	▪ 500,000 – 999,999
▫ 100,000 – 199,999	▪ 1,000,000 or more

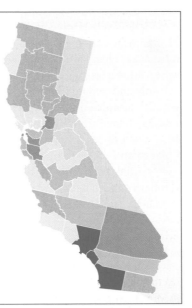

State Senate Districts, 2016

Population per district

Approx. 982,500

SOURCES: Join California, "Election History for the State of California" www.joincalifornia.com/ (accessed 12/19/16); Don A. Allen Sr., Legislative Sourcebook (1965); California Citizens Redistricting Commission, www.wedrawthelines.ca.gov/ (accessed 12/19/16).

forcriticalanalysis

1. Does the large population size of current Assembly and State Senate districts make it difficult for Californians to truly be represented in the legislature?

2. If the plan adopted by California in 1926 is unconstitutional because representation is unequal, why is it that the representation in the U.S. Senate is not invalid?

The Progressive Movement and Its Impact on California Politics

The development of California's distinctive constitution has been influenced by many different groups over the course of the state's history. One group whose influence is still deeply felt in California politics is the Progressives. The Progressive movement had roots in the economic and political changes that swept the United States after the Civil War. It was foreshadowed by the Populist movement, which dominated American politics from 1870 to 1896.

Some of the political concerns and much of the moral indignation expressed by the Populists about the changes taking place in the United States were subsequently reflected in the Progressive movement. From the Civil War on, the country rapidly industrialized, and wealth became concentrated in the hands of a new breed of corporate entrepreneurs. *Monopoly* was the word of the day. These corporate giants dictated economic policy, with significant social and political consequences. One huge corporation, the Southern Pacific Railroad, held a monopoly on shipping in California and could charge producers and retailers exorbitant prices. Its vast wealth and power gave it undue influence not only economically but also politically; along with a web of associated interests, it ruled the state to a degree previously unparalleled in the nation. Bribing public officials was not unusual, nor was handpicking candidates for the two major political parties.[10]

The Progressives countered the powerful corporations, specifically the Southern Pacific Railroad, by prosecuting the corrupt politicians who served them. Eventually, this tactic led to a series of regulatory reforms that loosened the choke hold of the railroad, corrupt politicians, and interest groups on state and local politics.

Local Politics

Progressive reforms began at the local level. The battle against the Southern Pacific Railroad and corporate influence in general started in San Francisco in 1906, with the reform movement fighting to rid city government of graft and bribery. President Theodore Roosevelt stepped in to help. Working hand in hand with James D. Phelan, the former mayor of San Francisco, Roosevelt sent in federal agents led by William J. Burns to investigate bribery and corruption charges.[11] Public officials were put on trial for the bribery, bringing to the public's attention the extent of graft and political corruption in municipal government, and 17 supervisors and a number of corporate leaders were indicted.[12] The mayor was forced to resign, and his henchman, Abraham Reuf, who implicated officials of the Southern Pacific Railroad and several utility companies, was convicted and sentenced to 14 years in jail. Although the graft trials largely failed to convict those indicted (Reuf was an exception), they were nonetheless an important step in breaking the power of the Southern Pacific Railroad and its political allies.

In 1906 the Southern Pacific Railroad also dominated local politics in Los Angeles.[13] During this time, a group dedicated to good government, the Non-Partisan Committee of One Hundred, was formed. They selected a reform candidate for mayor who was opposed by the two major parties, labor groups, and the *Los Angeles Times*. While the reform candidate lost his bid for the mayoralty, 17 of 23 reform candidates for other city positions were elected.[14] The nonpartisan reformers were on their way to ridding the city of the Southern Pacific machine.

This cartoon from 1882 depicts the Southern Pacific Railroad as a destructive octopus with farmers, miners, lumber dealers, and other victims of the company's monopoly on shipping entangled in its tentacles. The faces of Mark Hopkins and Leland Stanford, two of the railroad's founders, form the creature's eyes.

THE CURSE OF CALIFORNIA.

State Politics

The 1907 legislative session was one of the most corrupt on record, heavily controlled by the political operatives of the Southern Pacific Railroad. At the end of the session, the editor of the *Fresno Republican*, Chester Rowell, wrote, "If we are fit to govern ourselves, this is the last time we will submit to be governed by the hired bosses of the Southern Pacific Railroad Company."[15]

At the same time, Rowell and Edward Dickson of the *Los Angeles Express* began to organize a statewide movement to attack Southern Pacific's power. At Dickson's invitation, a group of lawyers, newspaper publishers, and other political reformers met in Los Angeles. They founded the Lincoln Republicans, later to become the League of Lincoln-Roosevelt Republican Clubs (also known as the Lincoln-Roosevelt League), dedicated to ending the control of California politics by the Southern Pacific Railroad and linking themselves to the national Progressive movement.

The Lincoln-Roosevelt League participated in the statewide legislative elections of 1908 and managed to elect a small group of reformers to the legislature. Two years later it fielded a full-party slate, from governor down to local candidates.

STATEHOUSE VICTORY In 1910, Hiram Johnson became the Lincoln-Roosevelt League candidate for governor. He campaigned up and down the state, focusing on one issue: the Southern Pacific Railroad. He claimed that the company, acting in concert with criminal elements, had corrupted the political process in California. He defined the battle as one between decent, law-abiding citizens and a few corrupt, powerful individuals who were determined to run the state in their own best interests.

Johnson won the election and met with leading national Progressives— Theodore Roosevelt, Robert La Follette, and Lincoln Steffens—to discuss a reform program for California. The new administration in Sacramento set out to eliminate every special interest from the government and to make government solely responsive to the people and Johnson. Through a series of legislative acts and constitutional amendments, they made significant progress in that direction. In 1911 the voters passed the initiative, the referendum, and the recall. These three reforms, widely known as **direct democracy**, placed enormous power and control over government in the hands of the voters. Now citizens could write their laws or amend the constitution through the initiative, approve or reject constitutional amendments through the referendum, and remove corrupt politicians from office through the recall.

In addition to these reforms, a new law set up a railroad commission that had power to fix rates beginning in 1911. Other reforms included the direct primary, which gave ordinary citizens the power to select the candidates of the political parties for national and state offices. Women obtained the right to vote in California in 1911. Legislation was also enacted that limited women to an eight-hour workday, set up a workmen's compensation system, put into practice a weekly pay law, and required employers to inform strikebreakers that they were being hired to replace employees on strike (and therefore might face verbal abuse and physical violence). These reforms were in part a reaction to what were viewed as harsh employment practices by Southern Pacific Railroad.

The Progressives in California made significant headway in limiting the influence of corporations and political parties in politics. In its first two years in office, the Johnson administration succeeded in breaking the power of the Southern Pacific Railroad.[16]

LAST HURRAH The national Progressive Party lost its bid to capture the White House in 1912 with Theodore Roosevelt on the ticket for president and Hiram Johnson for vice president. The failure to win an important national office weakened the party by lessening the enthusiasm of its supporters. It also meant that the party had no patronage with which to reward its followers between elections. Electoral failure was just one of several major problems that plagued the Progressives. Several other factors also contributed to the decline of the party: the public grew tired of reform; there was a major falling out among the leadership in California; the Progressives generally opposed World War I, which was supported by the overwhelming majority of the American public once the country got into the war; and the party failed to support reforms that labor so badly wanted.

When the Progressives learned that the Republican Party would not nominate Roosevelt in 1916, they offered him the nomination. Roosevelt declined. At a dinner in San Francisco in July 1916, the California Progressive Party disbanded and Hiram Johnson urged his followers to join either the Republican or the Democratic Party. Later that year Johnson, now a Republican, was elected to the U.S. Senate, where he served for 28 years.

If there was one major flaw in Progressive thinking, it was the belief in the active, informed citizen willing to participate in politics. Progressives believed that given the opportunity, citizens would be happy to support the democratic process and spend whatever time and effort was needed to participate in elections. Since the late 1940s, however, a host of studies have shown that many people neither vote nor pay attention to politics. But the Progressives leave behind the significant legacy of having gained tremendous political power for the people of California, if and when Californians choose to use it.

The Progressive strategies to gain power for the people were appropriate for 1910, when California had a population of 2.4 million. Since then, California has grown so much and so quickly that its constitution has been unable to catch up: in a state of now 39.3 million people, reforms that allowed "the people" to propose initiatives and recall public officials cannot now be exercised on a statewide[17] level without a great deal of money, organization, and professional help. The last initiative that did *not* use paid, professional signature gatherers was introduced in 1990, and it relied on a paid campaign coordinator. An initiative organized completely by volunteers has not been successful since 1984.

Direct Democracy

The Progressives established civil service reforms, nonpartisan commissions to control key state regulatory functions, nonpartisan elections to cripple local machines, office block voting (a ballot listing all candidates for a given office under the name of that office), and primary elections. Even if these innovations have failed to check the power of special interests, they have given voters the power of direct action through the initiative, referendum, and recall. Citizens activate these three mechanisms by circulating petitions to gather a required number of signatures and bring the measure to statewide vote. The number of signatures, as we shall see, varies depending on the mechanism.

Initiative

THE PROCESS Of the three direct voices in government, the **initiative** is the most well known and most frequently used. The process, also known as direct legislation, requires the proponent to obtain a title (for example, "Public Schools: English as Required Language of Instruction") and summary of the proposed initiative from the state attorney general. Upon obtaining the title and summary, the proponents have 150 days to circulate a petition to gather the required number of signatures to qualify for the ballot—5 percent of voters in the last gubernatorial election for statutes, and 8 percent for constitutional amendments. The secretary of state submits the measure at the next general election held at least 131 days after it qualifies or at any special election held before the next general election. The governor may call a special election for the measure.

Before 1960 initiatives appeared only on the general election ballot, thus limiting their use to the two-year election cycle. From 1960 to 2012 they appeared on the primary, general, and special-election ballots. In 2012 a new law, propelled by the Democratic majority in the legislature, again required that ballot propositions appear only on the general election ballot in November, motivated by the general consensus that the smaller and more conservative primary electorates disadvantage more liberal initiatives.

FREQUENCY OF USE Initiatives have become indispensable to California's political fabric. From 1912 to 2016 over 1,900 initiatives were titled and summarized for circulation. Of this number, 380 qualified for the ballot, 3 were removed by court order, and 135 were approved by the voters—for an overall passage rate of 36 percent. Of the 135 initiatives approved, 42 were constitutional amendments and 13 were constitutional/stationary changes.[18]

Figure 2.2 presents the use of initiative by decade. Note these two points: the increasing frequency of initiatives since 1970, and the varying, but generally low, level of success for the measures that made it to the ballot.

For discussion purposes, we can compress the 100-year history of initiatives into four time periods: 1912–39, 1940–69, 1970–99, and 2000–16.

1912–39 From the beginning, various individuals and special interests understood that the initiative could be used to forward their special causes. Social and cultural

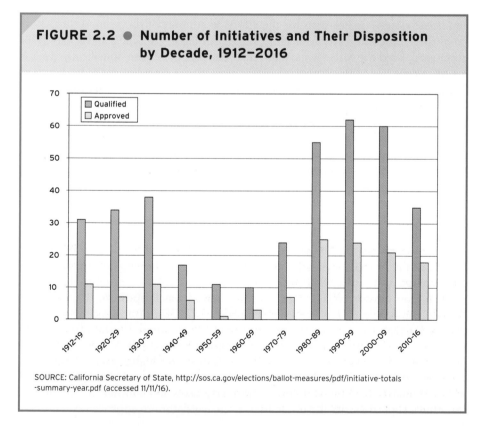

FIGURE 2.2 ● **Number of Initiatives and Their Disposition by Decade, 1912–2016**

SOURCE: California Secretary of State, http://sos.ca.gov/elections/ballot-measures/pdf/initiative-totals-summary-year.pdf (accessed 11/11/16).

issues, such as outlawing professional fighting, prostitution, gambling on horse races, and land ownership by Asian Americans, drew the highest voter turnout during this period. Labor issues (closed versus open shops) and tax propositions were also volatile issues.

No single issue, however, dominated the initiative process during this period more than the so-called liquor question.[19] These initiatives were among the most controversial, and they drew high voter turnouts. Twelve measures related to liquor control appeared on the ballot between 1914 and 1936, for and against full prohibition and anti-saloon measures, and state regulation versus local control. Voting was consistent throughout this period, with the anti-Prohibition forces generally prevailing on every measure. The issue, however, wouldn't go away; in 1948, after many failures to qualify an initiative, the anti-liquor forces qualified another local option measure, which was rejected by 70 percent of the voters. After this vote, the issue lost its appeal, never to appear on the ballot again.

1940–69 In this time period use of the initiative declined markedly. Compared to the previous 27 years, a higher percentage of proposed measures failed to gather enough signatures to qualify for the ballot. The subject matter of the initiatives also varied from those of 1912–39. Newer issues came to the forefront: race and civil rights, property taxes, and labor and welfare.

Proposition 14 (1964) was the most prominent of a number of initiatives that dealt with fair housing. The initiative was drafted to nullify the Rumford Fair Housing Act, which prohibited discrimination in the rental, lease, or purchase of housing on the basis of race and national origin. The Rumford Act, supporters of Proposition 14 claimed, interfered with their private property rights. Real estate and homeowners' associations led the efforts in support of the proposition; a coalition of Democratic Party leadership, organized labor, churches, and a variety of other groups led the forces against it. The broader issue of race, specifically regarding treatment of and biases toward African Americans, lingered in the background of the campaign; by all accounts, race was the deciding factor in how people voted. Proposition 14 passed by a 2-to-1 margin in November 1964. Its victory was a major impetus for the Watts riots during the summer of 1965, which lasted six days, resulted in 34 deaths, and damaged almost 1,000 buildings.[20] Over the next two years, Proposition 14 was overturned, first by the California Supreme Court and then by the U.S. Supreme Court, for violating the Fourteenth Amendment.

1970–99 In this period initiatives abounded, with over 1,000 initiatives receiving titles, 141 qualifying for ballot, and 56 approved by the voters. The subjects involved social, cultural, and economic issues, including the death penalty, gun control, busing, the property tax, nuclear power, water resources, air quality, coastal preservation, English as the official language, affirmative action, undocumented immigrants, and gay marriage.

The most controversial initiative of this period was Proposition 13, titled the "People's Initiative to Limit Property Taxation" (1978). Sponsored by longtime antitax activists Howard Jarvis and Paul Gann, Proposition 13 was a reaction to the spiraling appreciation of property throughout the 1970s. In just one year, some properties were reassessed at a value 50 to 100 percent higher, and their owners' tax bills jumped accordingly. Proposition 13 included several provisions, one of which dramatically reduced residential property taxes and another that required a two-thirds supermajority in both houses of the legislature to approve tax increases.

Proposition 13 was a grassroots effort, opposed by nearly every state employee and labor union and most Democratic leaders. The pro side raised $2.2 million, and the con side raised $2 million. On June 6, 1978, nearly two-thirds of California's voters passed the proposition, reducing property tax rates by about 57 percent.

Now, almost 40 years later, Proposition 13 is still hotly debated. Critics argue that it creates tax inequities by treating residential and commercial property as equivalent and by assessing similar properties in different ways based solely on when a homeowner bought a house. Supporters argue that pegging property taxes to the value of the property, assessed yearly, exposes homeowners to accelerated yearly property taxes, which leaves them vulnerable to losing their homes.

2000–16 During this period, California voters decided on 94 initiatives in 18 separate elections, 3 of which were special elections, including the special election to recall Governor Gray Davis. Initiatives that passed included measures on farm animal confinement practices, redistricting the state legislative boundaries, victims' rights, and parole procedures. (See Table 2.1 for a list of the top contributors for this period.)

The most controversial and long-lasting ballot issue deals with same-sex marriage, an issue that has been publicly debated for some 35 years. In 1977 the state legislature passed a law stating that marriage was a "personal relation arising out of a civil contract between a man and a woman." This was reaffirmed in 2000 when the voters passed Proposition 22, a statutory—not constitutional—amendment that revised the California Family Code to define marriage as between a man and a woman. However, in May 2008, the California Supreme Court ruled Proposition 22

TABLE 2.1 ● Top Contributors to Initiative Ballot Committees, 2000–16

Contributor	Amount
California Teachers Association	$154,714,998
Pharmaceutical Research & Manufacturers of America	70,549,206
Philip Morris	66,762,336
Pacific Gas & Electric Company	62,461,250
California Association of Hospital and Health Systems	60,448,154
California State Council of Service Employees	58,367,914
Charles Munger, Jr.	56,440,505
Stephen L. Bing	51,066,372
Pechanga Band of Luiseno Mission Indians	48,821,480
Morongo Casino Resort Spa	46,660,977
Chevron Corporation	44,527,500
Molly Munger	44,456,347
Thomas Steyer	39,854,000
RJ Reynolds Tobacco Company	36,680,569
Agua Caliente Band of Cahuilla Indians	34,940,025

SOURCE: National Institute on Money in State Politics, www.followthemoney.org/show-me?s=CA&y=2016,2015,2014, 2013,2012,2011,2010,2009,2008,2007,2006,2005,2004,2003,2002,2001,2000&m-exi=1#[(3|(1|gro=d-ad-st,d-eid (accessed 11/17/2016).

Two same-sex couples—Paul Katami and Jeffrey Zarrillo, and Kristin Perry and Sandra Stier—pictured here outside the U.S. Supreme Court, were the plaintiffs in *Hollingsworth v. Perry*. The Court held that the sponsors of Proposition 8 "lacked standing" to appeal the federal court ruling that upheld same-sex marriage under the Equal Protection Clause of the federal Constitution and thus paved the way for same-sex marriage in California.

invalid. At about the same time, fearing such a decision, proponents of Proposition 8 ("Eliminates Right of Same-Sex Couples to Marry") had already begun to qualify the initiative for the ballot, relying on a **constitutional amendment**, not a **statute**, to end debate on the issue.

The campaign over Proposition 8 was fiercely contested. In the end, the initiative passed by a margin of 52.3 to 47.7 percent. Both sides raised significant amounts of money: those supporting Proposition 8 contributed $39 million, while those opposing contributed $44 million, making it the second most expensive initiative campaign in state history (behind only Proposition 87 in 2006) and the highest expenditure on a same-sex marriage initiative campaign in the nation. After the election, six lawsuits were filed with the California Supreme Court by same-sex couples and government bodies challenging the constitutionality of Proposition 8. The court consented to hear three of the six jointly, but it denied the request to stay the enforcement of Proposition 8. On May 26, 2009, the court ruled that Proposition 8 was valid but allowed existing same-sex marriages to stand (in *Strauss v. Horton*).

Opponents of Proposition 8 then took their fight to federal court, which, on August 4, 2010, declared the ban unconstitutional in *Perry v. Schwarzenegger* (now *Perry v. Brown*). This decision was upheld by the Ninth Circuit in February 2012. The supporters of Proposition 8 (but not the state government) then appealed to the U.S. Supreme Court. The Court ruled in *Hollingsworth v. Perry* in June 2013 that the proposition's supporters could not appeal the case; only the state government could defend a proposition approved by the voters, and the state had declined to do so. As a result of this decision, same-sex marriage is legal in California.

How can we account for the increase in initiatives over the past four decades? The simplest explanation is that it is a consequence of several factors, including the complexity of modern society and the increased willingness of the government to regulate decisions previously left to citizens. Additionally, the legislature went from part to full time in 1968, which had a number of significant effects on California politics: more politicians made a career in the field, more legislation was passed, the budget grew, and decision making and power shifted to Sacramento.

These shifts, coupled with the other Progressive reforms designed to rid the capital of political corruption and an unresponsive legislature—direct primaries, term limits, regulation of campaign contributions, and various tactics to weaken political parties—undermined voters' influence on elected officials. Frustrated by the action or inaction of the legislature, voters have turned to the initiative to get what they want.

In addition to voters, special interests frequently turned to initiatives during this period to promote policies they could not get through the legislature. Money has increasingly become the only requirement for a successful initiative campaign. As a result, an industry of professional campaign managers and signature gatherers is flourishing. These so-called policy managers identify hot issues and then search for clients who will pay for the privilege of sponsoring the initiative.

Referendum

THE PROCESS The referendum allows voters to approve or reject constitutional amendments or statutes proposed or passed by the state legislature. There are two types of referendum: the legislative referendum, and the popular referendum.[21]

The **legislative referendum** exists when the legislature proposes a constitutional amendment or revision and the issuing of the majority of bonds (long-term borrowing to finance capital projects such as construction of buildings and infrastructure). This type of referendum must be approved by two-thirds vote of both houses of the legislature before it appears on the ballot.

The **popular referendum** is employed when voters are displeased with a law that was passed by the legislature. The requirements are the same as those for the initiative, and the two are sometimes confused. The process is as follows: the measure may be proposed by presenting to the secretary of state a petition with signatures equal to 5 percent of the voters in the last gubernatorial election. The filing of the signatures must take place within a 90-day period after the enactment of the statute. If the measure qualifies to be on the ballot, the law in question may not take effect until the electorate decides whether it should become a law.

FREQUENCY OF USE The referendum is used infrequently. In fact, it has almost faded from use. Between 1912 and 2016, 50 referenda have appeared on the ballot. Voters rejected 29 laws and approved 21. Of the seven approved since 1982, five dealt with Indian gaming. Proposition 29 (2000) rejected repeal of the Pala Indian tribe compact that authorized the operation of "video lottery terminals" if operated as lotteries, not slot machines. Propositions 94, 95, 96, and 97 (2008) allowed four individual tribes to operate additional slot machines and revised the environmental impact procedures. In 2012 voters approved a measure redistricting state Senate districts drawn by the Citizens Redistricting Commission, making districts more compact with near equal populations.[22] In the 2016 general election, voters upheld a law passed by the state legislature that prohibited grocery and other retail stores from providing single-use plastic or paper carryout bags at point of sale and placed a 10-cent charge on reusable paper bags.

Recall

THE PROCESS The **recall** allows voters to determine whether to eject an elected official from office before his or her term expires. Proponents first submit a petition alleging the reason for recall. They then have 150 days to present to the secretary of state a petition with the required number of signatures to qualify for the ballot. If the sitting official is recalled, a successor is elected. Most recalls are of school board or city council members at the local level.

For statewide offices, the number of signatures must be equal to 12 percent of the last vote for the office, with signatures from at least five counties equal to 1 percent of the last vote for the office in the county. For the Senate, Assembly, members of the Board of Equalization, and judges, the number of signatures must be equal to 20 percent of the last vote for the office. Upon receiving the petitions, an election must be held between 60 and 80 days from the date of certification of sufficient signatures.

FREQUENCY OF USE Recall of statewide offices or the state legislature are rare. There have been eight recall elections out of 118 filings against state officeholders. Seven of the eight were state legislators; Governor Gray Davis in 2003 was the other. Four of the state legislators were expelled from office. The recall was put into use against three state legislators almost immediately after its passage—twice in 1913, against Senator Marshall Black for involvement in a banking scandal, which succeeded, and against Senator James Owen for corruption, which failed. The next year, Senator Edwin Grant, who represented the red-light district in San Francisco, was recalled for opposing prostitution, which succeeded.

Four other state legislators faced a recall vote in 1994 and 1995. The National Rifle Association failed in its attempt to recall Senator David Roberti for his position on gun control legislation. Two Republican members of the Assembly, Doris Allen and Paul Horcher, were voted out of office for supporting Willie Brown for speaker in a battle between the parties for control of the Assembly. And an attempt to recall Democratic Assemblyman Mike Machado for backing Republicans failed.[23]

The most notorious recall, however, was that of Governor Davis. He is the only California governor to have been recalled, although there have been over two dozen previous attempts, including three against Ronald Reagan in the 1960s and one against Pete Wilson in the 1990s. During the 2002 campaign for governor, Davis, the incumbent governor, had claimed that the budget deficit was $18 billion, but a week after his election he revealed it was actually $35 billion. Proponents of the recall immediately accused Davis of misleading voters about the severity of the state's budget crisis during his reelection campaign. Other actions prompting the recall included the governor's efforts to prevent the anti-immigrant Proposition 187 from being appealed to the U.S. Supreme Court and his approval of two gun-control measures. The public also held Governor Davis partially responsible for the electricity crisis, during which some people's electricity bills doubled and even tripled. Supporters of the recall also blamed Davis for California's generally weak economy. After Representative Darrell Issa, who hoped to run for governor, funded the signature collection effort with a contribution of $2 million, the recall took off on its own momentum. Because the filing requirements to run as Davis's successor were relatively low, 135 candidates filed to replace him. Arnold Schwarzenegger's candidacy quickly gained the most attention and he easily won the two-part election, in which voters were asked to decide whether Davis should be recalled and to choose his successor. Only 4 of the 135 candidates received more than 1 percent of the vote.

Debating the Merit of Direct Democracy

The debate about the merits of direct democracy has been ongoing since its adoption in the early twentieth century. As we have seen, the initiative has been employed more than referendum or recall and is generally the focus of the debate on the value of direct democracy.

Many scholars believe that the initiative blurs the complexity of many issues and reduces them to clichés or sound bites for the voter. Some writers, such as journalists David Broder and Peter Schrag, believe that special interests with deep pockets dominate the initiative process, undermining the efficacy of representative government with its built-in system of checks and balances. Other writers, such as academics Elisabeth R. Gerber and Shaun Bowler, argue that money plays a vital role in defeating initiatives but not in passing them. They hold that successful initiatives are the product of grassroots movements that have more to do with easily grasped social and economic issues than with well-financed campaigns.

Most who have studied the initiative believe it to be a flawed method of forming public policy. Many initiatives are poorly drafted and are difficult to understand even for judges and legislators. The process is complex, and proponents cannot correct errors once circulation of petitions has begun. The legislature is discouraged from participating in the process at all. Reflecting the strong historic bias of its citizens against the legislature, California is the only state that prohibits the legislature from amending initiatives unless permission is written into the initiative itself. Even then, it usually requires a supermajority of two-thirds of the legislature to approve changes, a level of support difficult if not impossible to obtain on significant amendments. Qualifying initiatives by signature is too easy for a signature-gathering firm and too difficult in the five months allowed for those without one, meaning that a large amount of money is necessary in order to qualify an initiative.

Supporters of the initiative, on the other hand, claim that it is a more effective means of serving the majority in California than the legislative process. Therein lies the catch-22 that largely defines California politics: the legislature is supposedly hamstrung by the zealous use of direct democracy, while direct democracy is supposedly necessary to overcome an unproductive legislature.

A 2013 Public Policy Institute of California (PPIC) poll (see Figure 2.3) showed continued strong support for the initiative process, with 72 percent of likely voters viewing as positive the initiative's power to change public policy, and 60 percent agreeing that public policies made through the initiative are superior to those made by the governor and legislature. Likely voters support several reforms of the initiative process, however: more public disclosure of funding sources on initiatives; giving the legislature and the initiative's sponsors more time to seek a compromise before the initiative goes on the ballot; and increased public engagement, such as a citizens' commission to hold hearings on initiatives and make ballot recommendations. Oregon established such a program in 2011.

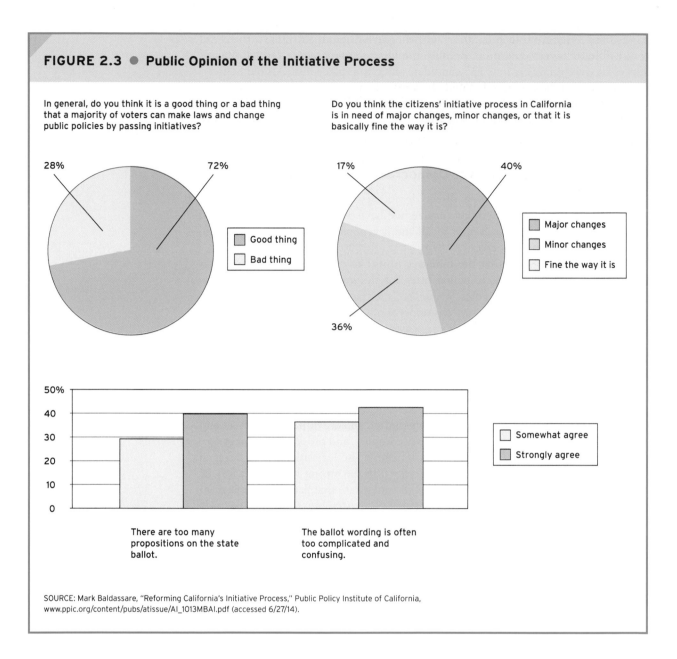

FIGURE 2.3 ● Public Opinion of the Initiative Process

In general, do you think it is a good thing or a bad thing that a majority of voters can make laws and change public policies by passing initiatives?

28% 72%

- Good thing
- Bad thing

Do you think the citizens' initiative process in California is in need of major changes, minor changes, or that it is basically fine the way it is?

17% 40%
36%

- Major changes
- Minor changes
- Fine the way it is

- Somewhat agree
- Strongly agree

There are too many propositions on the state ballot.

The ballot wording is often too complicated and confusing.

SOURCE: Mark Baldassare, "Reforming California's Initiative Process," Public Policy Institute of California, www.ppic.org/content/pubs/atissue/AI_1013MBAI.pdf (accessed 6/27/14).

California's Constitution: Where Are We Now?

California's constitution has been through three stages—establishment in the mid-1800s, rewriting in 1879, and extensive amendment during the Progressive Era. Since then, a fourth, ongoing stage has been defined by political scientists and others, in which numerous suggestions have been made to update the constitutional framework. Most notably, the 1996 California Constitutional Revision Commission made many suggestions to strengthen the governor and make state government less susceptible to interest-group influence. These suggestions included the following:

- Having the governor and lieutenant governor run as a team. Because the governor and lieutenant governor currently are elected separately, their political agendas may diverge.

- Having the other elected members of the executive branch appointed by the governor. The governor currently has no supervisory responsibility over the lieutenant governor, the secretary of state, the treasurer, the controller, the attorney general, the insurance commissioner, and the state superintendent of public instruction. The lack of supervisory authority significantly weakens the governor as a leader (see Chapter 6).

- Merging the several tax administration agencies. The state currently has three tax administration agencies; merging them would save money (see Chapter 6).

- Lengthening term limits for legislators. In 2012 the term limit for state Assembly members was lengthened from 6 years to 12 and for state senators from 8 years to 12, provided the total time in both chambers is limited to 12 years. This is an improvement over the stricter limits enacted in 1990, but the term limits still increase the likelihood that major, complex state legislation will be enacted by inexperienced legislators (see Chapter 4).

Most of these proposals have never come before the voters.

Study Guide

FOR FURTHER READING

Alexander, Robert. *Interest Group Involvement in Ballot Campaigns.* Westport, CT: Praeger Publishers, 2002.

Allswang, John M. *The Initiative and Referendum in California, 1898–1998.* Stanford, CA: Stanford University Press, 2000.

Broder, David. *Democracy Derailed: Initiative Campaigns and the Power of Money.* New York: Harcourt, 2000.

California Secretary of State. "History of California Initiatives." www.sos.ca.gov/elections/ballot-measures/resources -and-historical-information/history-california-initiatives/. Accessed 6/15/16.

Donovan, Todd, S. Bowler, D. McCuan, and K. Fernandez. "Contending Players and Strategies: Opposition Advantages in Initiative Elections." In *Citizens as Legislators: Direct Democracy in the United States,* edited by S. Bowler, T. Donovan, and C. Tolbert, 133–52. Columbus: Ohio State University Press, 1998.

Gerber, Elisabeth. *The Populist Paradox: Interest Group Influence on the Promise of Direct Legislation.* Princeton, NJ: Princeton University Press, 1999.

Hofstadter, Richard. *The Age of Reform.* New York: Washington Square Press, 1988.

Johnson, Hiram. "First Inaugural Address." January 3, 1913. http://governors.library.ca.gov/addresses/23-hjohnson01 .html. Accessed 6/20/16.

Matthews, Joe, and Mark Paul. *California Crackup, How Reforms Broke the Golden State and How We Can Fix It.* Berkeley: University of California Press, 2010.

Mowry, George. *The California Progressives.* Chicago: Quadrangle Paperbacks, 1963.

Olin, Spencer C., Jr. *California's Prodigal Sons: Hiram Johnson and the Progressives, 1911–1917.* Berkeley: University of California Press, 1968.

"Policy Forum: Do Ballot Initiatives Undermine Democracy?" *Cato Policy Report* (July–August 2000): 6–9. www .cato.org/pubs/policy_report/v22n4/initiatives.pdf. Accessed 6/20/16.

Schrag, Peter. *Paradise Lost: California's Experience, America's Future.* Berkeley: University of California Press, 1998.

Starr, Kevin. *Inventing the Dream: California through the Progressive Era.* New York: Oxford University Press, 1985.

———. *California: A History.* New York: The Modern Library, 2005.

Swisher, Carl Brent. *Motivation and Political Technique in the California Constitutional Convention: 1878–79.* New York: Da Capo Press, 1969.

ON THE WEB

Baldassare, Mark. *At Issue, Reforming California's Initiative Process.* Public Policy Institute of California, 2013. www.ppic .org/main/publication.asp?i=1071. Accessed 6/20/16.

Baldassare, Mark, Dean Bonner, Sonja Petek, and Jui Shrestha. *The Initiative Process in California.* Public Policy Institute of California, 2013. www.ppic.org/main/publication _show.asp?i=1072. Accessed 6/20/16.

California Secretary of State. *Ballot Measures.* www.sos.ca.gov /elections. Accessed 6/20/16.

California State Constitution. www.leginfo.ca.gov/const.html. Accessed 6/20/16. This site makes the California State Constitution searchable by keyword.

Center for Governmental Studies. *Democracy by Initiative.* May 2008. www.policyarchive.org/collections/cgs/index ?section=5&id=5800. Accessed 6/20/16. Search for "Democracy by Initiative."

Initiative & Referendum Institute. www.iandrinstitute.org. Accessed 7/20/16.

Southern Pacific Historical & Technical Society. www.sphts .org. Accessed 6/20/16.

SUMMARY

I. The history of the California Constitution comprises four stages.
   A. 1849: basic structure of government established. Includes separation of powers, bicameralism, federalism, and popular election of most state offices.
   B. 1879: a constitutional convention adds nine new articles and 8,000 words to respond to the reform needs of the time.
   C. 1910–17: the Progressive Era adds the initiative, referendum, and recall, as well as hundreds of reform laws.
   D. 1960–present: California voters have authorized a few significant reforms.

II. Proposing an amendment to the California Constitution is easy.
   A. Amendments can be proposed in three ways:
      1. Through a constitutional convention. The legislature can convene the convention by a two-thirds vote, or it can be convened by a majority vote of the electorate from an initiative. A Bay Area business group tried to collect sufficient signatures for a new constitutional convention in 2009–10 but gave up because professional signature-gathering firms refused to work with the group, feeling that the effort would imperil their future existence.
      2. Amendments may be proposed by collecting signatures through the initiative process.
         a) Signatures totaling 8 percent of the vote in the last gubernatorial election are required, collected over a five-month period.
         b) Most amendments are proposed this way. The cost is approximately $1 million to $2 million, mostly for signature gathering.
      3. The legislature may propose an amendment by a two-thirds vote.
   B. Amendments must go through a ratification stage. Regardless of the way in which an amendment is proposed, the electorate must then ratify the amendment before it goes into the constitution. A majority vote is required.

III. The Progressive reformers had several key goals.
   A. Ending the dominance of big business, especially the Southern Pacific Railroad, over the state.
   B. Reforming the corrupt political process.
   C. Removing from office corrupt political officials at the state and local levels of government.
   D. Returning political power to the people.

IV. Progressive laws and constitutional amendments wrought many significant changes.
   A. Ended child labor
   B. Established a state park system
   C. Enacted protections for working people
   D. Established nonpartisan elections
   E. Instituted primary elections
   F. Created office block voting
   G. Set in motion the process of direct democracy—the initiative, referendum, and recall

   H. Resulted in the great number of Progressive reforms that are still in operation today

V. Direct democracy is a vital aspect of California politics.
   A. The initiative is the most popular of the three direct democracy mechanisms.
      1. Proponents need to gather signatures equal to 5 percent of voters in the last gubernatorial election for statutes and 8 percent of the voters for constitutional amendments.
      2. Since 1912 roughly 34 percent of initiatives that have been voted on have passed.
      3. The initiative has increasingly become a mechanism by which special interests or wealthy individuals can pass legislation by circumventing the legislature.
   B. The referendum refers legislation to the voters for a direct decision. There are two types of referendum: legislative and popular.
      1. Legislative referendum allows voters to decide on statutes or constitutional amendments as well as most bond measures proposed by the legislature; it takes a two-thirds vote of the legislature to place a referendum on the ballot.
      2. Popular referendum allows voters to approve or repeal an act of the legislature. If the legislature passes a law that voters do not approve of, they may gather signatures to demand a popular vote on the law. Proponents need to gather signatures equal to 5 percent of voters in the last gubernatorial election.
      3. The referendum is infrequently used and has appeared on the ballot less than 50 times since 1912.
   C. The recall allows voters to remove a public official from elected office before his or her term is up.
      1. The number of signatures that needs to be gathered depends on the office: 12 percent of the last vote for statewide office from at least five counties equal to 1 percent of the last vote in the county; 20 percent of the last vote for office for Senate, Assembly, and Board of Equalization.
      2. Since 1912 there have been only eight recalls of statewide officials and legislative members.
      3. Governor Gray Davis is the only statewide official to have been recalled.

1. The popular direct-democracy process by which citizens can place a constitutional amendment or statute on the ballot is called a(n)
   a) referendum.
   b) initiative.
   c) recall.
   d) nonpartisan election.

2. The individual who served as governor during much of the Progressive period was
   a) Chester Rowell.
   b) Edward Dickson.
   c) Hiram Johnson.
   d) Samuel P. Huntington.

3. The process by which a petition signed by a specific percentage of those who cast votes in the last gubernatorial election enables voters to approve or reject a law enacted by the legislature is a(n)
   a) popular referendum.
   b) initiative.
   c) recall.
   d) nonpartisan election.

4. The process by which an elected official is removed from office before his or her term expires is called a(n)
   a) referendum.
   b) initiative.
   c) recall.
   d) nonpartisan election.

5. Progressive reformers pointed to this company whenever they spoke about machine politics and corporate privilege in Sacramento:
   a) Standard Oil Company
   b) Bank of America
   c) Southern Pacific Railroad
   d) Northern Securities Company

6. The only sitting California governor to be recalled from office was
   a) Ronald Reagan.
   b) Jerry Brown.
   c) Gray Davis.
   d) Pete Wilson.

7. Which of the following direct-democracy devices allows voters to approve or reject constitutional amendments or statutes and the majority of bond measures put on the ballot by the legislature?
   a) initiative
   b) direct primary
   c) legislative referendum
   d) recall

8. In which historical block was the greatest number of initiatives titled?
   a) 1912–39
   b) 1940–69
   c) 1970–99
   d) 2000–16

9. Which of the following is not a Progressive Era reform?
   a) nonpartisan elections
   b) primary elections
   c) the office block vote
   d) party caucuses

10. Which of the following is not a legal way to amend the California constitution?
    a) The legislature can convene a constitutional convention by a two-thirds vote.
    b) The governor can sign into law a proposed amendment passed by the legislature.
    c) The legislature may propose a constitutional amendment by a two-thirds vote.
    d) The electorate can propose a constitutional amendment through the initiative process.

CRITICAL-THINKING QUESTIONS

1. The California Constitution has gone through a series of revisions. Identify the periods of those revisions and discuss the contributions that each made to the state's political structure.

2. Suppose you worked for a coalition of interest groups supporting legislation to increase the state sales tax to fund a state-run health care system. The coalition is frustrated by the lack of action in the legislature. They come to you for advice about the initiative process and the possibility of success. What would you tell them, based on what you've learned in this chapter?

3. Some people argue that direct democracy provides citizens with another way to correct the behavior and deci-sion making of public officials. Others argue that it is merely the instrument of those special interest groups that have enough money to manipulate the political process. Present an argument for each position. Where do you stand in this debate?

4. California is the model Progressive state. The key components of the Progressive agenda, however, greatly weakened the role of political parties in the state. Identify and discuss how some of these Progressive reforms have weakened the state's party system. Is this a good or a bad thing? Do you think there are any correlations between weak parties and the increasing use of the initiative process?

KEY TERMS

constitutional amendment (p. 36)
direct democracy (p. 31)
initiative (p. 32)

Progressive movement (p. 21)
recall (p. 38)
legislative referendum (p. 37)

popular referendum (p. 37)
statute (p. 36)

3 Interest Groups and the Media in California

WHAT INTEREST GROUPS DO AND WHY THEY MATTER IN CALIFORNIA POLITICS

Consider the diversity of organizations that try to influence governmental policy or legislation:

- A **student organization** opposes legislation to raise tuition at state universities.
- A **business trade association** supports legislation that would reform the state's workers' compensation insurance system.
- A **beverage company** opposes legislation to tax sugar-sweetened soft drinks and label them with warnings of health hazards.
- A **citizens' group** supports legislation that would impose stricter penalties on people convicted of drunk driving.
- An **association of county governments** opposes legislation that prohibits the placing of certain juvenile offenders into group homes that are located in residential neighborhoods.
- A **public employees' union** supports legislation that prohibits state agencies from contracting with businesses unless the businesses pay their employees the equivalent of a living wage.

Each of these organizations is an interest group. Interest groups have always been part of California's (and the United States') political landscape. They are a product of freedom of association, a First Amendment right under our democratic system of government.

Interest groups are associations of individuals who seek to influence policy decisions in the legislature, the executive branch, and administrative agencies, as well as through direct legislation (the initiative). They are one method, as is voting, for individuals to voice their opinions on issues that concern them.

Interest groups are also called pressure groups, political advocacy groups, special interest groups, and lobbying groups. Because they focus primarily on influencing policy decisions in the legislature, interest groups are often referred to as the **third house**, a term that describes their standing and influence in the legislative process.[1]

In California, interest groups are especially influential because of the state's unique political landscape. As we shall see, open primaries, top-two primary elections, term limits, and nonpartisan elections at the local level have freed candidates from party dependence and pushed them toward interest groups for financial backing and help with mobilizing voters. At the same time, interest groups have realized that they can successfully use the initiative process to achieve political goals and have spared no expense in launching propositions, even when they are in conflict with broad-based citizen interests.

Character of Interest Groups

All Californians are represented, whether wittingly or not, by interest groups such as county and city governments, trade associations, labor unions, professional and religious organizations, educational institutions, and environmental groups. When a government recognizes the right of association, citizens will exercise that right, and groups of all types will form. There is much debate about the influence of interest groups in the political arena, especially about whether the theories of **pluralism** or **elitism** best explain their status and power in the political process.

Pluralist theory considers the political system as a marketplace in which a multitude of interests compete, where no single interest or combination of interests is powerful enough to dominate and government sits outside as an umpire or a referee. Pluralist theory argues that power is dispersed. To achieve success, interests often have to join together to bargain and negotiate with opposition interests, producing, by the end of the process, policy decisions. Pluralist theory acknowledges that some groups are stronger and more successful than others; however, it also contends that these groups do not necessarily succeed all or even a majority of the time—weaker but well-organized groups do sometimes succeed in achieving their goals or checking stronger groups.

Elitist theory acknowledges that there are many interest groups active in the political process but argues that most of them have minimal power. Power rests in the hands of a few groups, such as large national and multinational corporations, universities, foundations, and public policy institutes, where leaders (elites) set the agenda and determine the policy outcomes of government. Accordingly, when it comes to important policy matters, such as the economy and noteworthy social issues, elites representing a narrow range of groups determine the basic direction of public policy. Still, elite theory recognizes that less powerful groups, most commonly in coalition with other less powerful groups, are occasionally able to check the proposals of the elites. This is especially true when elites can't agree among themselves on policy choices.

But neither of these theories perfectly describes interest groups in California; in practice, California politics is a blend of pluralism and elitism. In each legislative session, there is widespread interest group activity, with literally thousands of interests competing for influence on more than 2,000 bills. Most of these groups, from child care facilities and auto repair shops to environmental organizations, trade unions, and businesses, focus on measures that directly affect their interests. Often these issues are of limited concern to the public at large. In these circumstances, the groups involved in the issue, whether supporting or opposed to it, work to create policy through competition and compromise. Here the pluralism theory fits well. Yet on some broad-based issues, a small number of (elite) groups, such as public employee unions and multinational corporations, influence decision making to favor their own special interests. They are able to exert power on the legislature, the public, and other interest groups because of their economic clout and ability to contribute great sums of money to candidates, independent committees, ballot initiatives, and public relations campaigns. In the end, California politics is a mixture of pluralism and elitism, depending on the issue in question and the stakes presented.

Diversity of Interest Groups

The term *interest group* is all inclusive, covering a wide range of businesses and organizations. The California secretary of state classifies interest groups into 19 categories and indicates the amount spent by each category for lobbying during a two-year legislative session. Table 3.1 lists the figures for the 2013–14 session.

Many organizations openly state under the About tab on their web sites that **lobbying** or advocacy is a major part of their activity; this is a principal reason why many individuals and businesses join the group. For example, the California Applicants' Attorneys Association claims to be "the most powerful and most knowledgeable legal voice for the injured workers of California"; the California Labor Federation, AFL-CIO, professes to promote "the interests of working people and their families for the betterment of California communities"; and the California Alliance of Child and Family Services claims it is "the champion and leading voice for organizations that advocate for children and families, and for advancing policies and services on their behalves."

Table 3.2 lists the top employers of lobbyists. This list has remained relatively stable over the past several years, with three or four groups moving in and out of the ranks from one year to the next, depending on their agenda in the legislative session. By most standards, the lobbyists for these groups are some of the most successful in Sacramento. Note how the top 10 employers of lobbyists match up with the categories in Table 3.1. The health sector, for instance, is third in total contributions, and the California Hospital Association and Kaiser Foundation Health Plan both make the list.

Individual businesses and educational institutions, however, rarely identify lobbying as one of their activities. This is understandable and perfectly legitimate: lobbying is not a primary reason for the existence of these organizations. They participate in politics to protect their chief interests: profits and education. But they are careful not to call attention to their involvement in politics out of fear that they

TABLE 3.1 ● Lobbying Categories and Spending, 2013–14

Category	Amount (in millions)
Miscellaneous*	$98.8
Government	87.9
Health	76.6
Manufacturing, industrial	46.8
Finance, insurance	40.0
Oil and gas	35.2
Education	31.1
Labor unions	30.5
Professional, trade	30.2
Utilities	27.1
Transportation	13.9
Entertainment, recreation	12.8
Real estate	12.0
Merchandise, retail	9.5
Agriculture	8.6
Legal	8.5
Public employees	6.9
Lodging, restaurants	3.5
Political organizations	.2

*Includes hundreds of interest groups, such as professional and trade associations, environmental organizations, and religious groups.

SOURCE: Data from California Secretary of State, http://cal-access.ss.ca.gov/Lobbying/Employers/list.aspx?view -category&session=2013 (accessed 6/15/16).

may alienate customers or tarnish their image. Accordingly, information about their lobbying activity must be obtained from newspaper accounts and public disclosure documents.

Many businesses do join professional or **trade associations** to give them a voice on issues that affect their industry. "We're the champion of California businesses, large and small," the California Chamber of Commerce proudly asserts on its web site. "For more than 125 years, CalChamber has worked to make California a better place to live, work, and do business by giving private-sector employers a voice in state politics." Its more than 13,000 member businesses give the chamber tremendous clout and stature. In turn, individual members enjoy several advantages—sharing of cost, strength in numbers, and, perhaps most important, anonymity.

Government also lobbies government. Taxpayer protection groups have come to call these interests—education, health, special districts, local government, state agencies—"the spending lobby" because they are motivated by the desire to maintain or increase their revenue. In 2014, for instance, Government was the second highest spender, after the catchall Miscellaneous category, among the 19 categories of lobbyist employers registered with the secretary of state.

According to governmental lobbyists, the passage in 1978 of Proposition 13, which limited property tax revenues to local government, is responsible for spurring the growth in governmental lobbying and the competition for funds. John P.

TABLE 3.2 ● Top Ten Lobbyist Employers, 2013–14

Organization	Cumulative Expenditures
Western States Petroleum Association	$13,553,943
California State Council of Service Employees	9,993,316
Chevron Corporation and subsidiaries	8,257,361
California Chamber of Commerce	7,639,130
California Hospital Association	6,118,525
Kaiser Foundation Health Plan Inc.	5,237,233
California Medical Association	4,125,207
AT&T	3,929,936
Pacific Gas and Electric Company	3,701,041
California Teachers Association	3,605,399

SOURCE: Data from California Secretary of State, http://cal-access.sos.ca.gov/Lobbying/Employers/list.aspx?view-category&session=2013 (accessed 6/15/16).

Quimby, Sr., a former assemblyman who lobbies for San Bernardino County, told the *Riverside Press Enterprise* in 1997: "I wish government wasn't for sale like this, but the fact is you have to hustle to get your share. Local governments without lobbyists see the ones with representation doing better so they say, 'We need to get our butts on board and get one [lobbyist] or they're going to steal everything from us.'"[2] Or, to put it another way, government agencies spend taxpayers' money to lobby government for more money to spend on taxpayers.

Proliferation of Interest Groups

In California over the last two and a half decades, the number of interest groups and lobbying expenditures has grown steadily. In 1990 lobbyists represented approximately 1,300 interest groups; in 2000 the number nearly doubled to 2,552; in 2012 it increased to 3,468; and in 2014 it swelled to 3,690.[3] During the same period, lobbying expenditures also grew substantially with just a slight dip in 2009–10, as seen in Table 3.3.

California continually ranks first nationally in number of interest groups and amount spent on lobbying activity. California accounts for one-third of all lobbyist activity in the country (but only 12 percent of the country's population). Texas and New York rank second and third behind California in population, and each spends around 60 percent of what is spent in California on lobbying activities.[4] What Carey McWilliams said about California politics during the 1930s and 1940s still holds true today: "Interests, not people, are represented in Sacramento. Sacramento is the marketplace of California where grape growers and sardine fishermen, morticians and osteopaths bid for allotments of state power."[5]

Several factors have encouraged the proliferation of interest groups:

WEAK POLITICAL PARTIES California has weak parties for a variety of reasons, but the main one is the Progressive reforms of the 1910s. These reforms were directed at the spoils system in government, the control of the political parties over

TABLE 3.3 ● Growth in Lobbying Expenditures

Legislative	Lobbying	Percent
1991–1992	$193,575,480	0
1993–1994	233,872,097	7.0
1995–1996	250,119,667	6.7
1997–1998	292,615,513	9.6
1999–2000	344,318,650	17.7
2001–2002	386,829,719	12.4
2003–2004	413,376,146	6.9
2005–2006	500,326,710	21.0
2007–2008	558,419,109	11.0
2009–2010	538,638,251	–3.5
2011–2012	563,003,065	4.5
2013–2014	579,995,079	3.0

SOURCE: Data from California Secretary of State, http://cal-access.ss.ca.gov/Lobbying/Employers/list.aspx?view-category&session=2013 (accessed 6/15/16).

which candidates would represent the party in general elections, and the influence of interest groups in the legislature. To balance these influences, the Progressive reforms granted voters the direct-democracy practices of initiative, referendum, and recall. These measures and subsequent reforms—many of which were considered citizen initiatives, such as the direct primary, term limits, redistricting by an independent commission, and top-two open primaries—greatly free officials from party structure and discipline. But politicians still need money, resources, and support to win reelection, and so they have looked to interest groups in lieu of parties for help. In this way, Progressive attempts to curb interest-group influence have instead strengthened it.

GROWTH OF GOVERNMENT California government has grown substantially over the past half century. Californians, like other Americans, initially were suspicious of government, perceiving it as a force whose powers had to be kept in check to protect individual rights. As time passed, however, citizens began to perceive government as a tool that could be used to solve myriad social and economic problems. The legislature has eagerly taken up the challenge. A by-product of government expansion has been that local levels of government have increased their lobbying efforts in the state legislature. For example, in 2013–14, counties, cities, special districts, school districts, and public employee unions spent over $87.9 million on lobbying legislation that would affect their interests. (See Table 3.1.)

TERM LIMITS In 1990, California voters approved term limits for all state and legislative offices. Term limits, it was argued, would break the cozy relationship between elected officials and lobbyists. Yet this has not been the case. As legislators with years of institutional memory left office, the legislature became more chaotic and less efficient. This opened the door for the "third house" of special interests to gain influence, as lobbyists had the institutional memory that new legislators lacked. Legislators now often rely on lobbyists to write intricate legislation and council them on the flood of complex issues that come across their desk.[6]

PUBLIC INTEREST GROUPS The growth of **public interest groups**, what some call the New Politics movement, began in the 1970s and continues through today. Examples of such groups are AARP, Sierra Club, and the Foundation for Taxpayers and Consumer Rights. As the textbook *We the People* explains, the public interest lobby sought to distinguish itself from other groups—business groups, in particular—by "purporting to represent the general good rather than its own economic interests."[7] Although these so-called public interest groups claim to represent *only* the public interest, they should be judged critically; they are sometimes facades behind which narrow private interests hide.

Interest-Group Strategies

Today, in California, politics *is* interest groups. Not all interest groups, however, are equal. Some have considerably more clout than others. The success of an interest group depends on several factors: a clear message, group cohesiveness, the alignment of the group's interests with those of other groups and elected officials, an understanding of the political process, technical expertise, and money. As we shall see, money is especially important.

Lobbyists

The people who do the work for interest groups are called lobbyists, and the work they do is called lobbying. Lobbyists are at the forefront of interest-group activity. They coordinate the efforts to secure passage, amendment, or defeat of bills in the legislature and the approval or veto of bills by the governor. Having a good lobbyist is paramount to the success of any group.

There are citizen lobbyists and professional lobbyists. A **citizen lobbyist** is not paid to advocate for a particular issue or set of issues. Citizen lobbyists interact with their representatives to express their personal views on an issue and to attempt to influence legislation on that issue. Professional lobbyists are paid for their services and must register with the secretary of state. They also must submit quarterly disclosure reports detailing for whom they are working, the amount of money earned, and payment such as gifts and honoraria made to public officials they lobby.

There are two types of professional lobbyists: contract and in-house. **Contract lobbyists** make up 50 percent of all lobbyists in Sacramento; **in-house lobbyists** account for the other half. [8] Contract lobbyists offer their services to the general public; they are advocates for hire and often represent multiple clients on a variety of issues at the same time. In-house lobbyists are employees of a trade, professional, or labor association and represent that group's interest only. Many of these interest groups also use contract lobbyists because the group is involved in too many issues for its in-house staff to handle, or it may want to use a lobbyist who specializes in a specific subject area such as health insurance. A group may also want to use a lobbyist who has a close relationship with a particular legislator or members of a specific committee whose support is vital for the group's success.

Lobbyists and special interests are often seen as the driving force behind politics in California, as illustrated by this cartoon from the *Los Angeles Daily News*.

LOBBYING THE LEGISLATURE Few issues are just lobbied—that is, discussed with legislators or their staff during the legislative process. Most issues are managed using a combination of techniques: public relations (marketing), grassroots mobilization, and coalition building.

The first job of the lobbyist is to know the group's objective. Is the goal new legislation? Is it to amend existing law? Or is it to stop another business or interest group from passing new legislation or amending an existing law that may affect the group's interest? The goal may not even be legislation. The group may want to amend current regulatory policy or shape the content of new regulations that will affect its members.

The lobbyist must also identify other groups that may have an interest in the issue and assess whether these groups, as well as legislators, the executive branch, regulators, or the general public, will support or oppose the group's activity. Moreover, lobbyists who can rely on the group's members, especially if they reside in the legislator's district, can more easily influence policy making. The most successful efforts are built around networks of activists who have made it a point to know their elected officials. These relationships can be built in many ways: working on election campaigns, commending representatives in writing for actions they have taken, contributing to political campaigns, and connecting in other ways so as to have a positive relationship with these officials.

With this preparation in hand, the lobbyist has a greater chance of success. Of course, several other factors are also important: knowledge of the legislation process, strong communication skills, established relationships, credibility, adaptability to change, and the ability to negotiate.

LOBBYING THE EXECUTIVE BRANCH The techniques used to lobby the executive branch are similar to those used in lobbying the state legislature. There are, however, two main differences between these two branches that make lobbying the executive more challenging. First, unlike most other states, California has a number (seven) of statewide elected administration offices composing the plural executive. This makes it more difficult to coordinate lobbying, especially when the elected officials of those offices are from different political parties. Second, the executive branch includes more than 85 agencies, 325 state commissions and boards, and 30 educational institutions (see Chapter 6). The agencies write and oversee the implementation of thousands of regulations that have a powerful impact on different sectors of society at different times. The regulations they write and implement are generally subject-specific and often very technical. This forces a lobbyist to develop expertise—and relationships—with a number of different agencies.

Campaign Contributions to Candidates

In addition to their expenditures on lobbying to influence legislative action, interest groups also make campaign contributions, which enable them to become familiar with and gain access to legislators. They do so through **political action committees (PACs)**.

There is a connection between lobbying success and campaign contributions. Those who invest heavily in lobbying generally invest heavily in PAC contributions, and vice versa.[9] Table 3.4 lists the top 10 contributors for the 2013–14 legislative year. The table shows only the amount directly contributed to candidates for the state legislature—the total of which was $146,268,911. This figure does not include what these organizations may have contributed to statewide offices ($68,771,707),[10] the Democratic or Republican Party committees ($60,317,306),[11] independent expenditures ($90,999,463),[12] or ballot initiatives ($184,207,934),[13] which, when totaled, comes to an additional $404,296,410. Campaign contributions enable a lobbyist to gain access to legislators. The lobbyist can then make his or her argument—at which time he or she can provide the legislator with important, often technical information. To put these numbers in perspective, consider

---

TABLE 3.4 ● Top Ten Contributors to Legislative Candidates, 2013–14

Organization	Amount ($)
California Association of Realtors	$1,516,600
California State Council of Laborers	1,013,700
California Teachers Association	975,087
California State Council of Service Employees	913,700
California State Association of Electrical Workers	795,700
Pechanga Band of Luiseno Mission Indians	754,300
AT&T	725,461
State Building & Construction Trades Council	702,550
California Professional Firefighters	679,294
The Doctors Company	611,200

SOURCE: National Institute on Money in State Politics, www.followthemoney.org (accessed 6/15/16).

that the average cost of a seat in the California Assembly was $821,396 and in the California Senate was $1,199,596 during the 2013–14 election cycle.

Studies show that incumbency (i.e., currently holding political office) is a strong factor in being elected to office. Incumbents hold an advantage over their opponents for a number of reasons: high visibility and name recognition; media attention; history of constituency service; experience in managing a successful political campaign; and, most important, strong ties to the fund-raising pipeline.[14]

For example, in the 2014 campaign for state Senate, 20 seats were up for election—10 with incumbents and 10 open seats. All 10 incumbents won reelection handily. The winning incumbents raised $13.4 million—an average of $1.3 million per incumbent—compared to their opponents who raised a combined $3.4 million. The latter number, however, is deceptive because Luis Chavez, the opponent of incumbent James Vidak, raised about $3.2 million of this amount in a losing effort to unseat Vidak.

In the 2014 campaign for state Assembly, all 80 seats were up for election. Fifty-seven of the candidates were incumbents, who raised $53.2 million—an average of $933,000 per incumbent. Their opponents raised $6.9 million—an average of $121,367 per candidate. Needless to say, the incumbents dominated, as all but four won reelection. Of the four incumbents who lost, three were in interparty contests in which the Republican challenger defeated the Democrat incumbent, and one was in an intraparty contest in which the Democrat challenger defeated the Democrat incumbent. In each race, the losing incumbent outspent the winning challenger.

In the Senate, the campaign for the 10 open seats (where there is no incumbent) showed expenditures of $23 million. Overall, the winning candidates raised 30 percent more money than the losing candidates did. In competition for the 23 open seats in the Assembly, candidates raised $38.7 million. The competition for monetary support was ongoing and spirited. In the end, the winning candidates outraised their competitors by the small margin of 4.4 percent.

In both the Senate and Assembly, 94 percent of incumbents were reelected to office, and 79 percent of those running for open seats who raised more money than their opponent won. What is the source of the campaign funds? The majority of contributions (91 percent) came from non-individual sources—that is, primarily from interest groups and to a much lesser amount from the candidate's political party, which also received significant contributions from the same interest groups that contribute to the candidate.[15] (See the "Who Are Californians?" feature on the opposite page for more on top interest group contributors.)

Incumbency and interest groups (and their campaign contributions) go hand-in-hand, since their interrelationship, as we have seen, plays a crucial role in sitting legislators getting reelected. As Jesse Unruh, former speaker of the Assembly, once said, "Money is the mother's milk of politics."[16] This adage still holds true today. Most interest groups and PACs carefully target their campaign contributions. They support individuals who are in positions of power (e.g., incumbent state officers, party leaders in the legislature, committee chairs, and rising stars). Contributions have little to do with a legislator's or party's political ideology. The only question is this: Can this legislator help me achieve my goals?

CALIFORNIA CORRECTIONAL PEACE OFFICERS ASSOCIATION An example of the dynamics of campaign contributions and lobbying can be seen in the California Correctional Peace Officers Association (CCPOA), one of the most powerful interest groups in Sacramento. It has achieved this status through a combination of

Who Spends Money in California Politics?

Funds Raised for Selected Ballot Measures, 2016*

■ Support ■ Oppose

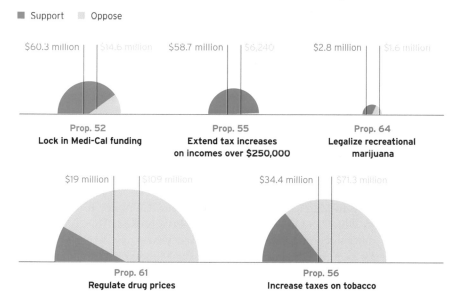

$60.3 million | $14.6 million

$58.7 million | $6,240

$2.8 million | $1.6 million

Prop. 52
Lock in Medi-Cal funding

Prop. 55
Extend tax increases on incomes over $250,000

Prop. 64
Legalize recreational marijuana

$19 million | $109 million

$34.4 million | $71.3 million

Prop. 61
Regulate drug prices

Prop. 56
Increase taxes on tobacco

Every election cycle, interest groups and individual donors spend massive amounts of money in California politics. In 2016 they contributed a record total of $473 million in support of or in opposition to ballot propositions, while only $99.5 million was raised by candidates running for the state legislature.

* As of December 2016

SOURCES: California Secretary of State, "Ballot Measure Total Contributions - 2016," www.sos.ca.gov/campaign-lobbying/cal-access-resources/measure-contributions/ (accessed 12/10/16); National Institute on Money in State Politics, www.followthemoney.org/show-me?s=CA&y=2016 (accessed 12/10/16).

Top Interest Group Contributors, 2016*

■ Donations for ballot initiatives ■ Donations to Democrats ■ Donations to Republicans

Donor	$0	$10M	$20M	$30M	$40M	$50M
CA Association of Hospitals and Health Systems						
Philip Morris USA						
RJ Reynolds Tobacco Company						
CA Teachers Association						
AIDS Healthcare Foundation						
Pfizer						
Johnson & Johnson						
Merck & Co.						
Dignity Health						
CA State Council of Service Employees						

forcriticalanalysis

1. Should more be done to limit the role of wealthy interest groups in California politics, or is this sort of campaign spending an important component of political speech?

2. What do you think contributes to the high cost of candidate and ballot measure campaigns in California?

aggressive lobbying, large campaign contributions, and skillful public relations. The CCPOA, a union, is one of the biggest contributors to candidates running for state-wide and legislative office. Over the past two decades, the union has spent over $40 million on lobbying,[17] contributing aggressively to the campaigns of its supporters and just as aggressively to defeat those who oppose its agenda. The union is one of the few public employee groups to give generously to both Republicans and Democrats. For example, when Pete Wilson ran for governor in 1990, prison guards gave $1 million to his campaign. Wilson reciprocated with substantial pay increases and stronger sentencing policies. The union made its most significant show of support, however, to Gray Davis. Besides granting him early endorsement in the primary, which guaranteed his selection as the Democratic candidate for governor, it contributed more than $3 million between 1998 and 2002 to his campaign war chest. During the same period, the union gave millions of dollars to members of the legislature, with especially large sums going to the leadership of both parties. Governor Davis responded in kind. Correctional officers' wages were tied to those of highway patrol officers. At that time, highway patrol officers earned $666 more than correctional officers. Moreover, highway patrol officers' pay, and by implication correctional officers' pay, for each year were brought in line with the pay of police officers in the five largest urban areas.

CCPOA also spent heavily—$1.8 million—in support of Jerry Brown's 2010 gubernatorial victory. In March 2012 the legislature and Governor Brown agreed on a new contract, which the union overwhelmingly approved. The contract increased officers' pension contributions, reduced their yearly pay by requiring one day of unpaid leave each month, and eliminated a state-funded, $42-million-a-year 401(k)-type plan that correctional officers had received in addition to their pensions. These changes sound like losses. However, as the *San Francisco Chronicle* pointed out, the contract eliminated limitations on accrual of vacation time, currently estimated at more than 33 million hours and with costs to the state calculated at $1 billion.[18]

Governor Brown argued that collective bargaining is about "give and take" and claimed that the deal with the correctional officers was comparable to what other public employee unions received under Governor Schwarzenegger. But some observers allege that the union contract is a bargaining chip to gain union support for the governor's prison reform agenda, which includes closing youth prisons and transferring up to 30,000 low-level offenders from state prisons to local jails. These reforms are intended to save the state millions of dollars. Still, the returns from CCPOA's campaign spending and lobbying suggest that the strategy has paid off handsomely for the union.

In March 2016, Governor Brown announced a new three-year deal with the union that includes annual across-the-board 3 percent raises for members. As a compromise, union members agreed to pay a small percentage of their salary into a reserve account for retirees' medical benefits. The state will match the employees' contribution. Today, "California's prison guards are the nation's highest paid, a big reason that spending on the state's prison system has rocketed from less than 4.3 percent of the budget in 1986 to more than 11 percent today."[19]

Grassroots Mobilization

Up until now, we have focused on the influence of interest groups on the state legislature and executive branch. Interest groups, however, flex their muscles in other

The California Correctional Peace Officers Association (CCPOA), the union representing the state's prison guards, is one of the most influential and aggressive lobbies in Sacramento. California's prison guards are now among the highest paid in the country.

ways in the electoral process: through get-out-the-vote and initiative (direct legislation) campaigns.

GET OUT THE VOTE Many interest groups engage in get-out-the-vote (GOTV) operations among their members to help a candidate (and political party) or an issue win at the ballot box. This is especially true during what are perceived as hotly contested elections. In such instances, GOTV can be the most important activity undertaken because there are many examples of an election being won or lost by a handful of votes.

GOTV operations are often considered "outsider strategies"—that is, they take place outside the traditional arena of interest-group activity (the legislature), and they are supported by groups that feel they have a vital stake in the outcome of the election. Examples of this are Hispanics' interest in 1994 in defeating Proposition 187, which declared undocumented people ineligible for public services, and the Protect Marriage Coalition's efforts in 2008 on behalf of Proposition 8, which eliminated same-sex couples' right to marry.

Some interest groups, such as organized labor, religious denominations, and minorities, have a long history of mobilizing their members to vote for or against a candidate or critical issue. Other interest groups, such as the LGBTQ community, environmentalists, and gender-based groups, have more recently begun to participate in GOTV activities. They mobilize their supporters at the grassroots level through a variety of techniques, including direct mail, door-to-door canvassing, telemarketing, poll watching, pickup, phoning, and assistance. Months of work go into planning the campaign. While the goal is simple—delivering members' votes—the outcome is unpredictable until the final tally of ballots.

INITIATIVES Chapter 2 explored the history of the initiative and the impact of some of those that have passed. What was initially considered a tool for citizens to check the actions of elected officials and the influence of interest groups in the legislature is still considered so today. The majority of voters support the use of the initiative because they believe that the public is better suited than elected representatives to decide "important government issues," although many believe that a few narrow economic interests also shape public policy through the initiative process.[20]

Yet, as Elisabeth Gerber shows, this may not be as big of an issue as voters think. Although there are now more initiatives and considerably more money spent on them, groups with different goals use the initiative process differently. On the one hand, narrow (economic) interest groups, whose members join because of their occupation or professional status, rely primarily on the mobilization of money for initiative campaigns. They use these monetary resources and, to a lesser extent, personnel in two ways: "to protect the status quo or to pressure the legislature." When they sponsor initiatives, the measures generally fail. On the other hand, citizen groups, whose members join as free individuals committed to some personal belief or social issue, rely primarily on the mobilization of personnel who "volunteer their personal time and energy . . . to pass new laws by initiative."[21] In the end, the measures that are backed by citizen groups succeed at a higher rate than those that are sponsored by narrow economic interests.

The Legislature, Bribes, and Scandals

Interest-group politics is not new; lobbyists have played a visible and sometimes controversial role in California politics for a long time. The most notorious figure was Arthur Samish, whose influence in the state legislature during the 1930s and 1940s drew national attention. Samish represented the most powerful industries in the state: oil, liquor stores, transportation, breweries, and racing. Samish was not shy about his influence. He once told a grand jury looking into his lobbying activities, "To hell with the governor of California. I'm the governor of the legislature."[22]

Samish's downfall came as a result of two articles in *Collier's* magazine in 1949 about "the man who secretly controls the state."[23] In one of the articles, when asked who had more influence, himself or Samish, Governor Earl Warren responded, "On matters that affect his clients, Artie unquestionably has more power than the governor."[24] Soon after the articles appeared, Governor Warren asked for legislation to regulate lobbyists and require the disclosure of lobbyists' financial activities. The legislature obliged first with the Collier Act and later with the Erwin Act, two of the earliest efforts to regulate lobbying in the state. The legislature also voted to ban Arthur Samish from the capitol building. Somewhat thereafter, Samish was convicted of income tax evasion and sentenced to three years in federal prison, thus ending his career as a Sacramento power broker.

As the preceding incident illustrates, interest-group influence has not remained on the sidelines; quite the opposite, in fact. It is not surprising that with the growth of the "lobbying industrial complex" in California, allegations of influence peddling follow and sometimes turn out to be true. For example, Clay Jackson, one of the most influential lobbyists in Sacramento, was accused in the early 1990s of offering large campaign contributions to Senator Alan Robbins in return for the lawmaker's support on legislation benefiting Jackson's clients. The FBI uncovered Robbins's part in the plan, and he agreed to wear a wire to expose Jackson in exchange for a reduced sentence. In the end, Jackson, Robbins, and former state senator Paul Carpenter (who funneled campaign money through a public relations firm for Robbins's personal use) were convicted of engaging in a money-laundering scheme.

Again, in 2014, the Senate was rocked by the indictment of three members—Rod Wright, Leland Yee, and Ron Calderon. All three were suspended by the Senate but remained on voluntary pay and benefit leave until their cases were ruled upon or their terms expired. This was the first time either the Assembly or Senate suspended members in its 164-year history.

In 2014, Senator Wright was convicted of voter fraud and perjury. He appealed the verdict; however, he lost the appeal. Later that year he was sentenced to 90 days in jail and ordered to complete 1,500 hours of community service. But Wright spent less than one hour in jail. Because of the nonviolent nature of his crime and overcrowding in the jail, he was quietly released. Senator Lee was not so fortunate. In April 2016 he negotiated a plea bargain and avoided a possible 20-year prison sentence. Ultimately he received a five-year prison sentence on the lesser charges of bribes for political favors and coordinating weapons sales to help pay down campaign debts.

In June 2016 former assemblyman Tom Calderon, the brother of Senator Ron Calderon, pleaded guilty to one count of money laundering and implicated his brother in the scheme. His conviction could have carried up to 20 years in prison; however, federal prosecutors recommended a one-year prison sentence. Because of significant health problems, he was ultimately sentenced to six months in prison and six months under house arrest wearing an electronic monitor. Senator Ron Calderon pleaded guilty to mail fraud, acknowledging that he accepted thousands of dollars in bribes from a hospital executive and FBI agents. He was sentenced to three and a half years in federal prison and will be required to do 150 hours of community service following his release. This brought to a close the FBI's Senate investigation and sting operation.

Because of these scandals, the Senate adopted resolutions to ban members from fund-raising during the last month of the legislative session and the month leading up to a budget vote, when special interests are especially active in trying to influence legislation. The resolutions also required the Senate Rules Committee to appoint an ethics ombudsman to accept allegations of wrongdoing and protect whistle-blowers from retaliation. In 2016, however, the ban on political fund-raising was killed after the Assembly did not adopt a similar rule—perhaps because it didn't suffer similar scandals—so all that is left is the ethics ombudsman position.

In the 2016 primary election, however, voters passed a legislative referendum (Proposition 50) that gave the Senate and Assembly the power to suspend members and prohibit them from receiving pay and benefits during the suspension period. This brought to a close the debate over legislative suspensions and the withholding of pay and benefits of suspended legislators.

These incidents raise questions about the connections among interest groups, money, and power in Sacramento. They reveal how a legal fund-raising system can be used to benefit legislators, especially in an environment in which there is a fine line between campaign contributions and influence over legislators' votes—even when these processes are conducted legally.

Regulating Campaign Contributions

This dubious history of influence peddling prompted numerous efforts over the years at reform. With the passage of the **California Political Reform Act (PRA)** of 1974, California lobbyist and interest groups are required to report campaign

TABLE 3.5 ● **California Contribution Limits**

	Individuals*	Single Candidates Committees	PACs	Small Contributor Committee**	Political Party	Super PACs***
Governor	$28,200	$4,200	$28,200	$28,200	unlimited	$0
Statewide Candidate	7,000	4,200	7,000	14,100	unlimited	0
State Senate	4,200	4,200	4,200	8,500	unlimited	0
State Assembly	4,200	4,200	4,200	8,500	unlimited	0
Party Committees	35,000	35,000	35,000	35,000	$35,000	0
Ballot Measures	unlimited	4,200	unlimited	unlimited	unlimited	0

*Corporate and union contribution limits are the same as individual limits.

**A small contributor committee is one that has been in existence for at least six months, receives contributions from 100 or more persons but no individual contributions of more than $200 in a calendar year, and makes contributions to five or more candidates.

***Super PAC: an independent expenditure organization that can spend unlimited amounts for or against candidates and ballot measures, but cannot give directly to candidates, PACs, or committees.

SOURCE: California Fair Political Practices Commission, California State Contribution Limits, www.fppc.ca.gov/learn/campaign-rules/state-contribution-limits.html (accessed 6/1/16).

and lobbying expenditures. At the same time, the PRA shifted the filing of lobbying statements from the state legislature to the independent Fair Political Practice Commission.

Since its passage, the PRA has undergone numerous amendments, the most significant being in 2000 with the passage of Proposition 34. The following rules now govern interest groups and lobbyists:

● A lobbyist or lobbying firm cannot present a gift to a state-elected official or legislative official in aggregate of more than $10 a month. Anyone who is not a registered lobbyist can give up to $250 in gifts in any calendar year.

● A lobbyist cannot contribute to state candidates or officeholders if he or she is registered to lobby that candidate or officeholder's agency. However, the various interest groups that employ lobbyists have no such restrictions.

● Interest groups, individuals, and businesses have specific limits on election contributions to candidates or officeholders (see Table 3.5).

A controversial issue involves campaign contributions not directly tied to the candidate or political party. Much of the publicity and discussion of this type of organization, called Super PACs at the national level, centers on presidential, U.S. Senate, and House of Representatives campaigns in which millions of dollars are raised in support of or in opposition to a federal election candidate.

At the state level, these organizations are sometimes referred to as Super PACs but more often as **independent expenditure committees**. Like their federal counterpart, these committees may raise unlimited sums of money from corporations, unions, associations, and individuals and then spend unlimited sums to overtly advocate for or against a political candidate.

Independent expenditure committees have come under scrutiny for a variety of reasons: they infuse large sums of money into a campaign without having to comply with the limits for direct contributions to a candidate; they allow for great sums of money from outside the state to influence the state's politics and elections; and they sometimes make it difficult to identify donors by contributing money, one step removed from the independent expenditure committee, through contributions to affiliate nonprofit organizations.

Interestingly, for all the focus on independent spending, while not an insignificant amount, it has hovered around 10 percent as a percentage of total direct contributions to political campaigns. In a recently revised study of independent expenditure committees in California, Linda Casey of the National Institute on Money in State Politics (FollowTheMoney.org) compares the amount of independent expenditure spending to the amount given directly to candidates and ballot measure committees. From 2006 through 2014, independent expenditure committees spent $258,197,427 on candidates who ran for state offices and ballot measures; and, as Table 3.6 shows, this number is significantly less than the $2,212,747,644 contributed directly to candidates and ballot measure committees—just 11.7 percent of the total expenditures.

In 2010 the U.S. Supreme Court in *Citizens United v. Federal Elections Commission* held that these independent expenditure committees were legal and could raise unlimited funds. While not directly deliberating on independent expenditure committees in California, *Citizens United* confirmed the practice in California, since California had allowed such open expenditures before the Supreme Court ruling.

In 2015, however, the California Fair Political Practices Commission took action to clarify the meaning of "coordination" between candidates and organizations in

---

TABLE 3.6 ● Independent Spending Compared to Direct Campaign Contributions, 2006–2014

	Independent state campaigns and ballot measures	Direct contributions to state campaigns and ballot measures	Independent spending as percent of direct campaign contributions
2008	$35,413,175	$591,753,664	9.40%
2010	84,055,049	640,346,256	13.13
2012	47,638,234	581,215,152	8.20
2014	82,660,044	399,432,572	20.69
Total	167,106,458	2,212,747,644	11.70

SOURCE: Linda Casey, "Independent Spending in California, 2005–2010," September 20, 2011, revised and updated June 1, 2016, National Institute on Money in State Politics, www.followthemoney.org/research/institute-reports/?q=&b=0&b=1&t%5B%5D=16&p=3 (accessed 12/19/16).

order to make sure that independent expenditures were clearly independent of the candidate. It clarified within the definition of "coordination" these activities:

- the group cannot be established or run by former members of the candidate's staff,

- the candidate cannot participate in fund-raising for the outside group,

- the group cannot be established or funded by the candidates' family members, and

- political consultants cannot work for both the candidate and the outside group.

While these changes may seem minimal, they are intended, within the scope of law, to help bring transparency to the relationship between candidates and independent expenditure, which, as we mentioned earlier, topped $90 million in 2014.

Some public interest groups, such as Common Cause, Clean Money Campaign, and the League of Women Voters, have called for further restrictions on lobbying expenditures and campaign contributions by both individuals and interest groups. Such measures, they argue, would constrain the power of special interests and allow public-policy decisions to reflect the overall interests of society.

Recommendations to restrict the power of interest groups fall into three categories: clean-money elections, contribution restrictions, and conflict-of-interest laws.

Clean-Money Elections

The first category, clean-money elections, would provide public funding to candidates who demonstrate a base of public support by obtaining a qualifying number of voter signatures and a certain number of small contributions and who agree to forgo any other private donations. Such measures would cover all state legislative and statewide offices and have recently been adopted by Maine and Arizona. In California, it would be difficult to get the political parties and most legislators, who are tied to the current funding system, to support the idea. It would also be difficult to convince the public that they should subsidize campaigns for elective office. Over the years, only 35 to 40 percent of California voters have supported public financing of election campaigns.

Contribution Limits

The second category, contribution limits, has been a focal point of campaign reform for some time. Most of the effort has come from citizen groups disgruntled with the current system. Together they have established stricter reporting requirements and limits on campaign contributions and loans to state candidates and political parties. The changes have been accomplished almost wholly through initiatives sponsored by these groups over the past decade—Propositions 63 and 78 in 1993, Proposition 208 in 1996, and Proposition 34 in 2000. These efforts will continue in the future as various groups attempt to rein in the free flow of money into political campaigns.

Conflict-of-Interest Laws

The last category, conflict-of-interest laws, covers a multitude of situations. These laws are based on the belief that government officials owe their loyalty to the public, and that personal gain should not be part of the political process. Conflict-of-interest laws prohibit government officials from participating in decisions in which they have a vested interest, such as a business or real estate investment, or in any variety of situations in which they or their family would stand to gain financially.

There are, however, government-official lobbyist activities that technically fall outside of conflict-of-interest laws but may give the impression of conflict of interest. For example, the California Senate offers lobbyists who contribute to its charity, the California International Relations Foundation, the opportunity to travel with the lawmakers to various foreign countries.[25] Each donor contributes $2,000 to $3,000, which gives the donor a seat on the foundation's board of directors and the invitation to travel with legislators on trade and cultural trips to foreign countries. Since 2004 there have been 18 trips to places such as Tokyo, Jerusalem, and Rio de Janeiro. The foundation operates out in the open, and it does not underwrite the expenses of either the traveling legislators or the supporters. Critics, however, contend that it creates a conflict-of-interest situation by providing a unique opportunity for supporters to gain the goodwill of and access to legislators. This is especially convenient when the supporter's interest group has a bill pending in the legislature.

The Media

For most Californians, the **media**—news stories, paid political commercials, public debate, direct mail—are the most influential sources of information on the activity of interest groups, the amount of money spent on lobbying and political campaigns, and the increasing frequency and amount of money spent on initiatives. The media keep citizens actively involved in politics.

The term *media* refers to the dispensers of information, including broadcast media (radio and television), print media (newspapers and magazines), and electronic media (the Internet). An individual source is a *medium* (the Latin singular of *media*). Sometimes we speak about mass media but most often the limiting adjective (*mass*) is assumed.

Television

For many years, television has been the medium of choice for obtaining political information for the vast majority of Americans, and Californians are no exception. Although the rise of digital media has challenged television's dominance, TV retains a slight edge.[26] This medium can spread messages quickly, covering a wide variety of topics, including car chases, earthquakes, and the latest political scandal. Television is particularly important for conducting political campaigns in a large state with a diverse population such as California. Yet for all its speed and ability to reach large numbers of viewers, television is a medium that provides little information on government.

Two facts account for this lack of information: (1) California is so big and diverse that it is difficult to cover statewide political and governmental news, and (2) Californians in general are not that interested in state government and policy. These dynamics, along with a fragmented political structure, produce a stark reality—the largest state in the nation, with some of the largest media resources and markets in the nation, provides relatively little political and governmental news, particularly on television news programs.[27] There are few media correspondents in Sacramento. More important, because there is no newspaper distributed statewide, there is no incentive for television networks to cover news on a statewide basis.

The nightly news stations compete with one another for viewers. But the news programs provide little in the way of important political information. The half-hour news format is crammed with commercials, weather reports, entertainment news, sports coverage, and a host of other topics that do little to inform the viewer about the political problems that affect the state and the nation. Those topics that are reported with any depth are calculated to achieve ratings and are structured to last over several newscasts.

Each local station has its own version of some type of "action" news team or consumer protection group bringing audiences the latest artificially hyped crisis. From the nature of the issues covered, it is clear that local television, for the most part, has made a concerted effort to treat political news as a secondary issue. Issues related to political parties, government, or interest groups in California don't have the power to reach and energize large populations on a day-to-day basis.

Local television stations focus our attention on issues such as crime in a way that government representatives cannot. Sensational undercover stories are frequently broadcast, such as the financial deceptions practiced by automobile dealers, the unsanitary conditions in local restaurants, and the health risks of cosmetic surgeries. These exposés help identify dishonest practices in our communities, but they are also examples of how the ability to identify important political issues has passed from the political parties to the media. The media place an issue on the agenda, often based more on its sensational appeal than its practical importance, and the next day government representatives are telling the public what must be done to fix the problem. They are reacting to the media's promotion of the issue.

In California, where voters have the ability to put statutes and constitutional initiatives on the ballot, local television plays a major role in disseminating information to voters about these issues through extensive advertising campaigns. These messages are drafted and paid for by the interest groups that support the initiatives, and the political parties may or may not play a role in the process. The broadcast media have the power to reach a vast audience, something the parties cannot do on their own.

Newspapers

The number of newspapers across the United States has fallen during the last 25 years, and newspaper circulations have steadily declined in every recent year as well. Those who claim they get most of their information about politics from newspapers dropped from 87 percent in 2007 to 73 percent in 2010 to 66 percent in 2014.[28]

Newspapers still remain active in identifying political corruption, reporting the workings of state and local government, covering political campaigns, and helping keep the public focused on important political issues. But in the final analysis, newspapers are businesses and must be able to generate revenues and profits. To adequately cover state government, reporters and news staff have to be located in Sacramento. At the same time, on-the-spot coverage of county and local government requires a second set of reporters and news staff. The expense is prohibitive, and, over time, newspaper coverage at the state and local levels has noticeably declined. The public is not as fully informed about the activities of its various levels of government as it needs to be. The *Los Angeles Times* and the *Sacramento Bee* cover developments in Sacramento more extensively than other newspapers, but both have become victim to cost pressures and the need to reduce news reporting staffs.

The drive for profits has reduced the news-reporting capabilities of broadcast and print media, which cover only the big stories at the state government level. Ultimately, this means the public receives little information about the political activities of state and local government. This leads to a public that constantly finds itself surprised by political crises that seem to develop suddenly, such as rising state deficits, electricity shortages, declining state bond ratings, school facilities that are falling apart, and an overwhelmed freeway system. But for all their failings, broadcast and print media still play an important role in the election process and in formulating the political agenda. The media continue to identify the major political issues, report on the political progress of candidates at all levels, question the candidates and officeholders, and edit the replies the public is allowed to hear and read. These powers continue to undermine the role of political parties in California.

With Arnold Schwarzenegger's election as governor in October 2003, the public gained a renewed interest in state politics. People were curious. A few stations that had closed their Sacramento news bureaus announced their reopening. This wasn't surprising: nationally known figures have generally drawn more media attention than regional or local personalities. There was more coverage of governors Edmund G. Brown, Ronald Reagan, and Jerry Brown, each of whom was a presidential contender, than of governors Deukmejian, Wilson, and Davis, who were not.[29]

As time passed, however, though the increase in coverage remained, it was due no longer to Schwarzenegger's celebrity but to the state's economic woes: record budget deficits, sinking bond ratings, high unemployment, and staggering foreclosure filings. These concerns still persist today under Governor Jerry Brown. Local government, interest groups (especially public employee unions whose members are affected by the budget deficits), and the general public have turned to Sacramento for solutions. Economic, environmental, and social justice issues are the big concern, not the political personalities to whom have been thrown the responsibility for resolving these problems.

The Internet

Online and digital news are the only forms of news media that have increased in the number of users over the past six years. Americans are turning more frequently to their tablets and smartphones to obtain news—64 percent of tablet owners and 62 percent of smartphone owners use these devices to get their news on a weekly basis, while 37 percent of tablet owners and 32 percent of smartphone owners use them for news on a daily basis.[30]

Smartphones and tablets offer instant access to political information and the opportunity to quickly communicate one's views to political leaders, news outlets, interest groups, and other individuals through blogs, Twitter, Tumblr, Facebook, other social media channels, and YouTube videos. Twitter and Facebook have become instrumental in organizing campaigns. The "share" function on Facebook and "retweet" feature of Twitter allow like-minded activists to easily share news and information such as fund-raising appeals and get-out-the-vote efforts.

The Internet doesn't change politics, but it does make it easier for elected officials to share with the public their opinions unfiltered by traditional media, and for the public to share their unfiltered opinions with public officials.

At the state level, Californians are at the forefront in experimenting with the Internet by using crowdsourcing techniques and wiki-style web sites to reach into the political arena. While still in its infancy, **crowdsourcing** is proving to be a useful fund-raising tool. In 2012, Steve Hansen was running for the Sacramento City Council. Hansen, a young openly gay Democrat, had very little name recognition or backing from community leaders. But that didn't stop him. "In just one day, Hansen built a web site on WordPress, joined MailChimp, and set up an account on Rally. Hansen's campaign raised more than $80,000 from donors who contributed $250 or less."[31] He now sits on the Sacramento City Council.

In the California state legislature, Assemblyman Mike Gatto became the first lawmaker nationally to utilize the Internet to encourage citizens to craft legislation. In 2016, for the second session in a row, Gatto encouraged individuals to draft legislation directly by going to a "Wikibills" web site which has an interface similar to Wikipedia's. There the users could propose, draft, or edit the bill, which, after a consensus emerged, Gatto committed to introducing. We have no analytics on the number of respondents, but the outcome appears to be Assembly Bill no. 83, which requires businesses and corporations to strengthen privacy standards for personal information including social security numbers, driver's license numbers, financial information, medical information, and travel information (such as one's Uber trip log). The bill made it through the Assembly (66 yea, 4 nay) but ended up on the inactive file in the Senate.[32]

The most ambitious use of the Internet came in 2014, when Tim Draper, a California venture capitalist, initiated a campaign using a web page to gain support for a ballot initiative. The measure was to divide California into six states. The effort failed and didn't make it to the ballot. But this didn't stop Draper. In 2015 he founded a nonprofit organization called Innovate Your State and launched a web site (www.fixcal.org) to allow citizens to help draft what would become the first crowdsourcing initiative in the nation. The idea, in Draper's words, "bridges private sector innovation and ingenuity with policy and government to improve the lives of constituents through a 'Venture Governance' approach."[33]

One such idea is the Fix California Challenge. The campaign has already generated over 300 ideas, and as it picks up steam, Draper plans to select the best ideas for a 2018 ballot initiative. So far most of the suggestions fall into three categories: improve representation and the legislative process (42 percent), address infrastructure and water conservation problems (22 percent), and enrich the state through business incentives (14 percent).[34] Political consultants and elected officials are watching this campaign and, if it is successful, will likely consider incorporating some sort of crowdsourcing approach to drafting future legislation and initiatives.

Many experts see the Internet as a catalyst for enhancing the democratic process. It offers candidates the opportunity to communicate rapidly with supporters and to recruit campaign workers. During the presidential election season, it has proven to be an excellent tool for raising campaign funds. The Internet offers political parties the opportunity to disseminate their issue positions quickly and inexpensively to millions of potential voters. Whether it will restore some of the power that political parties have lost remains to be seen. The Internet is open to all users, and in that environment, political parties will still have lots of competition over control of the political agenda.

Even with these innovative uses of the Internet, when it comes to social media, politics still lags behind other domains such as advertising and marketing. Most often, political campaigns use the Internet to develop web sites that outline a candidate's or party's position on important issues in hopes that possible supporters will visit the web sites and donate to the campaigns that they represent. However, campaigns are beginning to recognize and harness the power of social media networks and digital media to influence the electorate.

The example of Proposition 32, a 2012 initiative, demonstrates how the strategic implementation of new media campaigns can transform voting behavior. Proposition 32 sought to limit the money that unions could spend on lobbying and prohibit them from putting money that had been gained through automatic dues deductions from members' paychecks toward campaign contributions. By the end, the amount spent in the election was great—$75 million against and $60 million for the proposition. Midway through the campaign, however, with support for the "No on Proposition 32" cohort lagging, union leaders concluded that young voters—those under 30 years old—weren't being influenced by the union television ads because they weren't watching them. Therefore, the unions switched tactics. Employing sophisticated data-mining techniques and research via Facebook, they identified patterns of behavior among younger voters that gave clues about their political beliefs. In turn, the unions began speaking the language of these voters through their medium of choice, particularly through smartphones and tablets, in an attempt to influence their voting. They sent online messages, ads, and even some direct mail to individuals whom they had targeted through their research. Within a couple of weeks, support for "No on Proposition 32" among young voters rose from 40 percent to 60 percent, and the measure was ultimately defeated in the statewide election.[35]

With the growth of social and digital media, access to California's political and news sources has expanded exponentially. Today, major newspapers provide daily emails that focus on topics of the reader's interest, while research organizations, libraries, and blogs provide political information, background, and research. A list of some of the major sources covering California politics is provided in Table 3.7.

Media and Political Campaigns

Running for office is a very expensive endeavor, and it requires highly focused political messages. Because of these requirements, electronic media are the media of choice to reach large numbers of citizens. The media are also very useful in mobilizing supporters on Election Day. Mobilizing a candidate's base of support is essential to winning elections. Without the media, no effective message is conveyed to the electorate, and consequently no money can be raised to fuel the modern type of media campaign that candidates must use to get elected.

In some cases, the media themselves and their coverage can become a central issue in the campaign, with a candidate running against the media and positioning him- or herself outside the political establishment. During the recall election of 2003, the *Los Angeles Times* ran a story just before the election about inappropriate sexual behavior on the part of Schwarzenegger during his acting days. Many citizens reacted by asserting that the newspaper was taking incumbent Governor Gray Davis's side, not that it was uncovering important information that citizens might want to consider in their voting decisions.[36]

TABLE 3.7 ● Online Sources Covering California Politics

MAJOR NEWSPAPERS

Capitol Weekly (www.capitolweekly.net)
Los Angeles Times (www.latimes.com)
Sacramento Bee (www.sacbee.com)
San Francisco Chronicle (www.sfgate.com)

ORGANIZATIONS

Around the Capitol (www.aroundthecapitol.com)
Calitics (www.calitics.com)
Calbuzz (www.calbuzz.com)
California Political Review (www.capoliticalreview.com)
California Watch (www.californiawatch.org)
Flashreport (www.flashreport.org)
Fox & Hounds (www.foxandhoundsdaily.com)
Rough & Tumble (www.rtumble.com)

PUBLIC POLICY SITES

Public Policy Institute of California (www.ppic.org)
California Health Care Foundation (www.chcf.org)
California Policy Center (http://californiapolicycenter.org)

UNIVERSITIES

University of California at Berkeley, Institute of Governmental Studies
   (http://igs.berkeley.edu)
California State University Bakersfield (www.csub.edu/library)

MAJOR COLUMNISTS

Joe Garofoli of the *San Francisco Chronicle* (www.sfgate.com)
George Skelton of the *Los Angeles Times* (www.latimes.com)
Dan Walters, Daniel Weintraub, and Dan Morain of the *Sacramento Bee*
   (www.sacbee.com)

Interest-Group Politics in California: Where Are We Now?

Interest groups play an important and often dominant role in California politics. The continued growth in the number of groups and their lobbying expenditures attests to this fact. Moreover, if the past decade is any indication, the number of interest groups doing business in Sacramento will continue to grow, and lobbying expenditures will continue to increase. The size and structural deficit of the state budget, weak political parties, mandated term limits, the increase in public interest groups, and the continued dependence of local governments on Sacramento for financial assistance are all factors that will continue to promote interest-group politics.

Much of the time, these groups are self-regulating, checking one another and forging broad-based coalitions of interests to achieve important policy decisions. Of course, interest groups will always be able to win on narrow issues affecting their members, and the most powerful will generally be the most successful, as long as they can convince a group of legislators to fall in behind them. That's why interest-group disclosure rules, campaign expenditure limits, and other reporting requirements are necessary. They enable us to keep these groups in check. That's the theory, at least.

Today, however, there is a disjunction between theory and practice. Interest groups have undue influence on politics in the state. Without some limit on the amount of money an interest group can spend on lobbying and campaign contributions, the only check on their power may be divided government, whereby one party controls the executive and one controls one or both houses of the legislature, so that no single interest or coalition of interests can ride roughshod over government.

That's the state of affairs in California today. California's politics is not broken, but unless these concerns are addressed, California will continue to hobble along, and interest groups will continue to flourish and prosper at the expense of the general public.

Study Guide

FOR FURTHER READING

Alexander, Robert, *Interest Group Involvement in Ballot Campaigns.* Westport, CT: Praeger Publishers, 2002.

Baldassare, Mark. *The California Initiative Process—How Democratic Is It?* Public Policy Institute of California, February 2002. www.ppic.org/content/pubs/op/OP_202XXOP.pdf. Accessed 11/16/16.

Boyarsky, Bill. *Jesse Unruh and the Art of Politics.* Berkeley: University of California Press, 2007.

Gerber, Elisabeth R. *Interest Group Influence in the California Initiative Process.* Public Policy Institute of California, 1998. www.ppic.org/main/publication.asp?i=49. Accessed 11/16/16.

Lajos, Maria, "California Interest Groups Hedge Their Bets, Give Cash to Anyone in Power." KQED News, May 14, 2015.

McWilliams, Carey. *California: The Great Exception.* Berkeley: University of California Press, 1999.

Michael, Jay, Dan Walters, and Dan Weintraub. *The Third House: Lobbyists, Power, and Money in Sacramento.* Berkeley: Berkeley Public Policy Press, 2000.

Miller, Kenneth P., Thad Kousser, and Frederick Douzets. *The New Political Geography of California.* Berkeley: Berkeley Public Policy Press, 2008.

Morain, Dan, "An Out of Control System Creates Instant Campaigns and Candidates." *The Sacramento Bee*, June 4, 2016. www.sacbee.com/opinion/opn-columns-blogs/dan-morain/article81726957.html. Accessed 6/4/16.

Rasky, Susan F. "Covering California: The Press Wrestles with Diversity, Complexity, and Change." In *Governing California: Politics, Government, and Public Policy in the Golden State*, edited by Gerald C. Lubenow and Bruce E. Cain, 157–88. Berkeley: Institute of Government Studies Press, University of California, 1997.

Samish, Arthur H., and Bob Thomas. *The Secret Boss of California.* New York: Crown Publishers, 1971.

ON THE WEB

Around the Capitol. www.aroundthecapitol.com. Accessed 11/16/16. A portal to California legislative information.

Capitol Alert. www.sacbee.com/news/politics-government/capitol-alert/. Accessed 11/16/16. California and national political news and commentary.

Capitol Weekly. www.capitolweekly.net. Accessed 11/16/16.

Lobbying activity. http://cal-access.ss.ca.gov/lobbying. Accessed 11/16/16. The secretary of state's office reports on lobbying in California politics.

SUMMARY

I. Interest groups are at the center of California's campaign and lobbying activities.
   A. Interest groups are associations of individuals who join together for the purpose of influencing governmental or legislative policy. They can be individual businesses, trade and professional associations, or labor unions.
   B. Some believe that interest groups play a necessary role in our democratic society, advocating a pluralist theory to explain their power.
   C. Others see them as detrimental to our political system, because only a few, elite groups have power.

II. The number of interest groups (and registered lobbyists) has grown substantially in each legislative session since 1990.
   A. In the 2013–14 legislature, interest groups employed over 3,600 lobbyists.
   B. In the same legislature, interest groups spent more than $500 million on lobbying activities.
   C. Interest groups have proliferated over the past three decades for four reasons: weak political parties, growth of government, term limits, and a greater number of public interest groups.

III. Lobbyists do the work of interest groups. There are three different categories of lobbyists: citizen lobbyists, contract lobbyists, and in-house lobbyists.
   A. Citizen lobbyists are individuals who have an interest in an issue and want to make their view known to their public official.
   B. Contract lobbyists and in-house lobbyists are professionals who must register with the secretary of state and submit a variety of disclosure statements yearly regarding their activities.

IV. Lobbyists perform a variety of activities to accomplish their goals.
   A. The first job of the lobbyist is to know the interest group's objective.
   B. The lobbyist must also identify other organizations that could support or oppose their goals.
   C. Lobbyists may work with a grassroots network of activists in a legislator's district to establish a relationship with a legislator.
   D. Lobbying the executive branch is more difficult to coordinate because of the large number of regulatory agencies and commissions within the branch.

V. There is a strong correlation between lobbying expenditures and campaign contributions.
   A. Interest groups that invest heavily in lobbying also invest heavily in political campaigns. Interest groups contribute to candidates' and officeholders' campaigns to leverage their influence.
   B. The California Correctional Peace Officers Association (CCPOA) is a prime example.

VI. Many efforts have been made to regulate the relationship between lobbyists and legislators.
   A. The Political Reform Act of 1974 was passed to regulate lobbying practices and requires the disclosure of lobbying financial activity.
   B. Proposition 34, the most recent amendment to the act, includes new restrictions:
      1. Lobbyists cannot contribute to the campaigns of anyone for whom they are lobbying.
      2. Lobbyists are limited in the amount of money they can contribute during any election cycle.

VII. The media are important vehicles for mobilizing and informing voters and candidates' supporters.
   A. Television and newspapers have traditionally had the greatest influence on politics.
   B. Today the Internet and social media, as well as the increased use of smartphones and tablets, are changing the way political messages are conveyed. Given the current growth in usage of these devices, digital media, among specific age groups, has surpassed all other media as the primary source for political news and campaign management.
   C. Little of this mobilization, however, comes from news programs, which generally provide scant political information. Television news programs cover scandals and dishonest practices of politicians and focus viewers' attention on the latest special investigation, which indirectly mobilizes citizens.
   D. California politicians are at the forefront among those in other states in using social media to raise money for campaigns and to enlist citizens to help draft legislation and initiatives. This demonstrates how the power to set the political agenda has passed from the political parties to the media.

PRACTICE QUIZ

1. The term *third house* refers to which of the following entities?
   a) judicial branch
   b) executive branch
   c) interest groups
   d) media

2. Over the past two decades, interest-group expenditures in California have
   a) declined.
   b) increased.
   c) remained relatively the same.
   d) fluctuated from year to year.

3. An individual who offers his or her lobbying services to multiple clients at the same time is called a(n)
   a) contract lobbyist.
   b) "hired gun."
   c) citizen lobbyist.
   d) in-house lobbyist.

4. The principal function of an interest group is to
   a) provide its members with educational and social opportunities.
   b) contribute money to candidates for public office who favor its programs.
   c) attain favorable decisions from government on issues that it supports.
   d) seek to inform the public on the role of interest in the economy.

5. Political action committees (PACs)
   a) have declined in popularity in recent years.
   b) must disclose campaign contributions and expenditures in connection with state and local elections.
   c) may make unlimited contributions to political candidates.
   d) provide candidates with public funding for their campaign.

6. According to the text, all of the following factors are involved in the media's decision not to cover more political and governmental news except:
   a) Californians are not that interested in political and governmental news.
   b) The ratings for political and governmental news are lower than other kinds of news, such as the weather, consumer news, and sports coverage.
   c) So many news programs cover California political and governmental news that there is little for each station to report.
   d) Political and governmental news, except during election campaigns, does not lend itself to sensational coverage.

7. Which former speaker of the California Assembly said "Money is the mother's milk of politics"?
   a) Jesse Unruh
   b) Willie Brown
   c) Antonio Villaraigosa
   d) Fabian Nuñez

8. Over the past two decades, the number of newspapers across the United States has _____, and newspaper circulations have _____ in every recent year as well.
   a) risen, increased
   b) remained the same, increased
   c) risen, declined
   d) fallen, declined

9. What is the process called of obtaining ideas, fundraising contributions, or policy support by enlisting online a large group of people?
   a) direct appeal
   b) crowdsourcing
   c) web-based business pattern
   d) outsourcing

10. Many experts see digital media as a catalyst for _____ the democratic process.
    a) threatening
    b) enhancing
    c) having little effect on
    d) undermining

CRITICAL-THINKING QUESTIONS

1. Over the past several decades, interest groups have grown and expanded their influence over public-policy decisions in the legislature and at administrative agencies. Identify the reasons for this phenomenon.

2. Interest groups use a variety of techniques to accomplish their goal. Suppose you worked for an interest group that opposed stricter requirements for the recycling of plastic bottles. Outline a campaign to achieve your goal. Justify why you would take the action you propose.

3. Some people argue that interest groups provide citizens with another way to become involved in the political process. Others argue that interest groups undermine the political process. Discuss the arguments for both positions. Give your opinion on the controversy.

4. Interest groups play a significant role in the funding of political campaigns. Should more restriction be put on their activity? If you decide that interest groups should be limited or altogether prohibited from contributing to political campaigns, how would this policy affect political campaigns? What would be the outcome of this reform?

5. What are the factors that have led to relatively low levels of media coverage of politics and government in California?

KEY TERMS

California Political Reform Act (p. 61)
citizen lobbyist (p. 53)
contract lobbyist (p. 53)
crowdsourcing (p. 68)
elitism (p. 48)
independent expenditure committee (p. 63)
in-house lobbyist (p. 53)
interest group (p. 47)
lobbying (p. 49)
media (p. 65)
pluralism (p. 48)
political action committee (PAC) (p. 55)
public interest group (p. 53)
third house (p. 48)
trade association (p. 50)

4

Parties and Elections in California

WHAT CALIFORNIA GOVERNMENT DOES AND WHY IT MATTERS

California is a trendsetter in many ways: culturally, economically, and politically. Since it is the most populous and diverse state in the nation, laws passed in California attract a lot of national attention. Initiatives passed by California voters often set a trend as other states adopt similar ballot measures. This means that the voters of California can influence politics way beyond their state border. This is quite a responsibility! In spite of their influence, California voters are somewhat lackadaisical about voting. A recent study by Nonprofitvote.org ranked the 50 states and Washington, D.C., according to the percentage of eligible adults who actually voted in the 2012 presidential election. California ranked 41st—nearly at the bottom! While 76 percent of the eligible voters turned out to vote in Minnesota (ranked number 1), less than 60 percent of Californians voted. This ranking, moreover, was determined during a presidential election, when voter turnout is highest. During less exciting elections, such as primaries and midterm elections, the turnout rate is much lower. For example, the June 2014 statewide primary election had the lowest turnout rate in California's history, at less than 20 percent. Only 14 percent of eligible voters in Los Angeles, the state's largest county, cast ballots. And in one of the more bizarre results of the June primary, candidate Leland Yee finished third in a field of eight candidates for the office of secretary of state, despite having publically withdrawn from the race after being indicted on charges of political corruption and conspiracy to run guns. He received nearly 400,000 votes.

However, it must be noted that the June 2016 presidential primary was an election that did engage voters: Nearly 50 percent of those registered turned out to vote. Why such a high turnout for one of the last primaries held in the nation? One reason is that people knew their votes would matter. Votes cast in the hard-fought Sanders versus Clinton primary impacted that race, giving the nomination to Clinton. Lots of media attention generated voter excitement, resulting in nearly 650,000 Californians registering to vote in the final six weeks of the registration period. November's general election had 54 percent of eligible voters participating. This high-profile, media-driven, controversial presidential election resulted in a lower-than-usual voter turnout—not surprising considering the high negative ratings of both candidates and the fact that the presidential contest was not competitive in California.

If voting, and particularly the voting choices of Californians, is so important to the American democratic process, why aren't more Californians paying attention to and participating in elections? This chapter will look at the many factors that affect patterns of voting in California.

Political Parties

A political party is an organization of people with roughly similar political or ideological positions who work to win elections in order to gain greater control of the government and change public policy. Political parties perform many valuable functions in a democratic society. One of their most important roles is to mobilize voters at election time. They are directly involved in political campaigns: providing workers, raising money, and identifying important political issues. In theory, parties help bring about consensus on important political issues and serve as two-way communication channels between government and the people. Consequently, most political scientists consider them vital to the health of a democratic state.

California has a **winner-take-all** system of voting in which the candidate receiving the highest number of votes wins the election. Political scientists have long known that such a system promotes two dominant political parties, and, as expected, the Republicans and the Democrats dominate the political process in California. But as you will discover below, California has what is considered a weak political party system, a consequence of the reforms brought about by the Progressive movement, which took a considerable amount of power away from organized political parties.

The Progressive Impact on Political Parties

The Progressive movement (1890s–1920s) viewed political parties as corrupt organizations operating in concert with big corporations to control and manipulate the political system for their own benefit. Spencer Olin describes the attitude of Progressives toward political parties:

Accompanying their democratic faith in the wisdom of the individual voter was a distrust of formal party organizations, which were viewed as the media of special-interest power. . . . Furthermore, it was argued by progressives that science and efficient management would solve the problems of government; parties were irrelevant and unnecessary.[1]

The Progressives attacked the power of the political parties with reforms such as party primaries. **Primary elections** are used to select the party candidate who will run for office against candidates of opposing parties in the **general election**. Before primaries were established, party leaders typically selected their candidates in proverbial "smoke-filled rooms," outside of public view. Primaries were designed to allow voters, not parties, to select candidates for office. The primary system also opened up the opportunity to run for office to anyone capable of meeting the basic qualifications, which included age and residency requirements. Historically, the party leadership and their corporate allies had selected candidates and subsequently manipulated them while they held office; with the Progressive reforms, the people could participate in a whole new class of elections, forcing candidates to direct their political messages and loyalty to the average voter.

The Progressives also introduced a new type of ballot, the **office block ballot**. This type of ballot made it difficult to vote the straight party ticket, a method popular in many other states where ballots list all the candidates running for each office by party. Political parties preferred this party column ballot because it made it easy for voters to select only candidates from their party. The use of the office block ballot in California discourages such behavior by listing each office separately and has resulted in more split-ticket voting, where people vote for candidates from different parties.

Another Progressive reform was the introduction of nonpartisan elections, which further weakened parties by preventing party designations from appearing on the ballot for most local contests (city councils, board of supervisors, school boards, and judges). Instead, voters were given only the current occupational status of the candidate, and thus could no longer use their party loyalties to make voting decisions at the county and city level on Election Day. The Progressives wanted the electorate to research the candidates by reading up on them or attending forums.

Political scientists believe that the weakening of political parties through nonpartisan elections at the county and city levels has an impact on voters. Despite the hopes of the Progressives, most voters do not devote a lot of time to conducting research on each candidate to determine how to cast their vote. County and city races are typically low profile, so forbidding party labels on ballots further diminishes the voters' already limited information. Voters who identify with a political party view the party affiliation of candidates as important and rely on it to make their voting decisions. As Schaffner, Streb, and Wright describe it, "Party identification is a, or even the, central component of voter decision making. As an effective attachment, it motivates individuals to participate as a display of party support."[2] Therefore, nonpartisan elections may have lower turnout rates than partisan ones.

The Democratic and Republican Parties in California

Currently, California is considered a very Democratic state. Democratic candidates running for the presidency are fairly confident that they will win the popular vote in California (e.g., Clinton won 62 percent of the vote), and they visit our state not to sway voters but to hold expensive fund-raisers. Republican candidates don't spend too much time campaigning in California, as they are certain they will lose the popular vote—although, like Democrats, they do visit to collect campaign contributions. For over 20 years, our state has had two Democratic U.S. senators and the Democratic Party has controlled the state legislature.

But California has not always been in the Democratic camp. From 1952 to 1988, Republican presidential candidates won every presidential vote in California except for one (Democrat Lyndon Johnson defeated Republican Barry Goldwater in 1964). Richard Nixon and Ronald Reagan were both hugely popular in California: Nixon represented California in both the U.S. House and Senate before being elected president, and Reagan served two terms as governor of California before serving in the White House.

What caused the Republican Party to lose support? Many experts believe that demographic changes in the state help explain the ascendancy of the Democratic Party. White and older voters, an important part of the Republican Party coalition, are declining in numbers. As of July 2014, Latinos are the largest ethnic group in California, just edging out the white population. It is projected that by 2060, Latinos will comprise 49 percent of the state's population. Young and ethnically diverse voters prefer the Democratic Party. Non-whites now amount to a majority in the state, and these voters have not supported some of the more strident anti-immigrant policies touted by Republican candidates. Conservative, right-wing Republicans do not do well in statewide elections: California voters largely prefer centrist leaders who advocate moderate policies. And, California appears to be a harbinger of national trends. As one analyst proclaimed, "Where L.A. goes is where the rest of the state goes and where the rest of the country goes," he said. "We announce, demographically speaking, the future for the rest of the country."[3]

Third Parties in California

The American political system, which is a federal system, delegates power to three levels of government: national, state, and local. One of the powers that states retain is to determine how political parties may organize and gain access to the ballot. By dominating the legislature in California, Republicans and Democrats have not made it easy for third parties to qualify for the ballot, and consequently the two parties dominate California politics. Third parties then are defined as any party other than Republican or Democrat.

Traditionally, third-party candidates do not win in a winner-take-all system, a fact that both major parties emphasize to warn voters against throwing their votes away. However, a significant percentage of voters continue to vote for third-party candidates anyway.

There are two ways in which political parties can qualify to get on the ballot in California. The first method is by registration; the second is by petition. Both methods are based on a percentage of those persons who voted in the preceding gubernatorial election. In the election held in November 2014, 7,513,972 persons turned out to vote. To qualify a new party by the registration method, the law requires that .33 of those who voted in the 2014 gubernatorial election officially register with the new party. The law also requires that voters complete and mail their registration by the 154th day preceding the upcoming primary. The petition method is just as difficult and tedious. It requires that a new political party petition to be included in the upcoming primary; the party must collect signatures equal to 10 percent of those who voted in the last gubernatorial election. Currently, that number stands at over three-quarters of a million signatures. Qualifying as a new political party clearly is not an easy task and requires time, personnel, expertise, and resources. In 2016,

TABLE 4.1 ● Qualified Political Parties in California, 2014

AMERICAN INDEPENDENT PARTY	www.aipca.org
DEMOCRATIC PARTY	www.cadem.org
GREEN PARTY	www.cagreens.org
LIBERTARIAN PARTY	www.ca.lp.org
PEACE AND FREEDOM PARTY	www.peaceandfreedom.org
REPUBLICAN PARTY	www.cagop.org

California had six qualified parties (see Table 4.1): the American Independent Party, the Democratic Party, the Green Party, the Libertarian Party, the Peace and Freedom Party, and the Republican Party. So what is the role of third parties in politics, particularly in California? One theory is that third parties act as spoilers, drawing enough votes from one or the other of the two major parties to alter the election outcome. Third parties also help focus public attention on important political issues. Once an issue attracts enough public attention, it will be taken over by one or both of the two major political parties. Sometimes, third parties can motivate people who do not usually vote to turn up at the polls because the third-party candidate better represents their views than the established Democratic or Republican candidates do.

Party Affiliation of California Voters

A plurality of California voters identify with the Democratic Party. As of October 2016, about 45 percent of voters are registered with the Democratic Party compared to 26 percent registered with the Republican Party. A substantial 24 percent of voters have **no party preference**, and 5 percent identify with one of the minor third parties. It should be noted that the name of one of these minor third parties, the American Independent Party, has confused voters who thought they actually were registering as independent voters (no party preference). Because the word *independent* appears in the party's name, tens of thousands of Californians mistakenly registered with this party that espouses ultraconservative, antigay, and antiabortion positions. After the *Los Angeles Times*[4] brought to light this confusion on the part of voters, nearly 32,000 voters who had previously registered with the American Independent Party changed their political party registration. The American Independent Party, however, still attracts over half a million voters, the most of any of the minor parties.

Party affiliation is fairly easy to determine because people are asked to declare **political party affiliation** when registering to vote (one of the options, however, is no party preference. As Figure 4.1 illustrates, since 1998 registration in the two major political parties has declined. The percentage of voters registering with the Democratic Party fell by 2 percentage points, while registrations with the Republican Party fell by 10 percentage points. The most dramatic change has been among those who have no political party preference (also referred to as independent voters). This group has nearly doubled its size over the past 20 years; nearly one in four voters now claim no party preference when they register to vote.

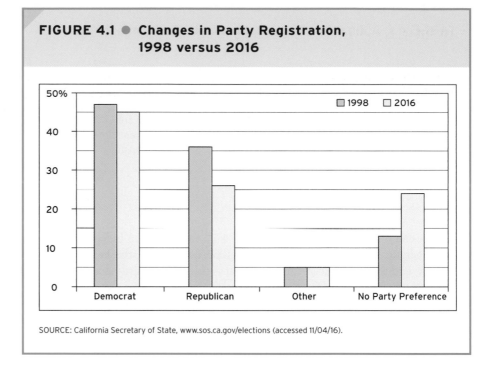

FIGURE 4.1 ● Changes in Party Registration, 1998 versus 2016

SOURCE: California Secretary of State, www.sos.ca.gov/elections (accessed 11/04/16).

Now let us look at political-party affiliation and some demographic factors. Figure 4.2 presents the results of a California statewide survey conducted in October 2016 that asked respondents about their party affiliation, age, gender, race, educational level, and place of birth. The results suggest that over 40 percent of all young, middle-aged, and older Californians prefer the Democratic Party. A recent California Field Poll (2011) found that the Republican Party is becoming the party of senior citizens. Currently, those 50 years of age or older make up 54 percent of the party, and this number is growing annually as the population ages. Many are questioning what the Republican Party of the future will look like in California with the passing of these older Republicans. Will the party be able to survive this demographic trend? Another important trend is young voters' movement away from organized parties to register instead as independent voters; nearly as many stated no party preferences (36 percent) as did those stating an affiliation with the Democratic Party (41 percent).

We also observe gender differences in party affiliation, with more women affiliating with the Democratic Party and more men than women registering as independents. The Democratic Party has more support than the Republican Party regardless of educational level. Race is also a key predictor of party identification, with Latinos preferring the Democratic Party at a much higher rate than whites do (58 percent compared to 38 percent). Some of these demographic trends suggest that politics in our state will change in the future. Older white males' proportionate decline in the population will continue to have an impact on the Republican Party as it loses a large segment of its support.

Another important demographic change is the increasing Latino population. Data from the Census Bureau demonstrate that from 2000 to 2015 the Latino population grew by nearly 30 percent to 15 million, whereas the white population

FIGURE 4.2 ● Party Registration by Demographic, 2016

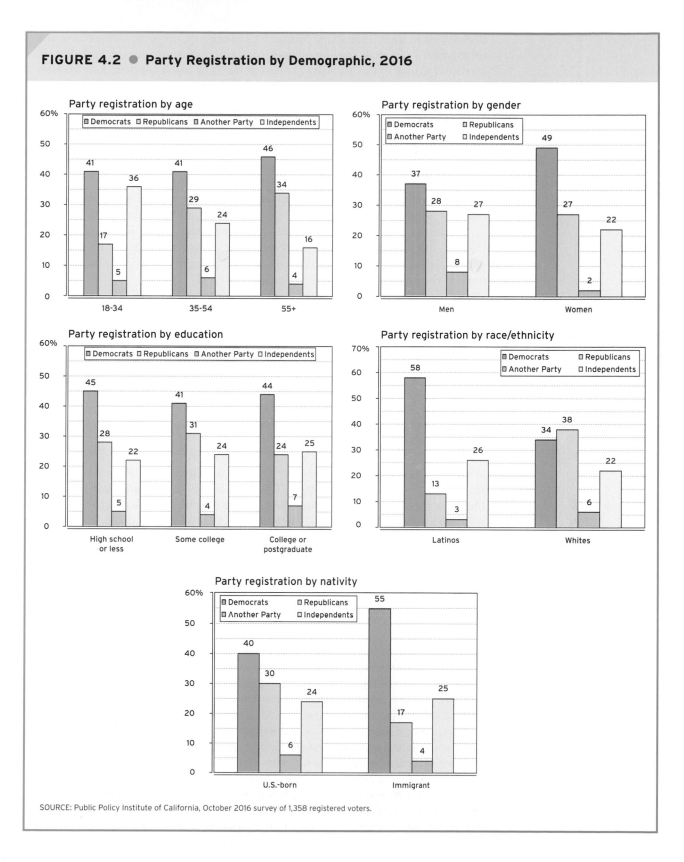

SOURCE: Public Policy Institute of California, October 2016 survey of 1,358 registered voters.

declined more than 5 percent to just under 15 million. Currently, Latinos favor the Democratic Party over the Republican Party by sizable percentages, and there is no reason to expect this to change in the future. Thus many are predicting an even stronger Democratic Party presence in the state in the future.

THE RED AND THE BLUE IN CALIFORNIA You may recall that most television programs focusing on the 2016 presidential election exhibited a color-coded map of the United States which represented the states that voted Republican as red and the states that voted Democratic as blue. The map nicely illustrated the national split between urban areas and rural, agricultural, and suburban areas: the West Coast, most of the Northeast, and the major urban areas of the United States were blue; the South, the agricultural regions, and the Great Plains states were red.

As the map in Figure 4.3 illustrates, the same geographic split appears within the state of California, between the coastal counties and the inland counties. Most of the Democratic counties are coastal and encompass major urban areas, whereas most of the Republican counties are inland and rural.

As reported by the *Los Angeles Times:*

> Over the last decade, Republican influence has grown more concentrated in conservative inland California—largely the Central Valley and Inland Empire but also the Antelope Valley, the Sierra and rural north. . . . At the same time Democrats have strengthened their domination of counties along California's coastline, building overwhelming advantages in the San Francisco and Los Angeles areas as Latino voters have expanded the party's base. And from San Diego's beachfront suburbs to the Central Coast, Democrats have eroded Republican support among moderates, especially women.[5]

What does this split mean politically? Overall, the Democratic Party has an electoral advantage in California; nearly 70 percent of the state's population resides in Democratic-leaning coastal regions. Republicans have an uphill battle to win statewide elections and are more likely to succeed if they nominate ideologically moderate candidates who are able to gain the support of Democratic voters. The fact that the urban and coastal population centers are largely Democratic and moderate to liberal, coupled with the tendency of the majority of independent voters to lean toward the Democratic Party, suggests that California will remain a distinctly blue state. However, this ideological split has potentially negative consequences. As described by Mark Baldassare,

> California seems poised to maintain its blue status this fall (2016). However, the geo-political segregation of the state—with Republican pockets of strength in California's northern, inland, and rural regions—means that federal and state legislators will be elected to represent the views of voters who are worlds apart. Indeed, the political polarization and antipathy of this year's election may result in a California Congressional delegation that will contribute to Washington gridlock and a California Legislature that will struggle to find common ground on solutions to the many challenges facing California's future.[6]

This is not to imply, however, that all populated coastal regions are the same politically and ideologically. As the next section illustrates, there are some interesting variations.

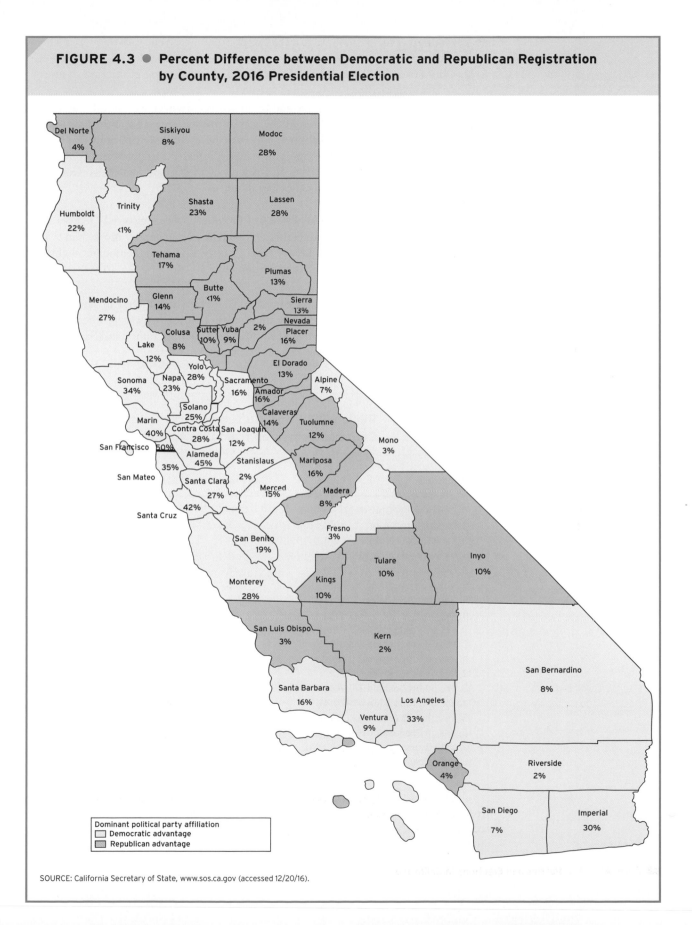

FIGURE 4.3 ● Percent Difference between Democratic and Republican Registration by County, 2016 Presidential Election

County	%
Del Norte	4%
Siskiyou	8%
Modoc	28%
Humboldt	22%
Trinity	<1%
Shasta	23%
Lassen	28%
Tehama	17%
Plumas	13%
Mendocino	27%
Glenn	14%
Butte	<1%
Sierra	13%
Nevada	2%
Colusa	8%
Sutter	10%
Yuba	9%
Placer	16%
Lake	12%
Yolo	28%
El Dorado	13%
Sonoma	34%
Napa	23%
Sacramento	16%
Alpine	7%
Solano	25%
Amador	16%
Calaveras	14%
Tuolumne	12%
Mono	3%
Marin	40%
Contra Costa	28%
San Joaquin	12%
San Francisco	50%
Alameda	45%
Stanislaus	2%
Mariposa	16%
San Mateo	35%
Santa Clara	27%
Merced	15%
Madera	8%
Santa Cruz	42%
San Benito	19%
Fresno	3%
Monterey	28%
Kings	10%
Tulare	10%
Inyo	10%
San Luis Obispo	3%
Kern	2%
San Bernardino	8%
Santa Barbara	16%
Los Angeles	33%
Ventura	9%
Orange	4%
Riverside	2%
San Diego	7%
Imperial	30%

Dominant political party affiliation
☐ Democratic advantage
▨ Republican advantage

SOURCE: California Secretary of State, www.sos.ca.gov (accessed 12/20/16).

California's Local Political Cultures from Left to Right

Political culture is difficult to define and to quantify. However, we can offer at least a few statistics to show how three of the state's most populous counties differ in terms of political partisanship, political ideology, political activism, political tolerance, and voting tendencies on important issues. Table 4.2 compares and contrasts the city and county of San Francisco, Los Angeles County, and San Diego County on these selected indicators of local political culture.

POLITICAL PARTY REGISTRATION As of October 2016, registered Democrats outnumbered Republicans in San Francisco by eight to one and by more than two to one in Los Angeles County. In San Diego County, however, Democrats slightly outnumber Republicans 37 percent to 30 percent.

POLITICAL IDEOLOGY Based on community surveys conducted in late 2000, 21 percent of San Franciscans identify themselves politically as "very liberal" and only 4 percent as "very conservative." In both Los Angeles County and San Diego County, conservatives outnumber liberals by about two to one.[7]

TABLE 4.2 ● Regional Political Cultures: Three California Counties Compared from Left to Right

Indicator	San Francisco	Los Angeles	San Diego
1. Democrats (2014)	58%	52%	37%
2. Republicans (2014)	7	19	30
3. Very liberal (2000)	21	8	6
4. Very conservative (2000)	4	15	14
5. High protest activity (2000)	47	30	30
6. Voter turnout (Nov. 8, 2016)	38	23	33
7. Voter turnout (Nov. 6, 2012)	57	52	56
8. Yes on Proposition 13 (1978)	47	67	60
9. Yes on Proposition 187 (1994)	29	56	68
10. Yes on Proposition 209 (1996)	29	45	63
11. Yes on Proposition 8 (2008)	25	50	54
12. Yes on Proposition 30 (2012)	77	60	46
13. Yes on Proposition 34 (2012)	70	54	45
14. Yes on Proposition 47 (2014)	79	63	55
15. Yes on Proposition 62 (2016)	71	52	44
16. Yes on Proposition 64 (2016)	74	58	56
17. Vote Brown for governor (2014)	88	66	50
18. Vote Obama for president (2012)	83	69	51
19. Vote for Clinton for President (2016)	85	72	56

SOURCE: Indicators 1–2, 6–19: California Secretary of State, various official statements of vote. Indicators 3–5: Analysis of sample survey data obtained from the Social Capital Benchmark Survey 2000.

POLITICAL PROTEST AND VOTER TURNOUT Those same surveys show that San Franciscans are much more inclined to engage in political protest than are their counterparts in the southland. Specifically, 47 percent of San Francisco citizens scored "high" on a nationally normed political-protest-activity index, as compared with only 30 percent of citizens in both Los Angeles and San Diego counties. In terms of more conventional forms of political participation, however, San Diego's County's citizens are on top, with higher voter turnout rates than San Franciscans and Angelenos in both the November 4, 2008, general election and the November 2, 2010, general election. The November 6, 2012, general election saw both San Diego and San Francisco with near equal turnout rates, with Los Angeles lagging behind. In November 2016 voter turnout dipped overall, but a similar turnout pattern held: San Francisco voters turned out at a near equal rate with San Diego voters, with the turnout rate in Los Angeles substantially lower.

SUPPORT FOR PROPOSITION 13 Proposition 13, the 1978 initiative that rolled back property tax rates and limited the government's ability to raise local property taxes in the future, is regarded by some observers "as one of the most significant political events in California's history."[8] It won by a landslide vote nearly everywhere throughout the state, including a 67 percent vote in favor in Los Angeles County and a 60 percent vote in favor in San Diego County. In San Francisco, however, it mustered only a 47 percent vote in favor, not even a majority.

SUPPORT FOR PROGRESSIVE POLICIES AND RACIAL AND CULTURAL DIVERSITY Table 4.2 reports county voting results on different statewide ballot propositions over the period 1994–2016. All results can be viewed as indicators of California voters' political tolerance and level of support for racial and cultural diversity and progressive policies.

- Proposition 187 was a 1994 initiative constitutional amendment that made undocumented immigrants ineligible for various public social services. The state's voters approved it by a wide margin, with 56 percent voting yes in Los Angeles County and 68 percent voting yes in San Diego County. Only 29 percent voted for it in San Francisco. After passage, Proposition 187 was challenged in the courts and was ultimately invalidated.

- Proposition 209 was a 1996 initiative constitutional amendment that prohibited state and local government agencies from giving preferential treatment to any individual or group on the basis of race, sex, color, ethnicity, or national origin. Widely viewed by friends and foes alike as an attack on affirmative action, this measure passed in the statewide vote, with 63 percent support in San Diego County. It received only 45 percent support in Los Angeles County, however, and a mere 29 percent support in San Francisco.

- Proposition 8 was a 2008 initiative constitutional amendment that eliminated the right of same-sex couples to marry. Backers of the proposition placed it on the ballot as a direct challenge to the California Supreme Court's ruling in May 2008 affirming the constitutionality of same-sex marriage. The measure was approved 52 to 48 percent in the statewide vote. Only 25 percent of San Francisco County's voters voted yes, however, compared with 50 percent in Los Angeles County and 54 percent in San Diego County. In June 2015 the

U.S. Supreme Court ruled in favor of same-sex marriage nationwide, declaring Proposition 8 unconstitutional.

- Proposition 30 was a 2012 initiative constitutional amendment that would temporarily raise taxes to fund education. Personal income taxes would increase for those earning over $250,000 for seven years and the sales tax would increase by 25 cents for four years. This increased state revenue would be used to fund education at the K–12, community college, and university levels, which otherwise faced budget cuts. Teacher unions and Governor Brown campaigned aggressively for the passage of this initiative. Failure of the proposition would result in extensive budget cuts to the already struggling public school and university systems. Proposition 30 was approved statewide by a vote of 54 to 46 percent. Over 75 percent of San Francisco voters approved of the measure, as did 60 percent of Los Angeles County voters. In San Diego County, however, only 46 percent voted yes. Proposition 55 on the November 2016 ballot sought to extend by 12 years the temporary personal income tax increases enacted in 2012. This proposition passed with 62 percent of the statewide vote. San Francisco voters approved it by 72 percent, Los Angeles voters by 67 percent, and San Diego voters by 60 percent.

- Proposition 47 was a 2014 initiative that would reform the state's Three Strikes law. This law resulted in harsh prison sentences for those convicted of a third felony offense, with the "third strike" for many being a nonviolent crime. Research has found that the Three Strikes law has disproportionately affected minority populations; over 45 percent of those serving life sentences under this law are African Americans.[9] Under the law as reformed by the initiative, those convicted of certain drug and property crimes would receive a misdemeanor sentence instead of a felony sentence if they had no prior convictions for serious or violent crimes such as rape, murder, or child molestation. Additionally, this measure would allow offenders currently serving felony sentences for nonviolent crimes to petition to have their felony sentences reduced to misdemeanor sentences. The measure passed with a statewide vote of 59 percent. It passed 79 percent to 21 percent in San Francisco and 63 percent to 37 percent in Los Angeles County. In San Diego County it passed by only 55 percent to 45 percent.

- Proposition 62 was a November 2016 initiative asking voters to approve the repeal of the death penalty and replace it with life imprisonment without the possibility of parole. This measure would apply retroactively to those inmates currently on death row. A very similar measure failed to pass in 2012 with a statewide vote of only 47 percent. November 2016 was no different: 54 percent of voters disapproved of this measure. San Francisco voters were very supportive of repealing the death penalty, with 71 percent voting in favor of the initiative. A slim majority (52 percent) of Los Angeles voters supported repeal. In contrast, only 44 percent of San Diego county voters were in favor of this measure.

- Proposition 64 on the November 2016 ballot legalizes marijuana and hemp under state law. With the support of 56 percent of the voters, this measure passed. Nearly 75 percent of San Francisco voters supported legalization, with Los Angeles and San Diego voters supporting passage at 58 and 56 percent respectively.

THE GUBERNATORIAL ELECTION OF 2014 In the 2014 race for governor, the winner, Democrat Jerry Brown, easily beat Republican Neel Kashkari by 75 percent in San Francisco and 32 percent in Los Angeles County. In San Diego County, however, Kashkari beat Brown by 241 votes.

THE PRESIDENTIAL ELECTION OF 2016 In the November 8, 2016, presidential election, California voters preferred Hillary Clinton over Donald Trump 62 to 33 percent. San Francisco County overwhelmingly voted for Clinton with a resounding 85 percent; voters in Los Angeles County supported her at 72 percent, and San Diego County at 56 percent.

TO SUM UP The statistics in Table 4.2 demonstrate that political life varies dramatically in California from region to region. If you happen to reside in San Francisco, you live in one of the nation's most liberal, tolerant, and activist political cultures.[10] The political environment in San Diego, on the other hand, is more conservative, less tolerant, and more passive. Los Angeles falls somewhere between these two. These three regions reflect the range of political cultural differences that exist across the state. You can easily see why local representatives in the state legislature fight so much and so fiercely and have a very hard time agreeing on anything.

Elections in California

The Battle over the Primary

The past decade has seen considerable controversy and upheaval and a number of court challenges regarding the type of primary system used in California. In primary elections, voters select their party's nominee for the general election. In the United States, there are three general types of primary-election systems, and states have the authority to determine the system under which they will operate.

- **Closed primary system**   Only voters who declare a party affiliation when they register to vote are permitted to vote in their party's primary election. Each party has its own ballot, listing the names of those who are competing to be the party's candidate in the general election. Voters receive the ballot of the party for which they are registered. Voters who decline to state a party affiliation when they register are not eligible to receive a party ballot; only party members can elect the party's nominees. Approximately 25 states use this system.

- **Open primary system**   Registered voters, regardless of their party affiliation, can vote in the party primary of their choice on primary election day. For example, a registered Democrat can decide if he or she would like to vote in the Republican Party primary and request that ballot. The choice of party ballot on primary election day does not affect the voter's permanent party affiliation. Approximately 20 states operate under this system.

- **Blanket primary system**   One ballot lists all candidates from all of the parties. All registered voters, including those not affiliated with any party, are permitted to vote, and all voters receive the same ballot. For instance, a voter who is not affiliated with a party may vote for a Democrat to run as the nominee for governor and a Republican to run as the nominee for the U.S. Senate. Under this system, voters who are not affiliated with a party help to choose that party's nominees. Alaska, Louisiana, Washington State, and California all use this primary system.

California operated under the closed primary system until the passage of Proposition 198 in 1996. Proposition 198 instituted a blanket primary system in which all voters received a single ballot containing the names of all candidates from all parties. California held two blanket primaries—in June 1998 and March 2000—before the U.S. Supreme Court (in the case of *California Democratic Party v. Jones*) invalidated Proposition 198. The Court ruled that, based on the First Amendment's guarantee of freedom of association, California's political parties have the right to exclude nonparty members from voting in party primaries. In an effort to include the growing number of nonaffiliated voters, California adopted a **modified closed primary system**. Beginning with the March 2002 primary election, political parties still had their own ballots but now had the option of adopting a party rule that would allow unaffiliated voters to vote in their party primary. If an unaffiliated voter was not allowed to request a party's ballot, he or she was given a ballot containing only the names of candidates for nonpartisan races and ballot measures.

Proponents of the blanket primary were not satisfied with the modified closed primary system, arguing that the blanket primary system is more inclusive and would result in more moderate candidates running in primary elections, thus producing more competitive races. The logic is that if independent, ideologically moderate voters participate in the primary election, they will bring a counterbalance to the more extreme and ideological views of traditional primary-party voters, the party loyalists. Primary candidates would, therefore, need to moderate their positions to attract the votes of independent voters. So, in June 2010, voters once more passed a proposition that changed California's primary-election system.

Proposition 14 mandates a form of a blanket primary system known as the "top-two vote getters" system. This primary system only applies to state legislative and congressional elections as well as to the election of statewide officials, such as governor and attorney general. (This system does not apply to candidates running for U.S. president, county central committees, or local offices. Presidential primaries continue to use closed or semi-closed primaries.) All registered voters, even those stating no party preference, receive a ballot listing all candidates from all qualified political parties. The two candidates who win the most votes for each office then participate in a runoff in November's general election. An interesting feature of this new primary election system is the possibility that the top two candidates can belong to the same political party.

The June 5, 2012, primary election was the first statewide election held under this new system, and the results were quite interesting. As a result of this new primary system, the November 2012 election saw 29 same-party runoffs for Congress, the state Assembly, and state Senate. This trend continued for the June 2014 and 2016 primaries. The June 2014 primary produced 24 same-party runoffs and the June 2016 primary resulted in 28 same-party contests. The June 2016 primary made history as it produced the first same-party runoff for a statewide office, the U.S. Senate seat replacing long-term senator Barbara Boxer. Kamala Harris, California's Democratic attorney general, faced off against Democratic House member

Loretta Sanchez in the November 2016 election (we will discuss this contest in more depth later in this chapter).

For statewide races only, this new primary system also allows candidates to designate whether they have a political party preference and how it should be stated on the ballot. According to California law, "a candidate for nomination to a voter-nominated office shall have his or her party preference, or lack of party preference, stated on the ballot, but the party preference designation is selected solely by the candidate." This means that candidates can state the party with which they identify or they can state that they don't have a party preference. In this age of voter frustration directed at party politics and legislative gridlock, electing to have the ballot state "Party Preference: None" appears to be a strategy adopted by some candidates. This is what happened in a race for a hotly contested congressional seat in Ventura County in 2012. The redrawing of the state's congressional district boundaries created a new swing district in the area. A swing district is one in which there are near equal numbers of Republican and Democratic voters and a significant number of independent voters—who often decide the winner. This new district consisted of 41 percent Democrats, 35 percent Republicans, and 19 percent independent voters. There were four Democrats, one Republican, and one independent running in this primary. The "independent" candidate was actually a Republican who switched her party registration to "no party preference" just before filing her papers to run, hoping to win the support of enough independent and moderate voters to be one of the top two winners. A number of candidates have used this strategy, hoping voters won't remember or even know that they have been party loyalists before the campaign. Unfortunately for this candidate, the only Republican on the ballot and the better-known Democrat captured the top two positions and competed against each other in the November general election.

Will this new primary system have the intended result of encouraging more moderate candidates to run in primaries and ensuring their success? Louisiana and Washington operate under similar primary systems, and analyses of their election outcomes found that these states have not seen more moderate candidates elected. However, some argue that blanket primaries can boost voter turnout by 3 to 6 percent because they attract voters with no party preference. The June 2014 primary election in California did not meet these expectations. Neither did the June 2016 primary, whose exceptionally high turnout of nearly 50 percent (with many voting for the first time) was largely a result of an exciting presidential primary and not the blanket primary.

Presidential Primaries: Maximizing California's Clout?

Until 2000, California held its presidential primaries in June of election years and was one of the last states to cast its votes for the parties' nominees. States holding earlier primaries and caucuses often determined the presidential nominees before Californians had a chance to go to the polls. To have more influence in the nomination process, California changed its presidential primary election date to March for the 2000 and 2004 presidential primaries.

Many believed it fitting that the most populous state should have an early primary date. However, this earlier primary date did not give California voters more clout in the presidential nomination process, because other states moved their primaries to even earlier dates. So for the 2008 presidential primaries, California changed the

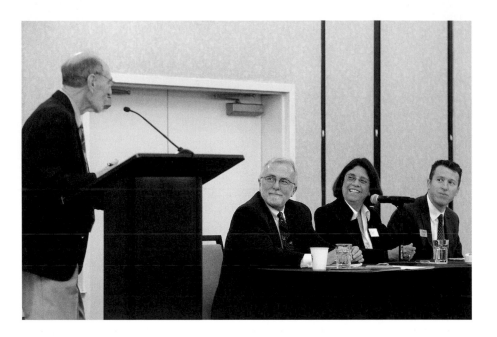

Three of the Democratic candidates for the District 4 seat in the California State Assembly participate at a March 2016 forum led by moderator Harris Nussbaum, left. Democrat Cecilia Aguilar-Curry (second from the right) and Republican candidate Charlie Schaupp won the most votes in the June 2016 primary election in order to compete on the November ballot.

date once again, to February 5, the earliest permissible date under national party rules.

Many political analysts and journalists heralded the early February presidential primary date. But did this move really have the intended effect, as reflected in a hopeful 2007 *Los Angeles Times* article titled "Earlier Primary Gives California a Major Voice"? Many who had argued for the 2008 presidential primary in early February believed that candidates would have to campaign early and hard in the Golden State and win support from a racially and ethnically diverse population, especially the growing number of Latino voters. To win voters' support, the candidates would need to address issues important to Californians, and all this would result in California's greater prominence in presidential campaign politics. Or so the theory went.

One of the unanticipated consequences of California's adoption of an early primary date was that a number of states with long-standing early primaries set their election dates even earlier, not wanting to be overshadowed by the most populous state in the nation. Twenty-three other states also moved their primaries to February 5, resulting in something akin to a national primary. California's dream of being in the electoral limelight quickly faded.

Another consequence of the early February presidential primary was additional cost for the state, as the primaries for statewide offices continued to be held in June. The June 2008 primary election for statewide offices cost the state and counties $100 million and resulted in a historically low voting turnout rate of less than 25 percent of the registered voters. Including the November 2008 general election, California voters were asked to vote in three elections in less than 10 months. Now California's presidential primary is once again back to the June date. However, the June 2012 California primary (which included primaries for presidential and statewide candidates) saw a record low turnout of only 22 percent of registered voters. Some believe that the frequent date changes for primary elections confuse voters and thereby contribute to California's less-than-spectacular voting turnout rates. We witnessed a slight improvement in June 2016, with 33 percent of registered voters casting ballots in the primary.

Initiative Campaigns: Direct Democracy or Tool of Special Interests?

One legacy of California's early-twentieth-century Progressive reform movement is the **ballot initiative** process. Californians can completely bypass the state legislature and their elected representatives and place proposed policies on the ballot for direct vote by the people. As the name suggests, the electorate *initiates* initiatives. Most people think of the initiative process as direct democracy in action—concerned citizens circulating petitions to qualify their issue for the ballot and then holding an election for the public to state its preference for or against the proposed policy. In reality, only a small number of ballot initiatives emerge as a result of grassroots efforts. Initiatives are largely a political tool used by special-interest groups to achieve their policy goals. Depending on the issue, interest groups sometimes find it politically expedient to bypass the legislature altogether, believing they have a better chance of achieving their policy goals if they take the issue directly to the voters.

For example, many members of the California legislature would find it politically unwise to introduce legislation to legalize marijuana, abolish the death penalty, or raise taxes. Positions on these issues are sure to outrage some voters, making re-election more difficult. That is why these types of issues find their way onto our ballots as initiatives or referendums. Likewise, legislation that would curb the power of special interests, interests that make sizable campaign contributions to legislators, also are unlikely to be dealt with by our elected representatives. Recently, some local ballot measures have passed that reduce retirement benefits for public employees. If an elected official introduced this type of proposal, he or she would be targeted for re-election defeat by unions representing public employees. So, for many of these types of issues, interest groups realize that the most productive route is to go directly to the voters via the initiative process. In addition, citizen groups have found the initiative process to be the only avenue for policy change in the areas of legislative term limits, nonpartisan redistricting, and the blanket primary system. These changes would never have been proposed or approved by legislators, whose power and that of their political party would be curbed.

Since 1912, the first year initiatives were permitted, nearly 400 statewide initiatives have appeared on the California ballot. These ballot initiatives have dealt with a wide range of issues, such as legalization of marijuana, campaign finance reform, same-sex marriage, taxation policy, legalization of gambling casinos, the establishment of a state lottery, environmental regulations, affirmative action policy, the criminal justice system, and labor issues. Of these hundreds of initiatives, only about one-third have been approved by the voters. In the past three decades, there has been a dramatic surge in the number of initiatives that have been proposed and that have qualified for the ballot. Many surmise that the reason for this increase is that special interests have become more sophisticated in their use of the initiative process to achieve their policy goals.

QUALIFYING FOR THE BALLOT For initiatives creating new laws (statutes) to qualify for the ballot, the state requires nearly 366,000 signatures of registered voters. For propositions aiming to amend the state constitution, the state requires

585,407 signatures. Signatures are gathered on petitions, which are then submitted to the secretary of state's office for verification. Collecting hundreds of thousands of signatures of registered voters is a daunting task. Rarely is this a grassroots movement in which ordinary citizens fan out across the state, knock on doors, and stand in front of supermarkets, asking strangers to support their initiative by signing a petition. More common is the hiring of professional signature gatherers, such as political consulting firms that hire people to go to college campuses, supermarkets, malls, and other places where voters congregate. Typically they are paid an average of $1.50 for every signature they acquire. However, the November 2016 election, with 17 ballot measures and many big-money donors, saw the average price of a signature rise to $4, with some companies paying $5 per signature collected. All total, to qualify for the November 2016 ballot, campaigns spent over $45 million just on signature-gathering activities. [11]

CAMPAIGNING To wage a successful campaign either in support of or in opposition to a more controversial initiative, one needs ample political resources, particularly money. Not only must a statewide initiative campaign hire political consultants, but it must also plan and implement a sustainable media campaign. Such campaigns are very costly because of California's size and expensive media markets. Therefore, it is not surprising that the more high-profile and controversial initiative campaigns cost tens of millions of dollars. In 2008 slightly over $80 million was spent on the highly controversial initiative Proposition 8, a constitutional amendment to eliminate same-sex marriage in California. Proposition 8 was put on the ballot in response to the state Supreme Court's May 2008 ruling (in a 4-to-3 decision) declaring that the state constitution protects a fundamental "right to marry" that extends equally to same-sex couples. Both sides of the issue collected near equal contributions, with the majority of the contributions in support of Proposition 8 coming from members of the Mormon Church throughout the United States.[12] As expensive as Proposition 8 was, it did not break the record for the most expensive initiative campaign. In 2006 both sides combined spent more than $150 million on Proposition 87, the alternative energy initiative, which was soundly defeated by a 55 percent vote. Breaking that spending record was a series of initiatives in 2008 (Propositions 94–97) that sought to expand the number of Native American casinos in the state. According to a recent report by the *Washington Post*, the two sides combined spent over $170 million on those campaigns.[13] This was, by far, the most expensive proposition campaign not only in California history but in U.S. history.

It should be noted that spending more money than the opposing side does not always guarantee victory. Case in point: Proponents of Proposition 34, an initiative to repeal the death penalty on the November 2012 ballot, spent over $8 million on the yes campaign, whereas the opposition spent only a paltry $400,000 to defeat the measure.

Political savvy is another important resource. The chances of winning an initiative campaign increase if one understands how the game is played. For example, the naming of the proposition can increase its chance of passage. In the November 1996 election, Proposition 209, officially titled "Prohibition against Discrimination or Preferential Treatment by State and Other Public Entities," appeared on the ballot. Its supporters referred to the proposition as the "California Civil Rights Initiative." Considering these titles alone, it would be difficult to imagine this proposition failing; in these progressive times, it is fair to say that most voters are opposed to discrimination and are supportive of civil rights. In reality, however, Proposition 209 was not what most would consider a civil rights statute. The proposition proposed to eliminate affirmative action programs in California for women and minorities in public employment, education (college admissions, tutoring, and outreach programs), and contracting. But the clever naming worked: Proposition 209 passed and is now state law.

CRITICISMS OF DIRECT DEMOCRACY Critics of the initiative process believe that too many complicated issues are presented to the voters as ballot propositions. In some recent elections, voters have had to vote for candidates for federal, state, county, and city elective offices as well as cast their votes for more than a dozen important state propositions and numerous county and city measures. Case in point—the November 2016 election had 17 ballot propositions and the Official California Voter Information Guide was 224 pages, the longest ever. It was estimated that it would take about 14 hours to read the guide. Not surprisingly, few voters will spend this amount of time educating themselves on the ballot propositions. David Redlawsk, co-author of *How Voters Decide: Information Processing in Election Campaigns,* describes the situation as follows: "People want to do what we would call a good job—that is make what they think is the right decision—but they want to do it essentially with the least amount of effort necessary." [14]

Some argue that many of the issues that appear as ballot initiatives are best suited for debate and deliberation by our elected representatives and should not be represented by misleading television ads aimed at the public. Sometimes the propositions are very confusing in name and in substance, and some question whether we are asking too much of the electorate to wade through all this information. Another problem with the initiative process is that the constitutionality of many propositions approved by the voters is later challenged. It takes years for the courts to render a decision, and it is not uncommon for the courts to declare the law based on the passage of the proposition to be unconstitutional, null, and void. Not only does this complicate the process, it also frustrates the public to see the courts invalidate its will.

The legislature understands some of the problems associated with the initiative and has created state commissions to investigate and reform the process. Some of these suggested reforms aim to accomplish the following: prohibit the use of paid signature gatherers whom only the well-funded interest groups can afford; increase the number of signatures required, with the goal of reducing the number of initiatives; restrict the types of issues that can appear as ballot initiatives; and review the constitutionality of initiatives prior to placing them on the ballot. In September 2014, the legislature enacted two bills that reform the initiative process. One bill provides for a 30-day public review period that commences when the initiative is first proposed. Reformers hope that public input during this time will result in constructive modifications to propositions before they appear on the ballot, and that such input may motivate supporters of the proposed initiative to work with lawmakers to find a legislative solution to the issue. The other bill requires that the secretary of state post online and continuously update the top ten donors contributing to both sides of an initiative. This provision creates more transparency by revealing exactly who is contributing big money in support of or in opposition to an initiative.

The 2003 Gubernatorial Recall Election: A Perfect Political Storm

On October 7, 2003, Governor Gray Davis made history. Only 11 months after he successfully won his re-election bid, he was recalled from office. He was the first and only governor in the state of California and the second governor in the nation's history to be recalled. The recall movement and election of Arnold Schwarzenegger were in every sense dramatic, historic, and stunning.

Davis was re-elected in November 2002, thanks in part to a very weak challenger, even though just before the election a majority of voters disapproved of his overall performance as governor.[15] Voters held Governor Davis responsible for the 2000–01 energy crisis during which Californians were forced to reduce their energy consumption and pay more for their electricity, experiencing or being threatened by blackouts. News reports focused on this issue for many months, which had a negative impact on Davis's popularity. Compounding the problem was a dramatic decrease in state revenues. The governor had to announce that the state was short $23.6 billion and that the 2003–04 budget shortfall would rise to nearly $35 billion. The state legislature could not produce a budget on time, and voters were very uneasy about the economic future of the state. Davis entered his second term as a wounded, unpopular governor, viewed as distant, too beholden to special interests, and ineffectual.

Darrell Issa, a multimillionaire Republican member of Congress from the San Diego area, was a dominant force in the movement to recall Davis. He injected nearly $2 million into the recall effort and had hopes of running for governor if the recall succeeded. Nearly 1.5 million voter signatures were collected on recall petitions, meeting the state requirement for an October 2003 recall election. Unfortunately for Representative Issa's hopes of capturing the governorship, a well-known, charismatic, moderate Republican anti-politician, antiestablishment actor/businessman appeared on the scene: Arnold Schwarzenegger. In the summer of 2003, Schwarzenegger announced his candidacy and immediately became the front-runner among Republican candidates, making national and international headlines with his decision to run.[16] Politically, it was a perfect storm: a weak and unpopular governor, an unhappy electorate, and an internationally known celebrity. On the day of the election, 9.4 million Californians cast ballots, 11 percent more than the turnout in Davis's 2002 re-election. Fifty-five percent voted to remove Davis from office. Schwarzenegger was elected governor in his place with 48.6 percent of the votes cast. Schwarzenegger's adoption of moderate positions—prochoice on abortion, moderate on the environment, and cooperative with the Democratically controlled state legislature—placed him in sync with voters, resulting in his re-election victory in 2006.

The 2008 Election: Demographic and Ideological Shifts

The 2008 election was somewhat unusual, even by California standards. A very popular, young, charismatic candidate, Barack Obama, topped the ticket as the Democratic candidate for the presidency, winning 61 percent of the popular vote compared to John McCain's 37 percent, the biggest margin in the state of California since 1964.

The *Los Angeles Times*, in an article aptly titled "State's Shifting Political Landscape," described the election results:

Those unpredictable decisions by voters, however, were accompaniments to the election's main theme: the demographic and ideological shifts that have delivered the state into Democratic hands and demonstrated anew the tough road ahead for the Republican minority.[17]

The Democratic Party was hopeful that it could continue to win the support and allegiance of the overwhelming number of voters who had cast their votes for Obama, including 83 percent of first-time voters. Seventy-six percent of those 18–29 years of age voted for Obama compared to only 48 percent of those 65 and older. However, some analysts were not confident that future elections would see high percentages of young voters turning out to vote or substantial increases in support for the Democratic Party.

By November 2, 2010, the evidence was in. The lead headline from Scott Fahey's Elections 2010 blog from Southern California Public Radio read, "Low youth voter turnout hurts Democrats." As he described it, "In California, one of every five voters in 2008 was between the ages of 18 and 29, compared with about 1 in 10 on Tuesday." California reflected the overall national trend with fewer young, liberal, and black voters casting votes in the November 2010 general election.

The 2010 General Election

While the nation witnessed a historic "shellacking" of the Democratic Party, as President Obama called it, with an unprecedented loss of Democrat-held seats in Congress, Californians voted to the beat of a different drummer. All of the Democratic candidates running for statewide elective office won, and nearly all of them won by respectable margins. The *Los Angeles Times*, in an analysis of the vote based on exit poll data, concluded that the strength of the Latino vote was a key factor in the success of Democratic candidates. Latino voters made up 22 percent of the California voter pool, a record tally that sunk the election hopes of many Republicans.

THE GOVERNOR'S RACE The costliest statewide race in the nation's history pitted novice politician and billionaire Meg Whitman against political insider Jerry Brown. Whitman spent a record-breaking $160 million on her general election campaign (see Table 4.3 on p. 105), with over $140 million from her own personal wealth. Of this total, she poured nearly $110 million into TV and radio advertising. Californians quickly became aware of her candidacy, and voters easily recognized her name. In contrast, Jerry Brown, who had served two terms as governor (1975–83), had been mayor of Oakland (1999–2007), and most recently had served as state attorney general, spent only $25 million on his campaign. In the end, Brown won by a very comfortable margin, 54 percent to 41 percent. Furthermore, Brown's cost per vote was only $1.24, whereas Whitman spent a whopping $51.82 per vote!

THE U.S. SENATE RACE Barbara Boxer, a liberal Democrat running for her fourth term in the U.S. Senate, had a tough re-election challenge, the toughest of her political career. Boxer, a career politician, ran against outsider and novice campaigner Carly Fiorina, a Republican and former CEO of Hewlett-Packard (HP). Typically, incumbents such as Boxer, running for re-election in a state where their political party dominates, have a relatively easy time keeping their seat. The situation was different this time around. California's economy was in shambles, Boxer's popularity had been declining, and Fiorina was a formidable opponent. In the end, Boxer prevailed, winning re-election with 52 percent of the vote compared to Fiorina's 43 percent. Many pundits believe that Fiorina's failure to moderate her position on social issues (she was ardently antiabortion and anti-illegal immigration), along with Boxer's stinging ads highlighting the layoff of 30,000 HP workers under Fiorina's stewardship, was responsible for Fiorina's loss.

PROPOSITION 20: REDISTRICTING CONGRESSIONAL DISTRICTS VS. PROPOSITION 27: ELIMINATING THE STATE REDISTRICTING COMMISSION Propositions 20 and 27 were actually competing initiatives. Proposition 20 is an extension of Proposition 11, which passed in November 2008. Proposition 11 created the 14-member Citizens Redistricting Commission that would be in charge of drawing the boundaries of state Assembly and state Senate districts after each U.S. Census. November 2010's Proposition 20 asked voters to remove the authority for congressional redistricting from the legislature and give this power to the newly created Citizens Redistricting Commission. The commission would then be responsible for drawing congressional district lines as well as continuing to exercise the power to draw state Assembly and state Senate district boundaries. The competing initiative, Proposition 27, on the other hand, would have eliminated the Citizens Redistricting Commission and returned to the legislature the power to draw state district boundaries (essentially repealing Proposition 11). California voters soundly endorsed the Citizens Redistricting Commission (defeating Proposition 27 with a 59 percent vote against it) and gave the Commission the power to determine congressional districts as well (Proposition 20 passed with a 61 percent vote in favor).

PROPOSITION 25: SIMPLE MAJORITY VOTE TO PASS BUDGET Proposition 25 changed the legislative vote requirement to pass the budget from two-thirds to a simple majority. In addition, all members of the legislature must permanently forfeit reimbursement for salary and expenses for every day the budget is late. At the time that Proposition 25 was introduced, California had not passed a state budget by the mandatory June 15 deadline in 23 years. Budget negotiations in 2010 extended 100 days past the deadline, just close enough to Election Day for it to be fresh in voters' minds. Californians passed Proposition 25 with a 55 percent affirmative vote. Supporters of this initiative were labor unions (especially teachers who received layoff notices when the budget was not passed on time), the League of Women Voters, groups representing retirees, and others who were able to devote resources to the "Yes on Prop 25" campaign. Since passage of this proposition, the state budget has been passed on time.

The 2012 Primary Election

The June 2012 primary was an interesting one. Usually, the major contest in the primary during a presidential election year is between the candidates competing for their party's nomination for the presidential race. But, as typically happens when states hold their primary late in the political season, Mitt Romney already had won enough delegates to secure his party's nomination, and President Obama had no Democratic challenger and was, by default, his party's nominee. Perhaps this explains why only one in three registered voters participated in this election, with one of the lowest turnout rates in Los Angeles County, at less than 22 percent.

As mandated by the passage of Proposition 14, this was the first statewide blanket primary using the new top-two candidates system. It was also the first election since the adoption of the newly drawn congressional and state legislative districts. The ballot looked different, all voters regardless of party affiliation were given the same ballot, the results were calculated differently, and some candidates found themselves running in new or very different districts. A very interesting election, indeed.

The 2012 General Election: More Demographic and Ideological Shifts

THE PRESIDENTIAL RACE The outcome of the November 2012 presidential election looked similar to that of the 2008 presidential election, with young and minority voters favoring President Obama and older and white voters supporting Romney. Statewide, Obama won 59 percent of the vote, slightly less than the 61 percent he won in 2008. He received 71 percent of the votes cast by 18- to 29-year-old Californians, which is close to the 76 percent he received in 2008. Of those 65 years of age and older, 48 percent voted for Obama, the same percentage as did in 2008. Other notable demographic results were based on race, marital status, and place of residence. While only 45 percent of whites supported Obama, 79 percent of Asian Americans and 72 percent of Latinos voted for him. Marital status also made a difference, with Obama receiving 67 percent of the votes of unmarried Californians and 51 percent the votes of married voters. Voters living in urban areas chose to re-elect the president by 65 percent compared to rural voters at 50 percent.

The 2012 election was interesting in terms of voter turnout rates. Although 5 percent fewer Californians voted in 2012 than in 2008, more young voters turned out to vote in 2012. The youth vote accounted for 20 percent of all votes cast in 2008 and 28 percent of all votes in 2012. That is a 40 percent increase in turnout among 18- to 29-year-old California voters. Nationwide, there was only a slight increase in the youth vote, which grew from 17 percent in 2008 to 19 percent in 2012. What accounted for this dramatic increase in the turnout of young California voters?

According to Peter Levine, California's new online voter registration system (described later in this chapter), made available shortly before the 2012 election, registered nearly 700,000 new voters, many of whom were young people.[18] Also, Proposition 30 (the initiative to fund higher education) was a salient issue for young voters. If the measure did not pass, college students would face another round of tuition increases, crowded classes, and cuts in enrollment to the California State University and University of California systems. This combination of an accessible online voter registration system and an important initiative impacting higher education motivated young voters.

CONGRESSIONAL RACES As mandated by the U.S. Constitution, all House members serve two-year terms in office. California has 53 House members, and in the November 2012 election, 11 new members were elected, the most in 20 years. Democrats won 38 of the 53 seats, and the number of seats held by Latinos increased. These changes were a result of the recent remapping of House districts and changing demographics. A number of incumbent House members retired when their districts were redrawn after the 2010 Census, and some found themselves in competitive districts where their re-election was not assured. Prior to the 2012 election, only one House seat had changed between the parties during the last five Congressional elections. In 2012, Democratic candidates won four more House seats than they had in 2010. A second factor related to the strong showing by Democratic candidates is the growing number and clout of Latino voters, especially in Southern California. As reported in the *Los Angeles Times*, "Voters in Riverside and San Bernardino counties elected three Democrats to Congress—two Latinos and a gay Asian American—after having sent only two Democrats to Washington in the last four decades."[19]

CALIFORNIA LEGISLATIVE RACES The *Los Angeles Times* headline on November 8, 2012, read, "Blue reign in Sacramento: Democrats' historic gains position them for unchecked power." Prior to the November 6 election, Democrats had controlled both the state Assembly and the state Senate. Amazingly, this election not only allowed the Democratic Party to maintain its majority status but also its electoral successes gave it *supermajority* status. Having a supermajority means that there are enough Democratic votes in each chamber to raise taxes without needing any votes from Republicans. The last time a party had supermajority power in California was in 1933 when the Republicans were in charge. The Democrats last had this power in 1883. This supermajority status was short-lived, however—three Democratic state senators were suspended in March 2014 after being indicted on felony criminal charges.

PROPOSITIONS There were 11 measures on the November 2012 ballot. Voters were asked to weigh in on a number of issues ranging from increased taxes to funding for educational programs to the repeal of the death penalty. A record-breaking amount of money was spent on these campaigns. George Skelton, a *Los Angeles Times* columnist, wrote, "It's almost unfathomable that $372 million was spent to promote or attack the 11 measures. To put it in perspective, that amount of money could pay for the annual tuitions of 31,000 undergrads at the University of California. The top 20 donors provided 69 percent of all initiative funding."[20] What follows is a description of some of the more high-profile measures:

- **Proposition 30: Taxes to Fund Education versus Proposition 38: Tax to Fund Education and Early Childhood Programs**   These two competing propositions dealt with ways to raise revenue to fund education. Proposition 30, backed by the governor, would temporarily raise the state sales tax for 4 years and increase taxes on the wealthy for 7 years. Proposition 38 would raise taxes on earnings for all Californians for 12 years. Since these were competing measures, if both passed, the one receiving the most votes would prevail. Proposition 30 passed with 55 percent of the vote. Proposition 38 received only 28 percent of the vote even though its sponsor, Molly Munger, spent $44 million of her own money on the measure. In addition, an outside political group from Arizona spent over $11 million to defeat both Propositions 30 and 38.

- **Proposition 34: Death Penalty**   This initiative statute would repeal the death penalty and replace it with life in prison without possibility of parole. Those currently on death row would have their sentences commuted to life imprisonment. Proponents of this measure spent over $8 million. Opponents spent a small fraction of that amount. The measure was defeated with a 52 percent "no" vote.

- **Proposition 36: Three Strikes Law: Repeat Felony Offenders**   This measure would revise the existing Three Strikes law to impose life sentences only when the offender is convicted of a new violent felony. Those previously convicted under this law for nonviolent felonies may have their sentences reviewed. The measure easily passed with 69 percent of the vote.

- **Proposition 37: Genetically Engineered Foods Labeling**   This proposition would require the labeling of food that is made from plants or animals containing genetically altered material. Agroscience opponents such as DuPont, Dow Agro, and Monsanto spent over $15 million to defeat this measure. The proposition failed, receiving only 48 percent of the vote.

The 2014 Election

Nationally, the contest between Democrats and Republicans over control of the U.S. Senate was the most important issue of the 2014 midterm elections. If the Republican Party gained six Senate seats, they would then control both chambers of Congress. The Democratic Party hoped to maintain control of the Senate but faced an uphill battle in a number of important U.S. Senate contests. The Republican Party prevailed and both chambers of Congress are now controlled by the Republican Party. In California, however, 2014 was a rather subdued election year, evidenced by the fact that fewer than three in ten voters participated in this election. California's two U.S. senators were not up for re-election, the governor's race was not very competitive, and only a few ballot initiatives engaged in media campaigns.

THE GOVERNOR'S RACE   Governor Jerry Brown, a popular incumbent, was re-elected by a comfortable margin. His opponent, Neel Kashkari, never stood much of a chance to win. Unlike Brown's 2010 challenger, Meg Whitman (who raised over $176 million, see Table 4.2), Kashkari was virtually unknown to the public and was seriously underfunded. Six weeks prior to the election his campaign had less than $700,000 to spend compared to Governor Brown's nearly $24 million. Brown agreed to only one 60-minute televised debate, which did not enjoy a large audience and did little to boost Kashkari's popularity. Kashkari's wecklong stint as an undercover homeless person in Fresno also failed to generate support for his campaign. Kashkari even gave away $25 cash cards to the first 100 people who showed up at one of his campaign events (most likely violating the state's election code that prohibits candidates from giving gifts to win votes). Brown beat Kashkari 54 percent to 41 percent and was re-elected to serve a historic fourth and final term as governor.

PROPOSITIONS   Six propositions appeared on the ballot, comparatively few by California standards. Below is a description of the initiatives that passed:

- **Propositions 1 and 2: Water Bond and State Budget**   These two measures were publicized as companion initiatives ("Save Water, Save Money") and had virtually no opposition. These propositions dealt with the water crisis in

California and ensured stricter enforcement of the state's "rainy day" surplus money fund. Both propositions passed overwhelmingly with 67 percent and 69 percent of the vote respectively.

- **Proposition 47: Criminal Sentences; Misdemeanor Penalties** As described earlier in this chapter, crimes such as drug possession, shoplifting, petty theft, and forgery would qualify as misdemeanor, not felony, crimes under this measure. The result would be lesser penalties for those with no prior convictions for serious, violent crimes. As reported in the *Los Angeles Times*, it is believed that 20 percent of criminals would face more lenient sentences and more than 7,000 current inmates could petition the courts to reduce their sentences.[21] Most law enforcement organizations were opposed to this measure, arguing that thousands of dangerous criminals would be released from prison and that our criminal justice system would be overwhelmed with petitions for reduced sentences. However, preelection polling found the public to be overwhelmingly in favor of this measure. The proposition passed with 59 percent of the vote.

The 2016 Primary Election

Many believed that California would finally have a June presidential primary that mattered. California's impact, however, was not as great as had been anticipated. All but one of the Republican candidates vying for the presidential nomination had dropped out prior to the June primary: Donald Trump was the last man standing on the Republican side and won the California Republican primary with over 75 percent of the vote. On the Democratic side, in the Clinton versus Sanders contest, Clinton had surged far enough ahead of Sanders in the delegate count that her nomination was a foregone conclusion prior to the California primary. Her victory in the California Democratic primary (winning nearly 56 percent of the vote to Sanders 43 percent) technically put her in the position where she could officially declare that she was her party's presidential nominee.

One positive consequence of this primary was that it engaged the public. As previously mentioned, the 2016 presidential primary motivated people to register to vote. From May 2012 to May 2016 California voter registration numbers had increased by over 760,000 people, with 650,000 people registering in the few weeks prior to the June 2016 primary.

The contest to fill retiring Democratic U.S. senator Barbara Boxer's seat saw two Democrats win the top-two primary, out of a field of 34 candidates. Kamala Harris, the twice-elected California attorney general, trounced Loretta Sanchez, a 20-year House member, in the primary. Harris, a daughter of Jamaican and Indian immigrants, and Sanchez, a daughter of Mexican immigrants, will ensure that the next U.S. Senator from California will be a woman of color.

The 2016 General Election

THE PRESIDENTIAL RACE The outcome of the November 2016 presidential race was a stunner! Virtually all the polls and predictions had Hillary Clinton winning the presidency. Surprisingly, on election night as the state by state results were coming in, it gradually became apparent that Clinton was losing the Electoral College vote. Donald Trump exceeded the necessary 270 Electoral College votes needed to win the presidency, in the end winning over 300 Electoral College votes. Clinton, however, won the popular vote count by more than two million votes. To say this was an upset victory would be an understatement: The nation was shocked. Young people across the country protested in the streets (a number of the larger protests were in California). It was calculated that if 1 out of every 100 Trump voters had shifted their vote to Clinton, she would have won the presidency with 307 Electoral College votes—that's how close of an election it was. California, not surprisingly, voted overwhelming for Clinton by a nearly 2-to-1 margin (62 percent Clinton; 33 percent Trump). Statewide, Clinton beat Obama's margin over Romney in 2012 by 6 percentage points. This was the widest margin in a presidential election in the past 80 years. In fact, southern California's Orange County, birthplace of the reactionary John Birch Society and historic Republican stronghold, voted for a Democratic candidate for the first time in 88 years. Clearly, California was out of step with the rest of the nation.

In the 2012 presidential election, Obama won 71 percent of the 18- to 29-year-old vote. Clinton fell slightly short of that number, winning 66 percent of the youth vote. Those 45 to 64 years of age had the highest turnout of any age group, contributing 38 percent of the total vote count in the state. This age group voted for Trump at a higher percentage (39 percent) than any other age group. Minority voters were overwhelming in favor of Clinton, but fell short of their support of Obama in 2012. Seventy percent of Asian Americans, 71 percent of Latinos, and 88 percent of African American voters supported Clinton. White voters voted for Clinton at a lower rate: 50 percent of white men and 57 percent of white women voted for Clinton. Similar to the national trend, whites with no college degree were more likely to vote for Trump. In California this group supported Trump at 59 percent, compared to 67 percent of this group nationally. Religion was another differentiating factor. Protestants were more likely to vote for Trump than any other religious group (51 percent). Slight regional differences were noted in this election. The areas that were the most supportive of Clinton were the Bay Area (79 percent), coastal communities (67 percent), and Los Angeles (71 percent). Trump drew support from inland and central California (45 percent) and parts of southern California (45 percent).[22]

Nationwide, voting turnout rates were the lowest in about 20 years. Of those eligible to vote, only about 57 percent went to the polls. In California even fewer eligible voters participated (approximately 50 percent), with the exception of Latino voters who flocked to the polls. This group mobilized in California most likely due to Trump's anti-immigrant positions. The Latino vote comprised nearly one-third of all votes cast, an increase of nearly 10 percent from the 2012 election. African American turnout was slightly below the 2012 turnout. White turnout fell by about 7 percent and Asian American turnout remained about the same. The youth vote declined by about 7 percent from 2012 and mirrored the national youth turnout, where 18- to 29-year-olds made up about 20 percent of all those voting.

CONGRESSIONAL RACES In 2016, California sent its first new Senator in 24 years to Washington. Kamala Harris, California's Attorney General, won the seat vacated by Senator Barbara Boxer. Harris also made history as the first African American to represent California in the U.S. Senate as well as the second African American woman ever to be elected to the Senate. In our new top-two primary system, Harris ran against another Democrat, Representative Loretta Sanchez. Overshadowed by the more media-driven presidential race, this race received scant attention and was not competitive. Harris easily beat Sanchez, winning 63 percent of the vote.

California's House delegation saw few changes in the 2016 election. No seats switched party and California sent 39 Democrats and 14 Republicans to the House of Representatives. A handful of Republican incumbents narrowly won reelection. One of these most watched contests was between six-term Republican House member Darryl Issa, representing a district that straddles Orange and San Diego counties, and newcomer retired colonel Doug Applegate. Issa had fended off challengers before with double-digit leads but Applegate made this contest highly competitive. Issa eked out a win by a very slim margin.

CALIFORNIA LEGISLATIVE RACES The Democratic Party again has firm control over both the state assembly and the state senate. Three Republican assembly incumbents lost their seats to Democrats. Two Democratic assembly incumbents lost their seats to fellow Democratic challengers—remember, we now have a top-two vote-getter primary system that makes it possible for the top-two candidates running against each other in the general election to be from the same political party. Democrats will have a supermajority in the state assembly with 55 seats; Republicans will have 25 assembly seats. Incumbent state senators all won their reelection bids. The Democrats also won a supermajority in the state senate and will have 27 seats to the Republican's 13 seats.

PROPOSITIONS There were 17 measures on the November 2016 ballot, the largest number of initiatives on a ballot since March 2000. Voters were asked to consider issues such as legalization of marijuana (again), repeal of the death penalty (again), background checks on purchases of ammunition, a ban on plastic grocery bags, caps on health care costs, and workplace rules for adult movie actors, to name a few. Let's look at some of the more high-profile, controversial initiatives:

- **Proposition 58: Repeal English-only Education** This proposition repealed Proposition 227, the initiative passed in 1998 that made California public schools English-only. Proposition 58 requires school administrators to solicit input from parents in developing language acquisition programs and allows schools to offer dual immersion language programs. This proposition had overwhelming support and passed with more than 72 percent of the vote. Proposition 227 passed in 1998 with more than 60 percent of the vote. The dramatic reversal in twenty years most likely reflects the demographic changes in the state and the growing Latino population and its strength at the ballot box.

- **Proposition 61: Drug Price Standards** This initiative would require that the state of California pay no more than prices paid by the U.S. Department of Veterans Affairs for prescription drugs. Over $125 million was spent on this campaign, with most of the money coming from major drug companies hoping to defeat this measure. Most experts agreed this was a poorly crafted measure that would not bring about the desired outcome of lower prescription drug costs. The measure failed with a 54 percent "no" vote.

- **Proposition 62: Repeal the Death Penalty and Proposition 66: Death Penalty Procedures** These were competing initiatives. Proposition 62 sought to end the death penalty in California. Prisoners already on death row would have their sentences commuted to life in prison with no chance of parole. Proposition 66 was an opposing measure that would retain the death penalty and speed up the appeals process, mandating that all appeals be completed within five years of the death penalty sentence. Proposition 62 failed with 54 percent of voters not wanting to repeal the death penalty. Proposition 66 passed by a slim majority of 51 percent. It is interesting to note that Los Angeles County and virtually all of the northern California coastal counties voted to repeal the death penalty and voted against speeding up the appeals process, whereas most of the inland counties voted against repeal and for the expedited appeals process.

- **Proposition 63: Background Checks for Ammunition Purchases and Ban on Large-Capacity Magazines** This measure requires individuals to have a permit to purchase ammunition, closes the loophole on allowing exemptions to the ban on large-capacity magazines, strengthens enforcement prohibiting felons from owning firearms, and makes the theft of firearms a felony. This initiative passed with a 63 percent vote. Proponents outspent opponents by a 5-to-1 margin. Surprisingly, the National Rifle Association, which opposed this measure, spent less than $100,000 on efforts to defeat it. And again, we see a regional split, with most inland counties voting against this measure and coastal and near-coastal counties in support of it.

- **Proposition 64: Legalization of Marijuana** California, along with Massachusetts, Maine, and Nevada, voted to legalize the recreational use of marijuana. In addition, Arkansas, Florida, North Dakota, and Montana all passed initiatives to make medical marijuana legal. Proposition 64 passed with 56 percent of the vote. Many of the counties voting against this measure are solidly Republican (as indicated in Figure 4.3).

- **Proposition 65: Disposable Bag Sales Revenue to Wildlife Conservation Fund and Proposition 67: Plastic Bag Ban** These two competing measures dealt with the legislative ban on plastic bags (Senate Bill 270). Proposition 65 was supported by the plastic bag industry and, if passed, would essentially kill Senate Bill 270. Proposition 67 would ratify SB 270, which outlaws single-use plastic bags and mandates that stores make available recyclable bags for a minimum cost of 10 cents. Revenue from the sale of these bags would be used to cover their costs and to educate consumers about sustainability. Proposition 65 failed to pass with a 55 percent "no" vote while SB 270 was ratified with 52 percent of the vote.

Campaigning in California

California politics presents many challenges to those seeking elective office or the passage of a ballot measure. First, the immense size of the state means that groups hoping to pass or defeat statewide propositions, candidates running for statewide office, and candidates vying for the U.S. Senate or the presidency must plan campaigns that reach voters throughout the entire state. California has 13 distinct media markets, making it very expensive to communicate to its 39 million residents about politics. Second, California's population is very diverse, with many ethnicities, racial groups, cultures, professions, occupations, and interests represented. Successful campaigns must find ways to effectively communicate their platform and messages to all of the state's 18 million registered voters. And third, California has passed a number of political campaign reform acts in an attempt to regulate campaign spending and to provide public information on contributions and expenditures. These laws have proved beneficial to some and not as helpful to others.

Whatever the challenges of campaigning in California, one thing is certain: California's campaign politics are watched by the nation. We are a campaign trendsetter.

Money and Politics: California Style

As the record-breaking spending in the campaigns of 2010 demonstrated, campaigning in California requires money, and lots of it. In fact, California is one of the most expensive states in which to conduct a political campaign. Table 4.3 illustrates how the candidates in the 2010 governor's race spent nearly $200 million, making it the most expensive governor's race in U.S. history.

Running for the California legislature is also very expensive. Citing a Pew Center on the States study, Osorio notes that California is the costliest state in which to win a state Senate seat ($938,522). The least expensive state is North Dakota at $5,713. In Arizona it costs $36,696; in Wisconsin, $140,287; and in North Carolina, $234,031.[23] The prohibitive cost of campaigning in California limits those who can realistically run for office, another factor contributing to the state's governance challenges. Incumbents far outspend challengers, and incumbents' spending has increased over time while challengers' spending has not. On average, challengers spend only a fraction of what incumbents spend. This discrepancy helps to explain the high re-election rates of those elected to the California legislature. Some competitive races for the California legislature cost in excess of $1 million.

The following are some reasons that California campaigns are so expensive:

MEDIA-DOMINATED CAMPAIGNS Because of the state's size and its 13 different **media markets**, candidates must run **media-dominated campaigns**, spending enormous amounts of money producing political ads and buying the broadcast time to air them. During the 2003 gubernatorial recall election, it cost approximately $2 million a week to run political ads statewide.[24] In the 2006 governor's race, Schwarzenegger's campaign alone spent $9 million on TV ads in the short time span between July 1 and September 30. As is shown in Table 4.3, an astounding $138 million was spent in the November 2010 governor's race just on TV, cable, and radio airtime and production. This cost is in addition to the $57 million spent on media during the primary campaign. As one media consultant described it, "There's a lot to be said for traditional politicking, kissing babies and shaking hands, but you have to get on TV to reach voters."[25]

POLITICAL CONSULTANTS Professional campaign managers and various **political consultants**—media consultants, pollsters, fund-raisers, direct-mail experts, and voter mobilization professionals—cost money. Because of California's love for direct democracy, especially the initiative process, many well-known political consultants have established offices in California. There is money to be made in California

TABLE 4.3 ● Spending in California's Gubernatorial Election: How the Money Was Spent, 2010

Expenditure	Whitman ($)	Brown ($)
Television and radio advertising	$106,930,505.28	$21,259,408.00
Campaign consultants	11,693,547.95	167,200.00
Campaign literature and mailings	10,582,303.93	2,532,801.36
Campaign workers' salaries	5,918,110.80	157,870.01
Radio airtime and production costs	5,472,228.17	0
TV or cable airtime and production costs	4,139,919.07	182,103.12
Information technology costs (Internet, email)	3,177,977.76	23,345.51
Office expenses	2,321,340.46	132,023.40
Meetings and appearances	1,772,342.56	0
Polling and survey research	1,410,893.36	93,728.30
Staff/spouse travel, lodging, and meals	1,260,616.12	2,618.30
Fund-raising events	1,241,158.66	70,626.38
Candidate travel, lodging, and meals	950,890.17	12,071.76
Professional services (legal, accounting)	880,044.13	39,310.00
Postage, delivery, and messenger services	668,059.56	2,117.00
Campaign paraphernalia/miscellaneous	633,946.72	65,129.65
Phone banks	549,904.75	0
Contribution	252,500.00	0
Print ads	153,440.00	0
Voter registration	66,710.00	0
Civic donations	16,383.00	0
Returned contributions	0	99,364.14
Candidate filing/ballot fees	0	3,579.74
TOTAL	**160,092,822.45**	**24,843,296.67**

SOURCE: Campaign Watch, http://californiawatch.org/dailyreport/how-whitman-spent-160-million-6292 (accessed 11/2/10).

politics, and candidates and supporters of ballot initiatives know that to win elections you must hire the costly services of top-notch political consultants.

WEAK POLITICAL PARTIES California has comparatively **weak political parties**. The Progressive reform movement of Governor Hiram Johnson (served 1911–17) implemented many rules that reduced the organizational strength and clout of political parties within the state, as described earlier. Because of California's weak party system, the party organizations are minimally involved in organizing and conducting the campaigns of candidates running for office. In addition, California has a relatively large number of registered voters who decline to affiliate with any political party and consider themselves politically independent. These unaffiliated, independent voters compose nearly one quarter of all registered voters. The combination of weak party structure and less party attachment means that candidates themselves have to work harder—raise and spend more money—to reach these voters.

Campaign Finance Reform in California

To create more transparency in the electoral process and to make public the flow of money in political campaigns, several **campaign finance reform** laws have been enacted in California over the past 100 years. Brief descriptions of the most recent laws follow.

1974: POLITICAL REFORM ACT In 1974 a group of reform-minded Californians crafted a statewide proposition that would require the most detailed campaign finance reporting in the nation. Proposition 9 appeared on the ballot during the Watergate scandal and passed with an overwhelming majority of votes. This act created the Political Reform Division within the office of the secretary of state to administer and oversee key provisions of the law. A new independent state agency, the Fair Political Practices Commission, was also created for the purposes of interpreting and enforcing the act.

1988: PROPOSITION 73 In 1988, California voters overwhelmingly passed Proposition 73, which limited contributions to legislative and statewide candidates to $1,000 per donor, including individuals, labor unions, and corporations. A federal judge struck it down in 1990.

1996: PROPOSITION 208 Voters approved Proposition 208 by a 61 percent vote in 1996. Contributions to candidates from individuals, political parties, committees, corporations, unions, and political action committees (PACs) were limited. Spending limits also were imposed on candidates, although these were voluntary. Candidates who abide by the spending limits are allowed to collect larger contributions, whereas candidates who do not abide by them have lower contribution limits. Proposition 208 was being challenged in the courts when Proposition 34 was proposed and passed.

2000: PROPOSITION 34 Proposition 34 was placed on the ballot by the legislature. Spending limits were substantially increased, as were contribution limits. For example, under Proposition 208, individuals were permitted to contribute $1,000 to gubernatorial candidates—$500 if the candidate decided not to abide by the voluntary spending limits. Proposition 34 increased individual contributions to $21,200. Many reform-minded organizations that had supported Proposition 208, such as the League of Women Voters and Common Cause, were opposed to Proposition 34. They saw Proposition 34 as an attempt by the legislature to replace the more stringent Proposition 208 that was then under review in the courts. Nevertheless, in November 2000, Proposition 34 passed with close to 60 percent of the popular vote and has replaced the provisions of Proposition 208.

Although it could be argued that Proposition 34 has resulted in less control of campaign financing, California does receive high marks when it comes to laws requiring public disclosure of campaign contributions and expenditures. The Campaign Disclosure Project conducted by UCLA in 2008 studied the campaign disclosure laws in all 50 states and ranked the states accordingly. California received a grade of A for its disclosure laws and ranked second in the nation; Washington State ranked first.

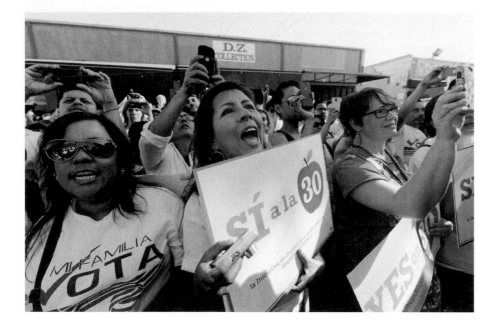

While Latinos in California currently vote at a significantly lower rate than whites do, the Latino population is poised to exert great influence over California's electoral outcomes as it increases in size and clout. For example, the Latino vote helped secure passage of Proposition 30 in 2012, which raised taxes to help fund public education and other programs.

Voting in California

Of California's 39 million residents, nearly 25 million are eligible to vote. Seventy-eight percent of those eligible (19.5 million) are registered. Contrary to some beliefs, registering to vote does not put one at higher risk of being selected for jury duty, nor does one receive more income tax scrutiny. To register to vote in the state of California, you must meet the following criteria:

- You will be 18 years of age on or before Election Day.
- You are a citizen of the United States.
- You are a resident of California.
- You are not in prison or on parole for a felony conviction.
- You have not been judged by a court to be mentally incompetent to register and to vote.

How You Can Register to Vote

Registering to vote is a simple process. Here are the options for doing so:

- **Obtain a voter registration form** from any U.S. post office or library. Forms are usually available on counters. Fill out the preaddressed, stamped form and mail it in.
- **Visit a branch of the California Department of Motor Vehicles.** The National Voter Registration Act of 1993 (also known as "**Motor Voter**") permits persons conducting business at a DMV office to register to vote or to update their

voter registration information while at the office. Since 1995 more than 12.5 million people have registered or reregistered in conformance with this law. California passed a new voter registration law, effective January 1, 2016. Now, at the DMV office, individuals will be asked if they are eligible to vote and, if so, their information will automatically be transmitted to the secretary of state's office where citizenship will be verified and names added to the voter registration rolls. An individual may opt out of this automatic registration.

- **Register online.** Go to the secretary of state's web site and use the new online voter registration system (registertovote.ca.gov). The process is very simple and can be completed entirely online if you have a California driver's license or identification card. Because voter registration applications must be signed by the individual, the online system retrieves your signature from your driver's license or ID card and electronically transfers it to your online registration application. This new system has proven to be extremely popular: of the record 1.4 million newly registered voters for 2012, over half of them registered online. California is one of only 15 states that offer electronic voter registration.

You will need to reregister to vote if:

- you move,
- you change your name, or
- you change your political party affiliation.

You must register at least 15 days before an election.

Who Votes in California?

There are demographic differences between those adults who are likely to vote and those who vote infrequently or who are not registered to vote. Table 4.4 clearly illustrates this. Of the individuals who are very likely to vote, 60 percent are white, 18 percent are Latino, 12 percent are Asian American, and 6 percent are African American. Likely voters live in urban areas, are older, are college educated, are U.S. born, and earn higher incomes. Over the decades the composition of the eligible voting population has changed and now there are more minority voters. But overall the same pattern has held: whites vote at a higher rate. Three factors help explain this discrepancy:

- **Eligibility**   A significant proportion of the Latino and Asian populations are not eligible to vote because they are not citizens.
- **Youth**   The Latino and Asian populations are both younger, and younger people are much less likely to vote than are older people.
- **Education**   The probability of voting increases significantly for those with college or advanced degrees.

Research shows that if you control for these three factors, Latinos vote at rates comparable to whites.[26]

TABLE 4.4 ● California's Likely Voters

	Percentage of registered voters likely to vote in California's next statewide election
Race/Ethnicity	
White	60%
Latino	18
Asian	12
Black	6
Other/Multirace	4
Region	
Los Angeles County	27
San Francisco Bay Area	21
Orange/San Diego Counties	18
Central Valley	17
Inland Empire	9
Other	9
Age	
18 to 34	18
35 to 54	35
55 and older	47
Education	
No college	17
Some college	41
College graduate	41
Nativity	
U.S.-born	84
Immigrant	16

SOURCE: "Likely voters" are registered voters meeting criteria on interest in politics, attention to issues, voting behavior, and intention to vote. Seven PPIC Statewide Surveys, September 2015 to July 2016, including 7,306 likely voters, 2,368 infrequent voters, and 2,128 unregistered adults. From Just the Facts: California's Likely Voters, www.ppic.org/main/publication_show.asp?i=255 (accessed 11/30/16).

The 2016 presidential election saw a decline in voter turnout nationally. According to an early analysis by political website FiveThirtyEight, a smaller percentage of eligible voters participated in the 2016 presidential election than in the previous two elections.[27] Only about 57 percent of voters went to the polls, down from about 55 percent in 2012 and 60 percent in 2008.

Who Votes in California?

Gender

▨ Female ▪ Male 👤 = 10% of eligible voters

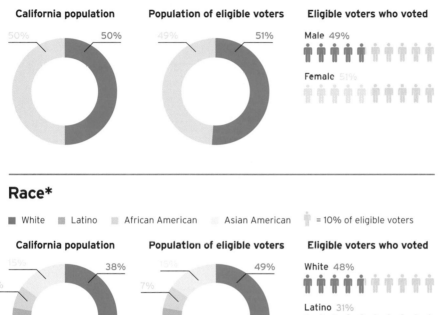

California population
50% 50%

Population of eligible voters
49% 51%

Eligible voters who voted

Male 49%
👤👤👤👤👤 👤👤👤👤👤

Female 51%
👤👤👤👤👤 👤👤👤👤👤

The active voting population in California is not reflective of general population demographics. Compared to their proportion of the population, white non-Latinos (Anglos) and older voters were overrepresented among active voters in the 2016 election. Despite the large size of the Latino population, they are a relatively small share of the electorate.

Race*

▪ White ▪ Latino ▪ African American ▪ Asian American 👤 = 10% of eligible voters

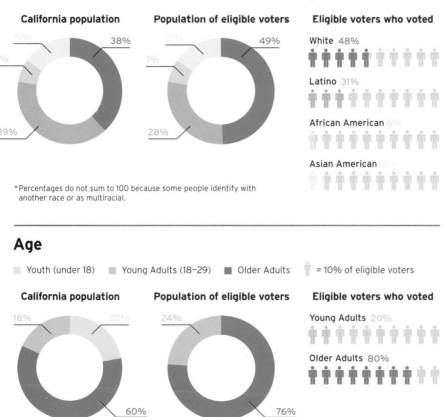

California population
15% 38% 7% 39%

Population of eligible voters
15% 49% 7% 28%

Eligible voters who voted

White 48%
👤👤👤👤👤 👤👤👤👤👤

Latino 31%
👤👤👤👤 👤👤👤👤👤👤

African American 6%
👤👤👤👤👤 👤👤👤👤👤

Asian American 12%
👤👤👤👤👤 👤👤👤👤👤

*Percentages do not sum to 100 because some people identify with another race or as multiracial.

1. What do you think might account for the differences in turnout rates among different groups in California? Why is turnout among whites and African Americans so much higher than among Latinos and Asians? Why is turnout among older voters higher than among young voters?

2. Looking ahead, what impact will the shifting electorate have on California politics, when the percentage of Latinos in the population increases and percentage of whites decreases, as discussed in Chapter 1?

Age

▨ Youth (under 18) ▨ Young Adults (18–29) ▪ Older Adults 👤 = 10% of eligible voters

California population
18% 22% 60%

Population of eligible voters
24% 76%

Eligible voters who voted

Young Adults 20%
👤👤👤👤👤 👤👤👤👤👤

Older Adults 80%
👤👤👤👤👤 👤👤👤👤👤

SOURCES: U.S. Census Bureau, Current Population Survey, 2010-2015; CNN Exit Polls, www.cnn.com/election/results /exit-polls/california/president (accessed 12/10/16); Projections from California Department of Finance Population Projections; and "Projections," State of California Department of Finance, www.dof.ca.gov/Forecasting/Demographics /projections (accessed 10/5/16).

As Figure 4.4 illustrates, California fits in with this national trend. Fifty-six percent of eligible voters turned out in 2012 and about 54 percent voted in 2016. It is interesting to note that nationwide, the decline in turnout was more prevalent in states that voted for Clinton, as evidenced in California. Although overall turnout declined in California, Latino turnout in the 2016 election substantially increased from previous years. Over 30 percent of voters self-identified as Latino compared to the 2012 election when that number was 22 percent. Latino voters were probably mobilized to vote in 2016 because of the anti-Latino, anti-immigrant campaign of Donald Trump.

(See the "Who Are Californians?" feature for a breakdown of California's voting population in 2016.)

THE EVER-EXPANDING GROUP OF VOTERS: VOTING BY MAIL California now has very liberal vote-by-mail laws. Before 1978 voters could only receive a mail ballot if they signed a sworn statement affirming that they would be away from their home precincts on Election Day or that they were infirm or bedridden and physically unable to cast a vote in person. All this changed in 1978 when California eliminated the requirement that voters present a valid excuse in order to vote absentee. Now, mail ballots are available to any voter who wants one. You are permitted to request a mail ballot for a particular election, or you may request permanent vote-by-mail status, meaning that a mail ballot is sent automatically to your home before each election.

From 1962 to 1978, the percentage of those voting by mail in primary and general elections averaged slightly under 4 percent of all votes cast. After the change in the law, voting by mail increased substantially. Of the over 11 million votes cast in November 2016, over 5 million were cast by mail ballots. Compared to the rest

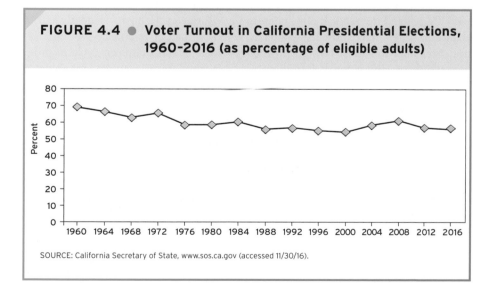

FIGURE 4.4 ● Voter Turnout in California Presidential Elections, 1960–2016 (as percentage of eligible adults)

SOURCE: California Secretary of State, www.sos.ca.gov (accessed 11/30/16).

of the country, California's approach is fairly distinctive: 29 states allow voting by mail without an approved excuse, but only 3 other states allow for permanent voting by mail.

EARLY VOTING There is a special type of voter in California: the early voter. In fact, in the November 2016 general election, nearly half of all voters were early voters. There are several ways in which Californians can vote early (casting votes before official Election Day).

Most early voters voluntarily request **vote-by-mail ballots**. Virtually all of these voters are classified as "permanent vote-by-mail" voters, which means they have requested to automatically receive a vote-by-mail ballot for every election. Otherwise, one needs to request such a ballot for each election. These ballots must be received by the county registrar's office no later than Election Day, often making it necessary to mail in the completed ballot at least a few days before this deadline. In fact, a number of voters fill out and mail their ballots weeks before Election Day because state law permits voting as early as 29 days before an election. A number of sparsely populated rural precincts in California, where staffing a traditional polling place makes little sense, have moved entirely to mail-in ballots for all voters. And in an attempt to lighten the volume of voters on Election Day, some counties have permitted "early voting," in which voters can go to various publicized locations (such as shopping malls, registrars' offices, and civic centers) to cast their votes as early as 29 days before an election. Nationally, states' approach to early voting is varied: early voting, requiring no special excuse, is permitted by 31 other states and prohibited in 15 states.

Many view these developments as positive changes, believing that making voting more convenient will increase participation in this important civic activity. However, as with many reforms, there are unintended consequences. One major consequence is that early voting has had a direct impact on campaign strategy. Traditionally, political campaigns approach the weekend before the election as their last opportunity to communicate with voters. Candidates spend an enormous amount of money in the last days of their campaigns trying to convince people to vote for them or their initiative, or at least not to vote for their opponent or opposing side, bombarding viewers with TV ads and messages. By this point in the election cycle, however, nearly half of California voters have most likely already voted by mail or at an early-voting location. So candidates must now spend money earlier in the campaign cycle in order to reach these early voters before they cast their votes. As an example, state senator Tom McClintock lost a race for state controller by less than one-half of a percentage point because he did not have enough money to buy TV ads until the final days of the campaign. Many absentee voters had already mailed in their ballots and did not see his campaign ads until after they had cast their vote. Earlier campaigning means more expensive campaigning in a state that is already prohibitively expensive.

HOW YOU CAN VOTE BY MAIL To apply for a mail ballot, you may use the application form contained in the sample ballot mailed to your home before the election, or you may apply in writing to your county elections official. Ballots can be returned by mail or in person to a polling place or elections office within your county on Election Day.

What Reforms Are Needed?

It is fascinating to observe electoral politics in California. We live in a state where ballot initiatives are frequently used to make law, bypassing our duly elected representatives and the deliberative process of the legislature. In recent elections voters have been asked to weigh in on important policy matters such as same-sex marriage, abortion and parental notification, renewable energy, legalization of marijuana, the state budget process, tax issues, and the process by which state and congressional district boundaries are determined. Many people question whether the initiative process is the best way to make public policy.

Although the recall, referendum, and initiative originally were established as Progressive reforms, during the past few decades these tools of direct democracy have been taken over by special-interest groups. Some believe that reforms are needed to make it more difficult to recall an elected official or to bypass the legislative branch through the initiative process. Suggested reforms have included the prohibition of paid signature gatherers, a judicial review of the proposed initiative before placement on the ballot, and a higher requirement for the number of signatures needed to qualify a recall or initiative for the ballot. For a recall to qualify for the ballot, California law currently requires the number of signatures to equal 12 percent of the votes cast in the last gubernatorial election. Other states require 25 to 40 percent. While progress has been made with the reforms recently signed into law, many serious issues with the initiative process remain.

Candidates and initiative campaigns spend enormous amounts of money in hopes of electoral victory. Proposition 34, the campaign finance initiative passed in 2000, substantially increased spending and contribution limits. California's limits on contributions to gubernatorial candidates are far more liberal than federal limits on contributions to presidential candidates. In fact, Californians can contribute more than 10 times the amount to gubernatorial candidates than they are permitted to contribute to presidential candidates ($25,900 versus $2,500). Many fear that these high limits will lead to spiraling campaign costs in a state where it is already expensive to campaign. The amounts of money spent in the 2010 governor's race seems to indicate that these fears are becoming reality.

Study Guide

FOR FURTHER READING

Cain, B. "The California Recall." Interview, Brookings Institution, October 8, 2003.

Cain, Bruce E., and Elisabeth R. Gerber. *Voting at the Political Fault Line: California's Experiment with the Blanket Primary*. Berkeley: University of California Press, 2002.

California Fair Political Practices Commission. "Proposition 34." www.fppc.ca.gov. Accessed 12/03/14.

California Secretary of State's History of Political Reform Division. www.sos.ca.gov/campaign-lobbying/history-political-reform-division/. Accessed 9/26/16.

Cohen, Micah. "Over the Decades, How States Have Shifted." FiveThirtyEight, October 15, 2012. www.fivethirtyeight.com/features/over-the-decades-how-states-have-shifted/. Accessed 9/26/16.

Douzet, Frédérick, Thad Kousser, and Kenneth P. Miller, eds. *The New Political Geography of California*. Berkeley: Berkeley Public Policy Press, 2008.

Lubenow, Gerald C., ed. *California Votes: The 2002 Governor's Race and the Recall That Made History*. Berkeley: Berkeley Public Policy Press, 2003.

Peterson, Pete. "Why Californians Don't Vote." *Business Insider.* www.businessinsider.com/why-californians-dont-vote-2014-6. Accessed 6/24/14.

Rarick, E. *California Votes: The 2010 Governor's Race*. Berkeley: Institute of Governmental Studies, 2012.

Rasky, Susan. Introduction to "An Antipolitician, Anti-establishment Groundswell Elected the Candidate of Change." In *California Votes: The 2002 Governor's Race and the Recall That Made History*, edited by G. Lubenow. Berkeley: Berkeley Public Policy Press, 2003.

UCLA School of Law, Center for Governmental Studies, and the California Voter Foundation. "Grading State Disclosure 2008: A Comprehensive, Comparative Study of Candidate Campaign Finance Disclosure Laws and Practices in the 50 States." 2008. http://campaigndisclosure.org/gradingstate. Accessed 10/16/14.

ON THE WEB

Baldassare, Mark, Dean Bonner, David Kordus, and Lunna Lopes. "PPIC Statewide Survey: Californians and Their Government." www.ppic.org/main/publication.asp?i=1218. Accessed 11/11/2016.

California Elections and Voter Information. www.sos.ca.gov/elections. Accessed 11/11/16. The California secretary of state offers a comprehensive guide to California elections, including information on how to register to vote.

California General Election Results. http://vote.sos.ca.gov. Accessed 12/3/14. Detailed breakdowns of California election results.

The California Voter Foundation. http://calvoter.org. Accessed 7/25/12.

Fair Political Practices Commission. www.fppc.ca.gov. Accessed 12/3/14.

Join California. www.joincalifornia.com. Accessed 12/3/14.

Los Angeles Times. "Did Your Neighborhood Vote to Elect Donald Trump?" www.latimes.com/projects/la-pol-ca-california-neighborhood-election-results. Accessed 11/12/16.

SUMMARY

I. Introduction.
   A. California as a political trendsetter.
      1. Laws and initiatives passed in California influence other states.
      2. California experiences low voter participation as a result of its younger and minority populations.

II. Political parties.
   A. An important function of parties is to mobilize voters at election time.
   B. The Progressives' (1890s–1920s) impact on parties was sizable.
      1. They disliked corrupt parties and passed legislation to weaken the power of parties.
      2. They created many nonpartisan elective offices.
      3. They introduced direct primary elections to select the party candidate who will run for office against candidates of opposing parties in the general election.
   C. California has two dominant political parties: the Democratic Party and the Republican Party.
      1. California is considered a very Democratic state.
   D. Third parties struggle to compete.
      1. There are six certified minor parties.
      2. Third parties can impact the political agenda by raising issues the major parties ignore.

III. Party affiliation of California voters varies by region and demographics.
   A. The Democratic Party represents a plurality of voters.
   B. There has been an increase in the number of independents ("no party preference").
   C. Demographics and party affiliation.
      1. Whites tend to vote Republican; Latinos tend to vote Democratic.
      2. Younger and middle-aged voters compose the highest percentage of independents.
      3. Women tend to prefer the Democratic Party, as do non–U.S.-born citizens.
   D. The Blue and Red in California. Similar to the nation overall, areas of California are distinctly Democratic or Republican.
      1. Coastal and urban areas tend to be Democratic.
      2. Inland and rural areas tend to be Republican.

IV. Elections in California.
   A. There have been many changes in the primary system.
      1. California operated under a *closed* primary system until Proposition 198 in 1996.
      2. Then a *blanket* primary system was in place from 1998 to 2000. In *California Democratic Party v. Jones* (2002), the California Supreme Court ruled this form of the *blanket* primary unconstitutional.
      3. A *modified closed* primary system was adopted from 2002 to 2010. "Decline to state" voters (also known as No Party Preference) were permitted to vote in party primaries if the party grants permission.

4. Proposition 14, passed in 2010, replaced the *modified closed* primary system with another version of the *blanket* primary.

B. Presidential primaries.
  1. California has changed the date of its presidential primaries in order to allow voters to have more of an impact in the selection process.
  2. The 2008 presidential primary was moved to an early February date. Unfortunately, the increase in clout for the state was unrealized.
  3. Since June 2012 the presidential primary has been moved back to June.

C. Initiative campaigns.
  1. Typically, initiatives are tools of special-interest groups or grassroots movements. Such groups find it easier to bypass the state legislature and take their issue directly to the people. Often, initiatives deal with controversial issues that legislators rather avoid.
  2. From 1912 to 2016 there were approximately 400 ballot initiatives.
  3. How to qualify an initiative for ballot.
     a) Nearly 400,000 signatures of registered voters are needed for an initiative to qualify for the ballot, and over almost 600,000 needed to place a constitutional amendment on the ballot.
     b) For an initiative to be successful requires millions of dollars and highly paid political professionals. As an example, the cost of collecting petition signatures for the 17 ballot propositions in the November 2016 elections exceeded $45 million.
  4. Criticisms of direct democracy.
     a) Critics say that issues presented as ballot propositions are often too complicated or confusing, and should be decided through legislative deliberation rather than a popular vote.
     b) Recent reforms have provided for a 30-day public review process for all proposed initiatives as well as more transparency regarding donations to initiative campaigns.

D. The 2003 gubernatorial recall election of Gray Davis.
  1. Only 11 months after he won his re-election bid, Davis was recalled from office. He was the first and only governor in the state of California and the second governor in the nation's history to be recalled.
  2. Voters held Governor Davis responsible for the 2000–01 energy crisis and for the fiscal struggles of the state.
  3. Arnold Schwarzenegger, an actor and a moderate Republican, was elected governor.

E. The 2008 election: ideological and demographic shift to Democratic side.
  1. Obama won 61 percent of the popular vote compared to John McCain's 37 percent, the biggest margin in California since 1964.
  2. Young people voted in historic numbers, solidifying the Democratic Party's dominance in the state.

F. The 2010 election was the most expensive governor's race in history.
  1. Brown, the former governor, beat a wealthy billionaire, Meg Whitman.
  2. Initiatives passed that have an important impact on state budget process and political representation and party politics.

G. The 2012 election: results similar to 2008 but more of a Democratic shift.
  1. The Democratic Party gained supermajority status in state legislature (lost it in 2014).
  2. Young voters' turnout increased but overall turnout declined.
  3. California adopted a new online voter registration system.
  4. Proposition 30 passed, increasing the state sales tax and taxes on the wealthy to fund education.

H. The 2014 election: a noncompetitive governor's race.
  1. Incumbent Jerry Brown easily beat underfunded challenger Neel Kashkari.
  2. For the more controversial ballot measures (Propositions 45, 46, and 48), the well-funded "no" campaigns were successful because the proponents were absent from the airwaves.

I. The 2016 election: Democratic Party remains strong.
  1. Decline in Republican Party registration and increase in number of no party preference voter registrations.
  2. Hillary Clinton won California by a 2-to-1 margin, but lost the presidential contest.
  3. Kamala Harris elected as first African American U.S. senator from California and second ever female African American elected to Senate.
  4. Democratic Party won supermajority in state assembly and state senate.
  5. Proposition 58 repealed English-only in public schools. Proposition 62 to repeal death penalty failed while Proposition 66 to expedite death penalty appeals passed. Proposition 64 legalized marijuana. Proposition 67 banned plastic shopping bags.
  6. Overall voter turnout declined but Latino turnout surged from 22 percent in 2012 to 33 percent in 2016.
  7. Voting by mail continued to be very popular.

V. Running for elective office in the largest state is expensive.
   A. The size of the state requires candidates to spend a lot of money on campaigns. California often attracts wealthy candidates with personal fortunes.
   B. Because of the size of the state, candidates need to spend a lot of money on TV ads in order to reach voters. Statewide campaigns are very expensive because of the need to broadcast political ads throughout the state.
   C. Numerous state laws have been passed to reform political campaigns and to minimize the influence of big money and create transparency.
      1. 1974: Proposition 9, Political Reform Act created the Political Reform Division and established the Fair Political Practices Commission.
      2. 1988: Proposition 73 passed, limiting campaign contributions but was later declared unconstitutional in 1990.
      3. 1996: Proposition 208 passed, limiting contributions.
      4. 2000: Proposition 34 passed, increased spending and contribution limits and invalidates Proposition 208.
      5. 2008: in a study of 50 states California gets an A for campaign-finance disclosure laws.

VI. Voting in California.
   A. With a population of 39 million, there are 18 million registered voters in the state.
   B. How to register to vote:
      1. Obtain a voter registration form from any post office or library.
      2. Visit the California DMV.
      3. Register online.
   C. Who votes?
      1. Whites are overrepresented in the voting population; Latinos and Asians are underrepresented; African Americans vote in equal proportion to their percentage of population.
      2. The November 2008 presidential election had the highest turnout since 1972.
      3. Over 50 percent of all registered voters cast their votes by mail.

VII. Reforms may be necessary.
   A. Is the initiative process the best way to make policy?
   B. Need for campaign-finance reform to limit contributions and candidate spending.

PRACTICE QUIZ

1. In the 2012 general election, 18- to 29-year-olds voted at a higher rate than they did in 2008.
   a) true
   b) false

2. In running for the state legislature, incumbents and challengers spend nearly the same amount of money on their political campaigns.
   a) true
   b) false

3. Political campaigns are so expensive in California because
   a) campaigns need to hire political consultants.
   b) campaigns need to spend a substantial amount of money on media advertising.
   c) political parties are not very involved in the planning and running of campaigns.
   d) all of the above

4. Special-interest groups often use the initiative process to achieve their policy objectives.
   a) true
   b) false

5. Which of the following is *not* true about Proposition 34, which deals with campaign finance?
   a) The League of Women Voters and Common Cause supported Proposition 34.
   b) Proposition 34 increased allowable individual contributions to candidates to $21,200.
   c) Proposition 34 has resulted in less control of campaign financing.
   d) Proposition 34 replaced the stricter campaign finance law enacted through Proposition 208.

6. Of California's 39 million people, approximately how many are registered to vote?
   a) 30 million
   b) 25 million
   c) 5 million
   d) 20 million

7. Democrats are the plurality party in California.
   a) true
   b) false

8. The number of voters who decline to state a party affiliation at the time they register is declining.
   a) true
   b) false

9. Most of the Democratic counties encompass major urban areas, whereas most of the Republican counties are more rural in nature.
   a) true
   b) false

10. California presently operates under which of the following primary election systems?
    a) open primary
    b) blanket primary
    c) modified closed primary
    d) fully closed primary

CRITICAL-THINKING QUESTIONS

1. How might the cost of campaigning be reduced in California? Because incumbents spend much more money than challengers do, what reforms might level the playing field of campaign politics?
2. What do you think have been the successes and failures of campaign finance laws in California? Do you think that additional reforms are needed? Why or why not?
3. How do you think the increase in unaffiliated voters and the increase in mail voters will affect campaigns and elections in the future?
4. Why do you think so many states follow California's lead in the areas of ballot propositions and recall efforts? Do you think this is a good or bad development? Explain why.

KEY TERMS

ballot initiative (p. 91)
blanket primary (p. 87)
campaign finance reform (p. 106)
closed primary (p. 87)
general election (p. 77)
media-dominated campaign (p. 104)
media market (p. 104)

modified closed primary (p. 88)
Motor Voter (p. 107)
no party preference (p. 79)
office block ballot (p. 77)
open primary (p. 87)
political consultant (p. 104)

political culture (p. 84)
political party affiliation (p. 79)
primary elections (p. 77)
vote-by-mail ballot (p. 112)
weak political parties (p. 105)
winner-take-all (p. 76)

5 The California Legislature

WHAT CALIFORNIA GOVERNMENT DOES AND WHY IT MATTERS

Californians give little if any thought to their legislature. We have a general sense that it is made up of a group of elected individuals who write laws, but beyond that our knowledge is limited.

Our lack of knowledge is related to the minimal media coverage that legislatures receive. The media find it difficult to cover institutions that have multiple members who are doing many different things and have no single voice. They find it much easier to focus on a chief executive who has a press office that provides news-ready stories. Moreover, media coverage of state politics is minimal. Prior to the election of Governor Arnold Schwarzenegger, no Los Angeles television station had a Sacramento bureau. But even the interest in a movie-star governor did not carry over to the legislature, and since the arrival of Governor Jerry Brown, who makes only a minimal effort to feed the news establishment, the media's interest in Sacramento has sharply declined. The last Los Angeles TV news bureau in Sacramento closed in 2013.

Accompanying our lack of knowledge is the general belief that the legislature does not work well. According to the Field Poll of California voters, a low was reached in May 2010 when only 16 percent of Californians approved of the job that the state legislature was doing (72 percent disapproved). Our dissatisfaction with the legislative process stems in part from a lack of understanding of how it works, but it has several other sources as well.

First, Americans dislike and distrust politics in general. They also like harmony and are turned off by conflict between the governor and the legislature and between parties. Since the legislature is the most observable political arena, conflict here is more obvious.

Second, the dysfunction that so often characterizes state government negatively affects attitudes toward the legislature. While the legislature is not the principal cause of this dysfunction, term limits and voting rules have led to gridlock and to elevated partisan conflict, which makes it difficult for the legislature to function well.

Third, while voters want their legislators to work together, these same citizens want their individual interests forcefully represented against competing ones. We have conflicting expectations of legislatures, and legislators' attempts to balance these expectations often contribute to our dissatisfaction. "Laws are like sausages; it is better not to see them being made." This quote, often attributed to the nineteenth-century German statesman Otto von Bismarck, has a point in suggesting that respect for the making of laws, like the making of sausages, decreases with our awareness of how they are made.

Finally, the occasional bad behavior of individual legislators brings the entire institution into disrepute. During the spring of 2014, three Democratic senators facing criminal charges were suspended by their colleagues. This was followed by a dip in the public's opinion of the legislature. However, the trend in public opinion since 2010 has been toward increased approval of the legislature, to the point where more voters approve than disapprove of the job it is doing. A Fall 2016 Field Poll found 50 percent of voters approve of the legislature, the highest in 28 years. (A May 2016 Public Policy Institute of California poll of all adults shows a favorable view of the legislature by a 6 percent margin.)[1]

Several factors have contributed to the legislature's improved reputation: redistricting by a nonpartisan commission, new primary election rules, removal of the two-thirds vote requirement to pass budgets, and changes in term limits. (Each of these factors will be discussed later in this chapter.) But perhaps most important, a Democrat was elected governor and the Democrats gained a two-thirds majority in each legislative house, greatly reducing both gridlock and conflict. The legislature became more harmonious not because Democrats and Republicans began to work together, but rather because the Republicans became marginalized. At the same time, the public's approval rating of the U.S. Congress—where power is closely divided and gridlock is common—dropped to a historic low of 9 percent in November 2013 and has risen only slightly since then.[2]

In spite of Californians' distrust of, and lack of interest in, their legislature, the influence it has on their lives—and yours—is significant. In the 2015–16 session alone, the legislature considered (and in some cases passed) legislation dealing with gun control, digital privacy, class material costs for California students, minimum pay, all-gender restrooms, housing for the homeless, and climate change. The range of issues could hardly be greater. In addition, the legislature funds all state government agencies, including parks, the Highway Patrol, and universities.

Legislatures, although poorly understood, play a critical role in our government. The framers of the U.S. Constitution, fearing a powerful executive, gave Congress the most significant and most explicit powers, including control over taxation and spending and the authority to write all laws. Today, the president gets the most media attention and some congressional powers have gravitated to the executive branch; however, Congress remains a very powerful body.

Most state legislatures, including California's, have been modeled on the U.S. Congress in structure, process, and function. California has a **bicameral** (two-house) legislature consisting of the 40-member Senate (sometimes called the upper house) and the 80-member Assembly. As in the U.S. Congress, members of both houses represent geographically determined districts and are elected in winner-take-all elections. As in Congress, bills become law by being approved by both houses and signed by the chief executive. The bulk of the work of each house is done in committees. Each house is organized by party, and party leaders determine committee membership. Despite these similarities, significant differences—such as the role of seniority in committee assignments—do exist. These differences will be explained in more detail later in the chapter.

The recent history of the California legislature has been remarkable in its extremes. In the 1960s, under the leadership of Assembly Speaker Jesse Unruh, the legislature was transformed from an often-corrupt, amateur body to a well-paid, well-staffed professional organization regarded by many as the best state legislature in the country. Then in 1990 California voters passed **Proposition 140**, imposing **term limits** on legislators. Although this did not change the basic structure of the legislature, it did change the collective knowledge, effectiveness, and power of the legislature by reducing the time that legislators were permitted to serve to 14 years, and by reducing the size of the staff that makes legislative work possible.

In 2012 term limits were slightly modified when voters passed Proposition 28, which further reduced the time that legislators could serve to 12 years. However, unlike Proposition 140, which limited members to 6 years in the Assembly and 8 in the Senate, Proposition 28 allowed for all 12 years to be served in one house. The principal result, in time, should be to increase the effectiveness of the Assembly by giving members and leaders more time to become knowledgeable in their jobs and thus become more competent players in the policy game.

Functions

Legislatures have two principal functions: **representation** and policy making. The tensions between these functions make it difficult for a legislature to perform as effectively as citizens might wish.

Representation

The legislature is the principal representative institution in our society, although the executive branch and interest groups also lay claim to this function. It is the duty of legislators (also called members, representatives, assemblypersons, or senators) to represent the voters and other residents (collectively known as **constituents**) within their districts, as well as to represent the dominant district interests. This is easier said than done. In the first place, the term *representation* has many meanings. Here we will simplify it to mean that our representative is our counterpart in Sacramento and that he or she will do what we would do if we were there, especially when it comes to influencing legislation or voting. Of course, there are many more constituents than there are legislators, and rarely do all people see things the same way. Some are wealthy and educated; others, destitute. Some see government as the means to solve society's problems; others see it as the main problem.

Furthermore, representatives face many different and difficult issues: same-sex marriage versus traditional marriage, lower taxes versus improved services, new highways versus neighborhood preservation, higher spending on prisons versus lower college tuition. How one approaches these issues depends in part on the way in which one understands the goal of representation: Is it to give constituents what they want or what they need?

Political scientists talk about two poles of representation style: the delegate who tries to find out what constituents want and then act according to their wishes, and the trustee who believes that he or she has been chosen to act based on his or her own best judgment. Delegates most often try to provide what constituents want, whereas trustees are more inclined to provide for their districts' needs *as they perceive them*. Both types of representation are difficult to achieve in practice. It is often impossible to know what constituents want because they do not communicate with their representatives very well. It is no easier to determine district needs, which are often diverse, conflicting, and influenced by ideology or other subjective factors.

In theory, a representative should act based on the wants and needs of each member of his or her district equally. But in practice, certain groups wield more influence than others. For instance, some legislators identify closely with a particular group, such as women, small business owners, or immigrants, and they view themselves as representatives of that group. (See the "Who Are Californians?" feature for more information on the party affiliation of the electorate and the legislature in California.) In addition, some groups are better organized than others and are particularly adept at gaining the representative's attention. These would include chambers of commerce, large employers, labor unions, and environmental organizations. Large campaign contributors do not give their donations without expecting something in return, so the legislator is unable to ignore them. Ultimately it is the constituents who have the vote, and this should force representatives to pay attention to the needs of the entire district, but even this principle has been weakened in recent years by big money and term limits. Rarely do voters have a realistic chance of keeping favored representatives in power or "throwing the rascals out."

In addition to representing our policy views, representatives try to look out for us when we have specific problems with government, whether it's not getting a disability check, being treated unfairly by an inspector, worrying that a new highway will be built through our property, or opposing the sale of liquor near our kids' school. This ombudsman function is called *constituency service* or *casework*, and it involves intervening with the bureaucracy to solve specific problems. Representatives also try to get favorable treatment for economic interests in their districts—when a restaurant owner wants a liquor license that he or she believes is

Who Represents Californians?

Among the 18 million registered voters in California, the largest proportion, approximately 45 percent, are registered with the Democratic Party, while only about 27 percent are registered Republicans. The remaining 28 percent are registered with a smaller political party or declined to state their preferred party.

As third party nominees rarely win elections, successful candidates for office tend to be members of one of the two major parties. This is reflected in the makeup of the California state legislature, where in 2016, 65 percent of members were Democrats and 35 percent were Republicans. While both major parties are thus overrepresented compared to the voting public, the size of the Democratic majority in the legislature is particularly disproportional.

Party Affiliation of the Electorate and Legislature, 2016

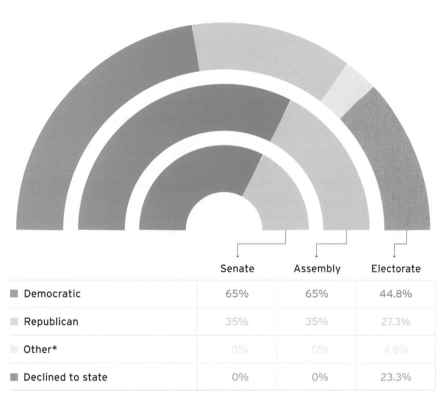

	Senate	Assembly	Electorate
Democratic	65%	65%	44.8%
Republican	35%	35%	27.3%
Other*	0%	0%	4.6%
Declined to state	0%	0%	23.3%

*Other includes the American Independent Party, the Green Party, the Libertarian Party, and the Peace and Freedom Party

SOURCES: Elections and Voter Information, "Report of Registration," www.sos.ca.gov/elections/report-registration/; California State Assembly, Members, www.assembly.ca.gov/assemblymembers; and California State Senate, Senators, www.senate.ca.gov/senators (accessed 6/20/16).

forcriticalanalysis

1. Why is the legislature so dominated by the Democratic Party? To what degree is this domination related to the population shifts discussed in Chapter 1, and to what degree is this a reflection of national trends?

2. Recent years have seen a dramatic increase in the number of Californians choosing to register as "Decline to State," rather than choosing to identify with either the Democratic or the Republican Party. Why do you think this is happening, and do you think it matters? Does the fact that only the two major parties are represented in the state legislature mean that Californians who don't affiliate with one of those two parties aren't properly represented?

It is easy to stay on top of what is happening in the legislature by using the Internet. Both houses have web pages. The Senate page is www.sen.ca.gov; the Assembly page is www.assembly.ca.gov. From these sites you can find out about the legislative process and about the status of individual bills. You can also find out how to stay in touch with your legislators. If you type in your address, the site will tell you who your legislators are and how you can contact them. Another useful site is that of the legislative counsel: http://leginfo.legislature.ca.gov.

State legislators are surprisingly accessible, especially in the district. If you have an issue for which you want to contact your legislator, be informed, call for an appointment, and be brief and forthright. Information is helpful, and a good anecdote is always useful! Thoughtful letters are also helpful. Email is used too much, and staff can recognize form mail as soon as it is opened.

Of course, working through a lobby is also effective, and you may belong to an organization that lobbies; environmental groups, unions, and student organizations are just a few of the many organizations that write, track, and try to influence legislation in their area of concern. Many of these organizations maintain websites discussing the status of legislation in which they have a stake.

being unfairly denied, for instance, or when a construction company wants to build more buildings at the local state university. Representatives will also take stands on issues that are largely symbolic but still important to their constituents, such as flag burning or prayer in schools.

Another important part of representation is being available to constituents. People want to see their representative, and representatives accordingly spend much of their time in their districts attending functions, speaking to groups about the activities of government, distributing commendations and certificates, and listening to constituents. Individual constituents as well as leaders of organized groups also visit with their representatives in Sacramento. See Box 5.1 for information on contacting your state representatives.

Policy Making

Representatives come together to make policy, most obviously through the complex process of making laws, which involves writing bills, holding committee hearings, conducting legislative debates, and adding amendments. These steps will be described in more detail later in the chapter.

Policy making also involves ensuring that legislation is carried out by the bureaucracy as the legislature intended and looking out for potential problems in the implementation of policy. This function, called oversight, is carried out through a variety of means, including staff follow-up on constituents' concerns, legislative hearings, budgetary hearings, and confirmation hearings. Legislators do not have much appetite for holding hearings that might make a governor of their own party uncomfortable, but any scandal involving a public agency almost automatically triggers such hearings. In recent years the legislature has held hearings on construction flaws in the new Bay Bridge, progress of the high-speed rail project, private (ex parte) meetings between coastal commissioners and developers, and the unnecessarily cumbersome college transfer process. Congressional oversight hearings at the federal level gain far more attention, in part because of divided government. While these hearings most often have a valid administrative or legislative purpose, they are also used to embarrass or damage the leaders of the opposite party. If they can do both, so much the better. Perhaps the most notable recent examples have been the hearings on Hillary Clinton's role in Benghazi and on her email servers, which were, at the very least, difficult to deal with in her presidential campaign, contributing to her loss.

Members and Districts

Unlike Congress, in which each state has two seats in the Senate regardless of population, both houses of the California legislature are apportioned by population. The state is divided into 80 Assembly districts and 40 state Senate districts. In each of these districts a single representative is elected by local voters, which means that these representatives will give serious attention to local interests. As former speaker of the U.S. House of Representatives Tip O'Neill once said, "All politics is local." Our legislative system is designed to favor local interests (and interests with money), and for representatives, these local interests often take precedence over statewide interests.

Legislators have offices in both Sacramento and in their districts. Mail, email, and phone messages are answered from both places. When representatives are in their districts, they listen to the concerns of their constituents and tell them about government activities, policy, and politics (e.g., they try to explain what life is like in the capital). In Sacramento they interact with those constituents who travel to the capital as well as with representatives of interest groups. In addition, they

Senate President pro Tempore Kevin de León (D-Los Angeles, left with infant) congratulates Senators Richard Pan (D-Sacramento, center) and Ben Allen (D-Santa Monica, right) after their bill requiring nearly all California school children to be vaccinated was signed by Governor Jerry Brown.

work on framing policy, primarily in committees. Legislators often spend Monday through midday Thursday in Sacramento and return to their districts for the remainder of the week; however, this varies with the time of the year, and special events often bring them back to their districts. It is essential to keep a high profile in the district to discourage potential election opponents. Being accused of ignoring one's district could be fatal in an election. Since minority party members often have little say in policy making, they may emphasize their availability to constituents to demonstrate that they have value in Sacramento.

Elections

Every member of the California Senate and Assembly must be elected by voters from a single geographic district. Most members with previous elective experience have served on school boards, city councils, or county boards of supervisors. Many are self-selected. Others are tapped to run for office by party leaders or interests who see them as viable candidates and friendly to their policies. Assembly members serve two-year terms while senators serve for four years.

Legislative elections are **winner-take-all** elections, which means that minor or third parties are generally excluded from the legislature even if they have substantial support statewide. Without a majority of votes in any single district, they cannot place a representative in Sacramento.

The process by which candidates are elected changed significantly in 2010 with the passage of Proposition 14. Prior to 2010, the primary elections were structured to select one candidate from each party to run in the general election. Candidates ran as Republicans, Democrats, or as representatives of a third party in separate contests against members of their own party only. Voters could choose one of those contests in which to vote. The winners faced off against each other in the general election in November. In districts where the voters were overwhelmingly of one party—typical of many California districts—the real contest was in the primary, and election was all but assured to the candidate of the majority party. Many believed that this resulted in the election of extremist legislators who were beholden only to the majority of the voters in their party, not to the majority of the voters in their district.

Proposition 14 instituted a single blanket primary, or "top-two" primary, in which all candidates run and all voters take part. Voters in the primary or preliminary election vote for the candidate of their choice for each office from a single list of all candidates, and the top two candidates go on to the November election regardless of party. Candidates need not state their party identification on the ballot. The expectation is that, even if both of the winning candidates are in the same party, the more moderate candidate will win the general election by appealing to voters in the minority parties (see Chapter 4). It is common for there to be more than two dozen contests (out of more than 150 legislative races) in which the top two candidates belong to the same party. In 2016 there were 28, and even the race for U.S. Senator was between two Democrats.

If there are only two candidates in the preliminary election, they will have to run against each other for a second time in the general election. While this may seem redundant, the electorate in November is almost always larger (and therefore less Republican) than in June, which can affect the outcome of the election. In

2012 the 65th Assembly District in Orange County provided an excellent example of an incumbent challenged by a single opponent—in this case, a Republican challenged by a Democrat. When they ran against each other in June, the Republican incumbent won with over 58 percent of the vote. In the runoff in November, the Democratic challenger won with about 52 percent of the vote, helping the Democrats gain a two-thirds majority in the Assembly. Contributing to this victory was a significant increase in voter turnout: about 50,000 people voted in June while over 120,000 voted in November. The new incumbent lost to a different Republican two years later when only 77,000 people voted and regained the seat in 2016 when there were over 140,000 voters.

Two other key features of California politics have a significant influence on who gets elected. First, the large size of each district means that campaigns are expensive and fund-raising is necessary. Second, the manner in which district boundaries are drawn influences the role of political parties and the strength of incumbents.

Fund-raising

Campaigns can easily cost millions of dollars (see Chapter 4), and campaign expenditures are likely to be much higher in the future because of the Supreme Court ruling in *Citizens United* (see Chapter 3), which rejected corporate spending limits, and because the California Citizens Redistricting Commission has created more competitive legislative districts. Fund-raising is one of the most significant obstacles to winning an election. The nature of California and the size of the districts make election victories unlikely through old-fashioned precinct work. Use of TV and radio advertising is also impractical in the larger media markets because of cost. Most candidates have campaign consultants and engage in polling, which help them come up with strategies for targeted distribution of literature, Internet advertising, and social media outreach.

Districting

Because of the relatively small size of the state legislature, its districts are among the largest in the country. Senate districts have over 950,000 constituents, and Assembly districts over 475,000. (For comparison, U.S. House districts in California have approximately 715,000 constituents.) Historically, district lines were drawn by the legislature, often leading to charges of **gerrymandering**. This term dates to the early 1800s, when Massachusetts governor Elbridge Gerry oversaw a redistricting that benefited his party and resulted in district lines that resembled, in a famous cartoon of the day, a salamander. To *gerrymander* means to draw district lines in a manner that favors one party over another, generally by packing most of the opponent's voters into a few districts and spreading the remainder thinly over the remaining districts. The courts have generally accepted this practice, saying only that districts must be equal in population and must not be drawn to diminish the voting strength of any minority.

Redistricting is done following each census and until 2012 had to pass both houses and be signed by the governor, like any other piece of legislation. However, after the 2000 census, despite Democratic control of both houses and the governor's office, the party did not create more gerrymandered Democratic districts. Instead, endeavoring (successfully) to avoid a lawsuit, they approved a set of maps known as the "incumbency protection plan," which maintained safe seats for both parties. Thus, the power of voters to hold their legislators accountable was diminished, as incumbents throughout the state were unlikely to lose a future election.

Therefore, before 2012, most action took place in the primaries, though incumbents rarely faced a serious challenge there following the advent of term limits in 1992. Knowing that an incumbent assemblyperson would be out of office in no more than four years, the astute challenger waited for that vacancy to occur rather than engaging in an expensive, divisive challenge. Term limits had the unintended consequence of inhibiting voters from "throwing the rascals out." The legislature was more immune from direct electoral challenge than ever before.

Since 2012, the situation that created safe districts with highly partisan incumbents has significantly changed. As a result of their continued frustration with the legislature, the voters approved two measures, Proposition 11 in November 2008 (followed by Proposition 20 in 2010) and Proposition 14 in June 2010, that have had an impact on who gets elected to the legislature.

The consequences of Proposition 14, the "top-two" primary law described above, have been overwhelmingly overshadowed by those of Propositions 11 and 20, both redistricting initiatives that unexpectedly resulted in a two-thirds Democratic majority in both houses. Proposition 11 took the task of drawing legislative districts away from the legislature and replaced it with a 15-person Citizens Redistricting Commission. This commission created districts with a closer partisan balance.

The expectation was that Proposition 11 would result in fewer safe seats and in the election of moderate legislators more willing to engage in bipartisan compromise. It will take several election cycles before these results can be assessed, because the large Democratic majorities currently in the state legislature make bipartisan compromise largely unnecessary. However, some observers believe that the smaller Republican minority is less moderate and less inclined to compromise, while the larger Democratic majority is more moderate.

Even though their two-thirds majority in the Senate was eliminated by the suspension of three Democratic members in March 2014, the Democrats still can carry out business with little regard for their Republican colleagues. (The supermajority re-appeared in 2017.) Thus, gridlock has been reduced, and the public's regard for the legislature has become correspondingly more favorable.

Still, the large majority of Democrats has not proven to be radical; they have not raised taxes or implemented draconian new regulations. This is partially because they have to work with a moderate Democratic governor, who would probably veto such measures. More important, many of these new Democratic legislators are from marginal seats that have many Republican voters (such as the 65th Assembly District in Orange County and the 32nd Assembly District in Bakersfield) and are reluctant to take bold action that might endanger their chances of re-election.

In addition, when contests in the general election are between two Democrats, big corporations (such as Chevron Oil) often spend large sums of money backing the candidate who is more supportive of their interests. While these candidates may or may not be moderates, they are definitely supportive of the corporations that have funded them.

There are enough business-oriented Democrats to form a loosely structured caucus that has designated leaders, has a PAC, and holds fund-raisers. Membership is not published but is probably around 20, more or less, depending on the issue. As the Democratic tent has grown bigger, the new members are most often from more conservative districts, and big business with big money has taken advantage of the "top two" primaries to aggressively support friendly Democratic candidates. One Assembly member, Cheryl Brown (D-San Bernardino), who was key to helping gut climate control bills in 2015, received over $1 million from Chevron in independent spending supporting her 2016 primary campaign, leading her opponents to label her "Chevron Cheryl." Brown was ultimately defeated in November 2016 in a race that cost $6.1 million in independent spending, mostly from the oil companies.

If the Democrats in the Assembly have 52 members, as was the case in 2015, then it takes only 12 "moderates" to join 28 Republicans to defeat legislation, as they did in 2015. In 2016, at the end of the two-year session, the governor and the Democratic leadership through intense politiking were able to pass meaningful climate control legislation with the minimum number of needed votes over the opposition of the oil companies. Although the governor and the Democratic leadership made a comeback, overcoming this opposition in 2016, to pass strong climate change legislation, it was a struggle. Business-oriented Democrats have demonstrated that they are an important third force in the legislature. A new chapter in California politics has begun, and no one knows exactly how it will be written.[3]

Organization

The process of policy making is complex, involving many steps and many actors. Over time, both the Senate and Assembly have, for reasons both practical and political, adopted principles of organization that structure how the legislature works.

Leadership

The leader of the Assembly is the **speaker**, and he or she has a remarkable array of powers (although these were diminished by the 6-year term limit on members of the Assembly). In an attempt to increase the power of the speaker by lengthening his or her time in the position, in 2003 and 2009 the Democrats elected a first-term legislator to the speakership. In 2014 they elected a member, Toni Atkins, in her second term. In 2016 she was replaced by another member in his second term, Anthony Rendon. Rendon, however, was elected to the legislature under new rules that allow him to serve 12 years in the Assembly. If he serves as speaker for the remainder of his allotted time—until 2024—he will have been one of the longest-serving speakers in recent history. This is a game-changer that should increase the speaker's effectiveness and thus the effectiveness of the legislature.

The Assembly speaker's powers are considerably more extensive than those of the Speaker of the U.S. House of Representatives. Beginning with control over assigning parking spaces and offices, these powers include almost complete control over establishing committees, assigning members to serve on them, and, if the speaker chooses, removing members from these committees. Because the bulk of legislative work is done in committees, members depend on the speaker to provide them with a meaningful role in the legislature. The speaker can also assign floor leadership of high-profile or popular bills to legislators of his or her choice, enhancing their reputations both inside and outside the Assembly.

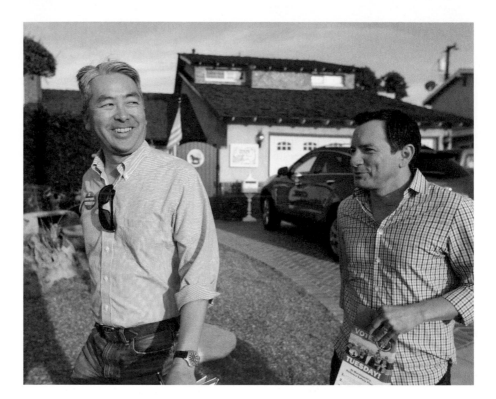

Assembly Speaker Anthony Rendon, right, helps Democratic Assembly candidate Al Muratsuchi canvass a neighborhood in the 66th Assembly District (Torrance) in 2016. Part of the speaker's job is to get fellow party members elected. Swing districts like the 65th and 66th tend to vote Republican in low turnout elections and Democratic when voter turnout is higher. Muratsuchi ultimately defeated the Republican who had ousted him 2014.

When the full Assembly meets, the speaker acts as presiding officer and thereby controls the debate; when not presiding, he or she designates the person who does. The speaker also appoints the majority floor leader, who assists in running legislative sessions. It is difficult to overstate the speaker's power, which can move bills, help supporters, and hurt opponents. Speakers can raise money as well, which in turn allows them to solidify support. Members find it advantageous to cooperate with the speaker. The speaker is elected by the entire membership of the Assembly, but in most cases the outcome is determined in advance by the majority party caucus, which consists of all of the members of the majority party meeting together. Only when the majority is split does the full Assembly vote become significant.

The minority caucus elects the Assembly minority leader, who is the public voice of the minority party and who works with the speaker to determine minority party assignments on committees. The speaker, however, has the final say.

The other important element of the leadership is the **Assembly Rules Committee**, which is made up of nine members, four elected by each party's caucus, plus a chair appointed by the speaker. The committee's responsibilities include hiring staff, assigning bills to committees, and reviewing legislative rules. Rarely does this committee operate independently of the speaker's wishes.

The organization of the Senate is similar to that of the Assembly, but the Senate leader, the **president pro tempore**, does not have the absolute power of the Assembly speaker. Many of the speaker's powers in the Assembly rest with the

Rules Committee in the Senate. Yet for a time the president pro tempore—most notably John Burton—was the most influential legislator in Sacramento, largely because of the impact of term limits. Prior to 2012, senators often served in the Assembly first, and their time in the Senate could last up to 8 years. Senate leaders could accrue 10 to 12 years of experience in Sacramento before assuming leadership roles. In contrast, Assembly leaders might have had only two or three years of experience. John Burton, who was the last of his breed, had far more experience than that, including experience in the U.S. Congress.

This pattern is now changing thanks to the passage of Proposition 28 in June 2012. Legislators elected in 2012 and after may now serve no more than 12 years in the state legislature, but those years can be spent entirely in one house or in a combination of both houses. Thus, Speaker Rendon may remain in his position for up to 8 years, potentially having greater influence than his immediate predecessors did. Senators will no longer be able to serve 14 years, which will level the playing field and provide members and leaders of the Assembly the opportunity to attain the same level of experience.

Committees

The bulk of legislative work is done in **committees**. Committees allow for greater specialization, greater expertise of those involved, and greater attention to detail. In 2015–16 there were 31 standing or permanent committees in the Assembly and 22 in the Senate (see Table 5.1). Each member sits on several standing committees. In addition to standing committees, there are many select committees that exist to study specific issues and joint committees to look at issues that concern both houses. Members may serve on a dozen or more of these less important committees.

Committees are at the heart of groups of players often referred to as **issue networks**. These networks consist of committee members and **staff**, senior members of the respective executive branch agency, and interest groups concerned with issues in a committee's jurisdiction. The bulk of policy details are worked out in these networks. Lobbyists and bureaucrats involved in issue networks tend to be specialists who spend their entire careers in a single subject area. It would be unusual for someone who has spent a career in transportation to move to education. Previously, legislators would spend their careers in specific issue areas as well. Term limits have changed that, or rather have shortened the length of careers. While policy is still worked out within these networks, the power to shape the policy has shifted to those who have greater permanency, experience, and expertise—namely, lobbyists and bureaucrats. The less experienced and less knowledgeable legislator is now more dependent than before on these individuals for policy details. Experienced staff can help, but since the severe staff reductions required by Proposition 140 in 1990, staff members are often no more experienced than legislators.

Staff

Without staff, the legislature cannot effectively do its job. Staff is crucial in both the policy-making and the representative functions of the legislature. All legislators have staff in both their Sacramento and district offices to help with constituency

TABLE 5.1 ● Standing Committees of the California Legislature, 2015–16

State Senate

Agriculture	Health
Appropriations	Human Services
Banking and Financial Institutions	Insurance
Budget and Fiscal Review	Judiciary
Business, Professions and Economic Development	Labor and Industrial Relations
Education	Natural Resources and Water
Elections and Constitutional Amendments	Public Employment and Retirement
Energy, Utilities, and Communications	Public Safety
Environmental Quality	Rules
Governance and Finance	Transportation and Housing
Governmental Organization	Veterans Affairs

Assembly

Accountability and Administrative Review	Human Services
Aging and Long-Term Care	Insurance
Agriculture	Jobs, Economic Development, and the Economy
Appropriations	Judiciary
Arts, Entertainment, Sports, Tourism, and Internet Media	Labor and Employment
Banking and Finance	Local Government
Budget	Natural Resources
Business and Professions	Privacy and Consumer Protection
Education	Public Employees, Retirement and Social Security
Elections and Redistricting	Public Safety
Environmental Safety and Toxic Materials	Revenue and Taxation
Governmental Organization	Rules
Health	Transportation
Higher Education	Utilities and Commerce
Housing and Community Development	Veterans Affairs
	Water, Parks, and Wildlife

contacts, including handling casework, scheduling appearances, and answering mail and phone calls from constituents. In addition, committees have staff, called consultants, to help with the policy work of that committee, and consultants are also critical components of the issue networks. Some of the best consultants will take their hard-earned experience and move on to become lobbyists, where the pay is often far higher and the job more secure. Each legislator is allotted an office budget for staffing. Legislators are permitted additional staff depending on whether they occupy a committee leadership role and on the generosity of the party leadership. In addition, the house leaders and caucuses have staff that may number more than 150 for the majority party. This staff helps with bill analysis for individual members and public relations for both individual members and the party.

There are over 2,000 legislative aides. It is not unusual for majority legislators to have 13 or 14 staff members. Minority members may have only 4 or 5. While most aides are modestly paid, some—especially highly valued committee consultants—make over $150,000 a year. The total personnel budget for legislative workers in 2015 was $216 million. The median salary for staff members is about $55–65,000. These aides often work alongside members of the prestigious Assembly and Senate Fellows program as well as many college interns.

There are three important and well-regarded groups of staff who are nonpartisan and who work for the entire legislature. The first is the Legislative Analyst's Office, which analyzes budget proposals and the fiscal impact of ballot propositions. The second is the Legislative Counsel, which helps write bills, analyze ballot propositions, and provide legal advice. The third is the State Auditor's Office, which handles management and fiscal audits of the executive branch.

Before Proposition 140 passed in 1990, the staff of the California legislature was considered the best in the nation. However, the proposition required a staff cut of 40 percent and resulted in layoffs and the departure of many of the most experienced staffers, especially the highly paid experts on which the committees relied. Staff is still a significant factor in the legislature, and over the years, it has inched back toward its previous size and influence.

Legislative Process

There are three types of items that may pass the legislature: bills, which if successful become laws; constitutional amendments, which require a two-thirds vote of both houses and a referendum by the voters; and resolutions, which are largely symbolic expressions of opinion. The remainder of this section is concerned primarily with bills.

Bills are introduced only by legislators, even if the content was originally proposed by someone as politically important as the governor. Indeed, bills are often written by someone other than the person who introduces them. Many bills may be written by, or in conjunction with, lobbyists; and the nonpartisan Legislative Counsel's office may help in drafting language. An individual senator may introduce no more than 40 bills in a two-year session, whereas assembly members may introduce 50 bills. Legislators may have a variety of motives for introducing a bill, such as impressing constituents or paying off a political favor, and most go nowhere. In the 2015–16 legislative session, 2,915 bills were introduced in the Senate and 1,481 in the Assembly for a total of 4,396. Of these, 1,991 reached the governor's desk. He signed 1,698 of them and vetoed 291, including some that were strongly supported by his allies. (Two became law without his signature.) This is far fewer than was common 20 years ago. In 1989 and 1990, for example, 3,174 new laws were enacted.[4]

Once a bill is introduced, the rules committee of the appropriate house assigns the bill to a standing committee or even two committees, depending on its content. There may be a political or strategic component to this assignment. The bill is also numbered and printed. Committees cannot act on a bill until it has been in print for 30 days, to allow comment from interested parties. Committees hold hearings, scrutinize the language to make sure that it clearly and accurately states what members intend, add amendments, and pass or reject bills. An absolute majority of the committee must vote favorably to report a bill out. If a bill is reported out of committee, it may go to the floor for discussion by the entire house; or bills with major fiscal impact may end up in the "suspense file" of the appropriations committee of either house to die, be amended, or be advanced without public vote and without explanation. These committees substantially reduce the number of bills reaching the floor, and may substantially change others. In the closing weeks of a legislative session, these committees may report out hundreds of bills in a single day, which adds to the end-of-session logjam. Once a bill reaches the floor, amendments may be added and require only a majority vote. Bill passage requires an absolute majority (41 in the Assembly, 21 in the Senate). Once a bill has passed one house, it goes to the other house for similar consideration. Bills must pass both houses with identical language before they are forwarded to a governor for his or her signature. If the governor vetoes a bill, a two-thirds vote in each house is required to override the veto. This rarely happens.

Most bills pass through each house with different wording. In this case one house may acquiesce to the wording of the other house, or a conference committee will be established to work out the differences. A conference committee is a joint committee consisting of three members from each body. Assembly members are appointed by the speaker, and Senate members are appointed by the Senate Rules Committee. They suggest compromise language that must pass both houses. If this attempt fails, two additional attempts may be made before the bill is put to rest. See Figure 5.1 for an illustration of how a bill becomes a law in the California legislature.

SHORTCUTS The process described above is the textbook approach, but much legislation is able to bypass some of these steps, especially near the end of a legislative session when bills tumble over one another and deals are made in back rooms in a rush to adjourn. (In the last weeks of the 2015–16 session the legislature dealt with over 1,500 bills.) Many bills reappear as amendments to other bills, attracting even less public attention than they would have in the normal process. At this time, the influence of party leaders is greater because they are able to grease the skids for compromises and logrolling. **Logrolling** is vote trading, the process by which members exchange votes: "You vote for my bill, and I will vote for yours." Another common end-of-session legislative tactic is to hijack a bill and then **"gut and amend"** it. An issue that may have been presumed dead suddenly reappears, without warning, in a procedurally alive bill that previously dealt with an entirely different topic. In an editorial denouncing the practice, the *Sacramento Bee* describes how "gut and amend" works:

> A bill on air pollution morphs into a bill on immigration. A bill on college tuition becomes a bill on shark fins. In the last three weeks of the 2011 session, legislators gutted and amended 48 bills, passing 22 of them. Gov. Jerry Brown signed 19 of them.[5]

Efforts to reform this procedure in the legislature by requiring bills to be in print for several days before coming up for a vote have never gained traction; so in 2016 wealthy Republican Charles Munger solely funded a successful ballot proposition that prohibits the legislature from voting on any bill until it has been in print and published on the Internet for 72 hours (Proposition 54). Work-arounds will no doubt be found.

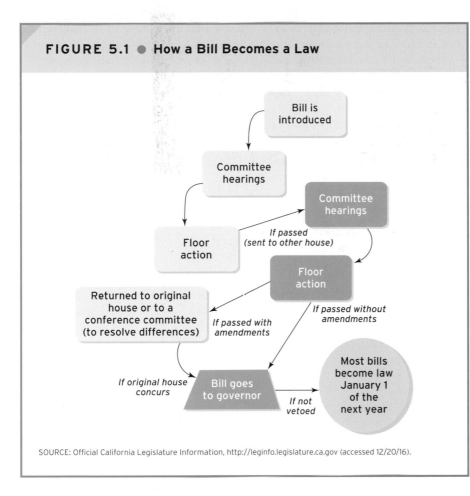

FIGURE 5.1 ● How a Bill Becomes a Law

Bill is introduced

Committee hearings

Floor action

If passed (sent to other house)

Committee hearings

Floor action

Returned to original house or to a conference committee (to resolve differences)

If passed with amendments

If passed without amendments

If original house concurs

Bill goes to governor

If not vetoed

Most bills become law January 1 of the next year

SOURCE: Official California Legislature Information, http://leginfo.legislature.ca.gov (accessed 12/20/16).

End-of-session periods in Sacramento reflect quintessential American politics: a system that favors insiders, corporations, and those with big money. While this goes on throughout the year, these backroom strategies work best when time is compressed and the media and other outsiders cannot follow what is going on or cannot do anything about it.

At the end of the session there is intense pressure to get things done. As noted earlier, 1,991 bills passed in 2015–16 and many others were in play. Insiders and lobbyists focus their attention on a single bill or a small number of bills that are important to their clients. Large corporations and other interest groups hire full-time lobbyists and lawyers, sometimes a full platoon of them, to follow their important bills, develop strategy, and take the necessary actions to ensure the desired outcome, all of which can be written off as business expenses.

These insiders work out deals behind the proverbial closed doors, and provisions to bills are added and removed at the last minute. Often the junior members voting on the floor have no idea of what they are voting on. Before the legislature was term-limited, members were extremely well-versed about their policy interests and had long memories about what tricks lobbyists and other legislators had pulled in previous sessions. This meant that it was more difficult to make unnoticed changes in legislation to benefit a special interest. Institutional memory is much more limited now among legislators. Experience, knowledge, and skills rest disproportionately with lobbyists and agency representatives.

Differences from U.S. Congress

While the California legislature is modeled closely on the national legislature, there are important differences that, collectively, make the California legislature a weaker body.

Term Limits

Unlike members of Congress, who can serve as long as they are re-elected, California legislators are limited to a total of 12 years, which can be served in one or both houses. Term limits enacted by the passage of Proposition 140 in 1990 limited members to three 2-year terms in the Assembly and two 4-year terms in the Senate for a maximum total of 14 years. Proposition 28 in 2012 instituted the current 12-year limit.

There were numerous reasons for the success of Proposition 140. First, it was a reaction to the highly effective Assembly Speaker Willie Brown, a flamboyant African American politician from San Francisco who was immensely unpopular with conservative voters. Second, it was an effect of public aversion to **gridlock** and divided government (generated by partisan conflict between the Republican governor and the Democratic legislature). Third, voters were protesting against the large fund-raising efforts of incumbents. Fourth, it was a reflection of the national trend against entrenched incumbents. Finally, it was the product of a belief among some Republicans that term limits could overthrow the Democratic majority. However, these term limits did not end divided government, gridlock, or large fund-raising (campaign-related spending has vastly increased), and they only briefly suspended the Democratic majority and in only one house, the 1994 Assembly. The proposition did reduce the ability of the legislature to act effectively. It is too early to know if Proposition 28 will ultimately make the legislature more effective.

Item Veto

In Washington, D.C., the president has to sign or reject bills passed by Congress in their entirety. The president cannot approve parts that he or she likes and reject those that he or she dislikes. In California, as in most states, the governor has a **line-item veto** on appropriations, including those in the budget. This power allows the governor to reduce or eliminate a specific spending item, although he or she cannot increase items. This means that the legislature cannot force the governor's hand by including an item that the governor opposes in a large spending bill that he mostly supports. In 2016 for the first time in over 40 years the governor did not use the line item veto when signing the budget.

Apportionment and District Size

Both houses of the California legislature are **apportioned** by population; in Congress, the Constitution allots two senators to each state, regardless of size. California has a population about equal to the populations of the 22 smallest states combined. While these states have 44 senators between them, California has the same number of senators as the smallest of these states, Wyoming. In fact, there are four states that have fewer residents than each of California's 53 congressional districts.

Because California is so populous (about 39 million people) and because its legislature is relatively small, its legislative districts are among the largest in the nation. Senate districts have over 950,000 constituents, while Assembly districts contain over 475,000 residents. Compare this to New Hampshire, with a population of about 1.3 million and with 400 members in its lower house, which results in one representative for about every 3,000 residents. While New Hampshire's representatives are very accessible and elections are not expensive, most representatives do not wield much influence in their very large chamber. California senators, unlike any other U.S. legislative body, represent more constituents than members of Congress and more than the U.S. senators of seven states. This means that they are considerably less accessible than their counterparts in other states and that their elections are considerably more expensive.

The fact that both legislative houses are apportioned by population has led some informed observers to suggest that a unicameral legislature of 120 members would make more sense. This would result in smaller districts and increased accessibility to legislators.

Media Visibility

In Washington, D.C., the media interpret the national government's actions by focusing on the president, who consequently dominates the news. The comments of members of Congress are generally used to give more depth to a presidential story. Most often, these are party leaders, committee chairs, or the occasional legislator who has managed to make a name for himself or herself on a given issue.

The same is true in California's capital, but the statewide media, especially television, rarely cover news in Sacramento. Only the four party leaders receive air time, and because they hold their positions for so few years, the public has difficulty keeping track of who they are. Speaker of the U.S. House of Representatives Paul Ryan is practically a household name, but California Assembly Speaker Anthony Rendon is not. Consequently, most of what happens in Sacramento occurs out of the spotlight.

Court Appointments

Some of the greatest legislative battles in Congress have occurred during the Senate's hearings to confirm judicial appointments, especially to the Supreme Court. In contrast, many judges in California are elected. Those who are appointed by the governor are approved by the Commission on Judicial Appointments. The Senate does get to approve many other gubernatorial appointments to executive positions and regulatory boards and commissions, including the governing boards of both the California State University and the University of California. In both the U.S.

Senate and the California Senate, legislators have rejected recent nominees over policy differences.

Filibusters

In the U.S. Senate, a body that is not apportioned on the basis of one person, one vote, 41 members (potentially representing slightly more than 33 million people—about 10 percent of the country's population) can block the passage of most legislation through use of the filibuster. California has no such provision. Indeed, in most cases the majority rules. The principal exceptions are tax increases and constitutional amendments, which require a two-thirds vote.

Initiatives

Unlike the U.S. Constitution, the California Constitution provides several means of taking issues directly to the voters. Of these, the most significant is the initiative. The initiative is important in the legislative context because those who are thwarted in their attempts to get legislation passed can always threaten to take it—or an even more extreme version of it—to the voters. This tactic is often used to persuade legislators to vote for measures that they would otherwise oppose, and it significantly weakens the legislature.

Seniority

In the U.S. Congress, seniority is used as an informal rule in appointing members to committees and in choosing each committee's majority and minority leaders; once members are appointed to their committee positions, they are almost never removed. In the California legislature, both the appointment and removal power resides with the Assembly speaker and Senate majority leadership, with seniority playing a much smaller role (with term limits seniority is, of course, limited). Both the speaker and the Senate majority leadership in 2007 and 2008 removed members of both parties from committee leadership roles for disagreeing with them over various issues.

Challenges Facing the California Legislature

When voters pay attention to the legislature, complaints and criticism of its actions often result. At times these objections are on target, at times not. State government tends to be perceived as dysfunctional, and the legislature is an easy target. It is easy to be repulsed by the contentious process of arriving at legislative agreements. Moreover, individual members often run for the legislature by running against it, emphasizing the legislature's shortcomings and foibles in order to play up their own importance to the legislature.

Scandal also gets the public's attention. In 2014 three senators were suspended for misbehavior: Rod Wright (D-Inglewood) was convicted of lying about living in his district in a 2008 race, and Ron Calderon (D-Montebello) and Leland Yee (D-San Francisco) were caught taking bribes in FBI sting operations. Yee was also charged with international gunrunning, not a typical legislative misdeed. In addition, Senator Tom Berryhill (R-Twain Harte) and his brother, a former assemblyman, were fined for improper handling of campaign funds. The misbehavior of any one of the 120 legislators is often generalized to reflect badly on the whole institution. To have several legislators in the news at the same time for improper behavior is especially damaging

While the Senate had the authority to suspend the three senators in 2014, it did not have the authority to cut off pay and benefits. As a consequence, Proposition 50, which would allow a house of the Legislature to suspend a member's pay and privileges with a two-thirds vote, was placed on the ballot and passed in June 2016.

In 2016, Roger Hernandez (D-West Covina) was removed from his committee positions after his wife, during divorce proceedings, claimed that he had severely beaten her throughout their marriage, and a judge issued a restraining order against him. He was not suspended and continued to receive his salary as well as per diem. (It was near the end of the legislative session and he was not running for re-election.)

Among the most common criticisms of the legislature are the following:

Money

In the California legislature, as is the case throughout American politics, money carries a great deal of clout. Elections are expensive, and the money for elections comes from many sources, including the candidate's personal wealth, small contributions from many individuals, and larger contributions from business, unions, and other special interests. Large contributions are generally given to ensure support for a particular interest. Although legislators claim that their vote cannot be bought and that contributors are buying access and nothing else, that claim is difficult to support. Moreover, simply having access that the ordinary voter does not have is a significant advantage for these contributors. We have the best legislature that money can buy, and short of moving to public financing of campaigns—an idea rejected by the voters in June 2010—those who have money will always have an advantage over those who do not. With increasing social inequality and more money available to big industries and a few very wealthy individuals (and less available to the rest of us), and with the Supreme Court having loosened the restrictions on campaign spending, this advantage is growing.

Money is usually distributed to legislators who support the position of a given interest or to those who might be swayed by an offer of monetary support. It also goes to party leaders, who then distribute it to other legislators or candidates to solidify their support both within their party and against the other party. Indeed, the amassing of a large war chest contributed to the distrust and dislike of Speaker Willie Brown and led to the passing of Proposition 140, setting term limits. However, term-limited legislators, having little background in fund-raising, have become more dependent than their predecessors on large donations from special interests. Jesse Unruh once said, "If you can't take their money, eat their food, drink their booze . . . and then vote against them, you don't belong here."[6] On this basis, there are probably more legislators now than before that "don't belong here."

Term Limits Lead to a Lack of Knowledge and Experience

When Proposition 140 was passed in 1990, many believed that term limits would remove a remote professional class of legislators and bring in a new breed with closer ties to their districts. The ballot argument said that term limits "would remove the grip that vested interests have over the legislature" and create a "government of citizens representing their fellow citizens."[7] The expectations for this proposition were too high, and the results were unfortunate.

Legislative politics works best as an ongoing game among a relatively stable group of experienced players. Many of the aphorisms about politics, such as "Politics makes strange bedfellows" and "Don't burn your bridges," are based on ongoing relationships played out over a period of years. With a short, fixed term limit, the players change too rapidly for legislators to learn whom they can trust, with whom they can work, and whom they should avoid. This knowledge would facilitate cooperation across party lines as legislators would come to learn that not all good is on their side of the aisle and not all evil on the other side. In a short six years, legislators cannot learn that well; the players change too rapidly. The people who can work out effective compromises seldom emerge, and even if capable negotiators materialized, they would not know with whom to work.

Nor can effective leadership emerge with term limits as short as six years. In recent years, to give leaders more time in office, the Assembly Democrats have often chosen freshmen legislators as committee chairs and as speaker. But a freshman legislator, no matter how talented, cannot effectively lead a large collegial body.

Nor in six short years is there time to develop expertise in process or subject matter, the ordinary skills of a legislator. This dilemma was summed up by a lobbyist:

> I feel sorry for the first-term members who faced the energy crisis. They don't know who's smart; they don't know who knows what they're doing; they don't know the policy; they don't know the politics. And they are faced with a crisis.[8]

Real power has shifted from the legislature to the permanent establishment—the bureaucracy and interest groups. Members in these institutions may spend a career in Sacramento outlasting five sets of Assembly members. Much as they were dissatisfied with the legislature, it is doubtful that the voters wanted to shift power to either of those two groups. In June 2012 voters made a change in term limits, which on balance may shift *some* power back to the legislature. Proposition 28 reduced the time a legislator could serve in Sacramento from 14 years (6 in the Assembly and 8 in the Senate) to 12 years, but now those years can all be served in one house. When this change is fully played out, it will give each house more stability and should result in more experienced leaders. Senators may be a little less experienced than they were previously, but whatever is lost in that body will be gained by the much greater experience that Assembly members will achieve before being forced to leave.

The result could be a more knowledgeable and effective legislature that is at least marginally better able to deal with lobbyists and bureaucrats. But we have not yet reached this point. Only those legislators elected in 2012 and after operate under the new term limits, and change is not likely to be significant until after 2018. Speaker Rendon, the first speaker chosen under the new limits, may serve for up to 8 years in that position. In the previous 8 years there were three different speakers.

If there has been a positive aspect to term limits, it is the increased diversity of the legislature. The percentage of Latino legislators rose from 6 percent in 1990 to 25 percent in 2009, before declining to 19 percent in 2015. In 2017 the percentage of Latinos rose slightly to 22.5 percent. In the 2017–18 session the Assembly membership was 54 percent non-white minority. The percentage of women in the legislature increased from 17.5 percent in 1990 to 32 percent in 2008 before dropping to 21.6 percent in 2017. The speaker of the Assembly prior to Anthony Rendon, Toni Atkins, was the first openly lesbian politician to hold that office (and the first speaker from San Diego). She was immediately preceded by John Pérez, an openly gay Latino, and before that by Karen Bass, an African American woman. Members of non-white ethnic groups and women regularly occupy positions in the Democratic leadership of both houses.[9]

Partisanship

Many believe that **partisanship** has increased in the legislature in recent years. This trend has often been attributed to safe districts, in which representatives who couldn't lose in a general election were elected by their party's—often extremist—majority. In these safe districts the general election is determined by the primary election outcome and results in representatives who are more extreme than average voters. According to the common interpretation, safe districts have resulted in increased partisanship and legislators who are less willing to compromise.

As usual, the issue is more complex than this, although the new, more competitive general elections that began in 2010 may have resulted in the election of more moderates. The problem with partisanship is not that there are strong partisans in the legislature—this has always been so. But in recent years, the quality of public discourse has become less civil, and the participants have come to have less regard for their opponents and less willingness to work with them. Part of this incivility is a reflection of the increasing homogeneity and polarization of the national parties and their leaders (epitomized by the in-your-face campaign style of the 2016 Republican presidential candidate). Term limits may play a role as well. Recognizing that they will not have to live with and deal with their opponents for years into the future, legislators make less effort to develop civil working relationships with them.

But legislators should be partisan. We elect representatives on a partisan basis. If we vote for Republicans rather than Democrats, then the Republicans should deliver on their partisan promises. Even those who rail against partisanship still want their interests to be forcefully proposed and protected.

Some of the greatest legislatures in the world, such as the British Parliament, are fiercely partisan and yet manage to govern. The difference is that in those bodies, the majority is permitted to rule. In our system, which permits a minority veto on taxation, bipartisan cooperation is essential; when it is not forthcoming, the system functions badly. If the California legislature appears to function better in recent years, it is not because of a reduction in partisanship, but because the Democrats' overwhelming majority makes cross-party cooperation less necessary. Proposition 25, passed in 2010, which removed the requirement for a two-thirds vote on the annual budget, also reduced the need for cross-party cooperation.

Gridlock, Minority Rule, and Lack of Accountability

While California does not have the filibuster that thwarts majority rule in the U.S. Senate, it does have two major checks on effective majority governance. The first is that the legislature and the governor are elected separately and may represent different parties. The second is that a **two-thirds vote** is required to raise taxes, necessitating, in the absence of an overwhelming one-party majority, that the two parties work together to produce realistic fiscal policy.

Perhaps no other provision of governance has contributed more to the dysfunctional state of California and to the **lack of accountability** that characterizes the legislature than the two-thirds vote to raise taxes. Californians may elect a majority in the legislature and even a governor of the same party, but unless that party controls two-thirds of each house, it cannot control fiscal policy. Voters blame the majority party for gridlock when in fact the control rests with the minority party, a political dynamic known as **minority rule**. This provision is even more restrictive than the filibuster, which can only work with 41 percent of the U.S. Senate actively backing it; California fiscal policy is held hostage to a one-third minority sitting on its collective hands, ensuring gridlock. As Peter Schrag describes it:

> More than any other structural flaw, it [the two-thirds rule] diffused accountability and brought on much of the budgetary gridlock that California became notorious for in the 1980s and early 1990s.[10]

This structural flaw has been in place for several decades, and in recent years the minority party has relied on it to refuse to compromise on the most critical issue before the state: the need for adequate and stable sources of revenue. The power of the minority to block taxation measures and the unwillingness of Republicans to vote for any tax increase can lead to harmful gridlock. If this has been less noticeable in recent years, it is partly because of the passage of Proposition 30 in 2012, which temporarily increased taxes and revenues, and partly because of an improving economy. Together, these have reduced the need for new or increased taxes. While the provisions of Proposition 30 expire in 2018, Proposition 55 on the November 2016 ballot extended these tax provisions for 12 years. But at some point, the economy will turn sour and gridlock will return.

Even Governor Jerry Brown, a political moderate, a skilled negotiator, and one of the most experienced individuals to serve as governor of California, was at first unable to find negotiating partners in the legislature's minority leadership. If he were governing amid the political culture of the 1970s, when he first served, he would have been very successful. According to a long-time associate of the governor, Jodie Evans, "He is aghast. He reports on some of his conversations like he couldn't believe the narrowness or lack of comprehending by public officials. . . . He said, 'Some of my old tools are not going to work.'"[11] Brown himself said that the Republicans have a "perverse fidelity to each point in the Republican gospel."[12] These points are reinforced in the party caucuses.

The Republicans, of course, saw it differently. Senator Bob Dutton stated, "He's all talk and no go. He throws a few scraps out there . . . let's demonize the Republicans, and that's supposed to fix a problem?"[13] *Los Angeles Times* columnist George Skelton wrote, "The entire legislative system has been corrupted by Democrats' fear of angering labor unions and Republicans' subservience to a few anti-tax opportunists and entertainers."[14] But while the governor has shown a willingness to oppose the unions (an important Democratic constituency) on pensions and organizing child care workers, the Republicans seem unwilling to agree to increasing revenues.

Change began in 2010 when enacting budgets with a simple majority vote became permitted. Budgetary gridlock tapered off further after the Democrats' overwhelming electoral victory in 2012 and the passage that same year of Proposition 30, which raised taxes and lessened the need for further immediate tax increases. These changes together greatly lessened the need for Republican cooperation for legislative action. Although the Democrats lost their two-thirds margin in the Senate in 2014, because of their overwhelming majorities, they could still largely ignore the minority. However, when Governor Brown decided to put a "rainy day fund" constitutional measure on the ballot for November of 2014 (ACA 4), he needed and—in a rare demonstration of bipartisanship—gained Republican support. Brown also secured bipartisan support for a $7.5 billion water bond for the same election. Both measures passed by healthy margins.

Initiatives

A further complication to effective policy making in California is the initiative, which is often used to bypass the legislative process. If an interest group believes that it can get an initiative proposition with a populist appeal on the ballot, then it has little incentive to submit legislation for careful consideration by committees in each house of the legislature or to engage in legislative bargaining. Taking a page from the interest groups playbook, Governor Brown in 2016 threatened to place an initiative on the ballot if adequate progress was not made on climate change legislation. In spite of his ultimate success passing that legislation, the possibility of an initiative to achieve far-reaching climate control regulations remains.

Moreover, initiatives have passed that have weakened the legislature or weakened the legislature's ability to make responsible policy. Proposition 140, which instituted term limits, greatly weakened the ability of the legislature to function effectively by ensuring that there were rarely any experienced legislators in Sacramento. Propositions 13 (1978) and 98 (1988) each limited legislators' ability to make responsible fiscal policy, the first by limiting the use of a stable tax tool (property taxes), the second by locking up a huge chunk of the available funds for a single purpose—education.

In 2014 modest changes were made to the initiative process through the passage of SB (Senate Bill) 1253, which provided a public review period for initiatives (see Chapter 4). Of most significance to the legislative process is the bill's provision that after 25 percent of the needed signatures for an initiative proposition are obtained, the Senate and Assembly must hold a joint hearing on the issue. These hearings could possibly result in compromise legislation that would make the initiative unnecessary. The process envisioned by SB 1253 worked in 2016 to help get a minimum pay bill passed and signed by the governor after labor unions had started the initiative process. However, that is the only example to date.

We will probably see many more propositions in the future: in 2016 there were 17 (resulting in a voter information guide of over 200 pages). It is easier to sway a majority of the voters than a majority of the legislature, and there are increasingly large amounts of money available to do just that.

Californians have done a lot of damage to effective legislative governance through the initiative process. Voters feel dissatisfied with the legislature and consequently, though not intentionally, pass propositions that result in the legislature working less effectively. That makes voters more dissatisfied, and they vote for more propositions. Since 2008 there has been a modest reversal in this trend and at the moment the state government is functioning more effectively.

California Legislature: Where Are We Now?

The legislature serves two principal functions: policy making and representation. The different requirements of these two functions create tensions. Legislators are also pressured by the needs versus the wants of the district, state versus local interests, and the demands of interest groups, campaign contributors, party leaders, and the governor. California is a large state with many competing wants and needs. Legislative districts are among the largest anywhere. These factors turn policy making into a complex and often unseemly process, a process moved by humans who will always be imperfect. Even before term limits were imposed, the once highly regarded legislature passed some bad legislation and left problems unaddressed.

Yet the legislature could work better than it does. It is valid to ask if the legislature is the creator of or the victim of this impaired system. In large part, problems of inefficacy have been generated by outside forces. Term limits, big money for campaigns and elections, and the two-thirds vote requirement for passing tax legislation are the most notable outside factors. The declining level of civility in the legislature is a reflection of the impact of term limits and of the increasing political polarization in the nation. But individuals are responsible for their own behavior. Regardless of outside forces, individual legislators of goodwill could make a difference.

Since 2008 a series of changes have taken place (mostly via the initiative process, ironically) that appear to have strengthened the legislative process and reduced gridlock, at least for the time being.

- **Proposition 11 (November 2008), Proposition 20 (November 2010), and Proposition 27 (November 2010, defeated)** Proposition 11 took redistricting of the legislature away from the legislature and put it in the hands of a Citizens' Redistricting Commission. It passed by only 50.9 percent of the vote. It was strengthened by the passage (by 61 percent) of Proposition 20, which extended the jurisdiction of the commission to congressional districts, and by the corresponding defeat (by 59.5 percent) of Proposition 27, which would have eliminated the commission. As a result of the commission's redistricting, which took effect in 2012, districts became more evenly balanced, and Democrats gained a two-thirds margin in both legislative houses.

- **Proposition 14 (June 2010)** Proposition 14 created the "top-two" primary system, with the expectation that more moderate legislators would be elected. It is too early to tell if that result was accomplished (and whatever impact this has is overshadowed by the impact of Propositions 11, 20, and 27), but in 19 districts two members of the same party ended up winning the primary election and running against each other in the general election. This kind of primary system offers an opportunity for minority party members to help select the more moderate of the opposing candidates. It also provides an opportunity for big businesses to put a lot of money behind the candidate who is most friendly to their goals, which has resulted in the rise of "business-friendly" Democrats in the legislature.

- **Proposition 25 (November 2010)** The requirement for a two-thirds majority to pass the annual budget was eliminated by this measure. This has substantially reduced the influence of the minority, whose involvement in this fiscal measure was required every year.

- **Proposition 28 (June 2012)** This proposition reduced the term limits in the legislature from 14 to 12 years, but it allowed members to serve all that time in a single house. This allows legislators the opportunity to gain more experience, especially in the Assembly, and presumably to achieve greater knowledge and effectiveness. It is too early to make that judgment.

- **Proposition 30 (November 2012)** Proposition 30 temporarily increased taxes, giving the state greater fiscal stability and reducing the need for the minority party's help in passing tax legislation. Proposition 55 in 2016 extended the tax provisions for 12 years.

The two-thirds Democratic majority did not reappear until 2017. During this off-year election, Republicans were more likely to vote than Democrats were, meaning that some marginal districts switched to the Republicans.

It is too early to make a long-term assessment of the impacts of these propositions on the legislature. The skilled moderate leadership of Governor Brown is an important factor in the current situation. But he will be in office only until 2018. The power of big money and the threat of dominating interests are always there to skew the process.

Given the sour national mood, the diverse nature of the state, and an electorate that is itself divided, positive change cannot be ensured. Moreover, the public has little understanding of legislative functions or of the legislative process, making further positive change through the initiative process unlikely. Draconian measures, such as a part-time legislature, have been suggested. As the cartoonist Walt Kelly's character Pogo said, "We have met the enemy and he is us."

But not always. We should be thankful for the current hiatus in gridlock that has permitted the legislature to address the many issues that face our state.

Study Guide

FOR FURTHER READING

Cain, Bruce E., and Roger G. Noll, eds. *Constitutional Reform in California: Making State Government More Effective and Responsive*. Berkeley: Institute of Governmental Studies Press, 1995.

California Journal and State Net. *Roster and Government Guide*. Sacramento: California Journal, 2004.

de Sá, Karen. "How Our Laws in California Are Really Made." *San Jose Mercury News*, July 10, 2010. www.mercurynews.com/politics-government/ci_15452125. Accessed 8/15/16.

Institute of Governmental Affairs. "IGS Goes to Sacramento to Assess Ten Years of Term Limits." *Public Affairs Reports* 42, no. 3 (Fall 2001).

Mathews, Joe, and Mark Paul. *California Crackup: How Reform Broke the Golden State and How We Can Fix It*. Berkeley: University of California Press, 2010.

Muir, William K., Jr. *Legislature: California's School for Politics*. Chicago: University of Chicago Press, 1982.

Schrag, Peter. *California: America's High-Stakes Experiment*. Berkeley: University of California Press, 2006.

———. *Paradise Lost: California's Experience, America's Future*. New York: New Press, 1998.

Wilson, E. Dotson. *California's Legislature*. Sacramento: Office of the Chief Clerk, California State Assembly, 2016.

ON THE WEB

California Choices. http://californiachoices.org. Accessed 8/16/16.

California Legislative Analyst's Office. www.lao.ca.gov/. Accessed 8/16/16. The LAO is a nonpartisan fiscal and policy adviser to the legislature.

California State Assembly. http://assembly.ca.gov/. Accessed 8/16/16.

California State Assembly Democratic Caucus. www.asmdc.org. Accessed 8/16/16.

California State Assembly Republican Caucus. http://asmrc.org. Accessed 8/16/16.

California State Senate. http://senate.ca.gov/. Accessed 8/16/16.

CALmatters. https://calmatters.org/. Accessed 8/16/16.

Legislative Counsel. www.leginfo.legislature.ca.gov/. Accessed 8/16/16. The Legislative Counsel of California's official site, maintained by law.

Los Angeles Times. "Essential Politics." www.latimes.com/politics/essential/la-pol-sac-essential-politics-updates-1471460386-htmlstory.html. Accessed 8/16/16. A daily news feed on California government and politics.

Rough & Tumble. www.rtumble.com. Accessed 8/16/16. Daily summary of California news.

Sacramento Bee. www.sacbee.com/news/politics-government/. Accessed 8/16/16.

Senate Democrats. http://democrats.senate.ca.gov/. Accessed 8/16/16.

Senate Republicans. http://cssrc.us/. Accessed 8/16/16.

University of California, Berkeley, Institute of Governmental Studies Library. http://igs.berkeley.edu/library. Accessed 8/16/16.

SUMMARY

I. Legislatures are not well understood, but they are critical to a democratic form of government. Indeed, a working legislature is practically the definition of a democratic government.

II. The California legislature is, for the most part, modeled on the U.S. Congress.
   A. It is bicameral.
   B. Members are elected from single-member, geographically based districts.
   C. Unlike the U.S. Congress, both houses of the California legislature are apportioned by population.

III. Legislators must both represent their constituents and make policy.
   A. These two items are not always compatible.
   B. In representing their districts, members must decide whether to follow the wants or the needs of their constituents and whether to follow directions from the district or use their own best judgment.
   C. Poor communication from constituents makes these actions difficult.
   D. Legislators have offices both in Sacramento and in their districts.

IV. Members of both the California Senate and Assembly are elected through a blanket or "top-two" primary followed by a general election. Two key features of California politics influence who gets elected:
   A. Candidates must engage in extensive fund-raising to increase their chances of getting elected.
   B. Redistricting, which follows each census, has a significant impact on who is elected. For example, redistricting by a Citizens Redistricting Commission in 2012 resulted in a Democratic supermajority in the legislature.

V. The leader of the Assembly is the speaker; the leader of the Senate is the president pro tempore.
   A. Each leader is elected by all of the members in that body, but the majority party caucus usually determines the outcome.
   B. The speaker controls most of the resources and is very powerful.
   C. The speaker and the president pro tempore are term limited.
   D. The president pro tempore shares powers with the Senate Rules Committee.

VI. The bulk of legislative work is done in committees.
   A. Bills are read and amended here.
   B. Issue networks are made up of a group of individuals—lobbyists, staffers, members, and bureaucrats—who make and control policy in a given substantive area.

VII. Professional staff members make the legislature possible.
   A. Some of them work in districts, some in members' offices, some for committees, and some for the leadership.
   B. The best-paid staff members are usually subject-matter experts working for committees.

VIII. The legislative process has several steps.
- A. Bills are first introduced by members and sent to committees.
- B. Bills must pass the floors of both houses (with identical wording) before they are sent to the governor for his or her signature.
- C. If the governor vetoes a bill, it takes a two-thirds vote in each house to override it.
- D. Tax bills also require a two-thirds vote, giving the minority party important power in the legislature and making it difficult for the majority party to govern.

IX. The state legislature is different from the U.S. Congress in several ways.
- A. Members are term limited.
- B. The governor has line-item veto power (he can cut or eliminate any item in a budget bill, while still approving the entire bill).
- C. Both houses are apportioned by population.
- D. Very little media attention is given to the California legislature.
- E. The legislature does not have a role in judicial appointments.
- F. The legislature does not have a filibuster, unlike the U.S. Senate. However, the two-thirds requirement for increasing taxes has a similar effect in thwarting the majority.

- G. California also has the initiative process, which allows the legislative process to be bypassed, most often by special-interest groups with deep pockets.

X. The effectiveness of the California legislature is limited
- A. by the power of big money;
- B. by term limits and members' lack of experience;
- C. by intense partisanship;
- D. by the two-thirds-vote rule on taxes, which limits the majority party's decision-making ability and makes accountability difficult; and
- E. by the initiative, which is often used to bypass the legislative process.

XI. Propositions passed since 2008 have reduced gridlock and made the legislature more effective by increasing the size of the majority party and by eliminating the two-thirds vote required for the budget.
- A. Propositions 11 and 20 took districting away from the legislature.
- B. Proposition 14 created the "top-two" primary system.
- C. Proposition 25 removed the two-thirds-vote requirement for passing budgets.
- D. Proposition 28 increased the amount of time that legislators can serve in one house.
- E. Proposition 30 temporarily increased taxes, and therefore state revenues.

PRACTICE QUIZ

1. A line-item veto allows
   - a) the governor to reject any single item in an appropriations or budget bill.
   - b) the speaker or the president pro tempore to pull any single item from the agenda.
   - c) a single member to block a single piece of legislation by signing a written objection.
   - d) a petition by a group of 10 legislators to block any single piece of legislation.

2. Proposition 140
   - a) limits the time that legislators can serve in Sacramento.
   - b) limits the legislature from raising property taxes.
   - c) sets aside 40 percent of the budget for education purposes.
   - d) requires the speaker to assign staff to the minority party.

3. The legislature is composed of
   - a) 80 members in the Senate and 40 in the Assembly.
   - b) 120 members in a single body.
   - c) 60 members in each body.
   - d) 80 members in the Assembly and 40 in the Senate.

4. A two-thirds vote is needed to pass
   - a) appropriation bills.
   - b) budget bills.
   - c) tax bills.
   - d) all of the above.

5. Partisanship in the legislature
   - a) has declined because of apportionment.
   - b) has declined because of the blanket primary now in effect.
   - c) has led to greater ease in getting budgets improved.
   - d) has increased in recent years.

6. The powers of the speaker of the California Assembly include all of the following *except*
   a) the power to assign parking spaces.
   b) the power to assign office space.
   c) the power to assign members to committees but not to remove them during the current term.
   d) the power to assign a member to a committee against both the member's wishes and the wishes and needs of his or her constituency.

7. Proposition 140 resulted in all of the following *except*
   a) an increase in office budgets.
   b) the establishment of term limits.
   c) a reduction of committee staff and personal staff.
   d) layoffs of some of the most knowledgeable staff experts from committees.

8. The legislative process is biased in favor of
   a) issues favored by the public.
   b) the status quo.
   c) change that interest groups favor.
   d) legislation proposed by the governor, who can introduce a limited number of bills directly to both houses, bypassing some of the steps of the legislative process.

9. California has some of the largest legislative districts in the nation. This means that
   a) elections in California tend to be expensive.
   b) citizen access to legislators is unusually good because legislators need to face the voters so often.
   c) Legislators appear in the media more often because they represent so many people.
   d) California has an unusually large number of legislators.

10. Term limits have resulted in which of the following:
   a) an increase in expertise among legislators, who have only a few years to make a name for themselves.
   b) an increase in citizen legislators, people with little or no political experience who are able to run because seats are open.
   c) an increase in staff members, who are needed to help legislators with little experience.
   d) a decline in the knowledge needed to pass good-quality legislation.

CRITICAL-THINKING QUESTIONS

1. Should a legislator vote for what his or her constituents want or what his or her constituents need?
2. Who should apportion the legislature?
3. What criteria should be used to apportion a legislature?
4. Should a legislator take orders from constituents or use his or her own best judgment, even if it is unpopular?
5. How much access should lobbyists have to legislators?
6. When should a legislature have rules that allow a minority to block legislation?

KEY TERMS

apportionment (p. 137)
Assembly Rules Committee (p. 130)
bicameralism (p. 121)
committees (p. 131)
constituents (p. 122)
gerrymander (p. 127)
gridlock (p. 136)

"gut and amend" (p. 134)
issue networks (p. 131)
lack of accountability (p. 142)
line-item veto (p. 136)
logrolling (p. 134)
minority rule (p. 142)
partisanship (p. 141)

president pro tempore (p. 130)
Proposition 140/term limits (p. 121)
representation (p. 121)
speaker (p. 129)
staff (p. 131)
two-thirds vote (p. 142)
winner-take-all (p. 126)

6

The Governor and the Executive Branch

WHAT CALIFORNIA GOVERNMENT DOES AND WHY IT MATTERS

Consider the following activities that recently took place in the executive branch of our state government:

- Following a mass killing in San Bernardino, Governor Jerry Brown signed six gun control bills into law and vetoed five others.

- Governor Brown's administration initiated an investigation of Caltrans after receiving reports of shoddy work on a segment of the Bay Bridge and learning that Caltrans had transferred or ended the contracts of the "whistle-blowing" project managers.

- In spite of declining public support and opposition within his own party, Governor Brown continued to pursue his vision of building a high-speed rail line connecting Los Angeles and San Francisco.

- Governor Brown, who has a reputation for being tightfisted, in 2012 helped convince overwhelming numbers of voters to approve Proposition 30, an initiative raising taxes for five years, by personally campaigning up and down the state.

- After twice vetoing similar bills, the governor signed into law a bill requiring motorists to give bicyclists three feet of clearance when passing from behind.

- Caltrans decided to replace high-occupancy vehicle lanes with toll lanes on an Orange County "freeway" over the objections of local governments and agencies.

- Through tough bargaining, Attorney General Kamala Harris negotiated a better settlement for California homeowners from a group of banks charged with foreclosure abuse than other states' attorneys general were able to achieve.

If you think you know little about the executive branch of California, you are not alone. The media rarely pay much attention to state government, and in 2013 the last out-of-town TV bureau in Sacramento closed. California government operates largely out of the public view. The governor's reputation is based mainly on his interactions with the legislature, which are often public and may be contentious—and therefore newsworthy. Barring major scandal, the governor's actions as the executive head of a huge bureaucracy are off the press's radar. Few reporters would be able to locate Caltrans or the Natural Resources Agency either physically or on an organization chart. Most of California's 200,000-plus state employees are known to the public only as friends and neighbors.

When Governor Brown came into office in 2011, it was not uncommon to hear that the state was "ungovernable." Now, government is said to be working well, and many credit Brown's widely acknowledged political skills with helping to increase the state's productivity. However, the government's recent successes are not only a result of Brown's abilities but also because of the overwhelming Democratic majorities in the California legislature. Recent changes in the state constitution that have made it possible to pass budgets on a majority vote have made a difference as well. When Brown had to deal with a larger Republican minority in the legislature, he was less successful.

If California government is viewed positively at this time, much of the credit is due to the party profile of the legislature, the temporary tax increases, and an improving economy. The governor, who is often the victim of circumstances and blamed when things go wrong, can also be the beneficiary of better times.

The Invisible Governor?

While the governor is the most visible political figure in the state, his visibility pales in comparison to that of the president of the United States. There are a number of reasons for this lack of visibility. We depend on the media for most of what we know about our government, and for the most part the media in California are not interested in state politics or governance. The media, after all, are a business, responding to the desires of their consumers and advertisers. For many Californians, and thus for the media, Sacramento does not capture much attention; it is a long way from the major population centers of the state, and what happens there just does not captivate an audience the way a good car chase does. The media have found that their business model works best by focusing on well-known or riveting personalities, and Governor Brown—who does not court the media—is often perceived as boring. With the exception of U.S. senators, long-serving, high-visibility politicians are rare in California's term-limited government. Media-wise, what happens in Sacramento stays in Sacramento.

The president's job is divided analytically into two roles: **head of government** and **head of state**. So, too, is the governor's job, but while the head-of-government

After winning re-election in 2014, Governor Jerry Brown addresses the media outside the Old Governor's Mansion State Historic Park accompanied by his wife, Anne Gust Brown, who is considered top aide to the governor.

role is similar for both leaders, the head-of-state role is vastly different. It is that role that gives the president the most visibility.

The role of the head of government is to govern—that is, to develop policy, get it passed through the legislature, and implemented via the bureaucracy. The governor's approach to these various tasks is often divisive. For example, think of the prime minister of Great Britain, who not only develops policy, gets it passed, and implemented, but actually appears on the floor of Parliament to answer questions, often shouted, from his or her own and opposition parties. In contrast, the queen is the head of state in Great Britain. Her role is highly visible, ceremonial, and important for bringing people together. She cuts ribbons, attends public events, greets foreign visitors, rides in parades, and goes on foreign tours to promote British businesses. In fact, this is her major role. Most of the time when you see the president between campaigns, it is in the role of head of state: welcoming the troops home, attending funerals, dedicating buildings, posing for pictures with foreign dignitaries, consoling victims of tornados or hurricanes, and making major or minor public announcements. Being head of state is largely a symbolic, positive, and noncontroversial role offering lots of photo ops for the media. In this role the president represents the entire nation, acting for all of us.

The governor does not have this range of opportunities for public visibility, and often the events are so insignificant that not many people care. Few dignitaries of note visit Sacramento, and the media simply do not warm to filming the governor talking to teachers or highway patrol officers. Because he was a showman able to generate his own buzz, Governor Arnold Schwarzenegger made as much as he could of the head-of-state role; Governor Brown simply has no interest in it. Indeed, Governor Brown offered the following advice to President Obama: "Minimize the fanfare and speechifying. Speaking a lot doesn't produce a lot."[1] Nothing else so clearly characterizes the difference between the chief executive of the United States and the chief executive of one of the most important states in the union as this difference in visibility.

There are important similarities between the two positions as well; most notably, both are offices with limited powers, as hard as it is for the public to understand that the most powerful political leader of the most powerful nation on earth is restricted in his or her authority. And no matter how important a state, California is not run by the governor any more than the president runs the nation. Our nation's founders feared a strong executive, having experienced such rule under a king and under capricious colonial governors. Consequently, they created a system in which the powers of all institutions were strictly limited, and in which the powers of the executive were secondary to those of the legislature.

The governor does have important **formal powers**, in some cases more than the president, but, according to Richard Neustadt, as with the president, the governor's power is mostly the power to persuade.[2] The governor's power to command and direct in any way he or she chooses is seriously limited, something that Donald Trump does not seem to understand.

As with the president, people have many incomplete, incorrect, and conflicting views about the governor. Tom Cronin and Michael Genovese compiled a list of what they call the paradoxes of the presidency:

- We want the president to be an effective politician while being above politics.

- We want the president to be a common person and an extraordinary person at the same time.

- We want the president to be powerful but not too powerful.[3]

In sum, we want the president to be all things at all times, and, of course, this is not possible.

The governor is not burdened with as much symbolic baggage as the president, yet many misperceptions carry over to this office as well. These misperceptions are amplified by the fact that people think that they understand the office. After all, it is an executive office, a position with which all of us who work in organizations have some familiarity. But the governorship is a *political* executive office, in an organization that often does not have a single, identifiable chain of command and which does not respond well, if at all, to direct orders.

Our greatest misperception is attributing more power to the governor than he or she has. The governor does not control the legislature and has trouble making policy without the cooperation, or at least acquiescence, of legislators who may have little reason to support the governor. He or she can win legislative cooperation only through persuasion—perhaps hardball persuasion, but persuasion nonetheless.

Within the executive branch, it is possible for the governor to exert influence more directly. But the executive branch is large and in many cases very remote from the governor. How does the governor get a Caltrans engineer in San Diego or a park ranger in Marin County to follow his wishes? Equally problematic is the insulation of much of the executive branch from direct gubernatorial influence. The executive branch includes several independently elected executives known collectively as the plural executive, who may be from the opposing party of the governor, and who are all focused on their own political ambitions. Some organizations, such as the University of California, are governed by boards that can be influenced only by appointments, budgetary threats, or strongly voiced public opinion.

Moreover, we often elect governors who are not especially knowledgeable about government agencies, Sacramento politics, or the many interests in our large and diverse state. For example, Arnold Schwarzenegger held no political office before being elected governor, and the unsuccessful 2010 Republican candidate for governor, Meg Whitman, did not even vote for many years. More important than formal powers are political skills and an ability to bargain, a long political memory, and friends and allies in important positions. A good economy, an absence of natural disasters, and luck can also be important.

Schwarzenegger's initial popularity was rare in California politics, even exceeding the popularity of Ronald Reagan. By sheer dint of personality and the threat to go to the public with initiatives, he managed a series of impressive victories in the early days of his tenure. His success did not last, however. He overreached himself, and he antagonized the members of his own party with his moderate positions on many issues. His attempt to pass four initiatives in a special—and costly—election in November 2005 was a disaster. Near the end of his time in office, his approval ratings had reached a low of 23 percent in a Public Policy Institute of California (PPIC) poll.[4]

Jerry Brown is the polar opposite of Arnold Schwarzenegger. He is one of the most knowledgeable governors that California has ever had. He loves the details of policy making, knows the intricacies of governing, and does not crave or need the limelight. He knows how to bargain and make deals. In 2011, at the start of his third term, he was faced with a bad economy, huge revenue shortfalls, and an opposition party that would not bargain on revenue issues. But things turned around with the emergence of favorable political and economic situations. Republican opposition became less important after new redistricting and primary laws provided the Democrats with overwhelming majorities in both houses of the legislature. Along with the improved economy and the passage of tax-raising Proposition 30—thanks in large part to the governor's political acumen and skills—and the earlier elimination of the two-thirds vote requirement for approving budgets, governing suddenly became much easier. In a PPIC poll during May of 2016, 52 percent of California adults approved of the job he was doing.[5]

Formal Powers of the Governor

The formal powers of the governor, while limited, are still significant. The governor has powers—the most important of which is the **line-item veto**—that are denied to the president. The true value of these powers, however, is as vantage points on which the governor bases his or her **informal powers**, or powers to persuade. (See Box 6.1 for a summary of the governor's formal and informal powers.) A governor who expects to use only formal powers to govern will not accomplish much. Those powers must be leveraged to persuade other political actors to support the governor's goals. For instance, using the power of appointment, the governor can try to persuade an important legislator to support the budget by promising to appoint one of the legislator's supporters to an important state commission.

The state constitution vests supreme executive power in the governor, a phrase that conveys both more and less than it seems. Less, because the governor's office is

> ### BOX 6.1 ● Powers of the Governor
>
> The governor has important formal and informal powers, which include the following:
>
> #### FORMAL POWERS
>
> Organizing and managing the executive branch, including appointing many top executives
>
> Taking independent executive actions
>
> Serving as commander in chief of the National Guard
>
> Appointing people to executive agencies, to independent boards and commissions, and to the judiciary
>
> Drawing up the budget
>
> Making legislative recommendations
>
> Vetoing legislation
>
> Employing line-item vetoes of budget and appropriation items
>
> Granting of clemency, including pardons and reprieves
>
> #### INFORMAL POWERS
>
> Bargaining with legislators and other independent power sources
>
> Having access to the public to make his or her case
>
> Developing a vision or an agenda for the state
>
> Raising money for political campaigns

an office of limited powers in which nothing is supreme. More, because executives often push established constitutional limits. However, given a supportive legislature that views most executive requests positively—as is true currently—most of the executive's goals can be reached.

Appointments

Making appointments is one of the governor's most significant powers. The governor appoints four distinct groups of individuals: **personal staff**, heads of major administrative divisions, some judges, and members of a number of **boards and commissions**. Some of these appointments require confirmation by other bodies, while others do not. Some appointees work at the governor's pleasure, while others serve for fixed terms. Some answer directly to the governor, but others are several steps removed or protected from executive intervention. Over the course of an administration, a governor can make more than 2,500 appointments, including about 500 positions that will be filled at the start of the term.

The governor's personal staff consists of about 100 individuals who craft policy recommendations, work with the legislature, or handle all the details to make the governor's life run smoothly, including providing structure, and packaging and presenting him or her to the public. Governors hire, fire, and move these individuals about at will. No confirmation is required.

Next closest to the governor are the members of the **cabinet**. The governor determines who will serve in the cabinet and what role, if any, the cabinet will play in policy development. The heads of the **superagencies** of state government (large organizations similar to federal departments, which contain a number of related bureaus and agencies) are in the cabinet, as are the director of finance and others whose presence the governor finds useful and appropriate. These positions require confirmation by the Senate, but the governor has the ability to remove them at will.

The governor also appoints the heads of the major bureaus or departments, which are mostly located within the superagencies. These individuals have the responsibility of overseeing the organizations and the more than 200,000 state employees that do the real work of government.

In addition, the governor appoints members to more than 325 boards and commissions, important and unimportant, visible and invisible. Once appointed, individuals do not have to answer to the governor, although the governor can apply political pressure, including threatening to cut the budget of the institution that the individuals administer.

Stating that "the state's bureaucracy is a labyrinth of disjointed boards, commissions, agencies and departments,"[6] Governor Brown in 2012 proposed a restructuring and consolidation of agencies, having eliminated 25 boards and commissions the previous year. There was no political payoff in this. Few outside of the government would notice. Not surprisingly, little came of this proposal.

Independent Executive Actions

The governor's powers are constitutionally restricted by the legislature, but in some cases he or she is able to act independently of it. Independent executive actions are permitted by the constitution or under laws passed by the legislature. They are most significant in times of an emergency.

Few laws passed by the legislature are self-implementing; most require positive action on the part of the administration. This process of implementation involves clarification of the law (e.g., what does the language used by the legislature imply?) and the assembling of finances and an administrative structure to allow action to take place. All of this requires prioritization and fund requests by the governor's appointees or the governor. This allows the governor considerable influence: using the line-item veto or failing to request adequate funds, for example, can effectively kill a program. Governor Brown has used these powers several times, in one instance eliminating both the California Postsecondary Education Commission and the duplicative office of the secretary of education, neither of which he found useful.

Commander in Chief

The governor is the commander in chief of the California National Guard. This role is of little significance until times of civil disorder or natural disaster, when the governor has the power to call out the guard, though not to direct its actions.

Organizing and Managing the Executive Branch

The governor is empowered to organize and manage the executive branch. *Organize* means that he or she can make a number of administrative appointments. *Manage* means that many of these appointees must report to the governor, at least indirectly, and the governor can remove them from office. Again, the limits of this power should be recognized.

First, the functions of the state government are not boundless. Much of the money that it collects is passed on to local government and school districts to spend.

Second, the rest of the elected executive branch, most notably the attorney general, limits the governor's actions, and some state employees report to these elected officials—over 4,500 report to the attorney general alone.

Third, some of the appointments made by the governor are to boards that can, and do, act independently of the governor. These appointments may be for fixed terms. The best known of these independent boards is the Regents of the University of California. This 26-member board consists of 7 ex officio members (members, including the governor, who sit on the board because they occupy another office), one student, and 18 members appointed by the governor for 12-year terms—terms that are longer than the governor's. Control over this board, if the governor wishes to exert it, is possible only through new appointments, the loyalty of previously appointed members, persuasion (including threats to cut the budget), and, in extreme cases, working with the legislature to restructure the body.

Fourth, the governor must make appointments to agencies about which he knows little, often appointing individuals about whom he knows little. Information coming out of these agencies is limited, so the governor is often in the dark about what is happening until something goes terribly wrong and it appears in the press.

The controversy over Caltrans' management of the rebuilding of the eastern span of the Bay Bridge provides a case in point. In 2006, Caltrans, perhaps the most visible of California's government agencies, hired a Chinese company with limited bridge-building experience to build key elements of the new span. According to the *Sacramento Bee*, numerous flaws and cost overruns followed, leading to questions of whether the bridge will meet its planned 150-year lifespan. The governor's public stance was that "stuff happens" (or words to that effect), but his administration initiated investigations, legislative and external, into the entire operation and culture of Caltrans. Were it not for aggressive reporting on the issue by California newspapers in the north of the state, the governor might never have acted to address long-standing issues within Caltrans.[7]

Intense public scrutiny over actions (or inactions) by the California Public Utilities Commission (CPUC) also led to a flurry of activity by the governor and the legislature (the governor appoints all five members of the CPUC). The handling of the Aliso Canyon (Porter Ranch) gas leak, the San Bruno gas pipeline explosion, and the closure of the San Onofre nuclear power plant with the ratepayers picking up most of the cost were all major scandals. In the latter case, the chair of the CPUC—a former Edison president—had an ex parte (secret) meeting with top Edison executives in Warsaw during which a settlement favorable to the utility was discussed. Subsequently, Edison donated $25 million to a program at UCLA favored by the chair. This meeting remained secret until the state Justice Department raided the chair's home on another matter.

After vetoing bills in 2015 to restructure the CPUC and to prohibit ex parte meetings, the governor worked with the legislature in an attempt to to pass legislation in 2016.[8] Ultimately, that effort failed, but due to the attention of the media, the State Auditors Office, and interest groups, this issue remains alive and will be addressed again.

Also, ex parte meetings between developers and members of the California Coastal Commission (the governor shares appointments with the legislature to the 12-member board) and the firing of its well-regarded executive director by more developmentally inclined commissioners drew intense public scrutiny that led to proposed—but as of yet unsuccessful—legislation that would limit such meetings.[9] The issue remains alive in the courts and media. Not only will the governor and the legislature ultimately have to deal with the ex parte issue, it will also be a factor in future appointments to the commission.

Budget

Perhaps the governor's most significant power is that of preparing the budget, coupled with the power to exercise a line-item veto of budget provisions. At the federal level, the president presents Congress with a budget proposal—but it is only a proposal; the House of Representatives has constitutional authority over fiscal matters. The California Constitution gives the power of preparing the budget to the governor. This means that all budget requests from executive branch agencies must pass through the governor. It is at this point that the governor has life-and-death power over a program and can have a critical impact on the policy that a program implements. The actual work on this process of preparing the budget is done by the Department of Finance.

The budget is prepared and sent to the legislature by January 10, with revisions following later in the spring (called the May Revise) as the financial picture becomes clearer. The governor shares the job of getting the budget approved by the legislature. Until the 2011–12 budget, a supermajority of two-thirds was required to approve a budget, and impasses and late budgets were common, while marginal votes were rounded up. Now only a simple majority in both houses of the legislature is needed and budgets come in on time.

Although a supermajority vote is no longer needed to pass a budget, it is still required to raise new revenues. Because budgets may not have adequate revenues, in the absence of a supermajority, the support of the minority party can be important, requiring expensive trade-offs with recalcitrant legislators who withhold their support until they receive an offer they cannot refuse. There are, in effect, five major players in the budget game: the governor and the leaders of both parties in both houses of the legislature. Because of his or her role at both ends of the budgetary process, and because one person needs to broker the deal, the governor usually has the key role. But even the governor can be held hostage by stubborn legislators. Although in recent years Republican legislators have been adamant in opposing any and all tax increases, the passage of the tax-raising Proposition 30 along with the improving economy has marginalized their influence. While neither the Republican Schwarzenegger nor the Democrat Brown has been able to persuade the two parties to work together to shape revenue legislation, the Democratic majorities in the legislature make bipartisan cooperation largely unnecessary at present. Proposition 30 expires in 2018, but an extension on the 2016 ballot (Proposition 55) successfully extended the tax provisions for 12 years.

Veto and Line-Item Veto

The second most significant power of the governor is the **veto**. Just as in Congress, all bills passed by the legislature can be vetoed by the governor. The legislature passes about 1,000 bills each year, and, since 1967, the governor has vetoed 13 percent of them on average. Governor Schwarzenegger vetoed about 26 percent of the bills that came to him, while Governor Brown from 2011 to 2015 vetoed 12.9 percent of the bills sent to him (from 1975 to 1982 he vetoed only 4.63 percent).[10]

The veto can be overridden by a two-thirds majority of each house of the legislature, but that has happened only seven times since 1946 (and four of those were against Jerry Brown in the 1970s). The most recent veto override attempt was on a 2012 bill that would have permitted local governments to take over the management of some state parks to keep them open during the fiscal crisis.

Equally important, and unlike the president, the governor has a line-item veto, which permits him or her to reduce or delete any appropriation in a spending bill. Consequently, legislators cannot force the governor to accept funding for a program that he or she does not like by burying it inside a large spending bill that the governor must sign. The governor cannot add items, but the ability to reduce or eliminate the favorite programs of legislators is a powerful tool. It is a key item in the governor's box of bargaining tools, and one that no other player has (although it is impossible to tell how often governors use it).

In recent years line-item vetoes have been minor, often correcting technical errors. However, they have also been used to kill programs that the governor feels are unnecessary or ineffective, such as Brown's 2011 veto of funding for the California Postsecondary Education Commission, a body that provided policy advice to the governor on the three branches of higher education. In the state budget for 2014–15, Governor Brown used the line-item veto only 10 times for cuts totaling $37.9 million (out of a budget of $156 billion).[11] Large majorities in the legislative houses that support the governor make the line-item veto less necessary, and in 2016, for the first time in over three decades, the line item veto was not used.

Legislative Powers

Much of the governor's success depends on having the ability to persuade the legislature to go along with specific programs. This is a difficult task because legislators owe little to the governor, who does not help elect them. Legislators represent smaller and different constituencies and often look out for local rather than statewide issues. They are on different career paths with different time constraints. Because they are term limited, they are relatively inexperienced in bargaining and do not have a long-term commitment to the Sacramento governing process. Their next jobs may be in the private sector, perhaps as lobbyists. If so, they may be more interested in pleasing potential employers (special interests) than in cooperating with the governor.

The governor's ability to persuade legislators depends on political skill as well as many factors beyond his control, including the partisan makeup of the legislature and the political and economic environment. Although much of this influence depends on informal and other formal powers, the governor does have several specific powers that are directed primarily toward influencing the legislature; these include preparing the budget, vetoing bills or provisions of bills, and making legislative recommendations.

Rather than twisting arms to get legislators to support his programs, Governor Brown is in the enviable—and nearly unique—position of having to persuade the Democratic legislature not to overreach and antagonize the electorate by passing too much legislation, spending too much money, or attempting to raise taxes.[12] However on some issues, especially the complex one of climate control, he has at times run into resistance from a group of "moderate" or "business-friendly"—some say "petroleum-friendly"—Democrats, especially in the Assembly. In 2015 they were able to gut his climate control bill, which would have reduced oil use by 50 percent by the year 2030; but in 2016 through astute politicking, the governor and the Democratic leadership made a successful comeback, persuading 17 Assembly members to change their votes (some agreed to the change only when the outcome was not in doubt) from the previous year.[13] As *Los Angeles Times* columnist George Skelton has pointed out, "Dominant Democrats in Sacramento hang together more often than not . . . ."[14] Still, this group is an emerging third force in the legislature (see Chapter 5).

Legislative Recommendations

At the beginning of a legislative session, as required by the constitution, the governor presents a State of the State speech to the legislature. This speech may be short or long, general or specific. It is normally not covered in detail by the media, unlike the president's State of the Union speech. Whether or not the State of the State contains the governor's legislative program, most governors have such a program, which addresses the state's problems as they see them and which they hope to get passed through the legislature.

The governor cannot introduce legislation but has allies who will introduce specific proposals. As the most prominent political figure in the state, the governor is in a position to press for action on these proposals. Success once again depends on a variety of factors, including his or her political skills. Because of his star power, Governor Schwarzenegger had greater access to the public through the media and, more than most governors, could bring outside pressure to bear on the legislature through public appearances. But Schwarzenegger's governorship is widely considered to have been filled with wasted opportunities, partly because of his support for ill-advised initiatives. Jerry Brown prefers to work on the inside, using his significant personal political skills. But he too needed public support for tax increases, and his successful public appearances to lobby for Proposition 30 may have had more impact simply because previously they had been so rare. Former state librarian Kevin Starr feels that the governor's reputation is enhanced by "everything he chooses not to say"—by staying, for the most part, out of the press.[15]

Judicial Powers

The governor has the power to grant pardons and commute or shorten sentences for state crimes. He can also reverse parole decisions or delay a death sentence. While these are significant powers, governors tend to use them with extreme care and caution, because appearing "soft on crime" can have serious political consequences. Among other judicial powers of the governor is the power to nominate justices to the Supreme and appellate courts, as well as the power to appoint other judges if positions are opened by retirement or resignation.

Public Roles of the Governor

While the governor's role as head of state does not provide as much access to the public as the president enjoys, the governor still is occasionally seen cutting a ribbon, bestowing an honor upon some citizen, leading an international trade delegation or, most often, signing a bill into law. These and other ceremonial and symbolic appearances may have little policy content, but they keep the governor in the public eye. Because of his—and the state's—longtime leadership on global warming, Jerry Brown received notable attention in Paris when he attended the important 2015 UN Conference on Climate Control.

While far less visible than the president, governors do not underestimate these appearances, which remind people that the governor is on the job and cares about their concerns, and that, in case of a disaster, the governor and the resources of the state will be available.

Occasionally issues arise of such overwhelming importance—the budget crises are prime examples—that the media are willing to give the governor significant air time. On other occasions the governor can stage policy-related events, such as showing up at a school to emphasize his education policies (or to mask opposition to certain education policies). Finally, disasters such as earthquakes, droughts, and fires require the governor to be publically active, and during these crises the media will broadcast every statement he or she makes.

The governor also moves into the public spotlight during elections, and not only when campaigning for re-election. California governors often think they have a chance to become president, considering that governors of far less populous or attention-getting states have been elected. When governors sense a chance for the presidency, they try to get into the national media as much as possible. Jerry Brown ran for president twice during his first two terms in office (and once afterward), to the detriment of his performance as governor.

Governors also campaign for political allies, including candidates for president or loyal legislators, although their influence in the latter cases is probably marginal at best. Additionally, they may take an active role in an initiative or referendum campaign, either to bolster the chances of an initiative that they support or to gain more public attention. In spite of his mixed success in this arena, Governor Schwarzenegger continued to be involved right through the elections of 2010, endorsing the successful Proposition 14 in June of that year and leading the successful effort in November to defeat Proposition 23, which would have suspended an air pollution control law (AB 32). Governor Brown's campaign for Proposition 30, which greatly enhanced his political reputation and helped put the state on a firmer financial footing, provides a critically important recent example. In 2014, Governor Brown also campaigned vigorously and successfully for Proposition 1, the water bond, and Proposition 2, the Rainy Day Budget Stabilization Fund Act. In 2016, Brown campaigned successfully against Proposition 53, which would require a public vote on public works projects of over $2 billion before bonds could be issued. This would make some of Brown's projects—especially the Delta tunnels—difficult to implement. The governor's extensive fund-raising appearances may also receive public attention, which is useful because it shows the opposition that the governor has a formidable war chest and convinces the party faithful that the governor is out there stumping on their behalf.

Jerry Brown as Governor

Jerry Brown is the son of Pat Brown, one of California's most popular governors, who in the 1960s helped develop the education system and infrastructure that made California the envy of the nation. In 1974, seven years after his father left office, Jerry Brown was elected governor for two consecutive terms. He earned a reputation as a fiscal conservative as well as a visionary and bold politician willing to ignore the wishes of his allies. He was also a frequent candidate for the Democratic Party nomination for president (in 1976, 1980, and 1992).

Governor Jerry Brown (center) and his wife, Anne Gust Brown (center right), sign a section of rail during a ground-breaking ceremony in 2015 for the controversial California High-Speed Rail.

As a visionary, Brown was often parodied as "Governor Moonbeam," because he promoted, for example, the establishment of a space academy and the purchase of a communications satellite for the state. His advocacy of fiscal restraints (which reflected his personal lifestyle) did not go over well in a state that still remembered his father, who had presided over an era of seemingly unlimited promise.

After his first two terms of office ended in 1983, Brown, still in his early 40s, was adrift. During the next 16 years, he studied Buddhism, ran for president (again), and chaired the California Democratic Party. In 1999 he reestablished his career as an elected official by starting at the local level as mayor of the economically troubled city of Oakland (1999–2007), and he held the position of attorney general from 2007 to 2011. In the 2010 governor's race, voters had the opportunity to select between Brown, an experienced if unpredictable Democratic politician, and Meg Whitman, a billionaire Republican Internet entrepreneur. The voters chose political experience over business acumen. Whitman had little political experience but a lot of money, and her self-financed campaign was the most expensive in California history. Brown spent far less and won by emphasizing his political experience and ability to work with the opposition Republicans.

Jerry Brown's predecessor in office, Arnold Schwarzenegger, was elected in the October 2003 recall of Governor Gray Davis. Davis was recalled partly because of the state's inadequate response to a manipulated energy crisis, legislative budgetary stalemates, fund-raising scandals, and his own remoteness. Hoping for change, the voters turned to the inexperienced but flamboyant movie actor who stood out in a weak field of possible replacements.

Most of Schwarzenegger's years in office were characterized by extreme state budget deficits that the governor and legislature were unable to close on a long-term basis. There were annual standoffs lasting for months with Republicans unwilling to raise taxes and revenues under any circumstances (a two-thirds vote was needed for a budget or for tax increases). In the end, the Schwarzenegger governorship failed to resolve the crises in California politics.

Although Brown is perhaps the most experienced non-incumbent to be elected governor of California, his first years in office were not easy. From his predecessor, Brown inherited a budget deficit of $25 billion as well as an established pattern of constructing budgets largely with smoke and mirrors. His greatest early accomplishments were initiating the process of cutting the structural deficit while offering budgets that were far more honest than those of recent years. He had to do this with no support from Republican legislators, and he was forced to make deep cuts in popular government programs, including cuts to higher education, which angered many Democrats.

By late 2012, Brown had cut 5,500 positions from government, convinced the e-commerce web site Amazon to pay state sales tax, "realigned" many services back to the local level, and eliminated local redevelopment agencies. Former Senate president pro tempore John Burton concluded that Brown "did as good as he could do with the cards that were dealt him."[16]

In the 2012 election Brown was dealt a decidedly better hand. The election resulted in the passage of the tax-raising Proposition 30 and overwhelming Democratic majorities in both legislative houses. Along with an improved economy and the elimination of the supermajority vote requirement for passing a budget, these results set a far more positive tone for state politics. Overnight, gridlock became a thing of the past; rather than encouraging the legislature to act, the governor had to caution Democrats about overreaching—advice that they appeared to take to heart. Journalists who a few years before had viewed California as a disaster area began talking about Jerry Brown's "political reboot," "turnaround," and "revenge."[17] He has been described as "the most interesting politician in America";[18] indeed he is an unusual combination of the intellectual and the practical. If he were younger he would have been a strong contender for the Democratic nomination for president in 2016. He remains a strong supporter of such future-oriented programs as building a high-speed rail and making California a leader in green energy and technology.

But California's problems, especially the fiscal problems, have not disappeared. While Brown engineered a change from a $25 billion budget deficit to a $4.5 billion surplus, the Proposition 30 tax increase is temporary. Although Proposition 55 in 2016 extended the tax provisions for 12 years, substantial long-term debts remain, along with vexing issues concerning water, transportation, income inequality, climate change, and infrastructure deficiencies. Because the California Constitution still requires a two-thirds vote on tax measures, the minority party has a veto so long as the majority does not enjoy a supermajority; without the minority's support, approving the increased revenues needed for significant infrastructure repairs or creating an adequate and stable source of revenue will not happen. Moreover, there are times when a coalition of Republicans and "moderate" Democrats will thwart attempts to pass environmental legislation or to regulate businesses and developers, as they did in 2015 when, in response to heavy lobbying by oil companies, they killed a provision that would have reduced gasoline use by 50 percent by 2030. The oil companies spent $10 million in that successful effort, only to fail in a similar effort the following year. No single individual is to blame for the long-standing political stalemate in California, and no single individual, not even Jerry Brown, can take credit for the current positive situation. However, the highly unusual supermajorities that the Democrats gained in 2012 and 2016, in addition to the large majorities which they enjoyed in the years in between, have made a difference. These legislators generally support the governor's program and pass bills that he is happy to sign.

How Does California's Governorship Compare?

The powers of the governorship vary considerably from state to state. In California, governors can serve a total of two four-year terms. They have full budget-making power as well as the power to veto line items in appropriations bills. How do the powers of California's governor compare to the powers of governorships in other states?

	Unlimited terms	Budget-making power	Line-item veto
AK		✔	✔
AL		✔*	✔
AR		✔	✔
AZ		✔*	✔
▶ CA		✔*	✔
CO		✔	✔
CT	✔	✔	✔
DE		✔*	✔
FL		✔	✔
GA		✔	✔
HI		✔	✔
IA	✔	✔	✔
ID	✔	✔	✔
IL	✔	✔	✔
IN		✔	
KS		✔	✔
KY		✔*	✔
LA		✔	✔
MA	✔	✔	✔
MD		✔	✔
ME		✔	✔
MI		✔	✔
MN	✔	✔	✔
MO		✔*	✔
MS		✔	✔

	Unlimited terms	Budget-making power	Line-item veto
MT		✔	✔
NC		✔	✔
ND	✔	✔	✔
NE		✔	✔
NH	✔	✔*	✔
NJ		✔*	✔
NM		✔	✔
NV		✔	
NY	✔	✔	✔
OH		✔	✔
OK		✔	✔
OR		✔	✔
PA		✔	✔
RI		✔	
SC		✔	✔
SD		✔	✔
TN		✔	✔
TX	✔	✔	✔
UT	✔	✔	✔
VA		✔	✔
VT	✔	✔	
WA	✔	✔	✔
WI	✔	✔*	✔
WV		✔	✔
WY		✔	✔

Key

Unlimited terms
✔ Yes

Budget-making power
✔ Full   ✔ Shared

Line-item veto
✔ Yes   ✔ Appropriations bills only

*Governor proposes budget; legislature amends; governor then signs or vetoes.

SOURCE: *Book of the States*, 2015 edition, vol. 47 (Lexington, KY: Council of State Governments, 2015).

forcriticalanalysis

1. What are the advantages or disadvantages of having term limits? What effect might a term limit have on a governor's actions?

2. What are the advantages or disadvantages of having a governor with full versus shared budget-making power? What about the ability to veto line items?

The popularity of both the governor and the legislature remain high, and the possibility of an electoral backlash is remote. As long as this continues, Governor Brown will be successful.

See the "Who Are Californians?" feature on the previous page for more information on how California's governorship compares to other states'.

Structure of the Executive Branch

The executive branch of California has several significant divisions: the governor's personal staff; the appointed cabinet and other department heads; the other elected officials of the executive branch (the plural executive); the appointed boards and commissions; and the more than 300,000 state employees (including those in state universities), who are divided into more than 85 agencies and 30 educational institutions. Not all of these agencies and employees are under the control of the governor. Figure 6.1 provides a graphic representation of the executive branch.

Personal Staff

Closest to the governor is the personal staff. The members of this staff include schedulers, speechwriters, and press officers. In addition, some staff members oversee the appointment process and the general development of policy, and act as liaisons with the legislature. They structure the governor's day, develop statements for the press and the public, arrange relations with various groups, and set up appearances throughout the state. Members of this staff tend to be young and transient and are expendable. Their positions depend on staying in the governor's good graces.

Governor Brown, preferring a flatter administrative structure, has not appointed a chief of staff. His principal (unpaid) aide, with the title "special counsel," is his wife, Anne Gust Brown, a former lawyer with Gap, Inc. She is credited with having strong political and personal skills and with softening many of the rough edges that Brown demonstrated during his first stint as governor in the 1970s. She has even been suggested as a possible successor to Governor Brown.[19]

The Cabinet and Agency Heads

The governor uses the cabinet as he or she sees fit. It has no official policy function as a body but can be used to help formulate policy. The cabinet is often more a symbolic body than an integral structure of governing. The executive branch is divided into seven superagencies, and the heads of these agencies, called secretaries, are generally in the cabinet. These are State and Consumer Services; Youth and Adult Corrections; Environmental Protection; Health and Human Services; Labor and Workforce Development; Business, Transportation, and Housing; and Resources. These superagencies contain most of the executive branch's agencies. It is the individual agencies, not the umbrella superagencies, that carry out functions, and they may act independently of the superagency secretaries. The governor appoints these agency heads, although he or she often does not have a free choice. Someone with expertise in the area needs to be appointed, and sometimes the qualifications are spelled out in law. These agencies and superagencies are called *line agencies*, the

FIGURE 6.1 ● Executive Branch of the California State Government

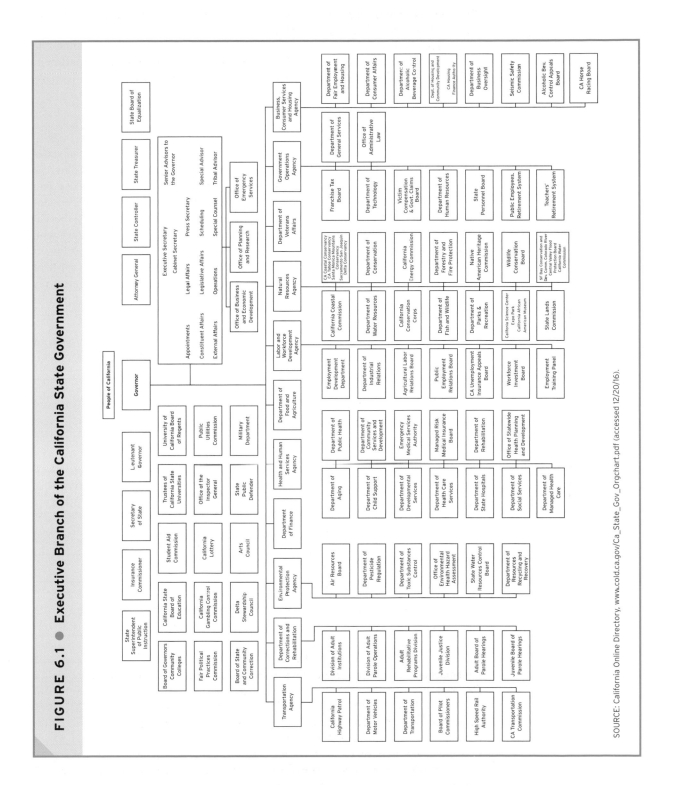

SOURCE: California Online Directory, www.cold.ca.gov/Ca_State_Gov_Orgchart.pdf (accessed 12/20/16).

term used to describe organizations that have their own statutory authority to carry out functions and provide services.

In addition, the governor has several staff advisory agencies, including the Department of Finance, the Office of Planning and Research, and the Department of Personnel Administration. Perhaps the most important of these is the Department of Finance, which prepares the governor's budget.

The Plural Elected Executive

One of the most notable features of California government is the number of state-wide *elected* administrative offices. There are seven of these positions, plus the Board of Equalization, which oversees the administration of property, sales, and excise taxes (see Box 6.2). This means that there are eight elected independent bases of power that do not report to the governor or need to adhere to gubernatorial wishes. This differs from other states that have a single elected leader who appoints lesser state executives. While California government's distribution of power may limit the governor's freedom to make or implement policy, most of these elected positions do not deal with substantial policy issues. The attorney general is usually the governor's only real policy competitor (and is sometimes an electoral competitor as well). Let's take a closer look at each of these seven elected administrative offices.

BOX 6.2 ● The Plural Executive

In addition to the selected duties listed below, all these officeholders sit ex officio on various state boards.

Governor: Organizes the executive branch, prepares the budget and legislation, signs or vetoes bills.

Lieutenant Governor: Replaces the governor if he or she is out of the state, incapacitated, or leaves office for any reason.

Attorney General: Enforces laws, oversees and assists district attorneys.

Secretary of State: Holds elections and oversees the records and archives of the state.

Treasurer: Manages state money.

Insurance Commissioner: Regulates insurance companies.

Controller: Monitors collection of taxes, provides fiscal controls for receipts and payments.

Superintendent of Public Instruction: Administers the state role in public education, sits on the state board of education.

Board of Equalization: Oversees the assessment and administration of property taxes, the collection and distribution of sales taxes, and the collection of excise taxes. The controller is a member of this body.

THE LIEUTENANT GOVERNOR The lieutenant governor exists to replace the governor if he or she becomes incapacitated and also acts in the governor's absence from the state. Since he or she is occasionally from a different party, this provides occasions for great mischief. The lieutenant governor can also preside over the Senate, breaking tie votes. Perhaps more than others, this position captures the imagination of those who would restructure government, either by eliminating the office or by linking the election of the lieutenant governor to that of the governor, as is the case in other states, such as Illinois. The lieutenant governor serves on several important boards, including the governing boards of both the University of California and the California State University system. The current lieutenant governor, first elected in 2010, is Gavin Newsom, the former mayor of San Francisco and a rising star in the Democratic Party. He has announced his candidacy for governor in 2018. The office does not provide much visibility, however, which can make campaigning challenging.

THE ATTORNEY GENERAL The attorney general (AG) oversees the Department of Justice, which employs more than 4,500 persons and is responsible for ensuring that the laws are enforced. The attorney general is free to determine which areas and which issues will receive the most attention and resources and has oversight responsibilities for local district attorneys and county sheriffs. The AG is legal counsel to the state and defends the state in lawsuits. There is no obligation to cooperate with the governor, and the AG is often viewed as a rival. In 2004 the governor ordered the attorney general to intercede with the state supreme court to stop gay marriages in San Francisco. The governor had no statutory basis for giving such an order, and although the attorney general ultimately followed the order, it was done on the AG's own authority. This office is very powerful, and incumbents often see themselves as leading candidates for governor. Although few have successfully made this transition, Jerry Brown used this office to launch his successful campaign for governor in 2010. The attorney general's office is able to set its own agenda, which may run counter to the governor's agenda; it can also use its substantial powers to counter or even embarrass the governor.

The most recently elected attorney general is Kamala Harris (2010 and reelected in 2014). Her star rose faster than that of the lieutenant governor who gained office in the same year (see above), and she was elected to the U.S. Senate in 2016. Unlike the lieutenant governor, she was able to grab the headlines on several occasions with her settlements against major corporations. Most notable have been settlements with mortgage banks that resulted in payouts to Californians that were much larger than had originally been proposed.

A vacancy in most of the plural executive offices, such as the attorney general, is filled by the governor, subject to the approval within 90 days of both houses of the legislature.

THE SECRETARY OF STATE The secretary of state's office oversees the records and archives of the state. It is also responsible for holding elections, including publishing election pamphlets, certifying initiative petitions, keeping records, and publishing election results.

THE CONTROLLER The controller is the fiscal officer for the state and oversees the state's money and the collection of taxes. The controller sits on a large number of boards, including the very important Board of Equalization and Franchise Tax Board.

THE TREASURER The treasurer manages the state's money after it comes in and before it is spent. He or she manages the investment of money and the sale of bonds.

THE SUPERINTENDENT OF PUBLIC INSTRUCTION The superintendent is the chief administrator of the Department of Education. Unlike the other elected statewide officers, the superintendent is elected on a nonpartisan basis. Education administration is a confusing policy area; the superintendent shares power with an appointed board of education. This arrangement ensures controversy and was even more confusing before Governor Brown eliminated the parallel position of the appointed secretary of education in 2011.

THE INSURANCE COMMISSIONER The insurance commissioner's office was made elective by Proposition 103 in 1988 and is the only position of the plural executive created by an initiative. The commissioner regulates the insurance industry, and Proposition 103 passed because the public felt that the appointed commissioner was not doing his job. It is not clear that making this an elective post has improved matters, because most of the contributions to the campaigns for this position come from the insurance industry.

In addition to these positions, voters elect by district four members to the Board of Equalization, which oversees the assessment and administration of property taxes, although much of the work is done at the county level. The board also oversees the collection and distribution of sales taxes and excise taxes. Income taxes are handled by a different nonelected body, the Franchise Tax Board.

Agencies and the Bureaucracy

Most of the work of California state government is carried out by more than 200,000 state employees (not counting employees in higher education) housed in over 85 agencies (see Box 6.3). Most of these agencies are located within the seven superagencies, and most are invisible to the general public, which tends to sustain the impression that state government runs by itself. A few agencies, such as the California Highway Patrol and Caltrans, are well known if not well understood. Others, such as the Office of Small Business Development or the Department of Aging, rarely make it into the news or the public consciousness. Few Californians could name anyone in the executive branch up to and including department heads; few governors could name more than a handful. Many of these individuals are professional experts on policy subjects who are quietly doing their jobs.

Most California employees have civil service protection. Many are also represented by unions. A few of these unions, notably the CCPOA (discussed in Chapter 3), are very powerful and politically well connected to the point where the wishes and desires of the union are more likely to become state policy than the wishes and desires of the governor, the head of the Department of Corrections, or the administration of the department.

There are more than 325 state boards and commissions. Positions on these boards are mostly filled by the governor and subject to the approval of another body, most often a legislative body (some are appointed by the legislature; some are ex officio). These boards and commissions include the Air Resources Board, the Public Utilities Commission, the California Coastal Commission, and the Gambling Control Commission. Probably the most visible are the Board of Regents of

BOX 6.3 ● How Many State Employees Are There?

How many people are employed by the state of California? We actually don't know, in part because the state's computer systems are out of date. The state also lacks a consistent definition of an employee. Some employees are full-time and have civil service protection. Others are full-time and temporary. Others are part-time with long-term contracts. Still others are part-time and temporary, although some of them work for the state for years. (Further complicating the situation, some are non-state employees who are employed under state contracts.) Many who are definitely not counted as state employees work for local government but with state funding.

Compared with other states, California has relatively few employees. The U.S. Census Bureau data show that in 2012, California had 1,049 full-time equivalent[1] state employees per 100,000 residents. This was the fourth lowest in the country. The average in the 50 states was 1,729 per 100,000 employees. Most of the states that are most "efficient" are larger states, suggesting that economies of scale for larger states will yield fewer employees to do similar amounts of work.

The Census Bureau estimates that in 2012, California employed 326,000 full-time employees and 156,000 part-time employees in the following sectors:

[1] Full-time equivalence counts part-time employees by adding up the amount of work they do and dividing it by a full-time workload (so one part-time worker who works 60 percent of full-time and a second who works 40 percent of full-time would count as one full-time employee).

SOURCE: U.S. Census Bureau, http://www.census.gov/govs/apes/ (accessed 6/19/14).

the University of California and the Trustees of the California State University, which together are responsible for more than 100,000 employees. On the other hand, boards such as the Board of Chiropractic Examiners and the Apprenticeship Council are probably known only to those with a direct interest in that area. Most members of these boards and commissions serve for fixed terms, some as long as 12 years, and, once appointed, do not have to respond to the governor's wishes.

California Executive Branch:
Where Are We Now?

In recent years several tentative steps have been taken toward tackling the biggest long-term structural problems facing the state and providing the governor with a greater capacity to lead. First, Proposition 25 removed the two-thirds vote requirement to pass a budget. Although this loses some of its force because revenues cannot be similarly raised, its impact has been greater than expected. Even in the absence of a supermajority in the legislature, Governor Brown has been able to largely ignore Republican legislators and work out legislative deals with the more accommodating Democrats. (This may come back to haunt the Democrats if someday the Republicans should control all parts of the state government and have the ability to cut programs at will.)

Second, Proposition 11, approved in November 2008, took the power to draw the state legislative districts away from the legislature and gave it to a citizens' commission. This commission created new districts that have a closer partisan balance and which initially pitted some incumbents of the same party against one another. The hope was to gain a legislature that was willing to cooperate and compromise both internally and with the governor. The result of Proposition 11 was different than expected, however: the overwhelming Democratic majorities that resulted made cooperation and compromise between parties largely unnecessary.

Along similar lines, Proposition 14, approved in June 2010, created a system of preliminary and final elections for the party primary (see Chapter 4). Again, the ambition was to create a less partisan legislature. As a result of these two measures, the reduced number of Republicans appear to be no less conservative than before, but the policies of the heavily Democratic legislature have not been as extreme as some feared. Even during the supermajority period following the 2012 election, for instance, there was no push to raise taxes, as might have been expected. The Democrats are held in check in part by having to work with a moderate governor who would veto extreme bills, as well as by some Democrats who were elected from marginal districts or who are backed by big business money and who are more likely to share some values with Republicans. While these changes have resulted, unfortunately, in a marginalized minority party, they have also given rise to an executive (and legislative) branch that is more effective, productive, and popular with the electorate.

However, nothing has been done to fix the distortions caused by Proposition 13 (the 1978 proposition that limited property tax increases) and the series of other initiatives that have locked in certain parts of the budget and have made it close to impossible to create a stable and adequate revenue stream for the state. California's revenues are far more volatile than those of other states, and Californians' willingness to govern by initiative remains undaunted. Given this situation, it is difficult to see how the state's revenue problems will be solved in the near future. And while the government seems to be functioning smoothly at the moment, there are many unfunded needs in the state—for instance, infrastructure, the homeless, and the costs of education—that are not being addressed.

Study Guide

FOR FURTHER READING

Cain, Bruce E., and Roger G. Noll, eds. *Constitutional Reform in California: Making State Government More Effective and Responsive*. Berkeley: Institute of Governmental Studies Press, 1995.

California Performance Review. *Prescription for Change, Report of the California Performance Review*. Vols. I–IV. California Performance Review, 2004. www.cpr.ca.gov/CPR_Report /pdf/GRP1.pdf. Accessed 8/25/16.

Gerston, Larry N., and Terry Christensen. *Recall! California's Political Earthquake*. Armonk, NY: M. E. Sharpe, 2004.

Lubenow, Gerald C., ed. *Governing California: Politics, Government, and Public Policy in the Golden State*. 2nd ed. Berkeley: Institute of Governmental Studies Press, University of California, 2006.

Mathews, Joe. *The People's Machine: Arnold Schwarzenegger and the Rise of Blockbuster Democracy*. New York: Public Affairs Press, 2006.

Schrag, Peter. *California: America's High-Stakes Experiment*. Berkeley: University of California Press, 2006.

———. *Paradise Lost: California's Experience, America's Future*. New York: New Press, 1998.

Simmons, Charlene Wear. *To Faithfully Execute the Law: California Executive Branch Agencies 1959–2003*. Sacramento: California Research Bureau, California State Library, 2004.

ON THE WEB

Around The Capitol. www.aroundthecapitol.com/. Accessed 8/25/16. Includes a daily blog, *The Nooner*.

California Choices. www.californiachoices.org. Accessed 8/25/16.

California Department of Finance. www.dof.ca.gov. Accessed 8/25/16.

California State Library. www.library.ca.gov. Accessed 8/25/16.

CALmatters. https://calmatters.org/. Accessed 8/25/16.

Governor of California. www.gov.ca.gov/home.php. Accessed 8/25/16. The official site of the Office of the Governor, where you can find background information and up-to-date news and even send an email to the governor.

Public Policy Institute of California. www.ppic.org. Accessed 8/25/16.

Rough & Tumble. www.rtumble.com. Accessed 8/25/16. A daily summary of California news.

University of California, Berkeley, Institute of Governmental Studies Library. http://igs.berkeley.edu/library/. Accessed 8/25/16.

SUMMARY

I. The office of the governor is modeled on that of the U.S. president, but there are significant differences between the two offices, mostly having to do with visibility.

II. Each job has two analytical roles.
   A. Head of state, which is largely ceremonial, symbolizing the unity of the state or country. In this role, the governor or president makes public appearances doing activities that bring people together. The president, in this role, is on TV almost every evening. The governor has less opportunity to play this role, and even when he does, the state TV stations seem uninterested.
   B. Head of government, which involves making policy and trying to get it passed by the legislature and implemented by the executive branch. This role is partisan and divisive. It is also an almost invisible role, especially on the implementation side.

III. The formal powers of the office are greater for the governor than for the president.
   A. The governor's formal powers include making appointments and organizing the executive branch; conducting independent executive actions that are permitted by law; being commander in chief; proposing the budget; making legislative recommendations; and exercising the veto, including the line-item veto.
   B. The governor has powers similar to those of the president in domestic policy but also can use the line-item veto, which gives the governor more control over the political process of constructing the budget.
   C. California has an initiative process that a popular governor can use to pressure the legislature into action.

IV. The governor's public roles as head of state include cutting ribbons, signing bills, and leading the response to natural disasters. Non–head-of-state public roles include campaigning and fund-raising as well as advocating for initiatives.

V. Like the presidency, the office of governor is one of limited powers, which are restricted by the legislature, the judiciary, the plural elected executive, and the permanent executive branch.

VI. The structure of the state government includes the following:
A. The governor's personal staff.
B. The governor's cabinet, which includes the heads of major departments (superagencies).
C. The plural elected executive, which includes the lieutenant governor, the attorney general, the secretary of state, the controller, the treasurer, the superintendent of public education, the insurance commissioner, and the State Board of Equalization.
D. The 85 or more agencies that comprise the major departments.
E. More than 325 boards and commissions, including the Public Utilities Commission and the Regents of the University of California.

VII. California employs the equivalent of more than 300,000 full-time employees to staff the government, including more than 100,000 in higher education, who are not under the direct control of the governor.

PRACTICE QUIZ

1. Which of the following is *not* part of the plural executive?
   a) the chancellor of the California State University
   b) the secretary of state
   c) the attorney general
   d) the controller

2. Which of these powers does the governor have that the president does not have?
   a) legislative veto
   b) line-item veto
   c) power to declare war
   d) power to appoint judges

3. Which of the following activities of the governor would be considered part of his or her role as head of government?
   a) proposing a budget
   b) vetoing legislation
   c) proposing new air quality standards
   d) all of the above

4. Which of the following groups of employees are under administrative control and report ultimately to the governor?
   a) legislative aides
   b) supreme court clerks
   c) highway patrol
   d) professors at California State University, Fullerton

5. How many state boards and commissions are there?
   a) fewer than 50
   b) between 50 and 150
   c) between 150 and 300
   d) more than 300

6. The California governor is "invisible" under normal conditions for all of the following reasons *except*:
   a) California's governors appear in events where they are visible to the public, but for the most part, there is little public interest in those events.
   b) For almost every recent governor, there has been little media interest in Sacramento.
   c) The governor splits his or her power with other state executives, who are also trying to attract the media.
   d) The governor's star power is only of interest to those who like superhero movies.

7. The governor manages the executive branch, but this power is limited by all of the following *except*:
   a) There are so many appointees of the governor, many of whom belong to agencies the governor doesn't know much about.
   b) Some of California government is outside the governor's power to supervise, such as the University of California and California State University.
   c) The boards and commissions whose members the governor appoints are mostly, except in extreme cases, outside of his or her power.
   d) The attorney general must approve appointments to many boards and commissions, and that appointment approval is difficult for the governor to obtain.

8. The line-item veto allows the governor to adjust any appropriations item up or down, including reducing it to zero.
   a) true
   b) false

9. All of the following are true of the governor's appointments to the cabinet *except*:
   a) Most cabinet appointments are routine, given to the governor's political supporters and campaign contributors.
   b) The cabinet as a whole has no official policy function, unless the governor wants to give it a role.
   c) Some cabinet and subcabinet positions require an appointment of someone with qualifications that are spelled out in law.
   d) The superagency heads are usually considered part of the governor's cabinet.

10. The job of the lieutenant governor, one columnist wrote not entirely in jest, consists of getting up in the morning, checking that the governor is still alive, and then making arrangements for lunch!
    a) This statement is probably true.
    b) This statement is probably false.

CRITICAL-THINKING QUESTIONS

1. Is the state government too large?
2. Does the plural elected executive contribute to effective or efficient government?
3. What is the value of having independent boards such as the Regents of the University of California that employ large numbers of people?
4. Which is more important for governing: the formal or informal powers of the governor? Think about this question in terms of "necessary" versus "sufficient" powers.

KEY TERMS

boards and commissions (p. 154)
cabinet (p. 154)
formal powers (p. 152)
head of government (p. 150)

head of state (p. 150)
informal powers (p. 153)
line-item veto (p. 153)

personal staff (p. 154)
superagencies (p. 154)
veto (p. 157)

7

The California Judiciary

WHAT THE CALIFORNIA JUDICIARY DOES AND WHY IT MATTERS

State courts are an integral and necessary component of state government. They ensure that a state's citizenry is guaranteed due process of law and that the other branches and levels of government within the state uphold state statutes, codes, and the provisions in the state constitution. Therefore, judges play a much larger role than simply punishing criminals or imposing fines on a polluting company. Courts make decisions that are often political and sometimes controversial, with the potential to affect more individuals than just those directly involved in the cases. Court rulings can have far-reaching consequences that not only ignite political debate but that also have an iterative effect. This is especially true in California, a state that witnesses a high rate of litigation and where politics can be very contentious. And while some cases that come before the California courts gain a significant amount of statewide and national media attention, many cases that remain under the radar still have an impact on citizens' daily lives.

California court decisions on immigration policy, for example, have the potential to influence national debates on immigration reform and are particularly salient in a state with a high population of undocumented immigrants. Questions of state policy regarding undocumented immigrants who entered the United States as children were tested in the case of Sergio Garcia, who came with his family to California only months after his first birthday. Garcia and his family moved back to Mexico when he was nine years old, but they returned to the United States eight years later, in 1994. This time, Garcia's father attained lawful permanent resident status for himself and filed a petition seeking the same for his family. But, because of limits on the number of visas distributed each year, Garcia graduated from high school, college, and law school while still undocumented. After obtaining his law degree, Mr. Garcia passed the California Bar Examination and applied for admission to the bar, at which point his undocumented status came under scrutiny from the Committee of Bar Examiners. The committee asked the California Supreme Court to determine whether state law or public policy banned Garcia's admittance. The court ruled that it did not, and it held that the intent of the legislature and the governor clearly indicated that Garcia's status should not be an impediment to his application.[1] Garcia's case effectively illustrates the complexity of contemporary immigration issues in the United States. It also serves as a good example of what it means to be an undocumented person versus a person with legal immigration status.

Structure of the California Judicial System

To understand the role that courts play in California politics, consider the following: from 2013 through 2014, approximately 7,500,000 cases were filed in California **superior courts** (trial courts of general jurisdiction).[2] Of these, over 80 percent were criminal in nature (crimes against the state or society, e.g., failing to pay state taxes or stealing a car) and the remaining almost 20 percent were civil cases (disputes between individuals). Each one of these seven and one half million cases had to be handled individually in one way or another by the appropriate state court until it was resolved. To put this into context, let's consider the number of people living in the state. According to the U.S. Census Bureau, as of July 2015, California's population was estimated at 39,144,818, which puts the case-to-person ratio at 1 to 5.

To adjudicate both criminal cases and civil cases, the state's courts comprise three levels: superior courts (trial courts), California Courts of Appeal, and the California Supreme Court.

The Lower Courts

Superior courts adjudicate cases that involve violations of state and local criminal and civil law. These are the trial courts of California. When cases come before the superior courts, a jury or judge reviews the facts of the case and determines guilt or innocence in a criminal proceeding. If it is a civil case, the jury or judge determines which side presents the best case and awards damages accordingly. There are 58 state trial courts (one in each county), with approximately 2,000 judicial officers presiding. This number includes judges, commissioners, and referees. The superior courts are the busiest courts of the state court system.

The California Courts of Appeal are intermediate courts with **appellate jurisdiction**; those who lose their cases at the superior court can appeal first to the California Courts of Appeal. The purpose of this intermediate appellate court is to review the trial or the superior court records for error. The California Courts of Appeal are divided into six districts across the state; 97 justices preside over these courts. These judges sit on three-judge panels to review cases.[3]

FIGURE 7.1 ● **Flow of Cases Through the California State Judicial System**

SUPREME COURT

COURTS OF APPEAL

TRIAL COURTS

Capital criminal cases

The Supreme Court

The California Supreme Court is the highest court in the state. Like the California Courts of Appeal, it is an appellate court that reviews decisions for reversible error, submitted by losing parties in the lower courts. When a party to a case is unhappy with the ruling of the California Courts of Appeal, the next step is to appeal to the California Supreme Court. In California, the supreme court has what is known as **judicial discretion**. Discretion allows the justices on the state supreme court to decide which cases they wish to review. Therefore, appeals filed with the California Supreme Court are not automatically reviewed. This is the only court in California with discretionary authority. Discretion is valuable because it provides the high court with a tool to moderate its workload. However, this discretion is not absolute: all death-penalty sentences are automatically appealed and go directly to the California Supreme Court for review (see Figure 7.1). The supreme court is also required to hear disciplinary cases involving judges or attorneys. The court includes one chief justice and six associate justices (see Table 7.1). Four out of the seven justices must agree in order for a party to win the case.

While the supreme court may seem remote, it often makes decisions that have an impact on Californians' daily lives. For example, on June 21, 2010, the California Supreme Court announced its ruling in *Kleffman v. Vonage Holdings Corp.* At issue in this case was the legality of commercial electronic advertising. Craig E. Kleffman sued Vonage on the basis that its use of multiple domain names to advertise its products and services through unsolicited emails (or spam) violated provisions in the California state code. The California high court ruled unanimously that "sending commercial email advertisements from multiple domain names for the purpose of bypassing spam filters is not unlawful under [the state code]."[4] This recent ruling serves to illustrate the importance of the California judiciary; in this case, the court's decision results in Californians receiving more spam email.

> **TABLE 7.1 ● Membership of the California State Supreme Court (as of July 2016)**
>
> Tani Gorre Cantil-Sakauye, chief justice, appointed by Governor Arnold Schwarzenegger in 2010
> Kathryn M. Werdegar, appointed by Governor Pete Wilson in 1994
> Ming W. Chin, appointed by Governor Pete Wilson in 1996
> Carol A. Corrigan, appointed by Governor Arnold Schwarzenegger in 2005
> Goodwin H. Liu, appointed by Governor Edmund G. Brown in 2011
> Mariano-Florentino Cuéllar, appointed by Governor Edmund G. Brown in 2014
> Leondra R. Kruger, appointed by Governor Edmund G. Brown in 2014

When individual citizens or groups of citizens believe that private entities or government has trampled on state law or on their civil liberties or civil rights, they turn to the courts. The judges serving on California's courts must decide if the state's laws or the rights of Californians have been violated.

Jurisdiction

Both criminal and **civil courts** in California are limited as to the cases and controversies they handle because of jurisdiction. Jurisdiction refers to the kind of law handled by a court. For example, there are criminal courts that deal with violations of state and local laws, and there are civil courts that hear cases involving disputes between individuals or classes of individuals. Civil courts may rule on cases involving breach of contract, tort liability, and wrongful-death suits, to name a few. Jurisdiction also refers to geographic boundaries. There are 58 superior court divisions in California, with at least one branch in each county. Cases are assigned to these courts depending on where the parties in civil suits reside or where alleged crimes have been committed in criminal cases.

It is easier for an individual to go to criminal court (just drive over the speed limit and get caught) than to civil court. Civil courts have rules about the types of cases they can hear. In civil disputes, parties must also have what is known as "standing to sue." To bring a case to court, an individual must suffer personal and real injury. Typically, an individual cannot sue on behalf of someone else. As well as requiring standing to sue, California courts, like the federal courts, will not handle collusive suits. Collusive suits are lawsuits in which both parties want a similar or the same outcome. Our legal system is an adversarial one, in which it is presumed that parties want opposite outcomes, and when one party wins, the other loses.

Access to the Court

The California Constitution and its statutes provide rights to the people of California regarding access to the courts. For example, Californians have:

- the right to sue for money owed and for other relief,

- the right to defend oneself against a lawsuit,

- the right to be presumed innocent if charged with a crime,

- the right to defend oneself against all criminal charges,

- the right to a public and speedy trial by jury if charged with a misdemeanor or a felony, and

- the right to an attorney at public expense if one is charged with a felony or misdemeanor and cannot afford an attorney.

These rights apply to citizens of the state and noncitizens alike. They do not mitigate against concerns about quality of legal representation for indigent persons. The lack of resources in some local court jurisdictions, especially in smaller localities, and the impact of the current budget crisis on the state's judiciary as a whole will affect access to the courts.

Federalism and the California Courts: The Case of Medical Marijuana

The California court system must occasionally negotiate discrepancies between federal law and state law in a particular policy area. For example, California's laws permitting medicinal marijuana use are at odds with federal laws that classify marijuana as a controlled substance. In 1996, through use of the initiative, voters in California approved Proposition 215, the Compassionate Use Act (CUA). This act provides for the medical use of marijuana for seriously ill persons. It requires that a physician recommend that a patient's health would benefit from using marijuana to alleviate symptoms of serious illness. In addition, the act also shields patients and their caregivers from criminal prosecution for cultivating or possessing marijuana for use approved under the act. More recently, voters approved Proposition 64, the California Marijuana Legalization Initiative, which allows persons 21 years or older to use and grow marijuana for personal use. The sale and taxation of marijuana will go into effect in January 2018. The passing of Proposition 64 expands the legalization of marijuana and may lead to future conflict between the federal government and the state. As you read the accounts below of the conflict over this controversial issue, think about the significance of this ballot measure with respect to growing one's own marijuana and the facts and ruling in the U.S. Supreme Court case, *Gonzales v. Raich*.

Confusion ensued shortly after the CUA was implemented. First, there were many (successful) attempts at expanding the scope of the law. Second, the state law came directly into conflict with federal law, which makes the cultivation, possession, sale, and consumption of marijuana illegal.

Seven years after the CUA was passed, Governor Gray Davis signed Senate Bill 420, the Medical Marijuana Program Act (MMPA), into law. The MMPA was designed to flesh out the parameters of the CUA. Among other things, the MMPA sought to create collective cooperatives in the state where marijuana could be cultivated and sold to qualified patients and caregivers. The cooperatives would be regulated by state and local agencies, and the patients and caregivers would be issued

U.S. Attorneys like Laura Duffy have been engaged in a protracted battle over medicinal marijuana in California. It remains to be seen what the new administration and Congress will do, especially with the legalization of recreational marijuana use in 2016.

identification cards that would help law enforcement more easily determine whether persons were covered by the CUA and, therefore, not subject to criminal prosecution under state law. The MMPA also allows for persons who can be classified as cooperatives, caregivers, or patients to raise a defense if they are charged with violating state laws involving the cultivation, possession, sale, or consumption of medical marijuana.

The MMPA had immediate implications regarding federalism. Although both the CUA and the MMPA are technically "good law" (meaning they are still current and enforceable), the national government has made various attempts to exercise preemption—a practice in which the government claims to have authority over a particular policy area when it comes to legislation, thus preempting state and local regulations. In 2005, for example, the U.S. Supreme Court reviewed the case *Gonzales v. Raich*. At issue was whether Congress's power to regulate the manufacture and possession of marijuana under the Controlled Substances Act (21 U.S.C. § 801) allowed the national government to preempt California's laws governing the medicinal use of marijuana. The Supreme Court ruled in a 6-to-3 decision that the Commerce Power gives Congress the authority to regulate and to punish the manufacture and cultivation of marijuana despite California law allowing for compassionate use. The dissenting Supreme Court justices argued that to preempt these laws was a violation of federalism and that, because the issue involved purely local or *intrastate*, rather than interstate, commerce, the state law should prevail.

Since this ruling in 2005, many local California governments have seized the opportunity to create new zoning ordinances to limit the expansion of marijuana dispensaries. In fact, one tactic commonly used by local governments to close down dispensaries involves calling the U.S. attorney's office. The U.S. attorney has the authority to order these shops to discontinue their operations under the threat of having their property forfeited or seized, as well as other criminal sanctions under federal law.

Despite the U.S. Supreme Court's ruling in *Gonzales v. Raich*, California courts have continued to try medical marijuana cases according to state law. For example, a 2009 case, *People v. Colvin*, involved a co-owner (William Frank Colvin) of two nonprofit medical marijuana dispensaries, Holistic I (in Santa Monica) and Holistic 2 (in Hollywood). The dispensaries are registered with the city of Los Angeles and have been incorporated for several years. In addition, they are often reviewed by local law enforcement to ensure that they meet the requirements and restrictions of the MMPA. Like other similar dispensaries, and in compliance with the MMPA, Holistic 1 and 2 grow some of their marijuana on site but also belong to a cooperative that includes growers in Los Angeles and Humboldt. In March 2009, Colvin was less than a block from Holistic 2 en route to Holistic 1. He was stopped by police, taken into custody, and charged with violating state laws for possession of cocaine, sale or transportation of marijuana, and possession of marijuana. He was carrying an identification card for medicinal use and showed it to the arresting officer at the time. He also presented evidence to the trial court that he was registered to run the Holistic dispensaries.

The trial court judge agreed that Colvin's dispensaries seemed to be in compliance with both the CUA and the MMPA, which are still California law despite the *Raich* decision. Colvin's attorneys argued that he was only transporting the marijuana (one pound) from one dispensary to another. However, the trial court judge disagreed and ruled that the MMPA did not cover the transportation of marijuana. Colvin was found guilty of all three charges, placed on probation, and given community service. Colvin appealed this conviction, and the court of appeal determined that the transportation of marijuana from one dispensary to another fell within the scope of the MMPA, reversing the trial court's decision with respect to two of Colvin's convictions (transportation and possession; the cocaine conviction was not appealed).

However, both parties to a case have the right to appeal, and the state appealed the decision of the court of appeal. The California Supreme Court had to determine whether it would take the case and rule on its merits or if it would choose not to hear the case and allow the court of appeal decision to stand (remain in effect). In May 2012 the California Supreme Court denied review, noting that medicinal marijuana remains an issue that has important implications for local, state, and federal law. It also cited the many cases dealing with this policy issue that continue to be filed in the courts. This is an interesting case study in the principle of federalism, particularly in those circumstances in which state and national law clearly conflict over a very controversial issue.[5]

In January 2014 the U.S. Court of Appeals for the Ninth Circuit disposed of a number of cases involving medical marijuana use. In their "unpublished" memorandum, the court wrote that states have no special protection from federal law when it comes to use, including medicinal, of marijuana.[6] One month later, the Ninth Circuit disposed of the case *Sacramento Nonprofit Collective v. Holder*. Here, the plaintiffs argued that because nine western states permit the use of marijuana for medicinal purposes, it should be recognized as a fundamental right. The court chose to dismiss the case in favor of the federal government. In fact, it dismissed with prejudice: the plaintiffs in this legal action are prohibited from ever bringing the case back to the court.

In a federal system, like ours, what may seem to be the end of a story isn't necessarily so. In October 2015, Governor Brown signed the California Medical Marijuana Regulation Safety Act (MMRSA) into law. This new law puts into place several state regulations of medical marijuana that had not existed in the past. Various state and local level agencies are given oversight authority with respect to the cultivation of medical marijuana, the operations of dispensaries, and the licensing and practices of prescribing physicians.[7] Given all of the state and federal court cases involving this issue, it might seem as if California were picking a fight with the federal government. This is not the case. In December 2014, Congress passed the "Consolidated and Further Continuing Appropriations Act of 2015" which includes Section 538 that basically prohibits the U.S. Department of Justice from spending any funds to interfere with California's laws regarding medical marijuana, including cultivation, dispensing, and possession.[8]

Judicial Selection

California's court system is the largest in the nation. Serving on the bench requires (1) qualifications and (2) having been selected to serve. The qualifications for judges are the same for all three court levels. In California, potential judges must have at least 10 years of experience practicing law in the state of California or service as a judge of a court of record.

The selection process for judges to serve on the California Supreme Court and California Courts of Appeal is the same. Judges are initially nominated by the governor to serve on the appellate bench and are then approved by the Commission on Judicial Appointments. The Commission on Judicial Appointments consists of the chief justice of the supreme court, the attorney general, and a presiding judge

In July 2016 the members of the California State Supreme Court were (from left to right) Mariano-Florentino Cuéllar, Kathryn M. Werdegar, Carol A. Corrigan, Chief Justice Tani Cantil-Sakauye, Goodwin H. Liu, Ming W. Chin, and Leondra R. Kruger.

on the California Courts of Appeal. In addition, all nominees for California's appellate courts are reviewed by the State Bar of California's Commission on Judicial Nominees Evaluation. This body evaluates the nominees by conducting thorough background checks on their qualifications as judges and as citizens. The governor may use the commission's decision as a source of information when making his or her selections but is not bound by the commission's findings. After a judge's appointment is confirmed, the judge holds office until the next **retention election**. To remain on the appellate courts in California, judges must win their retention elections. These elections are noncompetitive; the voters are simply asked whether the judge should remain on the appellate bench. If a judge does not receive a majority of affirmative votes, he or she is removed and the governor will appoint a new judge.

Likewise, judges serving on California's superior courts must face nonpartisan retention elections. However, their electoral process is different from the retention elections of sitting supreme court and courts of appeal judges. While appellate court judges run uncontested, simply against their own records, judges serving on California's superior courts can be challenged in their retention races. In addition, superior courts may have open seat races from time to time. These occur when a judge decides to retire close to an election. Finally, if an incumbent is up for retention and has no challengers, he or she may simply be declared re-elected; thus, no retention election is held.

Governors take advantage of opportunities to appoint judges to the courts by placing qualified jurists on the bench whose political beliefs most closely resemble their own. From time to time, a governor may be quite transparent about his or her preferences for those serving on the state supreme court. In the 1980s former governor George Deukmejian spoke out to the press and public about his desire to put more conservatives on the state supreme court because the liberals serving on the bench at the time were making decisions he vehemently disliked.

In addition, governors may have other political goals for the bench. They may, for example, seek to place more women and minorities on the supreme court so that it is more representative of the state's diverse population. Today's supreme court is diverse in regard to gender, race, and ethnicity: as of 2016 four of the justices are women and five identify as persons of color or of more than one race. (See the "Who Are Californians?" feature for more on the diversity of California's justices.)

However, the court is not so diverse ideologically. Four of the seven justices seated on the court were appointed by Republican governors. Generally, Republicans are more conservative than Democrats on issues of ideological preference, such as civil rights or civil liberties. For example, a liberal judge is more likely than a conservative judge to uphold laws that involve regulating business. This expectation, that ideology or party identification translates into differences in judicial

Who Are California's Judges?

Since 2006, the Judicial Council of California has produced an annual report with information about the demographic characteristics of the state's justices and judges. Over time, increasing proportions of the judiciary have been women and people of color, although the proportions do not yet reflect the general population. The ethnoracial composition of the California bar (lawyers who are qualified to practice law in California) is heavily white, at 79.3 percent Anglo and just 7.7 percent Asian/Pacific Islander, 4.2 percent Latino, and 2.7 percent African American; the bar is 39.4 percent female.

Justices and Judges in California, 2015

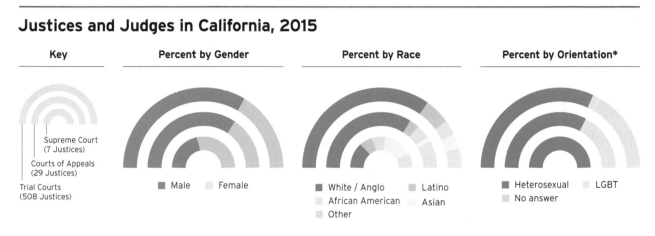

Key

Supreme Court
(7 Justices)

Courts of Appeals
(29 Justices)

Trial Courts
(508 Justices)

Percent by Gender

■ Male ■ Female

Percent by Race

■ White / Anglo ■ Latino
■ African American ■ Asian
■ Other

Percent by Orientation*

■ Heterosexual ■ LGBT
■ No answer

*33% of judicial officers did not provide information on sexual orientation/gender identity.

Gubernatorial Appointments, 1975–Present

■ Female
■ Latino
■ African American
  Asian
■ Democratic governor

Governor	0%	10%	20%	30%	40%	50%
Jerry Brown (2011–present)						
Arnold Schwarzenegger (2003–2010)						
Gray Davis (1999–2003)						
Pete Wilson (1991–1998)						
George Deukmejian (1983–1990)						
Jerry Brown (1975–1982)						

SOURCES: "Demographic Data Provided by Justices and Judges Relative to Gender, Race/Ethnicity, and Gender Identity/Sexual Orientation," December 31, 2015, www.courts.ca.gov/documents/2016-Demographic-Report.pdf (accessed 7/27/16); Judicial Council of California, "2013 Court Statistics Report: Statewide Caseload Trends," www.courts.ca.gov/documents/2013-Court-Statistics-Report.pdf (accessed 4/11/14); and Office of Governor Edmund G. Brown Jr., "Governor Brown Releases 2015 Judicial Appointment Data," www.gov.ca.gov/news.php?id=19323 (accessed 7/27/16).

forcriticalanalysis

1. Is it important for the judiciary to reflect the diversity of the California population? Why or why not?

2. Besides gender, ethnicity, race, and sexual orientation/gender identity, what other dimensions of diversity are important to consider and why?

decision making, is even more important when we consider issues such as same-sex marriage/LGBTQ rights, affirmative action, voting rights, freedom of expression, and capital punishment. Because the decisions of the California Supreme Court are binding on all persons residing in the state, the composition and dominating political ideology of the state's high court can be very important.

We may start to see some ideological shifts in the court. Since 2011, Governor Brown, a Democrat, has had the opportunity to appoint three justices, who will likely be more liberal than their predecessors. He has also demonstrated a commitment to diversifying the high court through his appointments. For example, in 2014 the governor announced his nomination of Mariano-Florentino Cuéllar to replace Justice Baxter, and the California Commission on Judicial Appointments unanimously confirmed the nomination. Cuéllar, who took office on January 5, 2015, is the first Latino immigrant appointed to the California Supreme Court.[9] Governor Brown has brought additional diversity to the bench by appointing an African American attorney, Leondra Kruger, to replace Justice Kennard. Ms. Kruger was previously a deputy attorney general in President Obama's administration. Kruger is the first African American to hold a seat on the court since 2005.[10]

Judicial Elections

Unlike the federal judiciary, which consists of appointed judges who serve life terms with good behavior, many states, including California, have some form of election system for selecting their judges. Federal judges are appointed to allow for **judicial independence**. Theoretically, appointed judges are less likely to be influenced by politics in their decision making because they do not have to rely on the electorate to maintain their positions on the bench. Most states, however, have adopted some kind of election system for selecting or retaining their judges in order to secure **judicial accountability**. Elections allow voters to select members of the courts and to remove them for decisions contrary to the public's preferences.

Justices Werdegar, Liu, and Cuéllar faced elections in November 2014, and all successfully retained their seats on the bench. Over 70 percent of California voters supported Werdegar's retention, while Liu and Cuéllar received approximately 67 percent of all votes. Although the voters rarely pay much attention to competitive judicial races or retention elections, there have been instances when judges have lost their seats on the bench because of voters' perceptions about judicial rulings. For example, in the November 1986 election, six justices serving on the California Supreme Court were seeking retention. Governor George Deukmejian spoke out against the retention of three of the six judges for their rulings on death-penalty cases and was especially critical of Rose Bird, the chief justice of the California Supreme Court at the time. While she served on the court, Bird participated in 61 death-penalty cases and voted every time to vacate the death sentence—an especially notable choice during a time of widespread public support among Californians for the death penalty. In fact, her appointment as chief justice occurred the same year that the death penalty was reinstated by a legislative override of a gubernatorial veto. One year later (1978), an initiative was adopted that expanded the number of special circumstances allowed for death-penalty cases. While she had many supporters, her decision making went against the tide of moneyed interests and those supportive of capital punishment.[11]

Governor Deukmejian warned Bird and two associate justices, Cruz Reynoso and Joseph Grodin, that he would oppose their retention elections if they did not change their rulings in death-penalty appeals and uphold the death-penalty sentences. Numerous interest groups and political action committees joined the governor's campaign against Rose Bird and her two colleagues. Political advertisements against the retention of Bird, Grodin, and Reynoso aired on radio and television. In response, Chief Justice Rose Bird produced a television ad explaining her decision-making record. Her explanations did not satisfy voters, however, and on November 4, 1996, Bird, Grodin, and Reynoso lost their seats on the California Supreme Court. Shortly thereafter, Governor Deukmejian appointed three justices to replace them, including Malcolm Lucas, who was nicknamed "Maximum Malcolm" for his rulings that sentenced convicted criminals to the maximum penalties, including death.

Despite the low visibility of judicial elections, these elections have many political scientists and jurists concerned, particularly over the amount of money being spent by candidates in judicial elections. A 1995 study of contested elections in Los Angeles County Superior Court reported that campaign spending by trial court judges had risen a great deal in the years between 1976 and 1994. In 1976 the median cost of a judicial campaign for a Los Angeles County Superior Court seat was approximately $3,000. By 1994 the median had skyrocketed to $70,000. Incumbents running for re-election spent, on average, $20,000 more than the median challenger, or $95,000, in 1994. Compare that to the $1,000 median campaign expenditure of an incumbent in 1976.

The Civil Justice Association of California (CJAC), a group of citizens, taxpayers, and professionals, reviewed campaign contributions to the California judiciary from 1997 to 2000 and found the following:

- From 1997 to 2000, contributions to candidates in contested superior court elections totaled over $3 million for four counties.

- In a single race in Sacramento County, over $1 million was raised.

- Attorneys are the largest contributors to most judicial races.

- Two supreme court justices seeking retention in 1998—in uncontested elections—received contributions of $887,000 and $710,000.

The escalation of campaign spending in judicial elections is controversial because it usually requires judicial candidates to seek funding support from outside sources. Like candidates seeking election to state legislative or executive offices, judges now receive and even solicit financial support from organized interests. This phenomenon has even spilled over into retention elections for the state supreme court, even though these elections are noncompetitive. Judges must solicit campaign contributions to retain their seats on the bench. Contributors often include trial lawyers' associations and other special interests. This connection has raised concern: financial contributions by interest groups to a judge's campaign increase the potential for influence over judicial decision making. The original intent by lawmakers in instituting elections for judicial candidates was to ensure judicial accountability to voters, not to the narrow preferences of an organized interest group. This concern has mobilized a national movement for reform. One of the most active reform advocates is former associate justice of the U.S. Supreme Court Sandra Day O'Connor. Retired Justice O'Connor has been a vocal critic of state judicial elections because of the amounts that judicial candidates are soliciting and spending and because of the public perception that money buys influence.

Most people consider the judiciary to be the least political of all branches of government, yet the increased spending in competitive and noncompetitive elections for judgeships compromises this assumption. Even judges are expressing concern. In 2001 an opinion survey, "Justice at Stake Campaign," revealed that 53 percent of California judges are dissatisfied with the current climate of judicial campaigning in the state. Over 80 percent of the judges surveyed believed that voters knew little about candidates for the bench and were electing judges based on criteria other than qualifications for office. The majority of judges polled agreed that reform of campaign financing for judicial elections is necessary and that public financing of these elections would be an appropriate alternative.

In response to stories in the media, including a series of articles published in the *Los Angeles Times*, and the concerns of the public, judges, public officials, and others, the Judicial Campaign Task Force for Impartial Courts was established in 2007. It consists of 14 members appointed by former California Supreme Court chief justice Ronald M. George, and it investigates several issues, including the structure of California judicial elections as well as the filing, reporting, and accessibility of judicial campaign contributions and spending. The findings of this commission to date were reported in a 408-page volume in December 2009.[12] Many problems with respect to judicial campaigns and elections were documented, most notably the amount of money spent by candidates for judicial elections and, ironically, the poor quality or low level of information disseminated by judicial candidates to the public. The commission is not finished with its work, and additional reports are expected. The following reforms have so far been successfully implemented:

- Judicial candidates are prohibited from making statements that commit or appear to commit them with respect to cases, controversies, or issues that could come before the courts.

- Judicial candidates may not knowingly misrepresent certain facts, including the identity, qualifications, or present position of themselves or an opponent.

- Any contributions to or expenditures of $100 or more by judicial candidates must be itemized.

- Judicial candidates for superior court may file a candidate statement to be included in the voter's pamphlet. These statements are very expensive, however, and the cost is prohibitive for most candidates.

There is one further caveat that should be mentioned. Whenever limits or rules are placed on campaign spending, the rights of freedom of expression and freedom of association guaranteed by both the California and U.S. Constitutions may be abridged. Campaigning for political office is guaranteed by the right to speak freely, and in today's political contests, it is becoming increasingly expensive. Therefore, it is almost impossible to impose limits on campaign spending. So judges running for retention on the California Supreme Court or running to serve on the state's trial courts must exercise their own restraint—not an easy task if your opponent or opposing forces are spending a lot of money to keep you off the bench. Added to this are concerns about the impact of the U.S. Supreme Court's 2010 ruling in *Citizens United v. FEC*. This decision allowed corporations and unions substantial freedom to spend money during elections through "independent expenditures." As long as corporations and unions do not coordinate their campaign advertising expenditures with candidates, they can spend practically without limits. In a 2011 report, "Spending in Judicial Elections: State Trends in the Wake of *Citizens United*," researchers suggested that California judicial politics may not be as influenced by this ruling as judicial elections in other states. The authors noted that the unions and corporations were already influential in the state's campaigns and elections.[13] Retention elections for the high court are uncontested and, therefore, spending remains relatively low. Moreover, most vacancies on all other state courts, including trial, are filled by gubernatorial appointment. Finally, campaign spending in trial court races is likely suppressed (compared with other states) because judicial incumbents are automatically re-elected if they are unopposed.

Removing Judges from the Bench

As we have already discussed in this chapter, voters may remove judges from the bench during an election. In addition, there are other means for removing judges in the case of public concern regarding judicial misconduct or judicial competency:

- **Impeachment**   California's judges may be impeached by the Assembly and convicted by a two-thirds majority of the state Senate.

- **Recall election**   Like the governor, California judges are subject to recall election petitioned by voters.

- **Regulatory commission investigation**   The Commission on Judicial Performance may, after investigation of complaints regarding misconduct or incapacity, punish, censure, or remove a judge from office.

Contemporary Issues in the Judiciary

Change in the Court

The new justices appointed by Governor Brown could influence the court's patterns of decision making. The California Supreme Court has had a conservative majority for a significant period of time, and Governor Brown will likely appoint justices who are more liberal than their predecessors. This will shift the ideological direction of the state high court from conservative majority to at least moderate if not liberal. Of course, we will not know the full impact of this change on the bench until the new justices participate in significant cases.

Legislative Redistricting

Every term, judges serving on the California bench across all court levels (trial, intermediate appellate, and supreme) are confronted with cases that require them to make political decisions or decisions that have political consequences. One example of this is political redistricting. The redrawing of electoral districts is always a political process. Political parties seek either to maintain or to increase their odds of getting candidates re-elected through the redrawing of district lines. It is common for redistricting plans to end up contested in the courts by political parties, elected officials, candidates seeking political office, or organized special interests.

Since the 1980s the California courts have been involved in many cases and controversies regarding redistricting. Perhaps the most controversial occurred in 2005 when Governor Schwarzenegger and others proposed an initiative, Proposition 77, which would reform redistricting procedures in the state. Rather than having legislators redraw district lines after each census, the responsibility would be given to a panel of three retired judges (selected by legislative officials). This ballot measure was contested in the California Courts of Appeal before it even appeared on the ballot. Those opposed to the measure argued that judges should not have the power to redraw or create new political districts. Although there was some success with procedural challenges to the initiative in the courts of appeal, attempts to block the initiative from the ballot finally failed, and in November 2005 the voters vetoed the measure by a margin of approximately 19 percent, prohibiting retired judges from redrawing the state's electoral district lines.

Judicial Review and the Statewide Initiative

Another issue of concern regarding the judiciary in California is the relationship between direct democracy and judicial review. California is one of 26 states in the United States that allow citizens to propose and enact their own legislation through the initiative. Like any piece of legislation coming out of the state legislature, the initiative is subject to judicial interpretation and review. When the initiative is used to enact controversial policies—such as anti–affirmative action laws, a temporary tax to fund education, the decriminalization of marijuana, or term limits for elected officials—it is usually debated in the press and often contested in the courts. In fact, the constitutional validity of each of the initiatives mentioned above has been challenged in at least one court of law. The outcomes of these court cases have been varied. But most central to the controversy is the ability of state court judges, like judges on federal courts, to conduct judicial review. When state judges have the power to overturn laws enacted by the people as well as laws composed by state legislators, the tension between lawmaking and law reviewing is heightened.

Is this tension all that important? Many scholars and many voters would argue that it is. In fact, the common opinion among the electorate in California is that the initiative as an alternative policy-making tool has become an exercise in futility, precisely because of legal intervention. The consensus among California voters is that once an initiative passes at the ballot box, it ends up in a court of law. In truth, courts are reactive bodies. Judges must wait until a case comes to their courtrooms to make a legal decision. So why do so many initiatives end up in the California courts? The answer is simply politics. California is a very diverse state, and our diversity can be measured in a number of ways. We are diverse in race and ethnicity, we are diverse in culture, we are diverse economically, we are even diverse in terrain and climate. Given so many dimensions of diversity, there is no dearth of conflict in our state regarding which political problems are important and which solutions to these problems should be adopted. Hence California courts also function as an arena for the continuation of political debate.

For example, the United States Supreme Court's landmark ruling in *Obergefell v. Hodges*, 576 U.S. ____ (2015) determined that the Fourteenth Amendment requires states to permit same-sex couples to obtain marriage licenses and to recognize the marriages of same-sex couples from other states. Although this case did not originate in California, the issue of same-sex marriage has been a subject of California politics for over a decade. It began in February 2004, when the county and city of

San Francisco began to issue marriage licenses to same-sex couples. The following month, the California Supreme Court issued an injunction ordering San Francisco to stop issuing these licenses. Several pending cases regarding same-sex marriage were consolidated and some traveled through the courts separately. Groups organized in support of and in opposition to same sex marriage as the cases percolated up to the California Supreme Court. In May 2008 the California high court ruled in favor of gay and lesbian couples, finding that denying them the right to civil marriage violates the state constitution. Meanwhile, opponents to same-sex marriage drafted an initiative, "Prop. 8," which was adopted by 52 percent of the voters. Proposition 8 amended the California Constitution to exclude same-sex marriage. All of these events, which occurred over a relatively short period of time, were part of the broader national debate regarding rights of same-sex couples to legally marry. Legal challenges to Proposition 8 were brought very quickly. A federal district court found Proposition 8 unconstitutional. There were subsequent appeals and the case went all the way to the United States Supreme Court in *Hollingsworth v. Perry*, 133 S. Ct. 2652 (2013). At issue was whether or not Proposition 8 violated the United States Constitution's Fourteenth Amendment rights to due process and equal protection. The Supreme Court did not decide these constitutional questions, however, because they determined that the petitioners, Hollingsworth and others, did not have standing and therefore couldn't bring this suit before the Court. The effect of the Supreme Court's ruling, even though it did not answer the questions on the merits, left lower-court decisions in place. Same-sex couples had the right to marry in California. Two years later this right was extended to gay and lesbian couples in all states in the *Obergefell* decision.

Caseload

While the caseload for all court levels in California has recently begun to decline after increasing over a period of several years, it remains very high when compared with other state court caseloads. And while the superior courts and appellate courts have managed this load fairly efficiently, there are legitimate concerns about the system's ability to continue to do so, given the state's continued fiscal crisis. As noted earlier, from 2013 to 2014, approximately 7.5 million cases were filed in California superior courts (trial courts of general jurisdiction).[14] There are many reasons for the high caseloads in the state court system. Following are a few examples: California, like many other states, has modified its laws to allow juveniles to be tried as adults in some criminal cases. Although the intent of this law may have been to let juveniles know that California has little tolerance for certain types of crime, regardless of the defendant's age, the effect has been to shift cases from the courts of judges who deal exclusively with juveniles to the already overburdened courts handling crimes involving adults. In addition, victims' rights legislation, which has elevated some misdemeanors (nonserious crimes) to felonies (serious crimes), increases not only the severity of the penalties for the accused but also the workload for the courts. California's Three Strikes law, originally enacted to punish repeat offenders, has had a similar impact. Keep in mind that these are just a few reasons for the high number of court cases in California.

To be sure, most of the cases filed in California's civil courts will be resolved through negotiation between the parties and their attorneys. For example, in 2013–14, 78 percent of unlimited jurisdiction civil cases were resolved without trial, while 94 percent of limited jurisdiction civil cases were disposed of before trial.[15] The courts are still involved, however, in processing the paperwork and dealing with the other administrative issues that each civil case may involve.

Similarly, most of the cases in the state's criminal courts will be resolved through plea bargaining, despite what we see in film or on television. Full court trials for the prosecution of high-profile crimes, like that of Conrad Murray, the personal physician found guilty in 2011 of involuntary manslaughter of his patient, singer Michael Jackson, are rare. A plea bargain is the norm. Even so, the courts are still involved in the process. Even if a criminal case never goes beyond the formal filing of charges against a defendant, judges are part of a plea bargain. As a referee, the judge's job is to determine if the plea bargain is appropriate and if the defendant entered into the plea bargain knowingly. If the judge decides that the terms of the plea bargain are inappropriate, that the defendant's ability to comprehend the terms of the plea was compromised, or that the plea was not entered into voluntarily, then a new plea may have to be negotiated or the case may actually go to trial. Regardless, a single case in the criminal courts involves many people, from clerks to administrators and, of course, a judge.

Despite this incredible workload, California's criminal courts typically resolve cases involving felonies within 12 months (89 percent were resolved in 2013–14). Civil cases are also resolved fairly quickly; on average, 75 percent of civil cases filed in a given year are resolved within 12 months. Most recently, California superior courts reported disposing of all civil cases within the 2013–14 fiscal year, including a backlog from prior years.

While these are impressive figures, problems remain. The lack of resources in some local court jurisdictions, especially in smaller localities, and the impact of the current budget crisis on the state's judiciary as a whole affect access to the courts and can compromise the quality of legal representation for indigent persons.

California Courts: Where Are We Now?

A number of issues currently confront California's courts. As discussed earlier, chief among these issues is the court system's ability to manage an increasing caseload as the state continues to face a tenuous fiscal situation. Courts are subject to constraints similar to those that affect state agencies. It is fairly easy to argue that the greatest of these constraints, aside from jurisdiction, is the state's economy and budget. Most recently, the court system in California has found itself constrained by the extraordinary challenges of the state's budget. Chapter 8 discusses the budgetary process and its political implications in greater detail, but here we can examine the impact of this budgetary crisis on the courts.

Taken at face value, a discussion about budgets and courts may not appear all that interesting. However, when Governor Brown signed the budget on June 27, 2012, it included $6 billion of automatic cuts—hundreds of millions to the court system—severely affecting both day-to-day operations and future construction plans. It is important to note that these cuts come on top of other actions that have been taken to reduce the size of court administration throughout the state. Because most courts are located at the local level, counties and municipalities have taken the brunt of these budget cuts. Responses to the ramifications of these cuts have included threatened strikes by state court administrative personnel and the elimination of some innovative, albeit controversial, programs at the local level. One such program focuses on nonviolent misdemeanor crimes by juvenile offenders in the Los Angeles area. This program is part of a relatively recent legal movement known as "problem-solving justice," or the good courts movement. It served as an alternative to traditional, more punitive, forms of addressing juvenile low-level crime. The nontraditional court served more than 100,000 children each year, but it has been shut down by the county because of budget cuts.[16]

In addition, Chief Justice Tani Gorre Cantil-Sakauye has had to respond to some criticisms by organized interests and other parties about wasteful spending on projects and the growth of the state's Administrative Office of the Courts (AOC). The Alliance of California Judges, established in 2009, has been pressuring the chief justice and the judicial council to respond to past and present budget cuts more proactively and to pay closer attention to wasteful spending, predicting (accurately) that, like his predecessors, Governor Brown would include more cuts to the state courts' budgets in the new fiscal year. More specifically, this organization targeted the now defunct electronic Court Case Management System. According to the *Courthouse News Service*, "Even as trial courts were closing, the [Judicial] Council voted repeatedly, with only one or two dissenting votes, to continue pouring hundreds of millions into that now failed IT project. That money came primarily from trial court funds." The same article claims that over half a billion dollars was spent before the Court Management Case System was terminated.[17]

On top of this, Chief Justice Cantil-Sakauye released a report "prepared by a committee of state judges" in late May 2012 criticizing the AOC for understating the number of its employees and for paying "hundreds" of its personnel six-figure salaries. The report noted that this growth in both size and salaries paid was taking place during a hiring freeze. The investigation concluded, among other things, that the AOC had circumvented the hiring freeze and had violated some of its own personnel rules; it recommended significant cuts to the staff and organizational consolidation to allow for more oversight and, presumably, more efficiency.[18]

Finally, reforming judicial campaigns in the state is also a critical agenda item. Some attempts at reform, such as campaign finance reporting, have been implemented and have not been found unconstitutional. However, when voters amended the state constitution in 1986 to prohibit political parties from endorsing judges who run in nonpartisan elections, the California Supreme Court found the initiative unconstitutional because it violated Californians' rights to freedom of expression and freedom of association. Obviously, judges have a lot of say when it comes to these reforms, and it is up to the individual judge to decide how much is too much when it comes to campaign spending.

Study Guide

FOR FURTHER READING

Bonneau, Chris W., and Damon Cann. "Campaign Spending, Diminishing Marginal Returns, and Campaign Finance Restrictions in Judicial Elections." *Journal of Politics* 73 (October 2011): 1267–80.

Bonneau, Chris W., and Melinda Gann Hall. *In Defense of Judicial Elections*. New York: Routledge Press, 2009. This book is a critique of previous empirical studies of judicial elections. Bonneau and Hall argue that elections as a selection method for judges are actually beneficial to democratic society.

California Courts. "Guide to California Courts." www.courtinfo.ca.gov/courts. Accessed 9/27/12.

Civil Justice Association of California. "Campaign Contributions to the California Judiciary 1997–2000." http://cjac.org/assets/finalrept2000.pdf. Accessed 8/16/12.

Hall, Melinda Gann, and Chris W. Bonneau. "Attack Advertising, the *White* Decision, and Voter Participation in State Supreme Court Elections." *Political Research Quarterly* 66 (March 2013): 115–26.

The National Center for State Courts (NCSC). www.judicialselection.us. Accessed 10/3/16.

Streb, Matthew J., ed. *Running for Judge: The Rising Political, Financial and Legal Stakes of Judicial Elections*. New York: New York University Press, 2007. This book is a collection of contemporary research conducted by professors who study state courts and judicial elections. Each chapter examines current issues and controversies that are confronted by state courts and state court judges.

Streb, Matthew J., and Brian Frederick. "When Money Can't Encourage Participation: Campaign Spending and Rolloff in Low-Visibility Judicial Elections." *Political Behavior* 33 (2011): 665–84.

ON THE WEB

California Courts. www.courts.ca.gov. Accessed 8/14/14. This is the official web site of the California court system.

The California Supreme Court Historical Society (CSCHS). http://cschs.org. Accessed 8/16/12. CSCHS catalogs and archives information about the history of the California Supreme Court.

Institute for the Advancement of the American Legal System. http://iaals.du.edu/. Accessed 8/14/14.

The National Center for State Courts (NCSC). www.judicialselection.us. Accessed 10/3/16. NCSC is an organization that provides services for court administrators, practitioners, and others interested in state courts. The web site includes information, data sets, and articles about state courts and court-related topics.

SUMMARY

I. Structure of the California courts.
   A. Court rulings, such as the recent rulings on undocumented immigrants, can affect all Californians.
   B. Superior courts are the trial courts of the California court system. They are courts of "first instance" and triers of fact. The California Courts of Appeal are intermediate appellate courts. They are divided into six districts across the state. All cases except for death-penalty cases are first appealed to the California Courts of Appeal.
   C. The supreme court is the highest court in the state. It is composed of seven justices and, like the courts of appeal, is an appellate court—that is, it reviews cases that were first heard in lower state courts such as the courts of appeal or a superior court.
   D. Jurisdiction limits the types of cases that civil courts and criminal courts can hear. Criminal courts deal with violations of state and local laws, and civil courts hear cases involving disputes between individuals or classes of individuals.
   E. Access to California courts is widely available. However, there is concern about the cost of litigation and legal representation.
   F. Federalism and California courts.
      1. Legal challenges to Proposition 215, the Compassionate Use Act (CUA), illustrate the tension between state and federal government. California permits the use of medical marijuana under certain conditions, but the federal government does not. There have been frequent attempts by federal law enforcement to close marijuana dispensaries that are operating legally under the CUA.
      2. Some local governments are adopting ordinances to regulate or even prohibit dispensaries from

operating in their communities. At times, local governments will call on federal law enforcement to assist them in closing dispensaries.

3. The California courts currently have a number of cases across all levels examining this policy.

II. Judicial selection.

A. Methods of selection for the California courts include nonpartisan elections for superior court and merit selection for appellate courts.

B. The California courts are diverse in terms of gender, race, and ideology. Governor Brown has appointed three justices to the court: Goodwin Liu, Mariano-Florentino Cuéllar, and Leondra Kruger. These appointments may give him the opportunity to shape the decision making of the California Supreme Court for years to come.

C. There are two competing theories regarding judicial selection—appointment and election. Those who favor judicial independence argue that appointment is a better method for selecting judges because it insulates judges from politics. Conversely, those who favor accountability argue that election as a method of selection is essential in a democracy and that judicial elections allow citizens to hold judges accountable for their decision making, similar to the way other elected officials are held accountable for their actions in office.

D. Recent controversies about judicial campaigning and campaign finance have led to some high-profile jurists (for example, retired U.S. Supreme Court associate justice Sandra Day O'Connor) and others to call for reforms. The most radical reforms proposed would eliminate judicial elections entirely. The increasing cost of judicial campaigns, which are low-saliency and low-turnout elections, have many members of the bar and legal community concerned.

E. Methods of removal from the bench include recall elections and impeachment. In addition, because all judges in California face some sort of election (direct or retention), voters may choose to vote for another judicial candidate or they may choose to vote against retaining an appellate court judge.

III. Contemporary issues in the judiciary.

A. Governor Brown's appointments of Goodwin Liu, Mariano-Florentino Cuéllar, and Leondra Kruger to the bench will shape and influence the court's decision making.

B. Judges serving across all court levels are confronted with cases that require them to make political decisions, including cases involving legislative redistricting.

C. State judges have the power to overturn laws enacted by the people through the initiative as well as laws composed by state legislators. There is a very strong likelihood that contested initiatives will end up in the courts, and the courts serve as an arena for continued political debate.

D. California courts have a very high caseload, though they remain fairly efficient and are able to dispose of a significant percentage of their criminal and civil caseload at all court levels.

PRACTICE QUIZ

1. All death-penalty sentences are automatically appealed directly to the California Supreme Court for review.
   a) true
   b) false

2. The California Supreme Court is similar to the U.S. Supreme Court in that it has nine justices.
   a) true
   b) false

3. Most civil cases in California are resolved before going to trial.
   a) true
   b) false

4. Voters in California are highly informed about the candidates running in judicial elections.
   a) true
   b) false

5. Initiatives passed in California are not subject to either judicial interpretation or judicial review.
   a) true
   b) false

6. In recent years, campaign spending in judicial elections
   a) has increased.
   b) has decreased.
   c) has remained the same.
   d) cannot be determined.

7. Chief Justice Rose Bird and Associate Justices Cruz Reynoso and Joseph Grodin were voted out by citizens who were angry about the judges' decisions concerning
   a) same-sex marriage.
   b) the death penalty.
   c) Proposition 13.
   d) term limits.

8. Judges selected by the governor to serve on the supreme court and the courts of appeal in California must be approved by
   a) the state legislature.
   b) the attorney general.
   c) the Commission on Judicial Appointments.
   d) none of the above

9. Superior courts in California adjudicate the following types of actions:
   a) civil and criminal cases.
   b) only civil cases.
   c) only criminal cases.
   d) only appeals.

10. One method of removing judges in the state of California is
    a) removal by the governor.
    b) censure by the state legislature.
    c) agreement between the speaker of the Assembly and the attorney general.
    d) a recall election.

CRITICAL-THINKING QUESTIONS

1. Given the concern on the part of lawmakers and the public over the role of money in judicial elections, what kinds of reforms might be implemented that would still allow for accountability? Is it possible to keep money and special interests out of judicial elections?

2. What factors do you believe are responsible for the tremendous criminal caseload in the California superior courts?

3. Is judicial independence important for state court judges?

4. What kinds of checks have been placed on the California judiciary? How do the other branches and political actors hold the state courts accountable?

KEY TERMS

appellate jurisdiction (p. 176)
civil courts (p. 178)
judicial accountability (p. 184)
judicial discretion (p. 177)
judicial independence (p. 184)
retention election (p. 182)
superior courts (p. 176)

8 The State Budget and Budgetary Limitations

WHAT CALIFORNIA GOVERNMENT DOES AND WHY IT MATTERS

Why does student tuition keep rising? The answer is simple. Higher education is a major category of the state budget, the third or fourth largest in most years, and charts circulating among politicians in Sacramento made it look as if California students until recently paid relatively low tuition and fees by national standards. The charts came from the Legislative Analyst's Office and the California Postsecondary Education Commission (CPEC), a research agency created by the legislature to be independent of the three systems of higher education. Everyone involved in higher education policy saw these charts: the governor's department of finance; the legislative committees and their staff; the bureaucracy; and two of this book's authors, who were members of the California State University (CSU) statewide academic senate for several years. After seeing these charts, legislators on the hunt for an extra several hundred million dollars to cut from the budget felt justified in saying, "Well, the students are paying relatively little by U.S. standards; just increase the university's fees to cover the difference."

And that was the process that occurred, year after year, for about a decade. Meanwhile the inequalities have increased. University of California (UC) students pay for more than half their education cost; community college students cover 15 percent. The Legislative Analyst's Office found that "UC's tuition and fees are higher than all but 10 of the 65 largest public research universities in other states. By contrast, tuition and fees at the CSU are lower than all but 42 universities among a group of 244 masters-level public universities in other states. CCC tuition and fees are the lowest in the country. . . ."[1] As the legislative analyst has stated several times, the "state currently does not have a tuition policy." Instead, when economic times are good, tuition and fees are frozen, but when the inevitable downturn comes, fees and tuition rise sharply. What kind of budget process produces such inequalities over time?

Ultimately, over the four years from 2008 to 2012, higher education lost $2.8 billion in funding, about 22 percent of its total, and by 2016, despite limited increases granted by the governor, the CSU had 19 percent less money to spend than it had in 2007–08.[2] Similar statements can be written about the University of California.

Figure 8.1 contrasts state spending on higher education with state spending on prisons and corrections. Forty years ago the state spent almost 18 percent of the state general fund on higher education and less than 4 percent on corrections. By 2008–09, the shares were almost equal at 11.1 percent for higher education and 10.7 percent for corrections. Since then, higher education spending has increased a bit and corrections spending has fallen, in part because the state has shifted inmates from state prisons to locally funded jails.

Students aren't the only citizens heavily affected by California's budget woes. With a budget of over $169 billion, plus almost $100 billion in federal funds, California represents one of the largest economies in the world. Its *deficit* in recent years has been larger than the entire budgets of all but the 10 largest states. Over 2.5 million workers in California (1 out of 6) work for the federal, state, or local governments, and some other workers are indirectly funded by the public sector.[3]

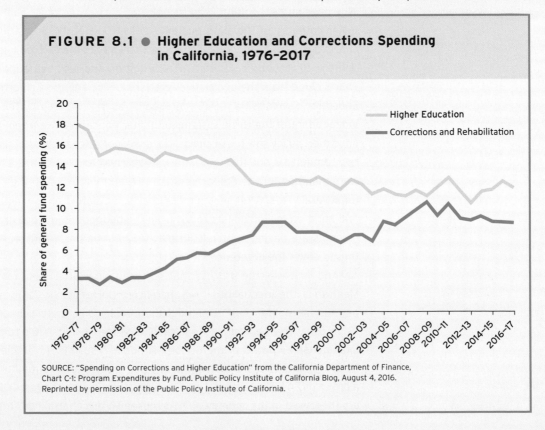

FIGURE 8.1 ● Higher Education and Corrections Spending in California, 1976–2017

SOURCE: "Spending on Corrections and Higher Education" from the California Department of Finance, Chart C-1: Program Expenditures by Fund. Public Policy Institute of California Blog, August 4, 2016. Reprinted by permission of the Public Policy Institute of California.

It is therefore unsurprising that the process to approve the budget, which controls the livelihood of so many people, is controversial. The public itself is split—most Californians are opposed to spending cuts in public programs as well as to increases in taxes or fees. They are also distrustful of state government and disapprove of the job their politicians are doing. One political party in the state legislature—the Republicans—won't increase taxes under any circumstances; indeed, some Republicans consider the entire budget so illegitimate that they won't vote for it under any realistic set of circumstances (one legislator didn't vote for a budget for over a decade). In 2002 the legislature came within one vote of increasing the sales tax, but that vote was impossible to procure. The amount and intensity of political controversy over the state budget, a document that embodies the values and decisions of the citizens, its legislature, and its leaders, is truly remarkable.

Passing the budget is at the center, both in difficulty and in scope, of what the state government does each year. Since the passage of Proposition 13 in 1978, the state government has received less revenue than it would have otherwise, and that revenue has become more volatile, rising and falling with the economy. The state constitution mandates that the legislature pass the budget by June 15. Since 1990, the legislature has met this deadline only ten times. Two of those were budget surplus years, when it is always easier to pass a budget. Six others have occurred since the passage of Proposition 25 in 2011, including 2014, 2015, and 2016. Proposition 25 requires only a majority vote to pass the budget and penalizes legislators by cutting their salaries when the budget is overdue.

How Is the Budget Formed?

The process of forming a budget has four steps. Most governments today follow a similar process—proposal by the executive branch, enactment by the legislature, approval by the governor, and implementation by the executive branch. Note that the preparation, enactment, and implementation of the budget for a single fiscal year takes almost three calendar years. See Box 8.1 for a summary of the budget process and Box 8.2 for the constitutional requirements for California's budget. The four steps of the budget process are discussed in detail below.

Executive Proposal

Each fall, state agencies send their budget proposals to the governor through the state **Department of Finance**. The governor formulates a proposal and sends it to the legislature in January. In late spring, he or she revises the proposal in what is called the **May revise**.

Before 1922, agencies proposed their budgets directly to the legislature; there was no **unified budget** proposed by the governor or anyone else. Instead, "budgeting was the domain of interest groups, department heads, and ranking committee members."[4] In 1911, upon finding little or no justification for the amounts contained in the appropriations bills sent to him, Progressive governor Hiram

BOX 8.1 ● California's Budget Process

CALENDAR YEAR 1

JULY–SEPTEMBER

- Agencies prepare requests and make proposals.
- Requests sent to Department of Finance.

OCTOBER–DECEMBER

- Department of Finance reviews requests and consults governor.

CALENDAR YEAR 2

JANUARY–MARCH

- California Constitution requires governor to send a balanced budget to the legislature by January 10.
- Governor's budget proposal is introduced in both houses as identical budget bills.
- Legislative Analyst's Office prepares extensive analysis.
- Budget hearings held in both houses.

APRIL–JUNE

- May: Governor sends revised and updated projections of revenues and expenditures to legislature (the May revise).
- June 15: California Constitution requires legislature to pass (by a majority vote) a balanced budget by this date. As of 2010, all members of the legislature permanently forfeit salary and expenses every day until the budget is passed.
- Governor signs budget, using line-item veto, if desired, to lower any appropriation items. Legislature can override by a two-thirds vote.

JULY–SEPTEMBER

- July 1: California's fiscal year begins. This is the first quarter. (The federal fiscal year, in contrast, begins October 1.)

OCTOBER–DECEMBER

- Second quarter of California's fiscal year.

CALENDAR YEAR 3

JANUARY–MARCH

- Third quarter of California's fiscal year.

APRIL–JUNE

- Fourth quarter of California's fiscal year.

Johnson created the Board of Control to advise him on the fiscal justification for each appropriation.

In 1922, California adopted its own version of new federal legislation that had been passed the previous year, thus *unifying* the budget process. The legislation called for a consolidated administration proposal in the form of a **governor's budget** that must be balanced, contain justifications for the amounts proposed, and be accompanied by bills introduced by legislative leaders in each house, thus providing a starting point for the negotiations and decisions each year. The existence of a governor's budget was an improvement over the situation before 1900, when "government structures . . . hid more than they revealed to the public."[5]

Legislative Adoption

The legislature adopts a balanced budget based on the governor's proposal. As of 2011, both the Assembly and the state Senate must adopt the budget by a majority of the entire membership. The Assembly and Senate budget committees and their subcommittees hold hearings on the budget bills, during which they receive testimony and input from individuals and groups, including the affected departments and agencies, the Department of Finance, the **Legislative Analyst's Office**, committee staff, and interest groups.

The Legislative Analyst's Office provides nonpartisan and independent review of the entire budget, including alternative ways to accomplish the same goals and objectives. The reviews are so nonpartisan that former legislative analyst Elizabeth Hill was called the "Budget Nun" because "her fiscal reports are incorruptible. They're the bible. The one source of truth. . . . She's the most influential non-elected official in the Capitol."[6] The current legislative analyst, Mac Taylor, was appointed in 2008 and has 30 years of experience in the Legislative Analyst's Office.

Before 2011 a **Budget Conference Committee** was appointed to work out the differences between the Assembly and Senate budget bills. Since the passage of Proposition 25 in 2010, however, a majority vote is now the sole requirement to pass the budget; the endless compromising with the Republican Party that used to occupy Sacramento through the summers of the 1990s and 2000s is over. The "Big 5" group, consisting of the governor, Assembly speaker, Senate president pro tempore, and Assembly and Senate minority leaders, used to be instrumental in soliciting a few Republican votes to pass the budget under the old two-thirds requirement. Their influence in the budget process is now irrelevant, or at least it has been in the first few years under the new system. From 2011 to 2016, the budget was passed by June 15, the official deadline in Proposition 25; if legislators miss this deadline, they lose their salaries on every day that the budget is late.

Raising a tax, however, still requires a two-thirds vote of both the Assembly and the state Senate (or the approval of the voters through an initiative). While the Democrats achieved majorities of over two-thirds in both the Assembly and Senate in 2012, the voters approved Jerry Brown's initiative proposal on the November 2012 ballot, Proposition 30, to raise the state sales and income taxes in the same year. Because of this new source of revenue, Governor Brown strongly urged the legislature not to pass any additional tax increases in 2013. The two-thirds supermajority disappeared in early 2014 after three Democratic state senators were suspended for their involvement in various scandals.

1. Within the first 10 days of the calendar year, the governor must submit to the legislature a unified budget that is balanced, contains an explanation for each proposed expenditure, and is accompanied by a budget bill itemizing the recommended expenditures.

2. The budget bills must be introduced immediately in each house by the respective appropriations chairs.

3. The legislature must pass the budget by June 15 of each year. Since 2004, the budget must be balanced.

4. Appropriations from the general fund must be passed in each house by a majority vote of the membership. Note that the requirement is a majority "of the membership," not just those present and voting.

5. When the governor signs the budget bill(s), he or she is allowed to reduce or eliminate an appropriated dollar amount. This is the line-item veto, a powerful tool.

Gubernatorial Action

The governor may use the **line-item veto** to lower any line-item appropriation in the budget, including lowering it to zero. The legislature may override the governor's veto by a two-thirds majority in each of the two houses and replace the lowered number with its own amount, although doing so is rare. Because of the line-item veto, the final budget is usually very close to the governor's May revise proposal.

Implementation

Agencies implement the budget as passed, with the fiscal year beginning July 1. The Department of Finance states explicitly that agencies and departments are expected to operate within their budgets and comply with any provisions enacted by the legislature: "The general expectation is that state agencies comply with the legislative intent."[7] There is some flexibility in implementation, but, compared to other states, the governor's flexibility is limited, as we shall see.

Other Groups Involved in the Budget Process

In addition to the governor and legislature, the agencies mentioned earlier—the Department of Finance on the executive side and the Legislative Analyst's Office on the legislative side—are closely involved in the budget process, as are two other groups:

- The courts have sometimes ruled on the constitutionality of particular budget actions, particularly on proposed administrative actions to be taken when the legislature has been late submitting a budget. They have also had to decide on the constitutionality of various budget provisions, such as the limits on property taxes established by Proposition 13 in 1978.

- **Moody's, Fitch Ratings, and Standard & Poor's** rate the ability of the states to repay their bonds. A "bond" is a loan where the investor is lending the government a certain amount of money for a certain length of time at a certain rate of interest. The rating is one of several factors that influence the cost of selling a bond issue. The lower the credit rating, the higher the interest rate that must be paid to induce investors to purchase the bonds. In 2003, Moody's rating of California's bonds was the lowest rating given for any state, but since then, California's credit rating has risen. Standard & Poor's raised California's credit rating in 2015, reflecting the budget discipline imposed by Governor Jerry Brown during his administration, but 31 of the 39 states rated still have a higher credit rating than California does. The 2015 ratings have come up to the AA level, meaning the state's bonds are of high quality but with more fluctuation or long-term risk than bonds at the AAA level. Of more significance perhaps was Moody's test in early 2016 of the four most populous states and their ability to withstand a potential recession in the next two years. Of the four (Texas, Florida, New York, and California), California was the least able because of revenue volatility and inadequate reserves.[8]

What Is in the Budget?

Every state budget contains the following information:

- economic assumptions—how the economy should respond during the forthcoming fiscal year, and what that response means for revenues and expenditures
- revenues expected in the various categories
- expenditures broken down by department and program

Revenues

The **general fund** includes all state revenues that are *not* **federal funds**, special funds, or bond funds. (See Box 8.4 later in the chapter for more on federal funds.) The state budget is usually assumed to consist of either just the general fund or the general fund plus special funds and bond funds. The general fund receives over 90 percent of its $100 billion–plus revenues from the sales tax, the income tax, and corporate taxes and consists of all state money that is not allocated to a special fund or a bond fund. **Special funds** are funds that are allocated for a specific purpose: thus there is a beverage container recycling fund, a fish and game fund, and almost 500 more, totaling some $45 billion in the 2016–17 budget. Each has a specific source of income and a specific use for which the fund is designated. **Bond funds** come from bonds that are repaid over spans of a few years to a few decades, but some of them substitute for current expenditures.

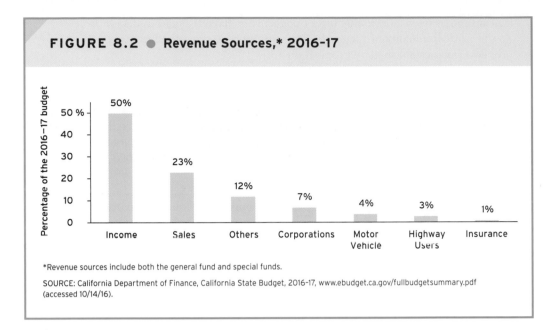

FIGURE 8.2 ● Revenue Sources,* 2016-17

Percentage of the 2016–17 budget

- Income: 50%
- Sales: 23%
- Others: 12%
- Corporations: 7%
- Motor Vehicle: 4%
- Highway Users: 3%
- Insurance: 1%

*Revenue sources include both the general fund and special funds.

SOURCE: California Department of Finance, California State Budget, 2016-17, www.ebudget.ca.gov/fullbudgetsummary.pdf (accessed 10/14/16).

Looking at all sources of revenue, both general funds and special funds, we see the revenue sources are as follows, according to the 2016–17 enacted budget (see Figure 8.2):

PERSONAL INCOME TAX Figure 8.2 shows that the **personal income tax** provides 50 percent of California's state budget, some $85 billion. California's personal income tax ranges from 0 to 13.3 percent of income, with a substantial credit per child or dependent. The income tax is considered highly **progressive**, with the top 1 percent of taxpayers paying over half of the income tax in 2012. The wealthiest 10 percent paid 80.4 percent of the income tax in the same year.[9] This is one of the most progressive personal income taxes in the nation. (See the "Who Are Californians?" feature for more on how California's income tax figures into its total revenue as compared to other states.) Regular income (salaries and wages) does not vary that much from year to year, but **capital gains** income (income from selling stock that has appreciated in value, for example) varies considerably from one year to the next, making revenues from the income tax fluctuate a great deal. Proposition 30 established three new brackets for taxpayers who make more than $305,100 per year: at 11.3, 12.3, and 13.3 percent of income. The new brackets are temporary, lasting from 2012 to 2018. They make the California state income tax even more progressive, reflecting the income level of the state (which is higher than the nation's; see Chapter 1). Proposition 55 on the November 2016 ballot extended those "temporary" brackets for 12 years.

SALES TAX Figure 8.2 shows that the **sales tax** provides about 23 percent of California's state budget, some $39 billion. The baseline state sales tax rate is 7.5 percent. Counties or taxing districts are allowed to add between 0.13 and 0.5 percent per local district for local services. In some areas there is more than one district tax in effect. The average sales tax in California is 7.75 percent. The minimum in

Where Does California Get Its Revenue?

There is wide variation in how states fund their programs and activities. Sources of state revenue usually include individual income taxes, sales taxes, property taxes, and corporate taxes; most states also collect a variety of smaller taxes, including gasoline and cigarette taxes. Fifteen states don't levy property taxes at all, while four states (Nevada, Texas, Washington, and Wyoming) don't levy taxes on individual incomes.

Share of State Tax Revenue, 2014

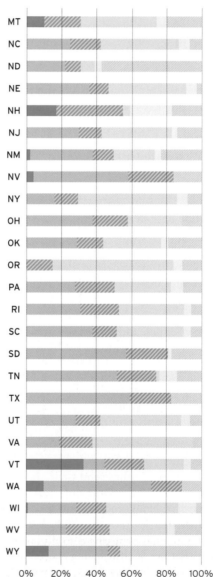

Legend:
- Property tax
- Sales tax (general)
- Sales tax (selective)
- Individual income tax
- Corporate net income tax
- License tax and other

SOURCE: Ben Casselman and Allison McCann, "Where Your State Gets Its Money," FiveThirtyEight, www.fivethirtyeight.com/features/where-your-state-gets-its-money/ (accessed 8/17/16).

forcriticalanalysis

1. How does the distribution of different types of taxes in California compare to the distribution of taxes in other states? For example, why do you think property tax makes up a smaller share of revenue in California than in New Hampshire?

2. California's largest revenue source, individual income taxes, is structured as a progressive tax: those with larger incomes pay larger percentages. Is this the best system, or would the state be better served by a flat income tax?

any area is 7.5 percent. The maximum is in Pico Rivera and South Gate, two cities in Los Angeles County, at about 10 percent. Economists consider the sales tax
regressive—that is, as individual or household income increases, the proportion of
income paid through the tax decreases, because lower-income households spend
a higher proportion of their incomes on consumption goods that are taxed compared with higher income households. In California, the state refunds 1.25 percent
of its share to the local city and county; this feature has led many cities to search
for businesses that are both clean industries and have a high sales volume (thus
increasing sales-tax revenue), such as **big-box shopping centers and automobile
dealerships**. A "clean industry" is one that produces little air or water pollution.
The process has been called the "**fiscalization of land use**."

A state sales tax has existed in California since 1933, with the rate raised on
average every five years. In 2013, Proposition 30 temporarily raised the state sales
tax one-quarter of 1 percent. The increase would have expired in 2016 but was
extended by Proposition 55 on the November 2016 ballot.

The sales tax was developed over 75 years ago and is based on an older conception of the economy consisting mostly of goods that are manufactured, bought, and
sold. Services make up over half of the modern economy, but these are not taxed in
California. In many states, at least some services are taxed. Having a broader base
on the sales tax would enable the rate to be lowered from its current high level,
but finding a two-thirds majority in the legislature to pass a tax reform act is close
to impossible. Even in 2013, when the Democratic Party had a two-thirds majority
in both the Assembly and the state Senate, the Democrats were unwilling and not
unified enough to modernize the tax code.

PROPERTY TAX Property tax revenues go to the local level of government, so
they are not included in Figure 8.2. All property owners pay California's property tax, limited under Proposition 13 to 1 percent of the assessed value in 1975
or the value of a more recent sale. Once acquired, annual tax increases are limited to 2 percent or the amount of inflation, whichever is smaller. Proposition 13
passed overwhelmingly in 1978 and contains provisions requiring special majorities greater than 50 percent for legislators and voters to raise taxes. Proposition 13
rolled back property taxes in California by more than half, and the state has endeav-
ored to make up the difference ever since. Local property tax revenue available for
cities, counties, and school districts has been substantially reduced. As a result, all
local government entities are more reliant on the state for revenue, and decision-
making power has substantially shifted, in the eyes of virtually all observers, from
the local level to the state level.

School districts are an excellent example of the effects of this shift. Whereas
California once had some of the best-quality and best-funded schools in the nation,
its expenditures per pupil have fallen in comparison to the rest of the nation. Its
staff-per-student ratio is now 70 percent of the average for other states. Its student
achievement levels lag behind the rest of the nation, and a greater proportion of
high-income families send their children to private schools compared to the pre-
1978 period. At the same time, teacher salaries are relatively high to accommodate
the cost of living and housing prices, and to attract good-quality recruits to the
profession.

Compared to other states, California's overall tax structure depends more on
taxes that are volatile, rising and falling with the economy (income tax, sales tax),
and less on taxes that don't vary with the economy (e.g., the property tax) because

California's public schools have suffered since the passage of Proposition 13, which decreased local property tax revenues and effectively transferred the responsibility for funding school districts from the local to the state level. Overcrowded classrooms have been one result of this shift.

of the Proposition 13 limits. The average state obtains 29 percent of its total state and local tax funds from the property tax, but because of Proposition 13's limits, California obtains only 22 percent. (See Box 8.3 for a more detailed explanation and assessment of Proposition 13.)

CORPORATION TAX The corporation tax is levied on corporate profits and provides about 7 percent of state revenues, some $11 billion. The corporation tax structure is cited favorably by *Governing* magazine in its appraisal of the state's tax system as "tough on the creation of tax-dodge subsidiaries, and the law covers a firm's property and assets, not just its sales."[10] The 2012 Franchise Tax Board Annual Report states that in 2011, out of the 734,315 corporations that reported their incomes, almost 43 percent either lost money or broke even. The 1.6 percent that earned $1 million or more paid about 85 percent of the total tax, while the top 1,322 corporations earning $10 million or more paid 71 percent of the total.[11]

INDIAN CASINOS Governor Schwarzenegger attempted to increase the amount of revenue received for the general fund from Indian gambling operations in California. In 2005–06 the state received only $27 million for the general fund of the $301 million from the tribal–state gambling compacts negotiated by the governor and ratified by the legislature. In 2008–09 the governor's budget projected $430 million in revenues, but much less was actually received. More recent budgets have no information on Indian gambling revenues, as they are so small as to be insignificant (less than one-tenth of one percent) in a budget of more than $100 billion.

STATE LOTTERY Lottery monies received by the state and allocated to education, projected to be $1.5 billion in 2016–17, would be meaningful if the state added them to the education budget. Instead, research shows that in California, as in other states, "lottery funds have merely substituted for normal levels of appropriations, despite the fact that lotteries had been promoted as boosting spending for education," according to the North Carolina Center for Public Policy Research.[12]

What is it? Proposition 13, passed overwhelmingly by the voters in June 1978, had the following provisions:

- All property taxes were rolled back to a maximum of 1 percent of the value of the property in 1975-76.

- The value of the property, and thus the tax paid, was allowed to increase by the rate of inflation, but the inflation rate was capped at 2 percent per year.

- When ownership changed, property would be revalued at the current market value.

- No new property taxes could be imposed, either by the state or by local governments.

- Any "special taxes" could be imposed only by a two thirds margin of the voters in the particular area (the state legislature was already under a two-thirds approval rule for raising taxes, a rule in force since 1933).

- All property taxes collected were to be distributed "according to law," and because no such law existed, the legislature had to create them.

THE EFFECTS OF PROPOSITION 13

Proposition 13 immediately affected local governments. Before 1978, local governments and agencies each established their own property tax rate, designed to produce sufficient revenues to accomplish the particular function of the agency. Now, each agency's property tax rate was irrelevant; the state would decide "according to law" how much money to apportion to each local jurisdiction. The total property tax collected decreased by over half. The state, however, had a $55 billion surplus, which helped bridge the gap in funds for several years.

The single biggest change set in motion by Proposition 13 is that the state assumed considerable authority over issues formerly handled by local government.[a] Local governments used to set the local tax rate to produce sufficient funds for public services necessary to the locality. Instead, those decisions are now made by the state, and "clearly, the property tax is now really a state tax."[b]

Another consequence stems from the provision that requires a two-thirds vote of the local area to impose or raise a tax. Many localities have seen election results of 60 to 66 percent in favor, just short of the required two-thirds, and have been powerless to initiate local projects, such as acquiring land for parks. Bond issues for the repair and construction of school facilities, however, were authorized by Proposition 39 in 2000 to require the approval of only 55 percent of local voters.

One of the most important consequences is called "the fiscalization of land use"—that is, the tendency of local governments not only to evaluate land use changes in terms of how much money will be brought to the local government but to make decisions on that basis. Because localities receive a share of the state sales tax, land use changes that produce a lot of sales tax revenues are preferred. Many cities favor big-box shopping centers and auto malls over housing developments, and rely increasingly on development fees and other ways to obtain revenue not available through the property tax.

Finally, we have seen the development of many "arcane" financing techniques, those so intricate that no one understands them except the few who developed them. These are also designed to help obtain revenues and replace property taxes.

(continued)

A Legislative Analyst's Office (LAO) study[c] completed in 2016 debunks some common claims about Proposition 13 and uses the best evidence on its current effects. Following the enactment of Propositon 13 and its one percent of assessed value property tax limit in 1978, property tax payments fell by 60 percent in California. The LAO study confirms that similar properties purchased at different times pay vastly different property taxes, depending on when the owner purchased the property. Higher-income Californians tend to own more homes and homes of greater value, and they therefore receive the majority of the tax relief dollars provided by Proposition 13. Property turnover has declined considerably since 1978, with Proposition 13 appearing to play some, but not the total, role in this decline.

One of the most significant findings was that homeowners pay only a slightly higher share of property taxes now compared to the period before 1978, and that residential properties do not turn over more than commercial properties. One of the justifications for the split roll reform of Proposition 13, in which commercial properties would be taxed at different and presumably higher rates than residential properties, was that residential properties were thought to be sold and resold at faster rates than commercial property.

[a]The best description of Proposition 13 and its implications is Jeffrey I. Chapman, "Proposition 13: Some Unintended Consequences," Public Policy Institute of California, www.ppic.org (accessed 7/27/12).
[b]Chapman, "Proposition 13," p. 22.
[c]Legislative Analyst's Office, "Common Claims About Proposition 13," www.lao.ca.gov/Publications/Report/3497 (accessed 9/19/16).

Why Do Revenues Vary So Much?

California's budget rises and falls each year, soaring when the economy is healthy and plunging in even the mildest recessions. Here is why:

- Revenues from the sales tax and the personal income tax depend directly on how the state economy performs each year.

- Compared to other states, the budget relies more on the personal income tax, the capital gains portion of which soars when stock options are cashed out, than on the property tax, which was limited in 1978 by Proposition 13 and is roughly constant every year.

How Well Does the Tax System Function?

The tax system seems to be functioning poorly. Little has changed since *Governing* magazine published "The Way We Tax" in 2003, comparing tax policy in all 50 states. The report gave California one star out of four in the category "Adequacy of Revenue," two out of four in "Fairness to Taxpayers," and two out of four in "Management of System."[13] Only Tennessee received a lower overall rating, and four other states were tied with California.

A more recent study of tax administration, conducted by the Council on State Taxation (COST) and published in December 2013, ranked California's tax administration in 49th place, tied with Louisiana, and graded it a D−, citing errors such as permitting the same people to serve on the boards at different levels of tax appeal and allowing officials unqualified in tax administration onto those boards.[14] Some of the problem areas include the following:

- The "highly progressive and volatile" income tax depends too much on capital gains being taxed at the same level as regular income. Thus tax revenues soared along with the stock market in 2000 and 2013–14, but typically these revenues fall just as quickly. In 2008, for example, the forecast for the income tax dropped 13 percent in just six months because of the downturn in the economy.

- Although the state income tax is highly progressive, both the sales tax and the entire tax system are regressive, meaning that those at the bottom of the income distribution pay a higher proportion of their income as taxes to the state than those at the top pay.[15]

- The sales tax focuses on goods that are sold, reflecting the manufacturing economy in place when the tax was developed. But the modern economy has shifted toward services, which are not taxed—for example, a doctor's office visit or the labor charge when your automobile is fixed. Broadening the base of the sales tax to include services would enable the high tax rate on goods (compared to the rate in other states) to be lowered.

- Ballot measures have imposed rigid spending demands (discussed in the section "Budgetary Limitations" later in this chapter).

- Tax administration is split among the Franchise Tax Board, the Board of Equalization, and the Employment Development Department, an arrangement that is widely considered to be inefficient.

Is California Overtaxed?

THE CONSERVATIVE VIEW Conservatives think California is overtaxed. The California Taxpayers Association makes the case that "the extraordinary level of taxation in California can provide more than enough in tax revenue to fund police and fire services, education for our children, and public works projects and health and welfare services for California's poor."[16] Taxes are so high, in their view, that the state is no longer economically competitive with other states. The Washington, D.C.–based Tax Foundation, which calculates the total tax burden, including taxes paid out of state (for vacation property, for example), found California's state and local tax burden for fiscal year 2012 to be the sixth highest in the nation.[17]

THE LIBERAL VIEW Liberals often argue not that California's taxes are low, but that they are moderate in comparison with California's income, ranked 15th to 20th among the states. The California Budget & Policy Center, for example, stated in 2014 that California was a "moderate" tax state, ranking 20th among the 50 states "with respect to total 'own source' revenues raised by state and local governments." California ranked 11th in the percentage of state taxes compared with personal income in the state in 2010–11. Personal and corporate income tax collections are relatively high in California, but the tobacco and alcoholic beverage taxes are relatively low.[18]

THE REALITY California is a relatively rich state. Its household and median family incomes are some $8,000 higher than the U.S. averages. The income and sales tax rates are among the higher tax rates of all American states, although there are numerous exemptions that bring the total tax rate lower.

The critical challenge to California's tax structure is not that taxes are high but that it is outmoded. It reflects the economy of the 1950s and Proposition 13 decisions made in the 1970s. The property tax collects less money proportionally than other wealthy states because of Proposition 13. The sales tax is based on the purchase of goods (with food exempted), not on services. Lower- and middle-class families with children are largely exempted from the personal income tax. The bottom line is that, like so many areas of the state's governmental structure, California's tax structure needs to be reformed.

Betty Yee, California state controller, established a Council of Economic Advisors on Tax Reform in 2015 to discuss the problems of California's present tax structure. Since Proposition 13 was approved in 1978, policymakers have adopted incremental changes to California's taxes, but no comprehensive restructuring has been adopted. Meanwhile revenues from the sales tax, the corporation tax, and the property tax have diminished relative to the size of the economy, and the resulting increasing emphasis on the personal income tax has led to greater unpredictability of state tax revenue and increasing challenges for budget policymakers. The commission found that comprehensive reform of the state's tax structure was long overdue and sought in its findings to discuss the underlying principles and tradeoffs that would be necessary in any legislation, without discussing actual proposals.[19]

Without comprehensive tax reform, California will continue to be a battleground for both liberals and conservatives, with conservatives seeking to lower the highest rates, and liberals seeking exemptions for the poor and middle class.

Conservative groups rate California's business climate as one of the worst of any state because of the high levels of taxes; the taxation of capital gains at regular tax rates; and the number of regulations and permits affecting citizens' ability to establish, run, and expand a business.[20] Nevertheless, many large corporations are located in California, particularly in Silicon Valley (the area between San Francisco and San Jose) because of the wealth of skilled talent in the area's labor market.

One question is whether California's tax levels hold down the state's economic growth. An analysis of the growth rates of nine states with high personal income taxes compared to the nine states that lack any personal income tax indicates no conclusive relationship. In fact, the states that grow the most seem to be those with high rates of population growth, and several of the non-income-tax states have economic resources (such as oil, which obviates the need for a state income tax) not available to other states.[21] Many observers point to the healthiness of California's recovery from the 2008 recession, especially compared with other states, as evidence that high tax rates do not correlate with low economic growth.

Expenditures

Figure 8.3 depicts the 2016–17 state budget, including the general fund, special funds, and bond funds.

It indicates that the largest spending category is health and human services (HHS), at 31 percent of the budget and some $53.8 billion. This category includes the state (but not the federal) contribution for Medi-Cal, California's Medicaid

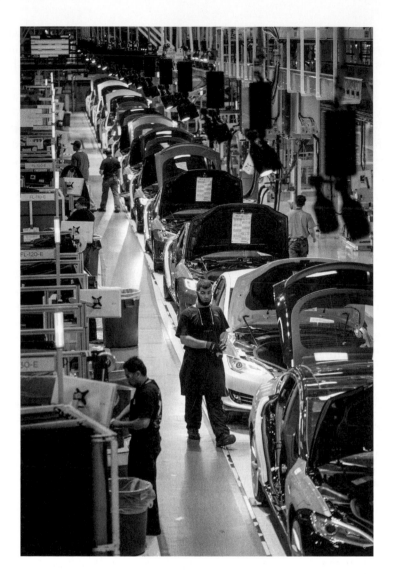

At Tesla's factory in Fremont, workers assemble cars on the line. Despite talk of California's unfriendly business climate, California ranks third for the number of Fortune 500 companies located in the state, with 53, exceeded only by Texas's 54 and New York's 55. The California economy in 2016 was the world's sixth largest, surpassing France and Brazil and exceeded only by the United States, China, Japan, Germany, and the United Kingdom.

program, which provides health coverage for the poor as well as for senior citizens in nursing homes. It also includes the public health system; Healthy Families, California's state children's health insurance program; welfare, including Temporary Assistance for Needy Families; and the state contribution to food stamps and to the Women, Infants, and Children (WIC) supplemental food program, among many others.

The second largest expenditure category in Figure 8.3 is elementary and secondary education, at $51.5 billion and 30 percent of total expenditures. With the passage of Proposition 13 in 1978, a gradually increasing proportion of the state general fund has been spent on K–12 education. The money in this category supplements property tax revenues for education, collected by each county.

Higher education is the third largest category at $14.9 billion and 9 percent of total expenditures. Higher education includes funding for the community college system (112 campuses, 2.1 million students), the CSU system (23 campuses,

FIGURE 8.3 ● **California Budget Expenditures* 2016-17**

Percentage of California's 2016–17 Budget

Category	Percentage
HHS	31%
K-12	30%
Univ.	9%
Corr.	8%
Bus.	7%
Gen'l	5%
Legis.	4%
Res.	3%
Env.	2%
Other	1%

*Expenditures include both the general and the special funds.

SOURCE: California Department of Finance, California State Budget, 2016-17, www.ebudget.ca.gov/fullbudgetsummary.pdf (accessed 10/14/16).

371,000 students), and the UC system (10 campuses, 5 medical centers, 3 national labs, 211,000 students).

Since 1980–81 there has been a trend downward in the proportion of the budget devoted to higher education, as discussed in the beginning of this chapter. In recent years, state funding for higher education was cut severely. A report from the Public Policy Institute of California demonstrates that funding for higher education composed more than 17 percent of the state budget as recently as 1975, but since then the proportion has declined to between 11 and 13 percent.[22] Another report, from the Center on Budget and Policy Priorities in Washington, D.C., compares spending-per-student cuts and tuition increases in all states from fiscal years 2008 to 2013.[23] All but two of the states cut their expenditures per student during this time period, and California is in the middle of the pack with a 29.5 percent cut. California's tuition increase percentage for the same time period, at 72 percent, is the second largest among the states. The recent budget augmentations from Governor Jerry Brown have partially restored the billions that were cut from higher education in the 2000s.

The corrections and rehabilitation category provides funding for state prisons and youth authorities. At $13.3 billion and 8 percent of the budget, this category increased steadily from 1980–81 through the mid-1990s as the public demanded the Three-Strike law and similar measures. It has since leveled off.

The fifth largest category is business, transportation, and housing, at $12.8 billion or 7 percent of the state budget. This area includes Caltrans, which maintains the state's roads; the Department of Motor Vehicles (DMV); and the departments that regulate corporations, alcoholic beverages, real estate, managed health care, and high-speed rail, among others. (The high-speed rail area includes only a few million dollars for state positions that manage the high-speed rail authority;

construction funds come from the federal government, local funds, cap-and-trade funds,[24] private funds, and bond issues.) Most programs in the business, transportation, and housing category are largely funded by special funds and taxes, not by the general fund.

Figure 8.3 contains several other smaller categories: general government administration; the legislative, executive, judicial category; the natural resources category (e.g., state parks); and areas covering state expenditures for the environment. The last category is "other," which covers everything else.

Budgetary Limitations

Through the use of initiatives California voters have not only passed bond issues but have also limited what the state government can do in some very significant areas. Many of these initiatives, such as Propositions 99, 111, 49, and 71, have placed money into various "special funds," which is why Figure 8.3 above includes both the general fund and special funds. Here are a few of the most significant initatives.[25]

- **Proposition 13 (1978)** cut property taxes to 1 percent of the assessed valuation of the property in 1975 and allows reassessment only when the property is sold. If justified by inflation, the tax can rise a maximum of 2 percent between assessments.

- **Proposition 98 (1988)** requires that at least 40 percent of the general fund be devoted to K–14 education, including community colleges; annual increases are to be at least equal to the increase in school enrollment and the cost of living.

- **Proposition 99 (1988)** mandated a 25-cent tax on cigarettes, with the proceeds to be spent on antismoking campaigns and medical research.

- **Proposition 111 (1990)** increased the gas tax and trucking fees; the proceeds must be spent on transportation projects.

- **Proposition 49 (2002)**, supported by then-potential Republican candidate for governor Arnold Schwarzenegger, requires that several hundred million dollars be spent on after-school programs.

- **Proposition 71 (2004)** authorizes the sale of $3 billion in bonds to fund stem-cell research in the state.

Of these, the two that have had the most effect are Propositions 13 and 98. Proposition 13 has made the state budget more reliant on taxes that vary with the economy and less reliant on sources of income that don't vary with the economy, particularly the property tax. Proposition 98 dictated that a certain proportion of the budget, almost half when higher education is included, must be devoted to one policy area.

Because the initiative requires only a majority vote, it is relatively easy to authorize expenditures through the initiative compared with doing so through the legislature. California has become a state in which it is easy to lower taxes/budget items through the legislature or to authorize expenditures through the initiative, but it has become increasingly difficult to raise the funds to pay for basic state functions, including higher education, health, and others. Voters in recent public opinion surveys find most items in the budget to be popular (except welfare), but they strongly resist paying extra for any of them.

Recent California Budgets and the Budget Process

In recent years, California lawmakers and the governor have closed the budget gap with the standard techniques used in other states—incremental tax or fee increases; cuts in education, health, and social services, the largest portions of the budget; and borrowing through bond issues that are repaid over a 5- to 10-year period to cover a portion of the yearly deficit. The capital gains tax produced extra funds for the budgets of 2013–14 through 2016–17, making the process easier, although Governor Jerry Brown strongly resisted legislators' push to make agencies that had been cut substantially in the previous decade "whole" again. Governor Brown also insisted that the state begin repaying the funds borrowed during the last decade to close budget gaps.

California Forward, a bipartisan group aimed at fixing some of California's perennial budget process problems, stated in 2008 that

> the current budget process is largely a relic of the mid-20th century, with the focus on how much to increase spending (or how much to cut), rather than the value that public services bring to Californians over time. These annual budget decisions often either push California's fiscal systems toward long-term solvency or away from it. The ongoing and chronic imbalance between revenues and expenditures is one indicator of system failure. Changing how budget process decisions are made could enable public leaders to deal with the more intractable and complex problems involving the revenue system and the state–local relationship.[26]

They identify, as we have, the key problems of budgeting:

> The costs of operating state programs are growing faster than the revenue base that supports them. The revenue system is highly sensitive to changes in the economy, producing significant volatility. The single-year budgeting horizon encourages short-term fixes, rather than long-term solutions. The budget does not take a strategic approach to ensure a return on public investments and there is a lack of public and legislative review of how money is spent.[27]

Many commentators noted the cumulative effect of the fees and caps that have been proposed more and more frequently in recent years.[28] Traditionally, California tried to supply sufficient services for all, on the principle that "if you're eligible, we'll serve you." The community colleges guarantee, for example, that any high-school graduate can go to college. That principle has been shifting, though. The Schwarzenegger budget for 2004–05 had caps on the number of individuals who could be served in various programs; immigrants in Medi-Cal and the program that supplies drugs for those with HIV/AIDS were both capped at the level of January 1, 2004. California's fees for students attending CSU and community colleges

BOX 8.4 ● Federal Funds

The 2014-15 budget included $98 billion in **federal funds**, about 50 percent of which was intended for use in the health and human services category. Most of this was for Medi-Cal, California's Medicaid program (medical care for the poor). Another quarter of the total was for labor and workforce development, mostly federal funds to supplement the Unemployment Insurance program. Another large portion was for education. None of the $98 billion included the additional $250 billion the federal government spent in California on wages and benefits for California-based federal employees, Social Security payments, Medicare payments to doctors, hospitals, and other providers (for those 65 and over, and some of those with disabilities), procurement contracts (defense and others), grants to universities and nonprofits, and so forth.[a]

Federal dollars are important to states during economic downturns, when states often cut back their budgets to meet balanced budget requirements. Federal money for unemployment insurance and stimulus packages typically increases substantially during recessions. Federal money received in California increased from $52.9 billion in 2006-07, just before the great recession of 2008-09, to $91.5 billion in 2010-11, according to the California Budget Project.[b]

Reports from the state controller's office indicate that cities in California received about 5 percent of their total income in 2011-12 from federal funds, and counties received some 21 percent, about $10 billion. Counties receive more because in California they are responsible for administering state and national health and welfare programs.[c]

Does California receive more from the feds than it pays in taxes? In spite of the large amounts discussed above, the answer is "no," because no wealthy state gets back more from the federal government than it pays in taxes. Federal funds, in general, redistribute money from wealthier states to poorer ones.

[a]Legislative Analyst's Office, "An Overview of Federal Funding in California," Sacramento: Legislative Analyst's Office, 2011.
[b]California Budget Project, "How Are Federal Dollars Spent in California?" http://www.cbp.org/publications/fed_taxes budget_land.html (accessed 7/30/2014).
[c]Controller's Office, State of California, 2014a, "Cities Annual Report," www.sco.ca.gov/ard_locrep_annual_financial .html; and Controller's Office, State of California, "Counties Annual Report," www.sco.ca.gov/ard_locrep_annual _financial.html (accessed 7/29/14).

used to be among the lowest in the nation, but they have increased substantially in recent years. Measures are often proposed as emergency measures, but few emergency measures have been repealed in the past.

In short, the lowered expectation for services has become particularly apparent in the Arnold Schwarzenegger and Jerry Brown eras but has been in the background for the last decade or more.

The California Budgetary Process: Where Are We Now?

We are optimistic in 2016 about California's fiscal prospects, more so than we have been in the past. Governor Jerry Brown has insisted that California live within the means that the voters have provided. Now that budgets are easier to balance, the governor has insisted that the budget surpluses from the capital gains tax be used to provide the state with a rainy-day fund (Proposition 44 on the November 2014 ballot) and to repay some of the bonds that were floated to pay for the deficits of the 2000s under Governor Schwarzenegger. It would be better to reform California's tax system, but this possibility is remote; any meaningful reform would engender substantial opposition (see the discussion of Controller Betty Yee's tax-reform report above).

The biggest fiscal problem facing the state is the voters' willingness to approve propositions (initiatives) that allocate money from the general fund or establish a special fund without having a funding source. Some of these are self-serving; others have more merit. While some initiatives divert money from the general fund by setting up special funds, others simply state that the money for a certain purpose shall be a specific amount to be paid from the general fund; this reduces the funds available for existing programs. Higher education in particular has been hurt by these actions.

Study Guide

FOR FURTHER READING

Barrett, Katherine, Richard Greene, Michele Mariani, and Anya Sostek. "The Way We Tax." *Governing*, February 2003.

California Budget Project. "An Incomplete Vision: Putting the Governor's Proposed 2014–15 Budget in Context." California Budget & Policy Center, February 2014. www.cbp.org/pdfs/2014/140219_budget_chartbook.pdf. Accessed 7/31/14.

———. "Principles and Policy: A Guide to California's Tax System." California Budget & Policy Center, April 2013. www.cbp.org/pdfs/2013/130411_California's_Tax_System.pdf. Accessed 7/31/14.

———. "Who Pays Taxes in California?" California Budget & Policy Center, April 2015. http://calbudgetcenter.org/wp-content/uploads/Who-Pays-Taxes-in-CA_Issue-Brief_04.14.2015.pdf. Accessed 8/6/16.

California Taxpayers Association. "Cal-Tax: Taxes Are a Heavy Burden in California." http://digital.library.ucla.edu/websites/2004_999_003/dynamic/downloads/individual_download_file_link_1_english_10.pdf. Accessed 10/10/16.

Johnson, Hans. "Defunding Higher Education. What Are the Effects on College Enrollment?" Public Policy Institute of California, May 2012. www.ppic.org/main/publication.asp?i=988. Accessed 7/28/14.

League of Women Voters of California. *Guide to California Government.* 15th ed. Sacramento: League of Women Voters of California, 2013.

Legislative Analyst's Office. "California's Tax System: A Primer," April 2007. www.lao.ca.gov/2007/tax_primer/tax_primer_040907.aspx. Accessed 7/30/14.

Oliff, Phil, Vincent Palacios, Ingrid Johnson, and Michael Leachman. "Recent Deep State Higher Education Cuts May Harm Students and the Economy for Years to Come." Washington, DC: Center on Budget and Policy Priorities, May 2013.

Public Policy Institute of California. "Just the Facts: California's State Budget: The Enacted 2016–17 Budget." Public Policy Institute of California, July 2016. www.ppic.org. Accessed 8/6/16.

———. "Just the Facts: Proposition 13, 30 Years Later." Public Policy Institute of California, June 2008. www.ppic.org. Accessed 7/30/14.

ON THE WEB

California Budget & Policy Center. http://calbudgetcenter.org/. Accessed 10/10/16.

California Forward. www.cafwd.org. Accessed 8/6/16.

Howard Jarvis Taxpayers Association. www.hjta.org. Accessed 8/6/16.

Legislative Analyst's Office. www.lao.ca.gov. Accessed 8/6/16.

Public Policy Institute of California. www.ppic.org. Accessed 8/6/16.

State of California, Department of Finance, Budget Update Site. www.ebudget.ca.gov. Accessed 8/6/16.

State of California, Department of Finance. http://dof.ca.gov/Reports/Demographic_Reports/. Accessed 10/10/16. California statistics and demographic information.

SUMMARY

I. How is the budget formulated?
   A. Agencies send their requests to the governor each fall.
   B. The governor sends a balanced budget request to the legislature each January for the fiscal year starting the next July 1.
   C. The legislature adopts a balanced budget by June 15 each year, for the fiscal year to start July 1.
      1. In recent years, the volatility of the state's revenues has caused the budget to be substantially readjusted during the fiscal year.
   D. The governor has a line-item veto, allowing him or her to reduce any line-item dollar amount downward, even to zero. However, the governor may not raise any line item.
   E. The legislature is assisted by its own neutral budget office—the Legislative Analyst's Office.
   F. If the Assembly and state Senate versions of the budget differ, a "budget conference committee" will attempt to iron out the differences.
   G. Agencies then implement the approved budget, including specific policy or budget studies to be carried out and presented to the legislature.

II. What is the California budget?
   A. The budget is the governor's and legislature's views of the future.
      1. The future of the state's economy (economic assumptions).
      2. The future income of the state (revenues).
      3. The future spending of the state (expenditures).
   B. The budget is at the center of the state's activities each year.

III. Revenues.
   A. Personal income tax—the largest source of income for the general fund, highly progressive, and subject to volatility because of its dependence on taxes derived from capital gains.
   B. Sales tax—the next largest source of income. Local governments can add a small amount to the state sales tax. A portion of the tax is refunded to them. Many localities have added businesses to their communities that produce sales tax, such as big-box shopping centers and automobile dealerships, specifically because of the revenues they then receive from the state.
   C. Corporate tax—the third-largest source of revenue. Most corporate taxes are paid by the larger corporations in the state.
   D. Property tax—severely limited by Proposition 13, composes only 22 percent of California's tax revenues.
   E. The California tax system is volatile compared to the tax systems of other states. It depends on the ups and downs of the economy and produces surges in revenue when the economy booms and precipitous falls when a recession takes place.

IV. Expenditures.
   A. Health and Human Services is the largest budget category, driven by the state expenditures for Medi-Cal and other health programs.
   B. Education (K–12) is the second-largest single expenditure and second-largest budget category. Proposition 98 requires that 40 percent of the state general fund be designated for K–12 expenditures.
   C. Higher education is the third-largest budget category; it includes expenditures for the community colleges, the California State University, and the University of California.
   D. The fifth-largest budget category is business, transportation, and housing.

V. Limitations on the budget.
   A. The most substantial limitations have come from initiatives passed by the voters.
   B. Proposition 13, which limits the property tax to 1 percent of the value of one's house, and Proposition 98, which guarantees a certain amount to K–12 education, are the most important of these limitations.
   C. Cumulatively, these budget limitations have guaranteed well over half the general fund and at least half of all expenditures, giving the governor and legislature less flexibility than they would have in other states. This is precisely the intended goal of initiatives—to limit the powers of the governor and legislature. The level of distrust the voters have for the governor and legislature is high in California.

VI. Recent state budgets have been characterized by huge and fluctuating gaps between revenues and expenditures.
   A. These gaps have made it difficult to find the middle ground necessary to obtain a two-thirds vote in the legislature for a budget. But starting in 2011, with only a majority required, the budget was passed six years in a row, more or less on time. The last four years, 2013–14 to 2016–17, had surpluses because

of a surge in income tax (capital gains) revenues. Governor Brown insisted that some of this money be set aside for a rainy-day fund, to be used when revenues inevitably turn downward, and that some of the money should repay the bonds used to balance the budget during the 2000s.

VII. Box 8.3 describes Proposition 13 and its restrictions on how property is taxed in California. Among the effects of Proposition 13 was an increased power for the state over local government and the "fiscalization of land use." Proposition 13 has resisted change, and legislators and interest groups seeking to change it have had little success. A proposal to split the tax roll and place a higher rate on commercial property has faced great opposition from the business community.

VIII. What is the future of budgeting in California?
   A. California seems to have turned a corner, with six budgets in a row passed on time and more or less balanced. The surge in revenues from the capital gains tax is being used to pay back old debt and to create a rainy-day fund for the future.
   B. The biggest fiscal problem facing the state continues to be the willingness of the voters to approve propositions (initiatives) that allocate money from the general fund or establish a special fund without having a funding source.

PRACTICE QUIZ

1. Both the governor and the legislature are obliged by the California Constitution to pass a balanced budget.
   a) true
   b) false

2. The state of California cannot pass its budget in 2016–17 unless the Assembly and state Senate pass the budget by
   a) 50 percent plus 1 vote.
   b) 55 percent.
   c) 66.7 percent.
   d) 75 percent.

3. The state of California cannot raise state taxes unless the Assembly and state Senate pass the relevant law by
   a) 50 percent plus 1 vote.
   b) 55 percent.
   c) 66.7 percent.
   d) 75 percent.

4. Proposition 13 requires
   a) property taxes to be lowered to the level when the property was last sold. Property tax values can rise 2 percent per year.
   b) property taxes to be set at 1975 levels; property is reassessed when it is sold. Property tax values can rise as much as 2 percent per year.
   c) property taxes to be lowered to 1945 levels; property is reassessed when it is sold. The level of the tax can rise 3 percent per year.
   d) Property taxes to be raised to the appropriate level when the property on both sides of a house or business has been sold—all the property is then reassessed at current values. The level of the tax can rise 2 percent per year if the property is not sold.

5. Proposition 98 requires education spending to be at least
   a) 50 percent of the entire state budget.
   b) 50 percent of the general fund.
   c) 33.3 percent of the general fund.
   d) 40 percent of the general fund.

6. What is the general fund?
   a) The general fund includes all revenues that are not otherwise allocated into special or bond funds.
   b) The general fund includes all tax revenue.
   c) The general fund includes all state revenue, including special and bond funds.
   d) The general fund includes all state revenue except bond funds, because these are used to construct state facilities and are paid back over a several decade period.

7. The governor's line-item veto allows
   a) the governor, if he or she wishes, to lower any appropriation item.
   b) the governor, in conjunction with an agency, to veto any bill in its entirety.
   c) the governor to "pencil out" any line or sentence in any bill.
   d) the governor to raise or lower any appropriation item, including lowering the item to zero.

8. The governor's line-item veto may be overridden by a 50 percent plus one vote in both houses of the legislature.
   a) true
   b) false

9. The credit rating assigned to the state of California by Moody's, Fitch Ratings, or Standard & Poor's is important because
   a) the credit rating influences the size of California's deficit or surplus in any given fiscal year.
   b) when the credit rating goes down, the interest rate that the state pays to float its bonds goes up.
   c) when the credit rating goes up, the amount of interest the state pays goes down.
   d) all of the above

10. Indian gambling revenues have become a significant source of income for the state of California.
    a) true
    b) false

11. The lottery is a significant source of income for K–12 education.
    a) true
    b) false

CRITICAL-THINKING QUESTIONS

1. How might California's tax system be made more predictable and less dependent on the economy than it is now? How might *Governing* magazine rate your proposed changes?

2. How should the budget process in California be reformed, assuming it should be reformed? What goals are important in reforming the process, and what changes in the process might achieve those goals?

3. Should the governor have more authority in the budget process? Leaving aside the opinion you might have of the current incumbent, what reforms might help with the long-term budget process in California?

4. The other major player in the budget process is the legislature. How might the legislature's consideration of the budget be changed to make California's budget more predictable and timely?

KEY TERMS

big-box shopping centers/automobile dealerships (p. 204)
bond funds (p. 201)
Budget Conference Committee (p. 199)
capital gains (p. 202)
Department of Finance (p. 197)
federal funds (p. 201)

fiscalization of land use (p. 204)
general fund (p. 201)
governor's budget (p. 199)
Legislative Analyst's Office (p. 199)
line-item veto (p. 200)
May revise (p. 197)
Moody's, Fitch Ratings, Standard & Poor's ratings (p. 201)

personal income tax (p. 202)
progressive (p. 202)
regressive (p. 204)
sales tax (p. 202)
special funds (p. 201)
unified budget (p. 197)

Local Government

WHAT CALIFORNIA'S LOCAL GOVERNMENTS DO AND WHY THEY MATTER

Governing California would be hard to imagine without the more than 5,000 local governments that help run the state. Local officials and workers in cities, counties, school districts, special districts, and regional bodies all play an essential role. The complexity of the state's local government system makes it difficult to generalize about what local governments do. But a short list would include the following:

- General-purpose local governments, like cities and counties, do everything from putting out fires to cleaning the streets and ensuring that the buses run on time. They protect the health, safety, welfare, and overall quality of life of all who live within their jurisdictions.

- Limited-purpose governments, such as school districts and other special districts, deliver specific public services such as public education, pest abatement, and irrigation to meet particular needs within defined territorial boundaries.

- Regional governments address problems such as air pollution and population growth that affect broad areas across many jurisdictions and that require comprehensive study and planning to solve.

- Many local governments do the actual work involved in implementing state and federal laws, from controlling water quality and producing affordable housing to carrying out duties related to homeland security.

- Most local governments provide citizens with opportunities to learn about public problems, express their opinions, practice hands-on democracy, and collectively exercise some degree of popular control on issues close to home that they really care about.

- Some local governments experiment and innovate to pioneer new ways of better serving citizens or improving the democratic process. Often these local initiatives spread and can have major impacts on how government works at the state and national levels.

California's local governments have been subjected to a severe stress test over the last few years, thanks to both the Great Recession and the political responses to it both inside and outside the system—a system that has evolved over decades to help different levels and facets of local government fit and work together. This chapter offers a description and analysis of the essential parts of that system and discusses its capacity to solve problems and function effectively in serving the public. The goal is to give the reader a basic knowledge and appreciation of California's local governments in all their variety, what they do, and why they matter.

The Legal Framework: Dillon's Rule, Home Rule, and Local Powers of Governance

The U.S. Constitution assigns power and authority to the national and state governments, but it says nothing about local governments. **Counties, cities, special districts**, and other forms of local government have no inherent rights or powers. What rights and powers they do have are conferred on them by the state constitution or state legislature.

The constitutional doctrine that gives state governments ultimate authority over local governments is known as **Dillon's Rule**. In 1868, Iowa judge John F. Dillon ruled that "municipal corporations" such as counties and cities were mere "creatures of the state" and could exercise only those powers delegated to them by the state.[1] Upheld by the U.S. Supreme Court in 1903 and again in 1923, Dillon's Rule is firmly established, at least in theory, as the basic legal framework for relations between state and local governments. In practice, however, only a few states, including Alabama, Idaho, and Nebraska, demand strict obedience to Dillon's Rule and require local governments to seek their permission in order to act. California, like most states, has passed government codes and **home-rule** laws that allow significant local discretion and autonomy. Within broad limits, county and city residents can select their own form of government, manage their own elections, raise their own revenues, and choose what kinds of functions to perform and at what levels of service.[2]

In California, under the provisions of Article 11, Section 5, of the state constitution and because of various court rulings,[3] most of the more populous cities and counties have adopted home-rule charters. The others are designated as general-law cities and counties that fall more directly under state authority and control. To get an idea of just how far home-rule powers can be taken in asserting local autonomy, see Box 9.1 on home rule and local autonomy in San Francisco.

A more practical restraint on state meddling in local government is based on the maxim that all politics is local. State legislators, after all, are elected by local constituencies to protect their local interests, and the legislators won't last long if they forget who brought them to the dance. These political realities have kept state power over local governments in check.[4] Finally, as part of the so-called devolution revolution that began in the 1970s, federal and state authorities have increasingly delegated responsibility to local governments to solve their own problems, using their own money.

In sum, Dillon's Rule is very liberally construed in California. The state's constitutional and legal framework confers broad formal powers of local governance, especially in charter cities and counties. Home rule on paper, however, does not necessarily translate into home rule in reality. In recent years, for example, the state's budget crises, public employee pensions, and other financial stresses have seriously limited the capacity of some local governments to govern effectively and serve the public well. Formal authority minus needed resources weakens home rule and diminishes local autonomy.

County Governments

At the first meeting of the California legislature in 1850, lawmakers divided the state into 27 counties for the purpose of administering state laws. Since then many new counties have been created, mostly by subdivision. The state's current 58 counties have been with us since 1907, when the last addition, Imperial County, was carved out of the old San Diego County (see Figure 9.1). Political movements have arisen from time to time that attempted to split an existing county to make a new one. An 1894 amendment to the state constitution, however, made it virtually impossible to do so by requiring a favorable majority vote in both the entire county affected and the territory of the proposed new county.[5]

California's 58 counties vary greatly in their territory, population, and demographic characteristics.

TERRITORY Just in terms of size, the differences are vast. You could fit 427 areas the size of San Francisco County (at just 47 square miles, the smallest county in California) within the borders of San Bernardino County (the largest county in California, at 20,053 square miles). The differences in physical geography are also striking, ranging from deserts to rain forests, flat farmlands to tall mountains. Some counties are densely urban and covered with cities, whereas others are so rural that coyotes outnumber people.

POPULATION Alpine County's grand total of 1,079 residents could all live comfortably in one San Francisco precinct. Los Angeles County, at the other extreme, is bursting with more than 10 million people, representing over 26 percent of the state's entire population. The lowest-ranking 29 counties combined contain only about 5 percent of the state's total population, while the 5 most populous counties (Los Angeles, Orange, San Diego, San Bernardino, and Riverside) hold about 54 percent of the state's total.

DEMOGRAPHY If you tour the state's 58 counties, you'll discover vastly different social and economic worlds. The populations of some counties are relatively poor, others relatively rich. Some are mostly white, others mainly nonwhite. Some are dominated by homeowners, others—for example, San Francisco—by renters.

The "Who Are Californians?" feature on page 225 reports the lowest- and highest-ranking counties on these and other indicators to illustrate the extremes that exist among California's counties.

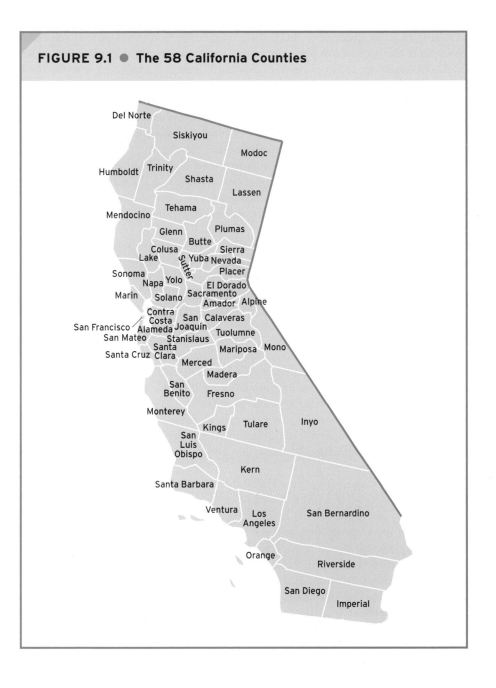

FIGURE 9.1 ● The 58 California Counties

Legal Framework

The state constitution provides a general legal framework for the governing of most counties, which are known as **general-law counties**. It prescribes the number and functions of elected county officials, how they are selected, and what they may or may not do as they raise revenue, spend money, deliver services, and so on. Fourteen counties, however, have adopted a home-rule charter, which gives voters greater control over the selection of governing bodies and officers, more flexibility in raising taxes and revenues, and broader discretion in organizing to deliver services. All of the state's most populous counties and one small county, Tehama, with its 57,000 residents, are now **charter counties**. Voters can adopt a charter for their county government by a majority vote.

Long content to live without a charter, the voters of Orange County finally adopted one in March 2002. They did so mainly to prevent the governor from filling a vacancy on the county board of supervisors with his own choice of representative, an act within his authority under the general-law provisions.

San Francisco is an unusual case. It is governed under a single charter as a consolidated county and city, an arrangement that is unique in the state and rare in the country. County charters vary widely in content and in the range of powers claimed for local control. Anything that goes unmentioned within a charter is governed by the general law.

County Government Organization

In all counties except San Francisco, an elected five-member board of supervisors exercises both legislative and executive authority. Given the extremes in the size of county populations, it shouldn't surprise you that small five-member boards yield huge disparities in political representation. For example, each board member in tiny Alpine County represents, on average, only 216 residents. In mammoth Los Angeles County, on the other hand, each board member represents more than 2 million people, nearly equivalent to the entire population of New Mexico.

County boards of supervisors, whose members are elected by districts for staggered four-year terms, not only pass laws, called **ordinances**, at the local level, but they also control and supervise the departments charged with administering these ordinances. This combination of legislative and executive authority gives county supervisors great power.

There is an exception: in the consolidated city and county government of San Francisco, an elected 11-member board of supervisors has legislative authority. An independently elected mayor has executive authority and some control, shared with many boards and commissions, over the bureaucracy.

In addition to the board of supervisors, other elected or appointed county officers required by general law include a sheriff, who enforces the law in areas outside the cities; a district attorney; and an assessor. A 1998 constitutional amendment consolidated municipal and superior trial courts into a single layer of superior court judges who are elected by county voters. Elections for all county offices are nonpartisan. In terms of appointed positions, charter counties have considerable latitude in creating departments and agencies to serve their needs, either by charter provision or by ordinance. Other offices are required or authorized by state law. Some charter counties, like Los Angeles County, have appointed a chief executive officer to manage their sprawling bureaucracies under board supervision.

Figure 9.2 shows Placer County's organizational chart, which is very simple and typical of counties with small populations. By way of contrast, Figure 9.3 shows Los Angeles County's organization chart. It illustrates the complexity of local government authority and responsibility that can be found in counties with large and diverse populations.

Who Lives in California's Counties?

Total Population

- ▪ Under 50,000
- ▪ 50,000–249,999
- ▪ 250,000–499,999
- ▪ 500,000–999,999
- ▪ 1,000,000 or more

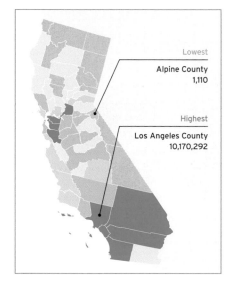

Lowest

Alpine County
1,110

Highest

Los Angeles County
10,170,292

Non-Latino White Population

- ▪ Under 30%
- ▪ 30–44.9%
- ▪ 45–59.9%
- ▪ 60–74.9%
- ▪ 75% or more

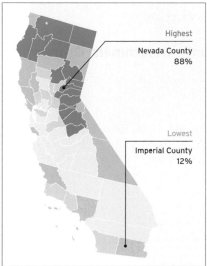

Highest

Nevada County
88%

Lowest

Imperial County
12%

California's 58 counties are extremely diverse in terms of their population size, ethnoracial composition, and economic conditions. Los Angeles, for instance, has the largest population, at over 10 million residents, and the second smallest white population, at 28 percent. In other ways, Los Angeles falls roughly in the middle: 30 percent of its residents have a bachelor's degree and the median household income is $56,000.

SOURCES: "Annual Estimate of the Resident Population," July 1, 2015, www.census.gov/quickfacts/table/PST045215/06 (accessed 8/15/16); and "2014 American Community Survey," U.S. Census Bureau, Population Division, www.factfinder.census.com (accessed 7/27/16).

Bachelor's Degree or Higher

- ▪ Under 15%
- ▪ 15–24.9%
- ▪ 25–34.9%
- ▪ 35–44.9%
- ▪ 45% or more

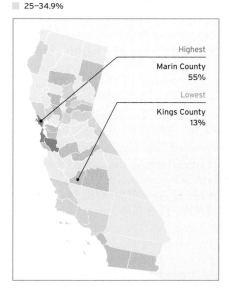

Highest

Marin County
55%

Lowest

Kings County
13%

Median Household Income

- ▪ Under $40,000
- ▪ $40,000–$49,999
- ▪ $50,000–$59,999
- ▪ $60,000–$69,999
- ▪ $70,000 or more

Lowest

Lake County
$35,997

Highest

Santa Clara County
$93,854

forcriticalanalysis

1. Why are the counties of California so different from one another? Are the four variables considered here related to each other, or to other factors not included here?

2. How do you think this range of ethnoracial diversity, educational attainment, and economic conditions affects California politics? How might this diversity affect local politics vs. state politics?

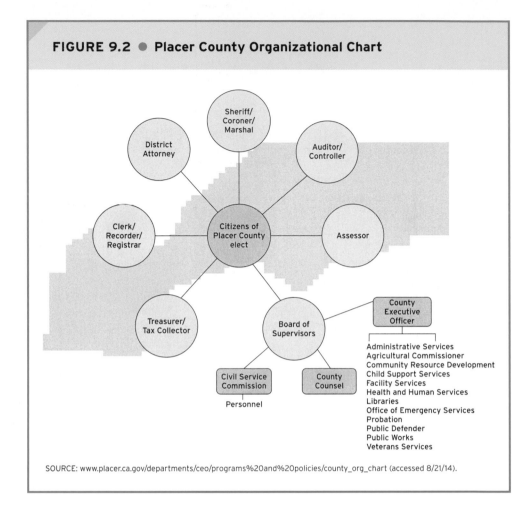

FIGURE 9.2 ● Placer County Organizational Chart

Sheriff/ Coroner/ Marshal

District Attorney

Auditor/ Controller

Clerk/ Recorder/ Registrar

Citizens of Placer County elect

Assessor

Treasurer/ Tax Collector

Board of Supervisors

County Executive Officer

Administrative Services
Agricultural Commissioner
Community Resource Development
Child Support Services
Facility Services
Health and Human Services
Libraries
Office of Emergency Services
Probation
Public Defender
Public Works
Veterans Services

Civil Service Commission

Personnel

County Counsel

SOURCE: www.placer.ca.gov/departments/ceo/programs%20and%20policies/county_org_chart (accessed 8/21/14).

County Government Functions and Responsibilities

County governments have major functions and responsibilities, most of them mandated by state or federal law, especially outside the jurisdictions of cities. County responsibilities include bridges and highways, public safety, public health, employment, parks and recreation, welfare and public assistance, public records, tax collection, general government, court administration, and land use. In the largest counties, the public workforce required to manage these responsibilities and the budget needed to pay for them can be truly massive. In 2016, for example, Los Angeles County had 108,093 employees and an adopted budget of $28.2 billion.[6]

Decisions on land-use policy are perhaps the most important and controversial ones a county board of supervisors can make. If you're ever in the mood to watch a good political fight, attend a typical county board of supervisors meeting in a place like Napa County or San Diego County. Areas like these still have plenty of open land outside the cities and fast-growing populations that fuel a demand for new housing construction, schools, and public infrastructure (sewers, highways, etc.). Landowners and developers typically badger the county board of supervisors to allow them to build, often with the result that conservationists, environmentalists, and other groups mobilize in opposition to push them back.

FIGURE 9.3 ● Los Angeles County Organizational Chart

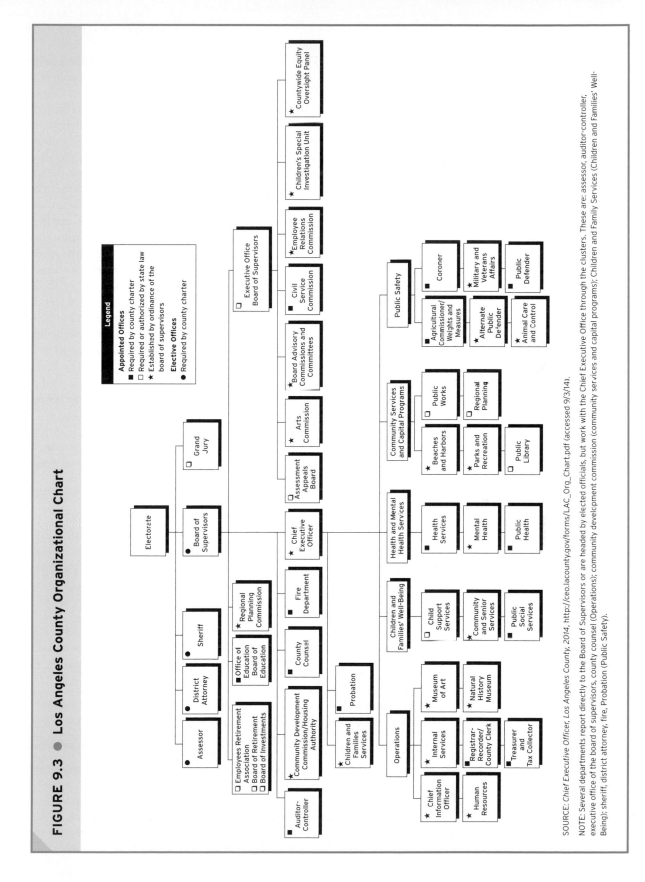

Legend

Appointed Offices
■ Required by county charter
□ Required or authorized by state law
★ Established by ordinance of the board of supervisors

Elective Offices
● Required by county charter

SOURCE: *Chief Executive Officer, Los Angeles County, 2014,* http://ceo.lacounty.gov/forms/LAC_Org_Chart.pdf (accessed 9/3/14).

NOTE: Several departments report directly to the Board of Supervisors or are headed by elected officials, but work with the Chief Executive Office through the clusters. These are: assessor, auditor-controller, executive office of the board of supervisors, county counsel; community development commission (community services and capital programs); Children and Family Services (Children and Families' Well-Being); sheriff, district attorney, fire, Probation (Public Safety).

For example, on July 31, 2012, the Riverside County Board of Supervisors met to decide whether to "fast-track" approval of Granite Construction's application to build a surface mine known as Liberty Quarry near the small town of Temecula. Fast-tracking would allow the project to skip the county planning commission's standard review and thus expedite the board's final decision. The debate at the crowded public meeting was impassioned on both sides. Orange-shirted opponents faced off against green-shirted supporters. Representatives of the chamber of commerce, labor unions, and other groups backed the proposal, arguing that the quarry would stimulate the local economy and create badly needed jobs. Temecula city officials, environmentalists, and leaders of the Pechanga Band of Luiseño Indians contended that the quarry would pollute the air, wreck the economy, and destroy a nearby sacred tribal site. One supervisor called Liberty Quarry "the most divisive project in county history." The board voted 3-to-2 to fast-track approval, prompting cheers from the green shirts and cries of outrage from the orange shirts. This story then ended abruptly and happily for all concerned. On November 15, 2012, just days before the board was scheduled to give its final approval, leaders of the Pechanga Band announced that they had reached an agreement with Granite Construction to purchase the Liberty Quarry site for $3 million and to pay the firm an additional $17.35 million to cover its project costs. Granite was permitted to build its mine elsewhere, miles from Temecula and the sacred tribal lands. The Pechanga Band promised to preserve the original site as it was. Temecula officials pledged to drop their lawsuit to stop the board from voting on a controversial decision it no longer had to make.[7]

As California's population continues to grow and spread from the cities into the state's remaining farmlands and rural areas, you can expect to see more land-use battles of this sort erupting in the political arenas of county governments.

Local Agency Formation Commissions

All 58 California counties have a **local agency formation commission (LAFCo)**, whose members are appointed by the county board of supervisors. These commissions play a critical role in resolving conflicts among the many local governments that often compete with one another for power and resources within their county jurisdictions. A county's LAFCo has the following responsibilities:

- reviewing and approving the incorporations of new cities, the formation of new special districts, and any proposed changes of jurisdictional boundaries, including annexations and detachments of territory, **secessions**, consolidations, mergers, and dissolutions

- reviewing and approving contractual service agreements between local governments and between local governments and the private sector

- defining the official spheres of influence for each city and special district

- initiating proposals for consolidation, dissolution, mergers, and reorganizations if such changes seem necessary or desirable

These powerful commissions are especially busy in counties that are rocked by large-scale land-use battles, such as in Riverside County, or that teem with masses of people and a multitude of governments, such as Los Angeles County.[8]

City Governments

Legal Framework

Like counties, California's cities derive their powers as municipal corporations from the state constitution and state legislature. Within that legal framework, as of July 2016, the state's 482 incorporated cities fell into three categories: **general-law cities** (372), **charter cities** (109), and the unique case of San Francisco's consolidated city and county. The California Government Code, enacted by the legislature, specifies the general powers and structure of general-law cities. Broader home-rule powers are granted to charter cities, giving citizens more direct control over local affairs. Under these different arrangements, all cities have the power to legislate, as long as their local policies don't conflict with state or federal law. They have the power to raise revenues, levy taxes, charge license and service fees, and borrow. They may also hire personnel as needed; exercise police powers to enforce local, state, and federal laws; and condemn property for public use.

Incorporation and Dissolution

The state grants powers to cities, and in that sense cities are indeed creatures of the state. But cities themselves are created only by the request, and with the consent, of the residents in a given area. In California, this process of **municipal incorporation** is typically initiated by a citizen petition or by a resolution of the county board of supervisors. Landowner petitions are also possible but rare. The following are some of the more important reasons that motivate residents to seek incorporation:

- to limit or accelerate population growth

- to provide more or better-quality services than those provided by the county

- to prevent annexation by a nearby city

- to create a unit of government more responsive to local needs and concerns

- to escape the tax and spending burdens imposed by county government rule

A petition for municipal incorporation must be submitted to the county's LAFCo. The LAFCo panel reviews the proposed plans for the new city, its boundaries, its service provisions, its governing capacity, and its financial viability. The LAFCo also studies the likely financial and other impacts of the proposed incorporation on neighboring local governments, including the county itself. If the petition for incorporation survives this initial review and a later public hearing and possible protests, it moves to an election. If a majority of voters living within the boundaries of the proposed new city approve, a new city is legally born.[9] The rate of incorporation of new cities has fallen dramatically in recent years. Only 9 have incorporated since 1999, raising the total number of cities to 482 in 2016.[10]

The heavy burden of legal obligations and fiduciary responsibilities that come with incorporation can be difficult for municipalities to handle, particularly in times of widespread financial stress. The trials and tribulations of Jurupa Valley, the state's youngest city, illustrate this point. Jurupa Valley, a community of about 100,000 people located in Riverside County, formally became an incorporated, general-law city in July 2011. The community thereby gained home-rule powers and greater local control over land use and service provision within its borders. The summer of 2011 proved an unfortunate time for the city of Jurupa Valley to be born, however, as the governor and state legislators faced yet another budget crisis. Only days after the community's incorporation, the state government diverted all of its vehicle license fee revenues away from local governments to bolster budgets for prisons and other law enforcement programs at the state level. This sudden diversion of funds hurt all California cities, but it hit Jurupa Valley especially hard; city officials had counted on their share of that money, which was several millions of dollars, to make ends meet. On January 16, 2014, after months of cutting staffing and services to the bone while searching in vain for state financial support, Jurupa Valley's city council members voted unanimously to petition Riverside County's LAFCo for municipal dissolution and a return to county rule.

It was the first such petition received by a LAFCo in more than forty years, and it triggered a legal process of disincorporation that could take up to two years to complete.[11] A local reporter warned her readers of some of the implications: "If home rule goes away, decision-making on land-use and other issues like code enforcement, public works and road repairs will revert to Riverside County. Traffic enforcement will be handled by the California Highway Patrol."[12]

This story, however, has a happy ending. On September 22, 2015, with the economy now booming and his budget balanced, Governor Brown signed a bill authored by State Senator Richard Roth (D-Riverside) that restored funding to Jurupa Valley and three other recently born cities in Riverside County. On October 1, Jurupa Valley's city council members joyfully passed a resolution rescinding the earlier dissolution request.[13] Thus did the new city of Jurupa Valley survive its near-death experience.

City Government Functions and Responsibilities

City governments provide a wide range of services and facilities that directly affect the lives of their residents: fire and police protection; street construction and maintenance; sewage and waste disposal; health, social, and recreational programs; and planning and zoning to determine land use that is consistent with the community's needs and values. Most city governments provide water, and some run public transit systems. A few, such as Los Angeles and Sacramento, own and manage municipal electricity or natural gas utilities.

Residents in most cities are content if basic services such as police, fire, and waste management are provided reliably and efficiently, either directly by the municipality itself or, as in many smaller cities, by contracting services from other local governments and the private sector.[14] In some places, however, residents demand more from their city government than just the basics. For example, in some cities, business leaders and entrepreneurs often pressure city hall to promote rapid economic growth and development. In other cities, community activists often pressure city hall to limit growth and development and to pursue ambitious social agendas on the world stage.

City Government Revenues and Expenditures

As shown in Table 9.1, the typical city budget in California relies most heavily on current service charges and taxes for most of its revenues. Most of what it spends

TABLE 9.1 ● Typical Sources and Uses of Municipal Funding (Excluding City and County of San Francisco)

Revenues (%)		Expenses (%)	
Current service charges	35.6%	Public safety	26.4%
Taxes	41.5	Community development and health	16.9
Intergovernmental agencies	9.3		
Special benefit assessments, licenses and permits, fines and forfeitures	2.3	Public utilities	20.5
		Transportation	18.0
		Culture and leisure	9.5
Revenues from use of money and property	3.7	General government	7.8
		Other	0.9
Other revenues and other financing sources	7.5		

SOURCE: California State Controller's Office, www.sco.ca.gov/Files-ARD-Local/LocRep/1112cities.pdf (accessed 9/3/14).

goes toward public safety, community development and health, public utilities, and transportation. We will have more to say about city finances later in this chapter in the context of the state's continuing budget crisis.

Forms of City Government and the Legacy of Progressive Structural Reforms

The overall vision and structural reforms advanced by the Progressives nearly a century ago have had an enduring impact on the form of municipal government in California. Progressive reformers sought to replace the corrupt bosses running partisan, ward-based, big-city political machines with government by reputable civic leaders and nonpartisan experts managing local affairs in the public interest. To implement that vision, the following structural reforms were necessary:

- strong managers and weak mayors
- nonpartisan elections
- at-large council elections
- the tools of direct democracy (the initiative, referendum, and recall)

Other Progressive reforms included civil service (merit-based) systems of municipal employment and, especially in the larger cities, professionally run city planning commissions and departments.[15] Reformers were particularly successful in the southwestern states, where populations were growing fast and new cities were popping up everywhere, isolated from the influence of eastern-style partisanship and urban machine politics.[16] Municipalities that have all or most of these institutional features are known as **reform governments**. Most medium-size American cities and nearly all of California's cities qualify for that label.

COUNCIL-MANAGER PLAN VERSUS MAYOR-COUNCIL SYSTEM Under the council-manager form of government, the voters elect a city council, which in turn appoints a professionally trained city manager to run the administration. The city manager directly controls the bureaucracy and supervises the performance of department heads. The council restricts itself to legislative policy making, while retaining the ultimate authority to fire or replace the appointed manager. Nearly all small- and medium-sized California cities, as well as San Jose and Sacramento, are governed by the **council-manager plan**.[17] Mayors are directly elected in about a third of these cities, but they perform mainly ceremonial duties and have no independent executive powers, such as the veto or budget control. (A partial exception is San Jose, whose mayor has very limited control of the budget and bureaucracy.)

The rest of California's cities are governed by **mayor-council systems**. Most are very small cities that can't afford a professional city manager and have weak mayors of the purely ceremonial type. Most of the state's largest cities, however, have strong mayor-council systems in which the mayor is elected independently of the council and serves as the city's overall chief executive. These are often called strong-mayor systems because the mayor proposes the city's budget, appoints department heads, and has veto power over council legislation. The council (or, in the case of San Francisco, the board of supervisors) is responsible for legislative policy making. Typically, as in Los Angeles and San Francisco, various appointive boards and commissions set overall policy and supervise administration of important city departments, such as police and fire, thus limiting the mayor's direct control of the bureaucracy.

In recent years, the voters in some council-manager cities have approved the switch to a strong-mayor system to make local government decision making more accountable, nimble, and responsive to changing political environments. When former governor Jerry Brown ran for mayor of Oakland in 1998, for example, he insisted that the voters support Measure X, which he had helped to draft, that would give the mayor the veto, control over budget preparation, and extensive appointment powers while reducing the then-powerful city manager to an administrator under mayoral authority. Oakland's voters approved the measure by a 3-to-1 margin and elected Brown as the city's new mayor. In 2004, San Diego's voters followed suit, changing one of the nation's largest council-manager systems into a strong-mayor system on a trial-run basis, and voted again in 2010 to make that new system permanent. On November 4, 2014, however, Sacramento's voters soundly rejected (57-to-43 percent) Measure L, a proposed charter amendment that would have changed the city's current council-manager plan to a strong-mayor system. It seems likely that Sacramento and San Jose will remain dug in as the state's two largest cities still sticking with the council-manager system in the years ahead.

In practice, formal and informal power arrangements vary widely across both the council-manager and mayor-council systems. Personal ambition, political skill, and leadership style are key factors that influence the degree of power accorded to a given mayor or manager to run local government and shape public policy.[18]

NONPARTISAN ELECTIONS California law requires that all local elections be officially **nonpartisan**. The Progressive Era reformers had pushed for nonpartisan elections as a means to insulate the important business of local government from what they saw as the distracting and corrupting influence of partisan politics. In nonpartisan elections, no information about a candidate's political party membership is shown on the ballot. In practice, of course, many local contests are fiercely partisan, even if the voters do not see a "D" or an "R" next to the candidates' names.

AT-LARGE VERSUS DISTRICT COUNCIL ELECTIONS More than 90 percent of California cities conduct at-large council elections, in which voters elect council members citywide rather than by districts or wards.[19] Under the **at-large elections** system, for example, if a number of candidates compete for one of the three vacant seats on the council, all of the city's voters have the opportunity to vote for any three of them, and the top three vote-getters are declared the winners. About 5 percent of cities use the **district election** method, which divides the city into districts and requires the voters in each district to elect one of the candidates running in that district to represent them on the council. The remaining cities—Oakland is an example—use some hybrid combination of at-large and district elections to elect their councils.

Local governments change their election systems infrequently, if at all, and they usually do so only after being pressured by political reform movements or lawsuits. (As an illustration of how lawsuits can force such change, see the discussion of the California Voting Rights Act below.) In 2000, for example, San Francisco switched from at-large to district elections for electing its board of supervisors in response to voter demand for greater representation of neighborhoods and minority groups, reduced influence of big money on elections, and a wider field of candidates who otherwise could not afford to run citywide campaigns.[20] Of course, the district system by itself doesn't guarantee a more neighborhood-oriented council, less costly campaigns, or political life on a smaller scale. The 15 members of the Los Angeles City Council, for example, are elected by districts. But each council member represents nearly a quarter of a million residents on average and must run expensive campaigns over vast territories to get elected.

The California Voting Rights Act of 2001 (CVRA) has catalyzed a recent wave of lawsuits throughout the state, with plaintiffs claiming racial disparities in representation under at-large systems. The CVRA expands on the federal Voting Rights Act of 1965 by eliminating the need for minority plaintiffs to identify a particular geographic district in their city in which a minority is sufficiently concentrated to result in a majority of voters. This crucial distinction makes it easier for plaintiffs to claim that at-large elections dilute their votes. CVRA-based lawsuits by minority groups in Modesto, Compton, Anaheim, Escondido, Whittier, Palmdale, and other cities have been successful, and more are coming. Local governments using at-large elections in racially diverse communities have been put on the defensive, and it's not hard to see why. Consider the egregious case of Palmdale, whose mayor, according to the *Los Angeles Times*, could not "explain why Palmdale, whose population is almost 55% Latino and nearly 15% black, has elected only one Latino and no African Americans to its council."[21]

The state's rapidly surging Latino population has been a major driver of CVRA lawsuits.[22] The Southwest Voter Registration Project, a Latino voting rights organization, has been particularly aggressive in suing local governments that have at-large systems and an underrepresentation of Latinos as a legally protected minority class. If such jurisdictions fight in court and lose, as they almost always do, they often must pay large settlements and fees. Palmdale, for example, fought such a lawsuit, lost, and had to pay about $4.6 million in attorneys' fees. Fearing such expensive lawsuits, officials in many jurisdictions have taken steps proactively to change from at-large to district systems. An example is the city of San Marcos, in which Latinos make up 37 percent of the population but have elected no Latinos to the city council in two decades.[23] Under the threat of such lawsuits, according to one report, more than 100 school and college districts throughout the state have also proactively decided to change their election systems.[24] Some advocates, like law professor Richard Hasen, see the CVRA as a "bright spot" in an era when other states are erecting barriers to minority voter participation. "In California, you have a large Latino population that's growing," Hasen told a reporter. "And you couple that with a Democratic majority in a state legislature that is willing to protect minority voting rights, then you get a very different situation than in Texas, where Republican legislators are making it harder for Latinos to vote."[25]

DIRECT DEMOCRACY At the local level of government, just as at the state level, ordinary citizens have access to the tools of **direct democracy** (the initiative, referendum, and recall) bequeathed to them by Progressive Era reformers. Specifically, if citizens gather the required number of valid signatures on formal petitions, they can accomplish the following:

- initiate direct legislation, including proposed ordinances and charter amendments, by placing such measures on the ballot for voter approval

- suspend implementation of council legislation until the voters approve it at a referendum election

- subject incumbent elected officials to a recall vote and possible dismissal before the next scheduled regular election

Local referenda are quite rare. Local recall elections are also rare, but they occur more often than statewide recalls do. For example, in the politically contentious town of Pacifica, voters have successfully petitioned for five recall elections over the last 40 years. The use of local ballot initiatives, however, is much more frequent and widespread, although not nearly to the extent observed at the state level. Direct legislation by citizen ballot initiative has become common in a few cities, such as San Francisco, especially around land-use and housing issues. Citizen initiatives appear on ballots less frequently in most other cities, but they are not uncommon. A 2002 study, for example, found that only 43 of 387 cities surveyed had even one citizen initiative on their most recent ballot.[26] A replication of that survey in 2016 would probably show a higher rate of citizen initiatives, given the rise of contentious politics and antiestablishment movements at all political levels.

Legal scholars Matthew Melone and George Nation III offer an important insight into the relationship between direct democracy and representative government:

> The importance of direct democracy is not diminished by the fact that representative democracy is the primary form of government because the importance of direct democracy is not determined by the frequency of its use. . . . [T]he mere fact that the tools of direct democracy are readily available in a state prevents many of the abuses associated with representative government despite the fact that such tools are actually used infrequently. . . . The institutions of representative democracy and the representatives themselves function better due to the possibility of the voters' resort to direct democracy.[27]

The Ralph M. Brown Act of 1953 required that "all meetings of the legislative body of a local agency shall be open and public, and all persons shall be permitted to attend any meeting of the legislative body of a local agency, except as otherwise provided in this chapter." The intent of the Brown Act, also known as the "open meetings law," was to support transparency and prevent secret meetings and backroom dealings of local government officials conducting public business. (The Bagley-Keene Act of 1967 later extended the same open-meetings requirement to state government agencies.) The Brown Act did allow closed meetings for personnel decisions and the like to protect community and individual rights. Critics such as Peter Scheer, however, argue that the original narrow exemptions were stretched too far in the 1990s to include meetings negotiating local collective-bargaining agreements, which the public may see only after they are signed—often too late to raise hard questions and objections about the financial implications. Despite its limitations, the Brown Act is consistent with the state's Progressive reform tradition. It gives citizens timely access to vital information about what local government officials say and do in their name.

SOURCE: League of California Cities, *Open & Public IV: A Guide to the Ralph M. Brown Act* (2007); Peter Scheer, "Public Employee Unions: Losing the Image Battle," *San Francisco Chronicle*, June 13, 2010, p. N5.

Some of the cases discussed later in this chapter will illustrate this point.

Also see Box 9.2 on the Brown Act, the "open meetings law" that gives citizens yet another tool of direct democracy to help them become more informed about the decision-making process and to hold their local government officials accountable.

LOCAL VOTER TURNOUT AND POLITICAL REPRESENTATION Despite the surge in voter turnout in the 2008 presidential election, the overall trend in voter participation since 1960 has been gradually downward in national elections (see Chapter 4). That trend continued in the 2016 presidential election, with preliminary estimates indicating that the national voter turnout was at a 20-year low.[28] According to Field Corporation pollster Mark Baldassare, however, California "bucked the national trend of depressed turnout" in that election, achieving a "record-setting 15.18 million counted and unprocessed ballots" as of November 16, 2016. Nonetheless, he observed, "only about half of the approximately 30 million California adults voted in this election."[29] Voter turnout rates in California's local elections tend to be much lower. A survey conducted in 2002, the most recent available, found that only 48 percent of a city's registered voters, on average, had cast ballots in the most recent council elections. It also revealed that "California residents who are highly educated, wealthy, old, and white are much more likely to participate than residents who are poor, young, less educated, and nonwhite."[30] As noted in Chapter 4, that same pattern holds for voter turnout in high-profile presidential election years, but the available evidence suggests that the active electorates (eligible voters who actually register and vote) in strictly local elections are smaller in size and even more demographically unrepresentative.

Certain institutional reforms could boost voter turnout and eventually produce more representative and responsive local government. Rescheduling local nonconcurrent elections to coincide with high-turnout presidential elections, for example, would likely have a major impact. Doing so in any given city, according to one study, "could well mean a doubling of voter turnout."[31]

Similar reasoning lies behind one of the arguments for ranked-choice voting, also known as the alternative vote or "instant runoff voting," which San Francisco adopted in 2002 (soon followed by Berkeley, Oakland, and San Leandro). Under ranked-choice voting, voters in the November general election rank the candidates for an office by order of preference (first choice, second choice, and so on). When all the ballots are counted, if no candidate receives a majority of first-choice preferences, the candidate receiving the fewest is dropped from the list and his or her ballots are transferred to the remaining candidates according to voters' rankings. (If a voter's lower-ranked candidates aren't among the survivors, his or her ballot is classified as "exhausted" and removed from the transfer flow of "continuing" ballots to be counted again in the next round.) Another tally is taken of continuing ballots, and if there is still no majority winner, the process is repeated until a majority winner is declared.

This system presents an alternative to the typical local election in California, in which the top two vote-getters face off in a typically low-turnout, low-interest runoff election in December if no candidate receives a majority of the votes cast in November. Under the ranked-choice system, these December runoff elections can be avoided.

Some critics of ranked-choice voting argue that many voters actually prefer December runoffs because they winnow the field of candidates and sharpen the voter's focus on only two choices. Further, voter turnout for mayoral elections and other high-profile local contests is sometimes even higher in the December runoff than in the November general election. These kinds of debates about the merits of ranked-choice voting and other proposed electoral reforms will continue.[32] This is considered a benefit by scholars who view local governments as ideal "laboratories of democracy" where innovations like ranked-choice voting can be tried and tested before being recommended to a wider public.[33]

Finally, and more controversially, a case can be made for greater political representation of noncitizens in local government. Noncitizens are not only tolerated but respected in many California cities, and their voices are heard and heeded by local officials. Leaders of immigrant-serving nonprofit agencies, community-based organizations, and worker centers are highly politically active in self-declared "sanctuary cities" such as San Francisco, where their efforts have led to assured equal access to city services regardless of immigrant status, the provision of municipal identification cards, and passage of wage-theft legislation to deter the economic exploitation of this vulnerable population. In 2004, with the knowledge that the California Constitution banned noncitizens from voting, advocacy groups and a broad coalition of supporters advanced a ballot measure giving noncitizen parents of children enrolled in the public schools the right to vote in the city's school board elections. That measure failed, just barely, in 2004, and it failed again in 2010 by a slightly larger margin. The third time was a charm, however. In the November 8, 2016, election, the city's voters approved the measure by an 8-point margin, 54-to-46 percent.[34] In the absence of comprehensive immigration reform at the federal government level, these kinds of initiatives in California's local laboratories of democracy will likely continue.[35]

Special Districts

Special districts are limited-purpose local governments. They fill the need or desire for services that general-purpose governments such as counties and cities cannot or will not provide. If residents or landowners desire new or better services, they can take steps to establish a special district to pay for them. As a popular guide to special districts notes: "Special districts *localize* the costs and benefits of public services. Special districts allow local citizens to obtain the services they want at a price they are willing to pay."[36] Examples of special districts include fire protection districts, cemetery districts, water districts, recreation and park districts, storm water drainage and conservation districts, irrigation districts, and mosquito abatement districts.

School and Community College Districts

California's **school and community college districts** are a unique type of special district. As of 2014–15 there were 1,022 K–12 school districts in the state, a number whittled down, mostly by consolidation, from the 1,630 districts that operated in 1962.[37] School districts derive their authority from the state's Education Code and are governed by locally elected school boards. Each board sets general policies and appoints a superintendent as chief executive officer, who serves at the pleasure of the board. The superintendent has overall responsibility for managing the system and its various schools and programs. In 2016 the state's community college system of two-year public institutions comprised 113 colleges organized into 72 districts. Serving more than 2.1 million students, it is the largest system of higher education in the nation.[38] In 1988 the California legislature enacted Assembly Bill 1725, giving community colleges status as institutions of higher education. AB 1725 also strengthened the advisory role of local academic senates and of the Student Senate for California Community Colleges in working with state government officials to make higher-education policy. Each community college district is governed by a locally elected board of trustees that sets general policies and appoints a chancellor as chief executive officer. As discussed elsewhere in this book, the state of California's K–14 public education system and especially the financial crises that surround it continue to be a major focus of policy debate and political battle.

Nonschool Special Districts

Excluding the school districts, the state had 4,711 special districts in 2011–12 according to the most recent California State Controller's report on special districts.[39] These special districts can be classified in three different ways: single-purpose versus multiple-purpose, enterprise versus nonenterprise, and independent versus dependent.

- About 85 percent of the state's special districts perform a single function, such as sewage management, water management, fire protection, or mosquito abatement. The others are multifunctional, such as the state's more than 800 County Service Areas (CSAs), which provide two or more services, such as enhanced recreation services and extended police protection.

- About one in four special districts are **enterprise districts**, which are run like businesses and charge **user fees** for services. Nearly all airport, harbor and port, transit, water, waste, and hospital districts are enterprise districts of this sort. In fiscal year (FY) 2011–12, the state's enterprise districts generated a total of $26.7 billion in user fees.[40] The state's many nonenterprise districts provide public services such as fire protection and pest control that benefit the entire community, not just individual residents. Typically, property taxes rather than user fees pay the costs.

- About two-thirds of the state's special districts are **independent districts**. An independent district is governed by its own separate board of directors appointed by an authorizing agency or elected directly by the district's voters. Dependent districts are governed by existing legislative bodies. Nearly all CSAs, for example, are governed by a county board of supervisors.

These three ways of classifying special districts are not mutually exclusive, and examples of all possible combinations exist.

Legal Framework

Like all local governments in the state, special districts must conform to the state constitution and to the legislature's government code. Statutory authority for special districts derives from either a principal act or a special act of the state legislature. A *principal act* is a general law that applies to all special districts of a given type. For example, the Fire Protection District Law of 1987 in the state's Health and Safety Code governs all 386 fire districts. About 60 of these principal law statutes are on the books and can be used to create a special district anywhere in the state. Another 120 or so *special acts* have been passed by the legislature to adapt a special district's structure, financing, and authority to unique local circumstances. The Alameda County Flood Control and Water District, for example, was formed under such a special act.

How Special Districts Are Created

To form a special district, the voters in the proposed district must apply to their county's LAFCo. After the LAFCo reviews and approves the proposal, it moves to an election in which only the voters residing inside the proposed district boundaries may vote. A simple majority is required for approval in most cases. A two-thirds majority is required if new special taxes are involved. The total number of special districts has decreased slightly in recent years, from 4,776 in 2007–08 to 4,711 in 2011–12, according to the latest available reports. However, the modest net change in total numbers can conceal a considerable churning of old districts dying and new ones being born. During the 2011–12 fiscal year, for example, 13 new districts were created and 74 were dissolved.[41]

The Advantages and Disadvantages of Special Districts

Following are the advantages claimed for special districts by advocates:[42]

- the flexibility that such districts allow in tailoring the level and quality of service to citizen demands

- the linking of costs to benefits, so that those who don't benefit from a district's services don't have to pay for them

- the greater responsiveness of special districts to their constituents, who often reside in smaller geographic areas of larger city and county jurisdictions

The disadvantages of special districts include the following:

- the overlapping of jurisdictions and the resulting duplication of services already provided by cities and counties or by other special districts

- the reduced incentives for needed regional planning, especially in providing water, sewer, and fire protection services, which are typically offered by a host of special districts governed by independent boards without any central coordination

- the decreased accountability that results from the sheer multiplicity of limited special districts, which overwhelms the average citizen's ability to find out who is in charge of delivering specific services

Some of the critics who make these kinds of arguments would abolish most special districts and centralize their functions in established general-purpose city and county governments. One contends that special districts "make a mockery of the natural connections that people have with a specific place. Special districts lie beyond the commonsense experience of most citizens; their very purpose is to divorce a narrow element of policy from the consideration of those charged with the maintenance of the common interest."[43]

Regional Governments

A number of **regional governments** have formed in California to cope with problems such as air pollution, waste management, growth control, affordable housing production, and transportation gridlock—problems that affect large geographical areas and millions of people living in many different city and county jurisdictions. Some of these regional bodies have strong regulatory powers. Others are mainly advisory in function.

Regulatory Regional Governments

Examples of state **regulatory regional governments** include the California Coastal Commission, the South Coast Air Quality Management District, and the San Francisco Bay Conservation and Development Commission.

CALIFORNIA COASTAL COMMISSION (CCC) Appointed by the governor and the state legislature, the 12-member CCC has state-empowered regulatory authority to control all development within the 1,000-yard-wide shoreline zone along the entire California coast. Exercising its powers to grant or withhold permits for development, the CCC has succeeded over the years in opening public access to beaches, protecting scenic views, and restoring wetlands.

SOUTH COAST AIR QUALITY MANAGEMENT DISTRICT (SCAQMD) The 12-member SCAQMD board has state-granted regulatory authority to control emissions from stationary sources of air pollution (e.g., power plants, refineries, gas stations) in the state's south coast air basin. This region encompasses all of Los Angeles

The California Coastal Commission, one of California's regulatory regional governments, can bring together citizens from all over the state through events like the annual California Coastal Cleanup Day, which encompasses the entire area under the CCC's jurisdiction—the length of California's coast.

and Orange Counties and parts of Riverside and San Bernardino Counties, an area of 12,000 square miles and home to more than 12 million people, nearly half the state's total population. This area also has the worst smog problem in the nation. Over the years, the board, which is appointed by city governments in the basin area, has conducted many studies, monitored air pollution levels, developed regional pollution abatement plans, and vigorously enforced federal and state air pollution laws. Thanks in large part to its efforts, the maximum level of ozone in the basin has been cut to less than half of what it was in the 1950s, despite the tripling of the population and quadrupling of vehicles in the region over that same period.

SAN FRANCISCO BAY CONSERVATION AND DEVELOPMENT COMMISSION (BCDC) The 27-member BCDC was created by the state legislature in 1965 in response to growing public concern about the future of San Francisco Bay, which was being dredged and polluted at an alarming rate by landfill projects. The commission includes members appointed by the governor, legislature, and various state and federal agencies, as well as four city representatives appointed by the Association of Bay Area Governments and nine county supervisors—one from each of the nine Bay Area counties. The commission is charged with regulating all filling and dredging in the bay; protecting the Suisun Marsh, the largest wetlands in California; regulating proposed new development within the first 100 feet inland from the bay to ensure maximum public access; enforcing the federal Coastal Zone Management Act; and other regulatory functions. By exercising its permit powers, BCDC not only stopped development that could have reduced the bay to a pond but also added hundreds of acres of new open water.

Advisory Regional Governments

In addition to regional regulatory bodies, the state also has a number of regional planning, research, and advisory institutions called **advisory regional governments**. The most important are various regional **councils of government (COGs)**. COGs are assemblies of delegates representing a region's counties and cities who join voluntarily and meet regularly to discuss common problems and regional issues. The state's two most prominent COGs are the Southern California Association of Governments (SCAG), the nation's largest COG, and the Association of Bay Area Governments (ABAG).

SCAG's regional jurisdiction encompasses 15 million people living in an area of more than 38,000 square miles, while ABAG's boundaries include 6 million people living in an area of 7,000 square miles. Both SCAG and ABAG have general assemblies that represent the broad membership of counties and cities located in each region. In both COGs, the serious work is done by smaller executive committees, a 75-member regional council in the case of SCAG and a 38-member executive board in the case of ABAG. Like most COGs, both SCAG and ABAG have professional staffs that conduct extensive research and planning studies of regional problems. Both regularly host regional conferences and forums on a range of substantive issues. And both have been designated by the federal government as metropolitan planning organizations for their regions, with the mandate to draw up plans for regional transportation, air quality, growth management, hazardous waste management, and production of affordable housing.

Both SCAG and ABAG have raised public awareness of regional problems and issues. They have also encouraged more regional planning and collaborative decision making. Neither COG, however, has the effective power or authority to enforce its policy recommendations on other local governments in their regions. Many Bay Area local officials, for example, pay lip service to ABAG's recommended fair-share quotas for production of affordable housing but then routinely ignore them when making decisions.

Occasionally, a serious organized effort is made to create a truly comprehensive regional government with broad regulatory authority and strong enforcement powers. In the early 1990s, for example, an attempt was made to establish a powerful Bay Area regional government under the banner of BayVision 2020.[44] That proposal failed, like all the others, because most of the region's local governments were unwilling to surrender local autonomy and delegate some of their powers to a new, higher authority.

California's Community Redevelopment Agencies: The Old and New Models

In late December 2011, 435 **redevelopment agencies** operated throughout the state in sponsoring cities and counties. By May 2012, only a few months later, they were all gone.[45]

While they existed, these agencies acquired property by the power of eminent domain, disposed of it by lease or sale without public bidding, cleared the land, constructed infrastructure needed for building on project sites, and made other improvements. Typically, the agencies would then transfer the developed land to private parties for residential and/or commercial development, which ideally would then attract new investment, businesses, and jobs to the area. These redevelopment projects were funded through property **tax-increment financing (TIF)**. If a project site generated higher property tax revenues than it otherwise might have produced without redevelopment, the increment in revenues over the baseline would be returned to the agency to pay for the project site investments. To ensure that these powerful agencies served a public interest priority, they were required to spend at least 20 percent of their funds on affordable housing.

When Jerry Brown became governor in January 2011, he faced a budget deficit of $25 billion. To help reduce it, he and the legislature passed a law abolishing all of the state's redevelopment agencies and redirecting their property tax revenues to pay for schools, health services, and other programs placed in jeopardy by the budget crisis. After the courts upheld the law on appeal, the agencies became officially extinct. This outcome illustrates Dillon's Rule, discussed earlier in the chapter, that local governments are creatures of the state, and the state's power to create such entities is also the power to destroy them.

By May 2012 redevelopment agencies no longer existed in California. The 1,500 or so employees who had worked for them were laid off or reassigned to other positions. A big chunk of redevelopment agency funds, about $1.5 billion, was redirected to support the state's public schools, health care services, and public safety programs. The remaining funds were assigned to counties for distribution to cities and their designated "successor agencies" to wind down existing redevelopment projects under the watchful eyes of the state controller.

In September 2015, Governor Brown signed Assembly Bill 2 authorizing local governments to create a stripped-down version of redevelopment agencies known as a "community revitalization investment authority" to be used as an economic development tool. Like the old redevelopment agencies, these new agencies would be allowed to use property tax-increment financing to improve project sites for development in low-income communities. Unlike the old models, however, the new ones would be prohibited from siphoning off tax revenues that would otherwise go to schools. And they would be subject to greater oversight and control by local residents.[46] Only time will tell whether these new agencies perform more effectively than the old ones and what their own lifespans will be.

Local Government: Where Are We Now?

By early November 2016, California's local governments had survived a gauntlet of economic and political crises. The Great Recession had severely weakened local economies and hit most of the state's city and county governments hard as tax revenues plummeted, which resulted in austerity in the form of slashed budgets, staff layoffs, and cutbacks in services. The cities of Vallejo, Stockton, and San Bernardino had been forced to declare bankruptcy, and other cities had teetered on the brink. As discussed earlier in this chapter, the state's newest city, Jurupa Valley, had barely survived a near-death experience. No financial rescue had come from the federal government, nor had the state government been of much help during the worst of it. Faced with its own budget crisis, the state abolished California's 435 redevelopment agencies to extract new revenues to help make ends meet. For some struggling cities, the loss of those revenues had been a crushing financial blow. The recession had also given rise to the **Occupy Movement**, whose participants had organized rallies in many of the state's larger cities. For the most part the movement had no clear agenda or even leaders, but the participants gave voice to the widespread rage against America's growing inequality, political domination by economic elites, and the evident failure of government at any level to do anything about it. Faced with such widespread economic hardship and political upheaval, leaders of the state's local governments had struggled and coped as best they could with limited resources, power, and authority.

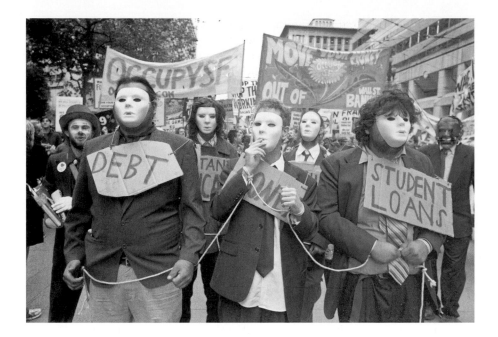

Occupy San Francisco demonstrators march up Market Street in November 2011. Their demonstrations voiced outrage at America's growing income inequality and demanded reform of governmental and financial institutions seen as serving the interests of only the nation's wealthiest 1 percent.

In the calmer seas and clearing skies of the current post-recession period, the state's local governments are now in a much better place than they were even a year or two ago. The state's economy overall has recovered from the recession. The state government's finances have improved to the point that for the last two years Governor Brown's budgets have shown surpluses rather than deficits, which has allowed him and the state legislature to give back to the cities and other local governments rather than taking from them. Funding was restored for public schools, health care, and social services. Plans for creating sustainable communities, improving transportation infrastructure, producing more affordable housing, and controlling greenhouse gas emissions, which had been placed on hold during hard times, were reactivated.

At the local government level, post-recession economic recovery continues in most cities, especially in the Bay Area and Los Angeles metropolitan regions. In some cities, like San Francisco, the tech-driven economic boom has created the problem of too much growth too fast, which has resulted in a housing affordability crisis, evictions and displacement, and growing political protest. In other cities, however, recovery from the recession still lags. The cities of Vallejo and Stockton, for example, are now released from bankruptcy. Bankruptcy court proceedings for San Bernardino should be completed by early 2017.[47] But all three continue to struggle with the same kinds of problems that forced them into bankruptcy in the first place: underfunded pension plans; limited tax revenues from slowly recovering businesses; and growing demands from citizens for better services, security, and employment opportunities. While cities in the state's coastal regions are once again thriving, many in the Central Valley and Inland Empire regions are still striving to attain prerecession levels of financial stability and economic well-being.

Perhaps the most important development to come out of the recession is the birth of a new urban-based political movement that is pushing the state government and many local governments to address the issue of growing income inequality and economic injustice, not only in California but throughout the entire country. The movement began with the formation of broad-based coalitions of labor unions, worker centers, and community groups in the Bay Area which demanded that local governments impose mandates on local employers requiring them to provide their workers with a higher minimum wage, paid sick leave, and other improvements in labor standards. Local governments in San Francisco, Oakland, San Jose, and a growing number of other, smaller cities in the region have responded, and both San Francisco and Oakland have raised their minimum wage standard to $15 an hour, which is quickly becoming the new regional norm. That movement has now spread rapidly to other regions in the state, including Los Angeles City and Los Angeles County, which recently adopted the $15 minimum wage policy, and even to the more conservative city of San Diego, whose voters in June 2016 supported a much higher minimum wage and the adoption of paid sick leave by a two-to-one margin. In April 2016, pressured by the state's largest labor union, the Service Employees International Union (SEIU), and other activist groups from across the state, Governor Brown signed a bill that made California the first state government in the country to adopt the $15 minimum wage along with the most generous paid-sick-leave policy in the United States.

This movement continues to grow in strength and numbers, not only in California but across the nation, especially in the big cities. Labor journalist Harold Meyerson has called this bottom-up, labor-union-driven movement "the revolt of the cities":

> What's happening in cities can be described as Obama's agenda trickling down to the jurisdictions where it has enough political support to be enacted—but it's also the incubation of policies and practices that will trickle up. With considerable creativity and limited power, the new urban regimes are seeking to diminish the inequality so apparent in cities and so pervasive nationwide. They are mapping the future of liberalism until the day when the national government can bring it to scale.[48]

Thanks in large part to this movement, which has taken root in California's cities, the time may yet come for the national government to "bring it to scale." After years of prolonged partisan polarization and legislative gridlock in the federal government, the issue of income inequality finally made its way onto the national political agenda and became a major focus of the 2016 presidential election. Donald Trump's surprising victory over Hillary Clinton in that election, however, will likely delay any major federal government action to deal with the issue for at least some time to come. Indeed, only days after the election, many of California's top elected officials, nearly all of them Democrats, were girding themselves for a prolonged "political war" with President Trump and the national Republican Party. Battle lines were being drawn on a wide range of issues, particularly immigration but also healthcare, abortion, homelessness, unemployment, housing, infrastructure, international trade, and climate change.[49] Of all the lessons learned from the Great Recession, perhaps the most important is that local governments cannot solve these kinds of problems alone. Empowered business leadership, public-private partnerships, and market-based initiatives have the potential to help, but the private sector is also limited in its capacity to solve public problems. Local governments and their business partners require the power and resources of the federal government to cope with such issues effectively. The years immediately ahead are certain to be politically turbulent and contentious, especially at the national level, and the future of California's state and local governments under the Trump administration is yet unclear.

Study Guide

FOR FURTHER READING

Baldassare, Mark. *A California State of Mind: The Conflicted Voter in a Changing World.* Berkeley: University of California Press, 2002.

Bridges, Amy. *Morning Glories: Municipal Reform in the Southwest.* Princeton, NJ: Princeton University Press, 1997.

DeLeon, Richard Edward. *Left Coast City: Progressive Politics in San Francisco, 1975–1991.* Lawrence, KS: University Press of Kansas, 1992.

Hajnal, Zoltan L., Paul G. Lewis, and Hugh Louch. *Municipal Elections in California: Turnout, Timing, and Competition.* San Francisco: Public Policy Institute of California, 2002.

Rodriguez, Daniel B. "State Supremacy, Local Sovereignty: Reconstructing State/Local Relations under the California Constitution." In *Constitutional Reform in California: Making State Government More Effective and Responsive,* edited by Bruce E. Cain and Roger G. Noll, 401–29. Berkeley: Institute of Governmental Studies Press, University of California, 1995.

Sonenshein, Raphael J. *Politics in Black and White: Race and Power in Los Angeles.* Princeton, NJ: Princeton University Press, 1993.

ON THE WEB

California Department of Finance. www.dof.ca.gov. Accessed 6/6/12. The Department of Finance produces detailed and up-to-date statistical reports and studies on local government finances, the state budget process and its impacts on localities, and a wide range of demographic and economic information on cities and counties.

California Employment Development Department. www.edd.ca.gov. Accessed 7/7/12. Valuable source of up-to-date statewide and county-level information on employment and labor market conditions.

California Secretary of State. www.sos.ca.gov/elections. Accessed 7/7/12. Excellent source of information on county-level election results for statewide candidate races and ballot propositions.

California Special Districts Association. www.csda.net. Accessed 7/7/12.

California State Association of Counties. www.csac.counties.org. Accessed 7/7/12. Useful source of wide-ranging news and information on California's counties, with a main focus on policy and administration.

Institute for Local Government. www.ca-ilg.org. Accessed 8/4/12. The research arm and affiliate of the League of California Cities and the California State Association of Counties. Good source for in-depth studies of key policy issues facing the state's local governments.

League of California Cities. www.cacities.org/index.jsp. Accessed 7/7/12. An excellent source of news, information, and data on all aspects of governing California's cities.

U.S. Conference of Mayors. www.usmayors.org. Accessed 7/7/12.

SUMMARY

I. Overview of California local governments.
   A. California has more than 5,000 local governments of various types, including general-purpose governments such as those in counties and cities, specific-purpose governments such as those for school districts and special districts, and regional governments.
   B. Local governments provide essential services, ranging from law enforcement and fire protection to waste management and street maintenance to air- and water-quality control.

II. Legal framework for local government: the state has ultimate authority over local governments.
   A. Under Dillon's Rule, local governments are "creatures of the state" and have no inherent rights or powers except those given to them by the state constitution or legislature.
   B. California, like most states, gives counties and cities significant powers to govern themselves, make policies, enforce laws, raise revenues, borrow, and generally control local affairs as long as their decisions don't conflict with state or federal laws.
   C. The more populous cities and counties have adopted home-rule charters, which allow maximum local autonomy in self-governance.
   D. The other cities and counties operate as general-law counties and cities, which have to abide more strictly by the state legislature's local government code.

III. County governments.
   A. California's 58 counties are extremely diverse in terms of territorial extent, population size, demographic characteristics, and political culture.
   B. Except for the unique case of San Francisco's consolidated county/city government, all counties are governed by five-member boards of supervisors that exercise both legislative and executive powers.
   C. Counties perform important functions, many of them required by state government laws and mandates.
   D. Counties also provide essential services, especially in unincorporated areas outside the cities and other jurisdictions, and they are major arenas for making large-scale land-use and development policies.
   E. Each county also has a local agency formation commission (LAFCo), which plays a critical role in creating, merging, or dissolving new local governments, such as those in cities and special districts, and resolving disputes among competing jurisdictions.

IV. City governments.
   A. The state has 482 cities, most of them general-law cities; the rest are charter cities with significant home-rule powers and local autonomy.
   B. Cities are legally created through a process of municipal incorporation that requires LAFCo review and approval as well as a final majority vote of the community seeking formal city status.
   C. Nearly all cities have a form of government modeled on the vision of Progressive Era reformers. Called reform cities, most of them have strong city managers, weak mayors, nonpartisan elections, at-large council elections, nonconcurrent elections, and direct democracy procedures (the initiative, referendum, and recall). Important exceptions to such reform cities are cities such as Los Angeles and San Francisco, which have strong mayors and, in the case of San Francisco, district elections.

V. Citizen participation in local government.
   A. The Brown Act of 1953, known as the "open meetings law," requires that all meetings of local legislative bodies be open and public unless specifically exempted, and that all citizens be permitted to attend such meetings.
   B. Voter turnout in city elections has been steadily declining in recent years.
      1. Those who do vote in city elections tend to be whiter, older, richer, and more educated than those who don't.
      2. In particular, the state's growing population of noncitizens has little political voice or formal representation in local government.
      3. Certain electoral reforms, such as a shift from nonconcurrent to concurrent elections, could markedly increase voter turnout levels.

VI. Special districts.
   A. Special districts are limited-purpose local governments.
   B. Excluding the state's 1,028 K–12 school districts and 72 community-college districts, California has nearly 5,000 special districts.
   C. Special districts provide a range of services—for example, irrigation, pest abatement, parks and recreation, water, and fire protection—which are not provided at all (or in insufficient amounts) by general-purpose governments such as those for counties and cities.
   D. Special districts are created by a LAFCo-approved citizen petition and a majority vote.
   E. Most special districts are independent agencies that provide one type of service received and paid for by residents in smaller territories of larger jurisdictions, like counties.
   F. Some special districts are enterprise districts that charge individual user fees for service.
   G. Most special districts are funded by taxes or special assessments from service recipients.
   H. The advantages of special districts include greater flexibility and responsiveness in tailoring service and requiring only the beneficiaries to pay the costs.
   I. The disadvantages of special districts include duplication of services, lack of coordination, and unclear structures of authority and accountability.

VII. Regional governments.
   A. The state's regional governments address problems such as air pollution and population growth that affect large areas and multiple local government jurisdictions.
   B. Some regional governments, such as the San Francisco Bay Conservation and Development Commission and the California Coastal Commission, have strong regulatory authority and enforcement powers.
   C. Other regional governments, such as the Southern California Association of Governments, the Association of Bay Area Governments, and other councils of government (COGs), mainly perform research, planning, and advisory functions and have little or no power or authority to impose their decisions on local jurisdictions.

VIII. Community redevelopment agencies.
   A. Over 400 redevelopment agencies were active throughout the state in 2011.
   B. These redevelopment agencies no longer exist, however. How and why they disappeared are discussed in the text.

IX. Four major transitions facing local governments.
  A. The transition from the Great Recession to geographically uneven economic recovery and prosperity.
  B. The transition from the death of urban redevelopment agencies to new institutions of physical and economic development in our cities.
  C. The transition from the massive but ephemeral Occupy Movement to a growing and durable network of progressive cities pushing for reforms at the local level.
  D. The transition from intercity competition, which was mutually destructive, to regional cooperation and sustainable economies.

PRACTICE QUIZ

1. Cities and counties that have home-rule charters have the authority to make their own laws even if they violate state and federal laws.
   a) true
   b) false

2. The U.S. Constitution gives local governments inherent rights and powers that cannot be taken away by state governments.
   a) true
   b) false

3. County boards of supervisors have both legislative and executive authority.
   a) true
   b) false

4. Most cities are governed by council-manager systems.
   a) true
   b) false

5. At the local government level, citizens cannot petition for a referendum or recall election.
   a) true
   b) false

6. Which of the following is *not* a characteristic of reform government at the local level?
   a) at-large council elections
   b) nonpartisanship
   c) city manager plan
   d) concurrent elections

7. Which of the following counties operates under a single charter as a consolidated city and county?
   a) Los Angeles
   b) Sacramento
   c) San Francisco
   d) Orange

8. Which of the following elected officials can be found only in county governments?
   a) sheriff
   b) mayor
   c) council member
   d) manager

9. ABAG is an example of a COG.
   a) true
   b) false

10. The Sustainable Communities Act (SB 375) prohibits California cities from making regional alliances with other cities.
   a) true
   b) false

CRITICAL-THINKING QUESTIONS

1. Do you think the Progressive Era reform vision for local governments is still a good one today? Should the state's local governments continue to be run by professional managers and insulated as much as possible from state and national party politics? Why or why not?

2. Should local governments, such as cities, be given more home-rule powers and greater local autonomy free of state interference? Test case: Would you support all California cities asserting their home-rule powers and local autonomy to the extent that San Francisco has? Why or why not?

3. Do you agree with some critics that most special districts should be abolished and their functions centralized under the control of county and city governments? Why or why not?

4. Do you agree with some observers that California needs more and stronger regional governments? Why or why not? If you agree, what are some of the problems facing those who seek to form such governments, and what steps would you take to create them? How would you balance your recommendations with the principles of home rule and local autonomy?

5. Do you support or oppose the rebellion of local governments against the state as a response to the state's attempt to use local government property tax revenues to solve its budget deficit problems? Why or why not?

KEY TERMS

advisory regional governments (p. 240)
at-large elections (p. 233)
charter cities (p. 229)
charter counties (p. 224)
cities (p. 220)
council-manager plan (p. 232)
councils of government (COGs) (p. 240)
counties (p. 220)
Dillon's Rule (p. 220)
direct democracy (p. 234)
district elections (p. 233)

enterprise districts (p. 237)
general-law cities (p. 229)
general-law counties (p. 223)
home rule (p. 220)
independent districts (p. 238)
local agency formation commission (LAFCo) (p. 228)
mayor-council system (p. 232)
municipal incorporation (p. 229)
nonpartisanship (p. 232)
Occupy Movement (p. 242)
ordinances (p. 224)

redevelopment agencies (p. 241)
reform governments (p. 231)
regional governments (p. 239)
regulatory regional governments (p. 239)
school and community college districts (p. 237)
secession (p. 228)
special districts (p. 220)
tax-increment financing (p. 241)
user fees (p. 237)

10 Public Policy in California

WHAT CALIFORNIA GOVERNMENT DOES AND WHY IT MATTERS

Riverside County, east of Los Angeles, has over 300 trailer parks, many inhabited by migrant agricultural workers who pick the vegetables and fruit that grow abundantly in the county's irrigated valleys. In 1999 the county accused several trailer parks that catered to migrant workers of substandard and dangerous conditions and subsequently shut them down. Harvey Duro, Sr., a member of the Torres Martinez Desert Cahuilla Indian Reservation, spread the word of a new trailer park on reservation land where the displaced workers could reside. Many farmworkers moved in, paying about $500 a month per trailer to live there.[1]

The conditions weren't good. The trailer park, officially called Desert Mobile Home Park but unofficially known as Duroville or Duros, was next to a dump that burned from time to time. Heaps of tires and construction debris littered the area, the streets were dusty (and muddy when it rained), and the area's sewage flowed into a pond next door. In 2002 the teachers in the local schools noticed that many of their students who lived in the park were suffering from asthma and rashes, and they determined that the dump was the likely cause. The Bureau of Indian Affairs, which had jurisdiction because the trailer park was on the reservation, moved to close the park because of the unsanitary conditions. In 2009 the local U.S. attorney cited in court the park's "leaking sewage, 800 feral dogs, piles of debris and fire hazards," as well as 5,000 tenants. The cost of bringing it into compliance would be more than $4 million, which the owner could not afford.

After several years of litigation, in 2009 a federal judge decreed that since there was no other place for the residents to go, the park could stay open. The population of the park numbered between 2,000 to 6,000 people, depending on the time of year and economic conditions. Many residents were undocumented. Many earned less than $10,000 per year. And many of them were Purépechas, an indigenous people from Michoacán, Mexico. Many, in fact, were from a single town in Michoacán.

By 2010 most of the people who sold drugs in the park were gone, the feral dog problem was substantially reduced, and the rotting garbage had been cleared. But there was still no place for the residents to move, and the quality of the trailers was no better. Riverside County then completed a public housing project for the residents, Mountain View Estates, six miles away from Duroville and composed of 181 units.[2] Duroville finally closed in June 2014, 15 years after it opened. Public housing projects require that residents be in the United States legally, so many undocumented former residents of Duroville moved to other trailer parks in the area.

While it was open, Duroville had its own Wikipedia entry and new-resident councils and representatives to help ensure residents' adherence to the rules. Articles about the community occasionally appeared in the *New York Times* and the *Los Angeles Times* as well as in the local newspapers. And while Duroville has been cleaned up because of legal intervention, a lack of quality housing and living conditions persists for many farmworkers, particularly the undocumented. For example, the *Los Angeles Times* reported in October 2015 that some families who work in the Coachella Valley have "pooled resources" to create livable trailer parks. Given their limited resources, the end result is that "they [have] jury-rigged almost everything. Electricity was tapped from a post meant to power one well, the dirt road was covered in rugs to keep down the choking dust." Similar trailer parks dot the area and most are vulnerable to power outages, storm damage, and sewage overflow. Residents are sometimes left with no option but to sleep in tents because of the heat index during the summer. Riverside County has responded to this problem by proposing $3.4 million dollars to pave dirt roads in a number of the trailer parks, and the county has "authorized the use of temporary construction power lines to return power."[3]

The issue of housing, along with many other policy areas in California politics, exemplifies the challenges posed throughout this book—challenges related to California's enormous diversity and unique institutions. Sites like Duroville can exist on Indian reservations, which have jurisdiction over most governmental areas except law enforcement. If not for this jurisdiction, the zoning and other laws in effect in most areas of California would have shut Duroville down much sooner.

You may have concluded by now that California is a land of contrasts. The same state that includes Beverly Hills and Silicon Valley also has its Durovilles. Public policy in California governs areas that are like Duroville—that is, areas that are not doing so well—and other areas that are in better shape. It is difficult to generalize as to the average state of affairs. California's high degree of heterogeneity is evident in the proposal to divide California into six states, an initiative that failed to collect enough signatures in 2014 to make the ballot. This plan would have created the richest state in the United States (the state that would have encompassed Silicon Valley) as well as the poorest (the state that would have included the Central Valley).

We know from earlier chapters in this book that California has come close to being ungovernable during the last two decades. We have a public that demands a high level of services but consistently refuses to pay for them. Many members of the public still feel that the free tuition and low fees in higher education during the Pat Brown era are still possible at a time when the state's people and politics have changed profoundly. Proposition 30, passed in November 2012, is one of the few exceptions, with a small permanent sales tax increase and larger temporary income tax increases on the wealthy, but these increases will expire in 2018. The public is sometimes willing to approve initiatives to undertake new projects that lack funding. It is also willing to pass special taxes earmarked for special purposes, many of which benefit the interests sponsoring the relevant initiative.

The lack of consensus among the public is reflected in our institutions, which in some cases barely function. However, major steps have been taken to improve the quality of the political process in California. While the legislature has been unable to change the state's tax structure, now over 50 years old, some new institutional changes—most notably the top-two primary system and the new nonpartisan legislative redistricting system—are designed to improve the functioning of our political system. The 50 percent majority now necessary to pass a budget has ended the budget haggling that used to paralyze Sacramento all summer and for part of the fall, but the cost of limited revenues in 2011 and 2012 was a substantial reduction in funds for the state's public schools. The top-two primary, the 50 percent rule for passing the state's budget in the legislature, and the commission to handle redistricting every 10 years in a neutral and nonpartisan fashion may be just the beginning of a wave of reform, though these reforms will take years to assess.

Meanwhile, our focus in this chapter is on the current state of public policy in California. The term **public policy** means what government actually does or "produces" in various policy areas, such as health, welfare, education, higher education, water, and the like. The policies in each of these areas are different in each state. For the California of the 1950s and 1960s, education and water policy were proud, if politically difficult, achievements, and the state was one of the nation's leaders in solving its problems and supporting its schools and colleges. For the California of the 2000s, these are areas of profound disappointment.

For example, even with Proposition 98 (1988) "guaranteeing" the public schools some 40 percent of the general fund, California's finances have been so tight that K-12 spending is below average, sometimes ranking in the bottom 40 percent of states.[4] *Education Week*, a national newspaper that covers issues in K-12 public education, gave California a C- for its "overall quality" of education. The grade includes evaluations of financial support, probabilities of success, and measures of student achievement. Only 10 other states received lower marks in early 2016.[5] Like 46 other states and the District of Columbia, California has adopted the Common Core Standards. Although the state adopted these standards in 2010, they were not implemented until 2012-13, so it is a bit soon to evaluate whether the Common Core Standards have improved student learning and achievement. According to Tom Torlakson, the State Superintendent of Public Instruction, it is hopeful that the Common Core Standards will improve college readiness. Results of the 2015 statewide standardized testing of students across all grades found that 44 percent met or exceeded the English language arts/literacy standard. Eleven percent fewer (33 percent) met or exceeded the standard for mathematics.[6] It is obvious from these measures that there is significant need for improvement. Advocates of the Common Core argue that over time the scores should improve because of the rigorous curriculum. One of the biggest problems facing public education in California is the achievement gap. It remains to be seen whether the Common Core will help narrow this gap given the many factors that need to be addressed, especially funding.

Likewise, the University of California, the California State University, and the state's extensive community college system have all seen cutbacks in faculty pay and course offerings as well as substantially higher costs for tuition and fees. How much higher these can go is a major, unanswered question, but there were few alternatives in the severe recession of 2009-10.

One could write several books about California public policy, so in this chapter we have confined ourselves to four areas of interest. They are typical in the sense that they show some of the best and worst areas in which the state is involved. The first of these is water policy. The second is health insurance. The third is the state's infrastructure, which has experienced spending issues similar to those endured by K-12 education. And the fourth is gambling, specifically the complex negotiations between the state and the Indian tribes regarding Indian casinos.

Water Policy

Of the water used in California, 20 percent is for households, business, and industry, while 80 percent is for agricultural purposes, including irrigation. Farm production and food processing compose about 2 percent of the California economy, down from 5 percent in 1960. Over the past decade or more, higher revenue perennial crops that require annual watering, such as grapes, nuts, and other fruits, have increased as a proportion of California's total agricultural output (as compared to annual crops, which enable land to be left fallow in times of drought). As a consequence, **agricultural water use** has been creeping up.[7]

Household water use is dominated by the two megalopolises of California: the San Francisco Bay region and Southern California. Residential and commercial water use is split 50–50 between use inside the house and landscaping outside. Total urban water use has been constant for the last two decades, despite increases in population, because water districts have instituted water conservation programs. Some of these are tiered pricing programs, so that large users pay more per unit, and some incorporate legal requirements to install low-flow toilets and showerheads. Even so, substantial differences among similar cities exist, depending on their closeness to the Pacific coast, density of the population, typical climate, and amount of industry. Coastal cities use less water; a dense population means smaller yards. Hot weather means more watering, and more industry can skew statistics because some industries may use a lot more water than others. A 2004 law requires that water meters be installed statewide by 2025. As of 2014 there were still cities with some unmetered customers; generally they are billed a flat rate each month.[8] (See the "Who Are Californians?" feature on the next page for more on variation in water use across California.)

The major **2013–14 drought** exposed the problems of water rights and uses in the existing system. Governor Jerry Brown proclaimed a statewide water emergency in January 2014, and local water agencies, depending on their particular situations, gradually imposed measures to restrict the use of water.

The drought has also highlighted problems in the water supply. A study by several University of California researchers released in 2014 pinpointed the central problem: California's freshwater runoff in an average year is about 70 million acre-feet, but since 1914, the state has handed out water rights totaling 370 million acre-feet. That's five times more water than nature, on average, produces.[9] An acre-foot of water (one foot of water in depth on an acre of land) is sufficient for two average households for a year.

Many solutions have been proposed, among them the following: building two 35-mile tunnels around the Sacramento–San Joaquin Delta to bring water to the California aqueduct, importing water from new sources, increasing water conservation efforts, and using rainwater or gray water at home. Four practical solutions were suggested in major studies released in June 2014 by Oakland's Pacific Institute, the Natural Resource Defense Council, and researchers from UC Santa Barbara. Taken together, these four solutions, listed below, point to the future of water supply.[10]

1. Increasing efficiency in homes and industries by replacing or improving inefficient appliances, reducing waste and leaks, and replacing traditional landscapes with low-water-use plants and gardens. The potential savings are 2.9 to 5.2 million acre-feet per year.
2. Increasing efficiency in agriculture through better irrigation techniques and practices, with potential savings of 5.6 to 6.6 million acre-feet per year.
3. Reusing treated wastewater for irrigation, landscapes, industry, and recharging groundwater basins. Savings here could total 1.2 to 1.8 million acre-feet.
4. Capturing storm water at homes and businesses, using it locally or to recharge groundwater basins. Savings could total 0.4 to 0.6 million acre-feet.[11]

At a minimum, the new sources over time could add 10 million acre-feet of water.

The other side of the water quantity problem is the water *quality* problem, involving problems of **groundwater management**, naturally occurring minerals such as arsenic in California's water, and, in the eyes of many Californians, hardness. (The latter isn't a water quality issue, but many feel that it is.)

Groundwater composes 35 percent of the total water used in California in an average year. In a drought year, pumping groundwater increases as users attempt to compensate for the lack of rain. While surface water is regulated in California, until September 2014 groundwater was largely unregulated. Some groundwater basins have been so heavily used that the amount taken out each year exceeds what can be reasonably replenished even in El Niño years with relatively heavy rainfall totals. When groundwater declines, the energy costs of pumping water from deeper wells increase, and the additional pumping can cause land to sink, damaging surface infrastructure such as roads and canals.[12]

Who Gets Water in California?

Most water in California goes to agriculture; in an average year, agricultural water use accounts for approximately 6 times as much as urban, including residential, water use. Water use became especially controversial in 2014, when the state experienced a historic drought, with groundwater at an all-time low (in the 119 years that the state has kept records). In 2014, Governor Jerry Brown issued a drought state of emergency, and in April 2015 he issued mandatory water use reductions. As shown in the right-side figure, most Californians complied with those reductions, despite population growth and record-high temperatures. In 2016 rainfall increased, leading Governor Brown to lift mandatory restrictions, but snowpack still lagged. As the left-side map shows, per capita water use varies significantly by region.

Per Capita Water Use by Region, 2014–2015

Residential water use, gallons per day

■ Less than 75   ■ 75-100   ■ 101-125   ■ 126-150   ■ Above 150

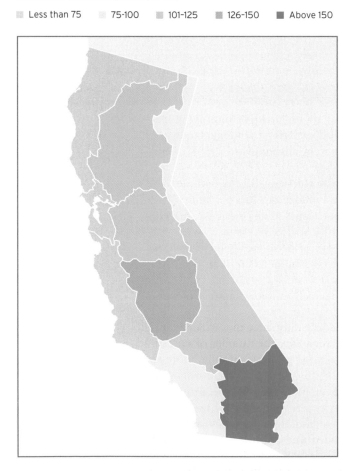

SOURCE: "June 2015 Statewide Conservation Data," California Water Boards, www.waterboards.ca.gov/waterrights/water_issues/programs/drought/docs/fs073015_june_by_the_numbers.pdf (accessed 9/6/16).

Compliance with Water Use Restrictions, 2015

Met or within 1% of standard

265 Suppliers

27.2 million people served

Between 1% and 5% from meeting standard

53 Suppliers

3.9 million people served

Between 5% and 15% from meeting standard

71 Suppliers

3.6 million people served

More than 15% from meeting standard

16 Suppliers

1.0 million people served

forcriticalanalysis

1. Why do some regions of California use more water than others? What drives the different rates of use in the ten hydrologic regions shown in the map?

2. Given the historic shortage of water, should restrictions be placed on urban/residential use, agricultural use, or both? What other strategies might California use to meet its water needs?

Contamination of groundwater is a growing problem in California, with some basins contaminated from fertilizers and manure, and others suffering because of salinity. Changes in water-use practices will help in the future, but some existing basins will need to be cleaned up.

Until 2014, California was the only western state in the United States without some level of state regulation of groundwater. The state took a major step in this direction as a result of the 2013–14 drought: the Assembly and state Senate passed three bills to compel water-basin managers in certain areas of the state to design groundwater management plans that would prevent overdrafting. All three bills were signed into law by Governor Brown. Together, they make up the Sustainable Groundwater Management Act (SGMA). The SGMA includes not only guidelines and regulations for the management of groundwater, but also regulatory language for areas that may not have groundwater basin managers.

In addition, a water bond issue of more than $7 billion was placed on the November 2014 ballot, as the drought provided the catalyst for the legislature to agree on a series of projects in the water policy area. The bond issue had previously been stalled in the legislature for several years. The water bond was approved by almost 67 percent of the voters.

Health Insurance

While many Californians are still without health insurance coverage, President Obama's Affordable Care Act (ACA) has already had a significant impact in California. During the first six months of enrollment, 1.4 million people purchased a policy on Covered California, the state's health insurance exchange.[13] Another 1.9 million people enrolled in Medi-Cal, now open to single adults and couples without children who qualify on the basis of poverty. These enrollments should reduce the number of people without health insurance in California by about 3 million; the exact number is unclear because some new enrollees replaced their private insurance plans with insurance through the exchange or Medi-Cal. Gallup polls taken in 2013 and in mid-2014 showed a reduction in those without health insurance in California from 21.6 percent to 16.3 percent, which is "in the ballpark" of what can be reasonably expected—a good start toward reducing the very high proportion of people in California without health insurance. More recently, a 2015 Gallup poll indicated that the trend has continued—only 11.8 percent of Californians were uninsured.

While the number of uninsured has declined steadily since the ACA's adoption and implementation, there are three major reasons why the number of uninsured has been so high in California. One is that many people in California, more than the national average, work in small firms, and small firms tend not to offer health insurance nearly as often as large firms do. The second is that the state's population has a large proportion of immigrants, and immigrants are much less likely to have health insurance than are native-born Americans. The third reason is that undocumented immigrants are not eligible to enroll in Medicaid (Medi-Cal is California's Medicaid program, see below), nor are they eligible to purchase health insurance through the ACA exchanges. About 2.5 million people are undocumented in California, a figure that has remained constant for over a decade. These statistics are unlikely to improve given the 2016 presidential election outcome. Donald Trump called for the repeal of the ACA in his campaign, and this position was a very popular one for many of his supporters and other conservatives. While he has also stated that he wants to replace the ACA with his own healthcare reform plan, doing so will take time and present many challenges for Californians in the interim. Trump's plan will significantly impact those who are eligible to participate as well as those who will remain uninsured because of their undocumented status. One proposed change is a tax deduction for the insured. Those who are working poor or have lower income are unlikely to benefit from a tax deduction in the way that wealthier Californians would, however.

Employer-Sponsored Insurance

In 2012 about 53 percent of Californians under age 65 had **employer-sponsored insurance (ESI)**—that is, they obtained their insurance through their employer, who typically subsidized some of the cost. ESI has been declining nationally, and the recession of 2008–09 accelerated the process. In California, ESI has historically been lower than in other states because of the size and structure of California's employers and the number of noncitizens in the state. As of 2015 the ESI numbers had stayed more or less the same after the first round of enrollment in the ACA, but there is some decline for eligible lower-income workers with families who may choose not to enroll in ESIs given the more affordable alternatives under the ACA.

Individual Health Insurance Marketplace

In California's state **individual insurance marketplace**, people purchase a health insurance policy directly from the insurance company. This is the market expected to be most directly affected by the ACA. Several provisions in the act reformed this market, which has been characterized in the past by extremely large price increases from year to year (one large insurer asked for a 39 percent price increase from 2010 to 2011) and by **rescissions**, cases in which insurers have dropped policyholders who have become sick and filed large claims, on the grounds that their applications were not truthful. The extent of these price increases and rescissions enabled by California's pre-ACA marketplace meant that it was a model other states would not want to emulate. The ACA now prohibits companies that provide insurance on the marketplace from charging higher rates for preexisting conditions, rescinding policies after policyholders file insurance claims, rating users by health status so that those with fair or poor health pay a higher rate, and enforcing lifetime limits on policies. In 2016 about 1.5 million Californians participated in this market. Most of the people in the market should eventually be receiving their health insurance through Covered California, the state's health insurance exchange.

Medi-Cal

Medi-Cal is California's version of the federal Medicaid plan for the poor. The federal government sponsors two large federal health insurance programs, **Medicare** and **Medicaid**. Medicare, aimed primarily at senior citizens, is paid for with federal funds, a tax on workers and their employers, and beneficiary premiums, deductibles, and co-pays. Medicaid, in contrast, is aimed at low-income people, and the financing is split between the federal government and the states. The federal government provides an average of 57 percent of the funding and some national standards, and the states provide the other 43 percent of the funding plus basic program administration and decision making. The proportion of the funding that each state provides is determined by a formula based on state per-capita income, and because California is a relatively rich state, it receives 50 percent federal funding, the minimum rate. Mississippi received the maximum federal funding rate at 73.6 percent in fiscal year 2015.

Under the ACA, Medicaid/Medi-Cal will expand by dropping requirements that excluded single individuals and couples without children and by accepting Medi-Cal enrollees solely on the basis of their income. These changes resulted in 1.9 million people signing up for Medi-Cal during the first enrollment period for the ACA, from November 2013 to March 2014. Medi-Cal now covers about 11.5 million Californians, almost 30 percent of the population.[14]

The downside to this expansion is that California's average cost per Medi-Cal recipient is the lowest of any state, mostly because provider payments—the payment to each hospital and doctor for providing a service covered by Medi-Cal—are the lowest in the country. Consequently, access to doctors, particularly specialists, is limited for Medi-Cal beneficiaries in many parts of the state. This is because, for financial reasons, many medical practices either will not take Medi-Cal beneficiaries at all or limit the number of Medi-Cal patients they will see.[15]

Medicare

Some 12.5 percent of Californians are over 65, and almost all of the 4.5 million people in that category are on Medicare. In addition, 2.4 percent of Californians under 65 also qualify for Medicare. All those under 65 who are on Medicare have a disability of some kind (although not all those with disabilities are eligible for Medicare): anyone with ALS (Lou Gehrig's disease) or end-stage renal disease is immediately eligible for Medicare, and those who are on Social Security disability are eligible for Medicare after a two-year wait. The Medicare numbers are not expected to be affected by the ACA.

TRICARE

TRICARE and other military-related programs are the health care programs for military retirees and their dependents, including some members of the military reserves, with some civilian health benefits for military personnel as well. The category also includes those who receive their health care from the U.S. Department of Veterans Affairs (VA). About 2.4 percent of those under 65, some 800,000 Californians, are on TRICARE. The ACA does not affect TRICARE.

The Uninsured

The California Health Care Foundation, using census data from the federal government, calculated the proportion of uninsured Californians under age 65 at 21.2 percent in 2010 to 2012.[16] Gallup, using its own surveys and a much simpler question, calculated the proportion as 21.6 percent in 2013 and 16.3 percent in mid-2014, and less than 12 percent in mid-2015. Clearly, the implementation of the ACA in early 2014 has resulted in a major drop in the number and proportion of the uninsured. Just as surely, there is still a long way to go. Basic information about those without insurance follows, although any specific numbers cited are from *before* the ACA.

- Some 23 percent of workers lacked insurance in California, compared with 19 percent in the nation.

- Most heads of household without insurance have a job, and most of those jobs are full-time.

- It is estimated that most *children* without insurance are eligible for Medi-Cal or Healthy Families, California's State Children's Health Insurance Program (SCHIP, which is a federal program aimed at those whose incomes are just above the Medicaid/Medi-Cal eligibility levels).

- 25- to 34-year-olds are the largest age group represented among the uninsured (26 percent), but every age group under 65 is represented. So-called pre-retirees, 55- to 64-year-olds, comprise 9 percent of the total.

- In terms of ethnicity, most people without health insurance in California are Latino (about 58 percent). Whites represent the next most frequent group, at 24 percent. Asians compose 11 percent of the total, and African Americans 5 percent.

- Of those without health insurance, 63 percent are American citizens and 37 percent are not.

California's Infrastructure

Infrastructure is the part of government with which citizens come into contact the most—highways, schools, universities, commuter buses, and railways. California's infrastructure deteriorated significantly from the 1970s into the 2000s, although recently the state has made some progress toward improving the system. One factor complicating the successful maintenance of the state's infrastructure is what Bruce Cain of U.C. Berkeley's Institute of Governmental Studies calls California's "infrastructure ambivalence." On the one hand, Californians want modern facilities and infrastructure, but "we don't want what often comes with those things. There are, for instance, unavoidable environmental costs. Water projects can endanger fisheries in the Delta. New roads and housing can separate and destroy ecosystems."[17] And, of course, we don't want to pay for them. Consider the following examples.

Highways

California's highway system was close to the best in the nation after World War II and into the 1950s and 1960s. Beginning in the 1970s, however, it declined severely. The "California Infrastructure Report Card 2012," issued by the American Society of Civil Engineers, gave California's infrastructure a grade of C, which is a bit better than the D grade for the nation as a whole.[18] A 2011 report on pavement conditions in the United States found 37 percent of California's roads to be "poor," with only 21 percent "good," making California the state ranked sixth from the bottom of the list.[19] A study of the structural quality of California's bridges found an improvement overall from 2007 to 2013. In 2007, 3,249, or 13.4 percent, of California's 24,189 bridges were structurally deficient; this number declined to 2,769, or 11.1 percent, in 2013.[20] There has been progress, partly the result of bond issues that were approved by the voters during the Schwarzenegger administration, but there is still much to be done.

The rebuilding of the Bay Bridge connecting San Francisco and Oakland is an extreme example of the substantial problems that have plagued the California state government's management of infrastructure projects. A 2014 report published in the *Sacramento Bee* indicated that the state agency responsible for the bridge construction chose a Chinese contractor who had never built parts for a bridge before to fabricate the steel structure of the bridge. The contractor ignored quality requirements built into the contract and fell behind schedule, necessitating the expenditure of hundreds of millions of dollars above the contract level. The result was a bridge built years behind schedule, costing more than twice the original price, and inspiring significant doubts about its quality.[21]

The management of California's transportation funds is clearly an issue. Dan Walters, who has been writing about California politics and management issues for the *Sacramento Bee* for several decades, points to "the labyrinth of interlocking transportation accounts" that direct money to infrastructure projects as the root of the mismanagement.[22] Others locate the problem in the increase in hybrid automobiles that use less gasoline, resulting in less income for the state from the gasoline tax. Another factor is the politicians who find few political benefits from maintaining infrastructure compared with building new projects. Additionally, there are governance problems. In a recent op-ed piece for the *Los Angeles Times*, George Skelton identified Proposition 13 as another factor that has affected potential revenues for California's highways and bridges. As noted in earlier chapters, Proposition 13 requires a two-thirds vote in both houses of the state legislature for any statewide tax increases. Governor Brown called for a special session of the legislature to address infrastructure problems. Representatives from Northern California, Senator Jim Beall and Assemblyman Jim Frazier, both Democrats, have co-sponsored a bill that would increase the gas tax on regular fuel by 17 cents a gallon and on diesel fuel by 30 cents a gallon, and it would require zero-emission vehicles to pay an annual fee of $165. Skelton, the author of this article, noted that it is unlikely for this 7.4 billion-dollar plan to pass, however, because of the two-thirds vote requirements and because of the current majorities in the state legislature.[23] One bright note in all of this is a change in California's car culture. As noted in the "Who Are Californians?" feature on the next page, recent survey results from the state's department of transportation show that increasing numbers of Californians are choosing public transportation, biking, and walking to get around over driving personal cars. Transportation is not the only persistent infrastructure problem that is confronted with political obstacles. When a water main broke in Los Angeles in 2014, it turned out that the main was 100 years old and that water rates were too

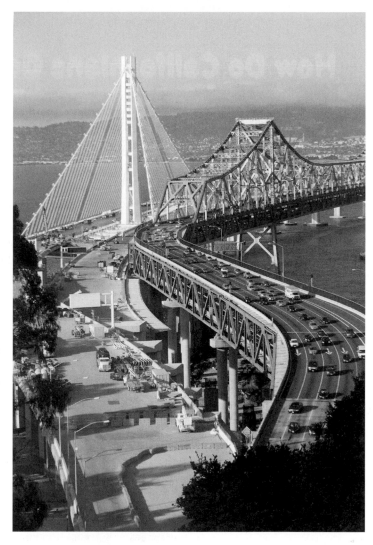

The new stretch of the Bay Bridge connecting Oakland and San Francisco (shown here alongside the old, structurally deficient stretch of the bridge that it is designed to replace) has been beset by construction and management problems that catalyzed a government investigation into Caltrans. Meanwhile, demolition of the old bridge is in process and a bicycle/pedestrian path linking the East Bay Bridge to Yerba Buena Island opened in October 2016.

How Do Californians Get Around?

Every 10 years, the California Department of Transportation conducts the California Household Travel Survey. The most recent survey covers the 2010–12 period and includes responses from 42,431 California households. Though the average household owns 1.8 cars, nearly 8 percent of California residents said that they don't own a car. When comparing the most recent survey data to the previous survey, conducted in 2000, we see that the percentage of people driving a car dropped by 11 percentage points, while the percentage of people walking, biking, and taking public transit doubled to 23 percent.

Percentage of All Trips by Travel Mode

2000

Private Vehicle (Driver)
60%

Private Vehicle (Passenger)
26%

Walk
8%

Public Transportation
2%

Bicycle
1%

Other
3%

2010–12

Private Vehicle (Driver)
49%

Private Vehicle (Passenger)
26%

Walk
17%

Public Transportation
4%

Bicycle
2%

Other
2%

SOURCE: U.S. California Department of Transportation, Statewide Travel Analysis Branch, www.dot.ca.gov/hq/tpp/offices/omsp/statewide_travel_analysis/ (accessed 8/1/16).

forcriticalanalysis

1. How do you travel to school? What role does the government play in your commute?

2. What, if anything, should government do to encourage people to use methods other than private cars to get where they need to go?

low to keep up on maintenance, because the city council, not a water agency, sets the rates. Although California's infrastructure is clearly beset by numerous problems, few people consider the maintenance of California's infrastructure, so critical to the movement of citizens, to be a top priority.

Levees

In 1986 a levee along the Yuba River broke and inundated the small town of Linda in the Central Valley, causing several hundred million dollars' worth of damage. In 2004, 18 years later, the state Supreme Court ratified a court of appeal decision that found the state of California liable because it had not repaired the broken stretch of levee. While the state resisted liability for the break and its consequences, the courts have determined that the state must pay for the consequences of its neglect.[24]

The *Sacramento Bee* published a series of articles detailing several governmental agencies that were responsible for flood control and maintenance of the levees along the Sacramento River. Although the agencies have not been able to find the funds to repair more than 150 sites where the levees could fail during a major flood, builders and developers have continued to construct large developments in the Central Valley near Sacramento in areas where levees hold back rivers that are capable of flood damage to thousands of homes and businesses.[25]

In mid-2004, just after the publication of the *Sacramento Bee* series, a dirt levee broke suddenly in the Delta region, instantly changing 12,000 acres of farmland into a 12,000-acre lake. Officials found that a second levee was in danger of breaking, and a third needed to be shored up to prevent a road from being flooded and cutting off the only connection to two islands housing 178 residents.[26] The total damage amounted to $35 million in damages to buildings and crops, plus another $36.5 million to fix the levees. Some of this changed when California lawmakers prioritized levee reconstruction after the destruction wreaked by Hurricane Katrina on the Gulf Coast and the subsequent failure of government in many places to fulfill its emergency responsibilities. The public-works package of bond issues approved by the voters in November 2006 included Proposition 1E, the Disaster Preparedness and Flood Prevention Act, which authorized $4.1 billion in bonds to rebuild flood-control structures, including the Delta levees. The authorized money has provided a starting point for rebuilding the eroding facilities.

In late 2013, Governor Jerry Brown proposed a $25 billion plan to build two 35-mile-long tunnels to carry water under and around the Delta and to rebuild the Delta levees, with construction starting in 2017. The plan would restore wetlands and, in the eyes of supporters, would provide a more reliable source for the 25 million Californians who use the Delta's water. Opponents, however, are concerned about the cost of the tunnels, the possible ecological damage from the additional water pumped out of the Delta, and the project's questionable financing. In April 2016 the *Los Angeles Times* reported that the previously projected impact of this project, now called California WaterFix, may have been overstated. According to the article, some federal agencies that have reviewed the plan are skeptical about its ability to do more than sustain the status quo of water delivery.[27] This skepticism is predicated on factors such as the complicated irrigation and other water delivery systems that currently exist in and adjacent to the Delta, as well as the existing federal regulatory policies that protect endangered fish species that would be affected by the proposed tunnel system. Water is obviously essential to California in myriad ways. It is a public policy problem that deserves to be at the top of the state's agenda. It illustrates, however, the challenges to solving critical public problems even when there is a consensus to act.[28]

The Future of California's Infrastructure

In addition to the Delta tunnels, Governor Brown's second long-term infrastructure priority is the high-speed rail system that would connect San Francisco, Sacramento, and Los Angeles. A ground-breaking ceremony was held in Fresno on January 6, 2015. Construction has been delayed by numerous lawsuits over the system's funding and other design and implementation problems. Currently the plan is projected to cost $68 billion, and the voters have authorized about $10 billion in bonds for the first phase of construction, along with federal stimulus funds from the 2009 recession. Many argue that the state cannot afford a project this large on top of its other needs.

The neglect of the state's infrastructure over time is obvious. There are many reasons why infrastructure repair and upkeep are not more pressing concerns, but the priorities of both politicians and the public are clearly part of the problem. Infrastructure is a long-term problem, and our political system, based on two- and four-year terms of office, thinks short term. This factor is magnified by the term limits imposed on the legislature, traditionally a body in which legislators spent several decades of their careers and could think in longer terms than the governor and the executive-branch officials, who are elected for only one or two four-year terms. Now with term limits, the members of the legislature are subject to the same short-term time constraints.

Indian Gaming in California

In 1931 the first casino opened in Nevada, which remained the only state with gambling casinos until 1976, when New Jersey voters legalized gambling in Atlantic City. Nine more states legalized gambling between 1989 and 1998, and some type of gambling, whether charitable, pari-mutuel, lotteries, commercial casinos, Indian casinos, or racetracks, is now legal in every state except Utah. In the early 1980s, Indian tribes in Florida and California began to operate bingo games with larger prizes than state regulators allowed. The cases in both states went to court, resulting in a Supreme Court decision in 1987 and the congressional passage of the **Indian Gambling Regulatory Act (IGRA)** in 1998. The act requires tribes to have a compact with the state specifying the type of gambling permitted on their lands. As of 2016, according to an Indian casino web site, at least 244 of the 562 federally recognized tribes run about 493 gaming operations in 28 of the 50 states.[29] Total national Indian gaming revenues in 2015 were approximately $30 billion.

In California, former governor Pete Wilson was reluctant to negotiate any compacts with the Indian tribes, asserting that any compact including slot machines violated the state constitution's prohibition on Nevada- and New Jersey-style casinos. The California Supreme Court subsequently suggested that some electronic gaming devices might qualify, possibly including slot machines. If so, then Wilson would have violated the IGRA's good faith requirement in his reluctance to approve any compacts. After Wilson "begrudgingly" negotiated an agreement with one tribe, citizens who found the agreement unacceptable launched **Proposition 5** in the

November 1998 election to force his hand.[30] Proposition 5, approved by a two-thirds vote in a hotly contested proposition battle, guaranteed that any tribe eligible for a gambling compact could have one with Class III games, including slot machines. However, the California Supreme Court overturned Proposition 5 on the grounds that its authorization of slot machines violated the constitutional prohibition against Nevada- or New Jersey-style casinos.

In the 1998 election Wilson left office and Gray Davis was elected governor. Davis was much more supportive of **tribal casinos** and drafted a model compact, accepted by the tribes pending the approval of Proposition 1A in 2000. Proposition 1A amended the California Constitution to exempt Indian tribes from the prohibition against Nevada- or New Jersey-style casinos and to authorize the governor to negotiate gambling compacts, placing casinos with slot machines and other gambling games in the same category. The proposition passed overwhelmingly. In 2016, 62 of the state's 109 tribes operated 69 casinos. The tribes are estimated to generate revenues of approximately $7 billion per year, purportedly the largest Indian gaming industry in the nation—and they have become major contributors to California election campaigns.[31]

In the past, the major policy issue regarding Indian gaming was the percentage of gaming revenues due to the state of California. At present, the tribes pay approximately $130 million per year to the state, about 2 percent of their revenues, to help other tribes that do not have gaming operations. They also make voluntary (often small) contributions to the local governments in the area of their casinos to offset increased expenses that may result from the casino. A court decision for the Ninth Circuit of the U.S. Circuit Court of Appeals involving the Rincon tribe of San Diego County held that California could not extract taxes from Indian casinos in return for permission to expand.[32]

Tribal casinos are not required to address environmental problems, such as "damage to local roads, animal and plant life, and water supplies and for public services." On his last day in office, after being recalled, Governor Davis wrote a letter releasing the tribes from any obligation to negotiate over these issues.[33] Another contentious issue is the exclusion of hundreds of persons who thought they were members of Indian tribes and thus entitled to receive the substantial annual payments generated from casino profits that go to lawful members. Several tribes in recent years voted former members out of membership on the grounds that they were not lineal descendants of the original members of the tribe. The governor has been urged to investigate the disenrollments, which in some cases are contravened by DNA evidence, and the disenrolled members have threatened to sue in state, federal, or Bureau of Indian Affairs courts; the courts have left membership issues to the tribes, however, and so the suits have not been successful.

One interesting feature of Indian casinos in California is that the tribes have **sovereign immunity** from lawsuits filed by those who work in the casino or by patrons of the casino. Injured employees and customers have sued the casinos, but the suits have been routinely dismissed because of sovereign immunity. Congress has been unable or unwilling to attempt any changes, and the Supreme Court might well refuse to uphold them, meaning that the tribes are not required to obey laws relating to environmental quality, workers' compensation, and so forth. (They are required to obey alcohol control laws, however.)

Another major issue currently facing the state and federal government is that some of the tribes want to expand their casinos closer to urban areas. The Obama Administration has loosened the rules on adding land to existing reservations. The

U.S. Supreme Court in 2009 issued a ruling that the Interior Department, which houses the Bureau of Indian Affairs, could not create reservations for tribes that were not recognized in 1914, but legislation could overturn that ruling. Indian gaming, then, raises a host of issues about the relations between historically deprived targets of discrimination and the current state and federal governments. These are difficult issues, particularly given the history of the treatment of Native Americans in California, and they promise to be in the news for years to come.

Conclusion

The Duroville case study illustrates the problems that arise in California because of fractured interests, complications of land (Indian reservations) that the state cannot control or regulate, and problems resulting from undocumented immigration. That a disgraceful trailer park finally closed after many years of dysfunction is good. That it took so many years to find a substitute location for the people who lived in the park is not good. That some families who work in this area are still residing in inadequate housing and lack basic amenities that are widely available to many Californians remains a problem. One characteristic of contemporary California is that years or decades can pass before even modest starts are made on solving problems.

Water policy and health insurance are two issues that illustrate how external changes, such as climate fluctuations or new federal policy, can dramatically affect state policy. When these kinds of catalysts do not exist, California is often slow or unable to make headway. For example, the health insurance situation only worsened in the two decades before the passage of the ACA, and the last great pieces of infrastructure affecting water policy were decided upon during the administration of Governor Edmund G. "Pat" Brown, from 1959 to 1967. Recent external events have finally prompted movement in both policy areas. The 2013–14 drought stimulated California's state government to pass pathbreaking legislation in August

A federal judge ordered the closure of Duroville, a mobile park residence in Thermal, California, but without funds for new public housing, residents have had to pool their own monies to get by and rely on make-shift resources for necessities like electricity.

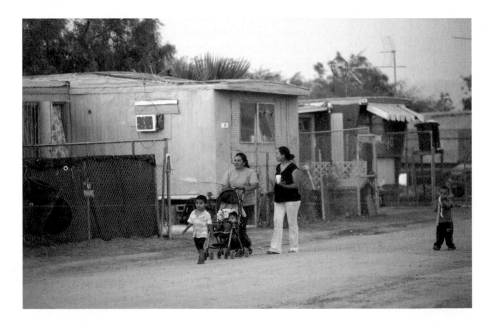

2014, making it the last western state to enact groundwater regulations. Regarding health insurance, the passage of the federal Affordable Care Act gave California the opportunity to insure a substantial proportion of its uninsured population at the minimum cost. California was wise to take advantage of this opportunity.

Water policy has become immensely more complicated with the growth of the environmental movement since the first Earth Day in 1969. But even under the senior Governor Brown in the early 1960s, the decisions made on water were not easy and involved prolonged political conflict. We often hear commentators discussing the "cultural breakup" of the old political consensus in the state, but the truth is, we are better for the multiplicity of voices that continually debate the best course of action for California to pursue. These differing voices make it more difficult to achieve public policy consensus and to make decisions, some long overdue, but water policy and health insurance are two important interests that need to be considered in the present day. We have begun the long road to reform on many issues discussed in this chapter and the book as a whole, and there is hope that California will be more governable in the future. But more steps have to be taken, and we need both visionary leadership and voters who pay attention and are interested in change. We hope the readers of this book will be those voters.

Study Guide

FOR FURTHER READING

"Arnold's Big Chance: A Survey of California." *The Economist*, May 1, 2004, pp. 1–16.

Barrera, E. A. "A Firestorm of Controversy—Still No County Fire Department Five Years after Cedar Blaze." *East County Magazine*, August 2008. www.eastcountymagazine.org. Accessed 8/17/12.

"The Drying of the West." *The Economist*, February 22, 2014, pp. 22–23.

Gleick, Peter H. "Solving California's Water Problems." *Huffington Post*, June 10, 2014. www.huffingtonpost.com/peter-h-gleick/solving-californias-water_b_5479569.html. Accessed 9/3/14.

Hanak, Ellen, Jeffrey Mount, and Caitrin Chappelle. "Just the Facts: California's Latest Drought." Public Policy Institute of California, February 2014. www.ppic.org. Accessed 9/3/14.

Hill, Laura E., Magnus Lofstrom, and Joseph M. Hayes. "Immigrant Legalization: Assessing the Labor Market Effects." Public Policy Institute of California, 2010. www.ppic.org/content/pubs/report/R_410LHR.pdf. Accessed 8/17/12.

Johnson, Hans, and Laura Hill. "At Issue: Illegal Immigration." Public Policy Institute of California, July 2011. www.ppic.org/content/pubs/atissue/AI_711HJAI.pdf. Accessed 8/17/12.

Light, Steven Andrew, and Kathryn R. L. Rand. *Indian Gaming and Tribal Sovereignty: The Casino Compromise*. Lawrence: University Press of Kansas, 2005.

Lustig, R. Jeffrey. *Remaking California, Reclaiming the Public Good*. Berkeley: Heyday Books, 2010.

Maiman, Bruce. "Priorities Are Not on Infrastructure Repair." *Sacramento Bee*, March 18, 2014. http://blogs.sacbee.com/capitol-alert-insider-edition/2014/03/bruce-maiman-priorities-are-not-on-infrastructure-repair. Accessed 10/17/16.

Matthews, Joe, and Mark Paul. *California Crack-Up, How Reform Broke the Golden State and How We Can Fix It*. Berkeley: University of California, 2010.

Pear, Robert. "Lacking Papers, Citizens Are Cut from Medicaid." *New York Times*, March 12, 2007, p. A1.

Piller, C. "Bay Bridge's Troubled China Connection," *Sacramento Bee*, June 8, 2014.

Rogers, Paul. "Is Jerry Brown's Delta Tunnels Plan Repeating the Errors of High-Speed Rail?" *San Jose Mercury-News*, December 9, 2013.

Schrag, Peter. *California: America's High-Stakes Experiment*. Berkeley: University of California Press, 2006.

Simmons, Charlene Wear. *Gambling in the Golden State, 1998 Forward*. Sacramento: California Research Bureau, California State Library, May 2006.

"Special Report: Democracy in California, The People's Will." *The Economist*, April 23, 2011.

State of California, Legislative Analyst's Office. *A Primer: The State's Infrastructure and the Use of Bonds*. Sacramento: Legislative Analyst's Office, January 2006.

Walters, Dan. "Politicians Often Ignore California's Aging Infrastructure." *Sacramento Bee*, August 9, 2014.

ON THE WEB

American Association of State Highway and Transportation Officials. www.transportation.org. Accessed 10/17/16.

California HealthCare Foundation. www.chcf.org. Accessed 9/3/14.

California Progress Report. www.californiaprogressreport.com /site/. Accessed 9/3/14. A daily briefing on politics and policy.

Field Poll of Californians. www.field.com/fieldpollonline /subscribers/. Accessed 9/3/14.

Huffington Post. www.huffingtonpost.com. Accessed 9/3/14.

Kaiser Family Foundation. http://kff.org/. Accessed 9/3/14. Health insurance information.

Pacific Institute. http://pacinst.org/ or www.californiadrought .org/. Accessed 9/3/14.

Public Policy Institute of California. www.ppic.org. Accessed 9/3/14.

State of California, Legislative Analyst's Office. www.lao.ca.gov. Accessed 9/3/14.

SUMMARY

I. Duroville was a trailer park located on an Indian reservation in Riverside County. Many of its residents were agricultural workers, and they experienced particularly squalid conditions during the 12 years of the park's existence.
   A. The federal government filed suit to close Duroville, but federal and state efforts to do so were stymied by the lack of an alternative location that the park's several thousand residents could afford.
   B. The state and county have constructed a new trailer park/public housing complex using redevelopment funds, and the Duroville trailer park was finally closed in 2014.

II. The 2013–14 drought worsened California's water supply problem.
   A. Twenty percent of the water used in California is for household and business consumption, half of which is used for landscaping. The other 80 percent is for agriculture.
   B. Urban water use has been constant despite increases in population, evidence of the conservation programs implemented in water districts in California.
   C. California water agencies have vastly overpromised the average amount of water that runs off each year in California.
   D. Practical solutions to increase the amount of water available for people to use in California include increased efficiency at home or in industry, increased efficiency in agriculture, reusing treated wastewater on landscapes and recharging groundwater basins, and capturing storm water.
   E. Water quality is also an issue in California because of pollution and naturally occurring minerals such as arsenic in the groundwater.

F. Groundwater makes up 35 percent of the water used in an average year, and the percentage is higher in drought years. Until 2014, California was the only western state that did not regulate its groundwater. In August of that year, the legislature passed a bill that allows the state to review groundwater management plans to be produced by many water districts in the state.

III. The lack of health insurance among Californians is a major problem, but President Obama's Affordable Care Act has had a major impact in the state, with 1.4 million people purchasing health insurance policies and another 1.9 million enrolling in Medi-Cal, California's Medicaid program during the first six months of enrollment.
   A. Employers insure a lower proportion of people in California compared with other states because there are more small firms in California and the state is home to many noncitizens.
   B. Proportionally, more people in California buy their own health insurance than people in other states do. The California health insurance market has been characterized by large price increases from year to year and by "rescissions," the cancellation of policies because of inaccurate applications (from the perspective of the insurance companies) or because high claims have been filed (from the perspective of the state). These are the areas that the Affordable Care Act will affect the most, by more closely standardizing policies and eliminating rescissions.
   C. Medi-Cal (the state's Medicaid program) covers 30 percent of Californians, a larger proportion than are covered by Medicaid in other states. California's average cost per beneficiary is among the lowest of the states because provider payments are so low. As

a result, access to providers is a major problem in some areas of the state.

   D. In California, Medicare covers some 600,000 persons under 65 with disabilities. A similar number is covered by TRICARE or the Department of Veterans Affairs (VA).

   E. Although we do not have good quality data on the statistics at this point, it appears that because of the Affordable Care Act, the percentage of uninsured adult Californians under 65 has fallen to 16 percent or less, down from 21 percent.

IV. California's infrastructure has noticeably deteriorated in the last 50 years.

   A. The state's highways were in poor condition but are being gradually upgraded through bond issues passed in 2006 at Governor Schwarzenegger's urging and through federal Recovery Act funds.

   B. The management of transportation funds is an issue, with the major contemporary example being the problems with the new San Francisco–Oakland Bay Bridge.

   C. The levees in the Delta and the Central Valley of California are the subject of a major and controversial plan that Governor Jerry Brown pushed for in 2014. Some levee work is being attended to by state funds provided in bond issues passed in 2006.

V. Indian casinos are widespread in California.

   A. There are presently 68 Indian casinos, with more than 60,000 slot machines. Some 2 to 3 percent of the proceeds from the casinos are paid to the state, mostly to a fund that compensates tribes that do not have casinos.

   B. *Sovereign immunity* for Indian tribes means that they control most areas of government that would otherwise be subject to the control of the state. One implication of this is that those who work at or patronize Indian casinos do not have the right to sue casino management for compensation in the event of injuries or other problems.

   C. Members of tribes that own casinos receive payments out of the money generated from casino profits. The tribes determine who is and is not a member, and some have excluded members after the casino has opened, thus increasing the money received by the other members. The state has given control of membership to the tribes, so former members have no recourse through state government.

PRACTICE QUIZ

1. Medicaid is
   a) a national program, administered by the federal government, with little state input.
   b) a state program, administered with little federal government guidance or funds.
   c) a federal/state program, with over half the money coming from the federal government.
   d) a federal/state program, with over half the money coming from the states.

2. Duroville was a particularly difficult public policy problem because
   a) the trailer park was located on an Indian reservation, where the state has little jurisdiction.
   b) many of the residents were undocumented, meaning they will have a difficult time qualifying for public housing.
   c) the many other trailer parks in Riverside County indicate that the problems symbolized by Duroville may be widespread.
   d) all of the above

3. In California, employer-sponsored health insurance or ESI
   a) has historically been higher proportionately than in other states because of the size and structure of California's employers and the number of noncitizens in the state.
   b) has historically been about the same as in other states.
   c) has historically been lower than in other states because of the size and structure of California's employers and the number of noncitizens in the state.
   d) has historically been higher than in other states because of the generosity of the state's medical programs.

4. The individual health insurance market in California, prior to the implementation of the Affordable Care Act, was a model that other states might emulate.
   a) true
   b) false

5. California's basic water allocation is as follows:
   a) Most is used for households and businesses, and only a small amount for agriculture. The water for household and business use is divided roughly 50–50 between inside and outside use.
   b) About half is used for households and businesses, with the other half for agriculture. The household and business portion is dominated by inside use, which is the greater proportion.

c) Most is used in agriculture. The portion used for households and businesses is divided about 50–50 between inside and outside use.

d) Most is used in agriculture. The portion used for households and businesses is mostly used outside for landscape watering.

6. The most likely solutions for increasing California's water supply rely on
   a) reusing treated wastewater.
   b) capturing storm water.
   c) increased efficiency at homes, businesses, and in agriculture.
   d) all of the above

7. California's infrastructure has been neglected for all of the following reasons *except*
   a) most recent budgets have had to cut expenses, and infrastructure is among the easier items to cut.
   b) the state legislature does not put a high priority on infrastructure issues.
   c) most politicians in California have long-term horizons.
   d) California's transportation funds are often mismanaged.

8. The amount of groundwater pumped during a drought is higher than the average amount pumped in most years.
   a) true
   b) false

9. Indian gaming issues in California have involved the following *except*
   a) tribal-sponsored initiatives.
   b) federal court decisions over the legality of Indian casinos in California.
   c) compacts negotiated by the governor and ratified by the state Senate.
   d) substantial gaming revenues received by local governments in California.

10. The example of the new San Francisco–Oakland Bay Bridge illustrates the following problem:
    a) Not nearly enough money was spent on the bridge.
    b) The management of bridge construction is a major problem for California state government.
    c) The bridge was built far too quickly, although by competent construction workers.
    d) The governor of the state should not be involved in constructing major projects like the new Bay Bridge.

CRITICAL-THINKING QUESTIONS

1. Discuss the condition of California's highways, both in your experience and as presented in the book. What do you think is the nature of the problem at the most fundamental level?
2. The involvement of many different groups makes Indian gaming a significant public-policy problem. Indicate the different groups that are involved; their goals, which may be different or conflicting; and something about their successes thus far.
3. What future reforms of California state government might help with the public policy problems illustrated in this chapter?

KEY TERMS

2013–14 drought (p. 253)
agricultural water use (p. 252)
employer-sponsored insurance (ESI) (p. 256)
groundwater management (p. 253)
household water use (p. 252)

Indian Gambling Regulatory Act (IGRA) (p. 262)
individual insurance marketplace (p. 256)
infrastructure (p. 258)
Medicaid (p. 256)
Medi-Cal (p. 256)

Medicare (p. 256)
Proposition 5 (p. 262)
public policy (p. 251)
rescissions (p. 256)
sovereign immunity (p. 263)
tribal casinos (p. 263)

Answer Key

Chapter 1
1. a
2. b
3. d
4. b
5. b
6. d
7. c
8. a
9. c
10. b

Chapter 2
1. b
2. c
3. a
4. c
5. c
6. c
7. a
8. c
9. d
10. b

Chapter 3
1. c
2. b
3. a
4. c
5. b
6. c
7. a
8. d
9. c
10. b

Chapter 4
1. a
2. b
3. d
4. a
5. a
6. d
7. a
8. b
9. a
10. b

Chapter 5
1. a
2. a
3. d
4. c
5. d
6. c
7. a
8. c
9. a
10. d

Chapter 6
1. a
2. b
3. d
4. c
5. d
6. d
7. d
8. b
9. a
10. b

Chapter 7
1. a
2. b
3. a
4. b
5. b
6. a
7. b
8. c
9. a
10. d

Chapter 8
1. a
2. a
3. c
4. b
5. d
6. a
7. a
8. b
9. d
10. b
11. b

Chapter 9
1. b
2. b
3. a
4. a
5. b
6. d
7. c
8. a
9. a
10. b

Chapter 10
1. c
2. d
3. c
4. b
5. c
6. d
7. c
8. a
9. d
10. b

Notes

Chapter 1

1. Joe Matthews, "What Is the California Dream? Commentary," Zocalo Public Square, January 14, 2015, http://curious.kcrw.com/2015/01/what-is-the-california-dream (accessed 7/7/16).
2. James Q. Wilson, "A Guide to Schwarzenegger Country," *Commentary* (December 2003): 45–49. Field Institute, "Legislation by Initiative vs. through Elected Representatives," November 1999, www.field.com/fieldpollonline/subscribers/COI-99-Nov-Legislation.pdf (accessed 11/16/16).
3. Ballotpedia, "History of the Initiative and Referendum in California," https://ballotpedia.org/History_of_Initiative_and_Referendum_in_California (accessed 11/16/16).
4. Initiative and Referendum Institute, "Initiative Use," University of Southern California Gould School of Law, September 2010, www.iandrinstitute.org (accessed 11/16/16).
5. United States Census Bureau, "Quick Facts, California." www.census.gov/quickfacts/table/PST045215/06 (accessed 7/3/16).
6. United States Census Bureau, "Educational Attainment in the United States: 2009," P20–566, February 2012, www.census.gov/prod/2012pubs/p20-566.pdf (accessed 7/3/16).
7. Sarah Bonn and Caroline Danielson, "Income Inequality and the Safety Net in California," Public Policy Institute of California, May 2016, http://ppic.org/main/publication.asp?i=1190 (accessed 7/8/16).
8. Public Policy Institute of California, "Just the Facts: Immigrants in California," May 2013, www.ppic.org/main/publication_show.asp?-258 (accessed 7/6/16).
9. Jeffrey S. Passel, Randy Capps, and Michael Fix, "Undocumented Immigrants: Facts and Figures," Urban Institute Immigration Studies Program, January 12, 2004, www.urban.org/UploadedPDF/1000587_undoc_immigrantsfacts.pdf (accessed 7/17/12). Public Policy Institute of California, "Just the Facts: Undocumented Immigrants," June 2015, www.ppic.org (accessed 7/6/16).
10. Dan Walters, "Ex-Governors Miss Chance to Discuss Complexities," *Santa Barbara News-Press*, February 21, 2004, p. A11.

Chapter 2

1. National Institute on Money in State Politics, www.followthemoney.org/show-me?s=CA&y=2006&m-id=30&d-et=3#[{1|gro=d-eid (accessed 6/23/16).
2. Joe Matthews and Mark Paul, *California Crackup: How Reform Broke the Golden State and How We Can Fix It* (Berkeley: University of California Press, 2010), 21.
3. Kevin Starr, *California: A History* (New York: Modern Library, 2005), 121.
4. Starr, *California*, 124.
5. Matthews and Paul, *California Crackup*, 23.
6. Carl Brent Swisher, *Motivation and Political Technique in the California Constitutional Convention: 1878–79* (New York: Da Capo Press, 1969).
7. The U.S. Constitution can also be amended by passage in a constitutional convention called by two-thirds of the states, followed by ratification by three-fourths of the states. This method has never been used, however. See Article V of the U.S. Constitution.
8. Spencer C. Olin, Jr., *California's Prodigal Sons: Hiram Johnson and the Progressives, 1911–1917* (Berkeley: University of California Press, 1968), 70.
9. John M. Allswang, *The Initiative and Referendum in California, 1898–1998* (Stanford, CA: Stanford University Press, 2000), 15.

10. George Mowry, *The California Progressives* (Chicago: Quadrangle Paperbacks, 1963), 9, 12–13.

11. Kevin Starr, *Inventing the Dream: California through the Progressive Era* (New York: Oxford University Press, 1985), 242–43.

12. Dean R. Cresap, *Party Politics in the Golden State* (Los Angeles: The Haynes Foundation, 1954), 12.

13. Mowry, *The California Progressives*, 12.

14. Mowry, *The California Progressives*, 15.

15. Quoted in Mowry, *The California Progressives*, 65.

16. Starr, *Inventing the Dream*, 254.

17. Many recalls take place at the local level; volunteer groups organize recalls of city council or school board members because they feel strongly about a particular issue. Statewide recalls, however, are rare.

18. California Secretary of State, "History of California Initiatives," www.sos.ca.gov/elections/ballot-measures/resources-and-historical-information/history-california-initiatives/ (accessed 11/15/16).

19. Allswang, *The Initiative and Referendum in California*, 33.

20. Allswang, *The Initiative and Referendum in California*, 75.

21. National Conference of State Legislatures, "Initiative, Referendum, and Recall," www.ncsl.org/research/elections-and-campaigns/initiative-referendum-and-recall-overview.aspx (accessed 6/23/16).

22. California Secretary of State, "Referendum," www.sos.ca.gov/elections/ballot-measures/referendum/ (accessed 11/15/16).

23. Jim Puzzanghera, "History of Recall Adds Fuel to Both Sides," *San Jose Mercury News*, June 18, 2003, http://digital.library.ucla.edu/websites/2003_999_022/latest.news/94/index.htm (accessed 6/23/16).

Chapter 3

1. Jay Michael, Dan Walters, and Dan Weintraub, *The Third House: Lobbyists, Power, and Money in Sacramento* (Berkeley: Berkeley Public Policy Press, 2002), 13.

2. Sam Delson, "Some Call Spending Money to Get Money Regrettable but Necessary for Inland Cities and Schools," *Riverside Press Enterprise*, July 6, 1997, A2.

3. California Secretary of State, "Employers of Lobbyists, 2013–14," http://cal-access.sos.ca.gov/Lobbying/Employers/list.aspx?view=name&session-2013 (accessed 6/23/16).

4. National Institute on Money in State Politics, "Election Overview," www.followthemoney.org/election-overview, 2014 data by state (accessed 6/23/16).

5. Cary McWilliams, *California: The Great Exception* (Berkeley: University of California Press, 1999), 198.

6. Mark Sappenfield, "Why Clout of Lobbyists Is Growing," *Christian Science Monitor*, July 23, 2003, www.csmonitor.com/2003/0722/p01s02-uspo.html (accessed 6/23/16).

7. Benjamin Ginsberg, Theodore J. Lowi, Margaret Weir, and Caroline J. Tolbert, *We the People, An Introduction to American Politics*, 11th ed. (New York: Norton, 2016), 424–25.

8. California Secretary of State, *The Lobbying Directory 2013–2014*, http://prd.cdn.sos.ca.gov/cal-access/lobbying/lobbying-directory.pdf (accessed 6/23/16).

9. Stephen Ansolabehere, James Snyder, Jr., and Mickey Tripathi, "Are PAC Contributions and Lobbying Linked? New Evidence from the 1995 Lobby Disclosure Act," *Business and Politics* 4, no. 2 (2002): 131–55, www.tandfonline.com/doi/abs/10.1080/1369525022000015586#preview (accessed 6/15/16).

10. National Institute on Money in State Politics, "Contributions to Candidates and Committees in Elections in California, 2013–14," www.followthemoney.org/show-me?s=CA&y=2014,2013&f-core=1#[{1|gro=pt-eid{1|gro=c-r-ot (accessed 6/23/16).

11. National Institute on Money in State Politics, "Party Committee 2013–14," www.followthemoney.org/show-me?s=CA&y=2014,2013&f-core=1#[{1|gro=pt-eid (accessed 6/23/16).

12. National Institute on Money in State Politics, "Independent Expenditures," www.followthemoney.org/show-me?dt=2&is-s=CA&is-y=2014 (accessed 6/23/16).

13. National Institute on Money in State Politics, "Ballot Measures," www.followthemoney.org/show-me?s=CA&y=2014&f-core=1&m-exi=1 (accessed 6/23/16).

14. The discussion of incumbent and open elections is based on data from the National Institute on Money in State Politics, "Incumbent Status 2013–14," www.followthemoney.org/show-me?s=CA&y=2014,2013&f-core=1#[{1|gro=c-t-ico (accessed 6/23/16). Click on Incumbents, then General Office.

15. National Institute on Money in State Politics, "Incumbency Status 2013–14," www.followthemoney.org/show-me?s=CA&y=2014,2013&f-core=1#[{1|gro=c-r-ot,c-t-ico (accessed 6/23/16). Click on Incumbents, Non-Individual, Contributor.

16. Robert Salladay, "Why Money Is Important," *Los Angeles Times*, September 11, 2006.

17. National Institute on Money in State Politics, www.followthemoney.org/entity-details?eid=3286 and www.followthemoney.org/show-me?dt=3&lby-f-fc=2#[{1|gro=lby-f-eid (accessed 6/23/16).

18. Maria Lagos, "Result of Furloughs—$1 Billion Liability," *San Francisco Chronicle*, April 23, 2011, www.sfgate.com/cgi-bin/article.cgi?f=/c/a/2011/03/07/MNSQ1I2ASB.DTL&ao=all (accessed 6/23/16).

19. Steven Malanga, "The Beholden State," *City Journal* 20 (Spring 2010), www.city-journal.org/2010/20_2_california-unions.html (accessed 6/23/16).

20. Field Research Corporation, "Statewide Ballot Proposition Elections," October 2011, http://field.com/fieldpollonline/subscribers/COI-11-Oct-California-Ballot-Propositions.pdf (accessed 6/23/16).

21. Elisabeth R. Gerber, "Interest Group Influence in the California Initiative Process," Public Policy Institute of California,

1998, www.ppic.org/main/publication.asp?i=49 (accessed 6/23/16).

22. McWilliams, *California*, 213.

23. Arthur H. Samish and Bob Thomas, *The Secret Boss of California* (New York: Crown Publishers, 1971), 13.

24. California Secretary of State, "History of the Political Reform Division," 2004, http://ss.ca.gov/campaign-lobbying /history-political-reform-division (accessed 6/23/16).

25. Patrick McGreevy and Nancy Vogel, "Senate Travel Perks for Sale," *Los Angeles Times*, March 16, 2008.

26. Pew Research Center for the People and the Press, "Digital: By the Numbers," *The State of the News Media, 2013*, http://stateofthemedia.org/2013/digital-as-mobile-grows -rapidly-the-pressures-on-news-intensify/digital-by-the -numbers (accessed 6/23/16).

27. Susan F. Rasky, "Covering California: The Press Wrestles with Diversity, Complexity, and Change," in *Governing California: Politics, Government, and Public Policy in the Golden State*, ed. Gerald C. Lubenow and Bruce E. Cain (Berkeley: Institute of Governmental Studies Press, University of California, 1997), 157–88.

28. Mark Baldassare, Dean Bonner, Lunna Lopes, and Jui Shrestha, "Californians' News and Information Sources," Public Policy Institute of California, October 2014, www.ppic.org /main/publication_show.asp?i=770 (accessed 6/23/16).

29. Rasky, "Covering California," 182.

30. Amy Mitchell, Tom Rosenstiel, Laura Houston Santhanam, and Leah Christian, "Future of Mobile News," Pew Research Center for People and the Press, October 1, 2012, www.journalism.org/2012/10/1/future-mobile-news/ (accessed 6/15/16).

31. David Pricco, "How Political Crowdfunding Killed Traditional Campaign Financing," CrowdExpert.com, http:// crowdexpert.com/articles/crowdfunding-in-politics/ (accessed 6/23/16).

32. Assemblyman Mike Gatto, press release, January 6, 2015, http://asmdc.org/members/a43/news-room/press-releases /assemblyman-mike-gatto-continues-groundbreaking -wiki-bill-project-invites-public-to-directly-draft-privacy -legislation (accessed 6/1/16).

33. Fix California Challenge, "About Us," www.fixcal.org/a /pages/about (accessed 6/23/16).

34. Gina Hall, "Tim Draper's Fix California Challenge Has 300 Ideas on How to Govern the State Better," *Silicon Valley Business Journal*, June 9, 2015, www.bizjournals .com/sanjose/news/2015/06/09/tim-drapers-fix-california -challenge.html (accessed 6/23/2015).

35. Joe Garofoli, "Labor Beat Prop. 32 via Social Media," *SFGate*, December 25, 2012. www.sfgate.com/politics/joe garofoli/article/Labor-beat-Prop-32-via-social-media -4145607.php (accessed 6/1/16).

36. Jim Rutenberg, "Working to Spin Distrust of Media Into Votes," *New York Times*, October 12, 2003, http://209.157 .64.201/focus/f-news/999985/posts (accessed 6/23/16).

Chapter 4

1. Spencer C. Olin, *California's Prodigal Sons: Hiram Johnson and the Progressives, 1911–1917* (Berkeley: University of California Press, 1968).

2. Brian F. Schaffner, Matthew Streb, and Gerald Wright, "Teams without Uniforms: The Nonpartisan Ballot in State and Local Elections," *Political Research Quarterly* 54, no. 1 (2001): 7–30.

3. Javier Panzar, "It's Official: Latinos Now Outnumber Whites in California," *Los Angeles Times*, July 8, 2015, www .latimes.com/local/california/la-me-census-latinos -20150708-story.html (accessed 9/26/16).

4. John Meyrs, "Tens of Thousands Have Left California's American Independent Party in the Last Month," *Los Angeles Times*, May 20, 2016, www.latimes.com/politics/la -pol-ca-american-independent-voters-registration-20160520 -snap-story.html (accessed 9/26/16).

5. Michael Finnegan, "The Race for the White House," *Los Angeles Times*, September 8, 2004, p. A1.

6. Mark Baldassare, "World Apart: California's Partisan Divide and the 2016 Election," *Viewpoints* (blog), Public Policy Institute of California, June 14, 2016, www.ppic.org /main/blog_detail.asp?i=2073#.V32JZcEPulI.email (accessed 9/26/16).

7. Roper Center for Public Opinion Research, *Social Capital Community Benchmark Survey: Methodology and Documentation*, February 17, 2001, http://ropercenter.cornell.edu /2000-social-capital-community-benchmark-survey/ (accessed 9/26/16).

8. Mark Baldassare, *A California State of Mind: The Conflicted Voter in a Changing World* (Berkeley: University of California Press, 2002), 47.

9. Stanford Law School Justice Advocacy Project, "Three Strikes Basics," https://law.stanford.edu/stanford-justice -advocacy-project/three-strikes-basics/ (accessed 9/26/16).

10. Richard Edward DeLeon, *Left Coast City: Progressive Politics in San Francisco, 1975–1991* (Lawrence: University Press of Kansas, 1992).

11. Christine Mai-Duc, "Get signatures, make money: How some gatherers are making top dollar in this year's flood of ballot initiatives," *Los Angeles Times*, August 10, 2016, www.latimes.com/politics/la-pol-ca-signature-gatherers -ballot-initiatives-california-20160627-snap-htmlstory.html (accessed 12/5/16).

12. "The Mormon Money behind Proposition 8," *The Atlantic*, October 23, 2008, www.theatlantic.com/daily-dish /archive/2008/10/the-mormon-money-behind-proposition -8/209748/ (accessed 8/13/12).

13. Reid Wilson, "The Most Expensive Ballot Initiatives," *GovBeat* (blog), *Washington Post*, May 17, 2014, www.washingtonpost.com/blogs/govbeat/wp/2014/05 /17/the-most-expensive-ballot-initiatives/?utm_term =.4f950116984b (accessed 12/5/16).

14. Carla Javier, "California's biggest ever election guide might not actually help voters decide," *Fusion*, September 22, 2016, http://fusion.net/story/349469/california-voter-guide-decide/?utm_source=emailshare&utm_medium=email&utm_campaign=socialshare&utm_content=theme_bottom_mobile (accessed 9/25/16).

15. Susan Rasky, "Introduction to 'An Antipolitician, Antiestablishment Groundswell Elected the Candidate of Change,'" in *California Votes: The 2002 Governor's Race and the Recall That Made History*, ed. Gerald Lubenow (Berkeley: Berkeley Public Policy Press, 2003).

16. Rasky, "Introduction."

17. Catherine Decker, "State's Shifting Political Landscape," *Los Angeles Times*, November 6, 2008, p. A1.

18. "Young Voters Help Secure Obama Victory, Passage of Progressive Ballot Measures," *Huffington Post*, November 7, 2012, http://www.huffingtonpost.com/2012/11/07/young-voters-2012-obama_n_2089789.html (accessed 9/26/16).

19. Phil Willon, "GOP Loses Grip on Inland Empire," *Los Angeles Times*, November 11, 2012, p. A37.

20. George Skelton, "Time for Initiative Reforms," *Los Angeles Times*, November 15, 2012, p. A2.

21. P. St John, "Prop. 47 would cut penalties for 1 in 5 criminals in California." *Los Angeles Times*, October 11, 2014, www.latimes.com/local/politics/la-me-ff-pol-proposition47-20141012-story.html (accessed 9/26/16).

22. "Exit Polls," *CNN*, November 9, 2016, www.cnn.com/election/results/exit-polls/california/president (accessed 11/17/2016).

23. D. P. Osorio, "The Cost of Winning a Senate Race," dposorio.com, May 9, 2012, http://dposorio.com/blog/822/the-cost-of-winning-a-senate-race (accessed 7/20/12).

24. Rasky, "Introduction."

25. William Booth, "In Calif. Governor's Race, It's Ads Infinitum," *Washington Post*, May 29, 1998, p. A1.

26. Carol A. Cassel, "Hispanic Turnout: Estimates from Validated Voting Data," *Political Research Quarterly* 55, no. 2 (June 2002): 391–408. Michael A. Jones-Correa and David L. Leal, "Political Participation: Does Religion Matter?" *Political Research Quarterly* 54, no. 4 (2001): 751–70.

27. Carl Bialik, "Voter Turnout Fell, Especially in States that Clinton Won," FiveThirtyEight, November 11, 2016, http://fivethirtyeight.com/features/voter-turnout-fell-especially-in-states-that-clinton-won (accessed 11/11/2016).

Chapter 5

1. Field Research Corporation, "California Voter Views of the State Legislature Turn Negative after the Arrest of State Senator Leland Yee," Poll release #2464, April 10, 2014, http://field.com/fieldpollonline/subscribers/ (accessed 8/11/14). Field Research Corporation, "Mixed View of the State Legislature . . . ," Poll release #2500, February 25, 2015, www.field.com/fieldpollonline/subscribers/Rls2500.pdf (accessed 8/16/16). Field Research Corporation, "Californians Hold Divergent Views . . . ," Poll release #2552, September 29, 2016, http://field.com/fieldpollonline/subscribers/Rls2552.pdf (accessed 10/28/2016). Mark Baldassare et al., "Californians and their Government," Public Policy Institute of California, May 1916, www.ppic.org/content/pubs/survey/S_516MBS.pdf (accessed 12/5/16).

2. Andrew Dugan, "Congressional Approval Rating Languishes at low Level," *Gallup Politics*, July 15, 2014, www.gallup.com/poll/politics.aspx?ref=b (accessed 8/11/14). Gallup, "Congress and the Public," www.gallup.com/poll/1600/congress-public.aspx (accessed 8/16/16).

3. Jeremy B. White, "Chevron Spends $1 Million to Boost Assembly Democrat Cheryl Brown," *Sacramento Bee*, April 14, 2016, www.sacbee.com/news/politics-government/capitol-alert/article71852047.html (accessed 8/24/2016). Patrick McGreevy and Chris Megerian, "With a record $24 million spent on the election so far, are special interests trying to buy their way into the Legislature?" *Los Angeles Times*, May 30, 2016, www.latimes.com/politics/la-pol-sac-california-independent-spending-20160530-snap-story.html (accessed 8/24/2016). Laurel Rosenthal, "Money Rains from Perfect Storm of Politics," *CALmatters*, June, 16, 2016, https://calmatters.org/articles/money-rains-from-perfect-storm-of-politics/ (accessed 8/24/2016).

4. John Meyers, "Political Roadmap: There's a Reason Why Jerry Brown Signs so Many Bills," *Los Angeles Times*, October 2, 2016, www.latimes.com/politics/la-pol-sac-roadmap-jerry-brown-signs-bills-20161002-snap-story.html (accessed 10/28/16). California Senate Office of Research, "How Often Do Governors Say No?" October 12, 2015, http://sor.senate.ca.gov/sites/sor.senate.ca.gov/files/styles/full_size/public/Governors%20Vetoes%202015%20%20final.pdf (accessed 8/24/16).

5. Editorial Board, "Editorial: Stop Disgrace of 'Gut and Amend' in Legislature," *Sacramento Bee Capitol Alert*, April 30, 2013, http://blogs.sacbee.com/capitol-alert-insider-edition/2013/04/editorial-stop-disgrace-of-gut-and-amend-in-legislature.html (accessed 9/15/16).

6. Lou Cannon, *Governor Reagan: His Rise to Power* (New York: Public Affairs, 2003), 166.

7. Peter Schrag, *Paradise Lost: California's Experience, America's Future* (New York: New Press, 1998), 244.

8. Institute of Governmental Studies, "IGS Goes to Sacramento to Assess Ten Years of Term Limits," *Public Affairs Report* 42, no. 3 (Fall 2001).

9. National Association of Latino Elected and Appointed Officials Education Fund, *National Directory of Latino Elected and Appointed Officials 2015*, https://d3n8a8pro7vhmx.cloudfront.net/naleo/pages/171/attachments/original/1440570181/2015_National_Directory_of_Latino_Elected_Officials.pdf?1440570181 (accessed 9/15/2016). The National Conference of State Legislatures, www.ncsl.org

/legislators-staff/legislators/womens-legislative-network/women-in-state-legislatures-for-2015.aspx (accessed 8/16/16). Leadership California Institute et al., "The Status of Latinos in California," July 2015, www.leadershipcaliforniainstitute.org/CALatino (accessed 8/16/16). Leadership California Institute, *Women: The Status of Women in California State and Local Government*, www.leadershipcaliforniainstitute.org/sites/all/files/Women_2014.pdf (accessed 9/15/2016).

10. Schrag, *Paradise Lost*, 143.

11. Adam Nagourney, "Political Shift in California Trips Brown," *New York Times*, September 20, 2011, www.nytimes.com/2011/09/21/us/politics/brown-says-california-gop-is-harder-to-work-with-decades-later.html?pagewanted=all (accessed 6/24/12).

12. Anthony York, "Brown and Obama Find Bipartisanship a Difficult Goal to Reach," *Los Angeles Times*, February 24, 2012, http://articles.latimes.com/2012/feb/24/local/la-me-jerry-brown-20120224 (accessed 6/24/12).

13. Nagourney, "Political Shift in California Trips Brown."

14. George Skelton, "California's Capitol—the Long View: A Columnist Looks Back on 50 Years Covering the Ups and Downs of Sacramento," *Los Angeles Times*, December 1, 2011, p. A2.

Chapter 6

1. Timothy Egan, "Jerry Brown's Revenge," *New York Times*, March 6, 2014, www.nytimes.com/2014/03/07/opinion/egan-jerry-browns-revenge.html?_r=0 (accessed 8/24/16).

2. Richard E. Neustadt, *Presidential Power and the Modern Presidents: The Politics of Leadership from Roosevelt to Reagan* (New York: Macmillan, 1990).

3. Thomas E. Cronin and Michael A. Genovese, *The Paradoxes of the American Presidency* (New York: Oxford University Press, 1998).

4. Public Policy Institute of California, "PPIC Statewide Survey: Time Trends for Job Approval Ratings for Governor Schwarzenegger," November 2010, www.ppic.org/main/dataSet.asp?i=927 (accessed 8/24/16).

5. Public Policy Institute of California, "PPIC Statewide Survey: Californians and Their Government," May 2016, www.ppic.org/content/pubs/survey/S_516MBS.pdf (accessed 8/25/16).

6. Office of Governor Edmund G. Brown, "Governor Brown Delivers Plan to Streamline and Simplify State Government to Little Hoover Commission," press release, March 30, 2012, http://gov.ca.gov/news.php?id=17476 (accessed 8/1/14).

7. Joshua Stark, "New Report Calls for Radical Reform of Caltrans," *TransForm*, February 4, 2014, www.transformca.org/trblogpost/report-calls-radical-reform-caltrans (accessed 8/24/16). Debra J. Saunders, "Jerry Brown on Bay Bridge: Don't Worry, Be Happy," *SFGate*, May 16, 2014, http://blog.sfgate.com/djsaunders/2014/05/16/jerry-brown-on-bay-bridge-dont-worry-be-happy/ (accessed 8/2/14).

8. Dan Walters, "California PUC's Big Scandal over San Onofre Closure Heats Up," *Sacramento Bee*, May 10, 2016, www.sacbee.com/news/politics-government/politics-columns-blogs/dan-walters/article76830107.html (accessed 8/24/16). Liam Dillon, "Overhauling the Embattled Public Utilities Commission," *Los Angeles Times*, August 23, 2016, www.latimes.com/politics/la-pol-sac-california-legislature-2016-public-utilities-1470682439-htmlstory.html (accessed 8/24/16).

9. Dan Weikel and Kim Christensen, "How a Ban on Ex Parte Communications by the Coastal Commission Could Change the Balance of Power," *Los Angeles Times*, May 14, 2016, www.latimes.com/local/california/la-me-adv-coastal-commission-20160515-story.html (accessed 8/24/16). Steve Lopez, "Cover Your Ears: Coastal Commissioner Martha McClure's on the Phone," *Los Angeles Times*, May 14, 2016, www.latimes.com/local/california/la-me-lopez-commission-sleepover-20160514-column.html (accessed 8/24/16).

10. California Senate Office of Research, "How Often Do Governors Say No?" October 12, 2015, http://sor.senate.ca.gov/sites/sor.senate.ca.gov/files/styles/full_size/public/Governors%20Vetoes%202015%20%20final.pdf (accessed 8/24/16). John Meyers, "Political Roadmap: There's a Reason Why Jerry Brown Signs so Many Bills," *Los Angeles Times*, October 2, 2016, www.latimes.com/politics/la-pol-sac-roadmap-jerry-brown-signs-bills-20161002-snap-story.html (accessed 10/28/16).

11. Eric McGhee and Paul Warren, "The Vanishing Line-Item Veto," *Viewpoints: The PPIC Blog*, Public Policy Institute of California, June 26, 2014, www.ppic.org/main/blog_detail.asp?i=1551 (accessed 8/24/16).

12. Steven Harmon, "Gov. Brown Warns Democratic Lawmakers Not to Overreach, Overspend," *Vallejo Times-Herald*, January 24, 2013, www.timesheraldonline.com/ci_22439612/gov-brown-warns-democratic-lawmakers-not-overreach-overspend (accessed 8/24/16).

13. Liam Dillon, "More than a Dozen Assembly Members Flipped Their Votes from Last Year to Support Climate Change Bill," *LA Times Essential Politics*, August 23, 2016, www.latimes.com/politics/essential/la-pol-sac-essential-politics-updates-more-than-a-dozen-assemblymembers-1471987788-htmlstory.html (accessed 9/24/16). Jessica Calefati, "California Climate Change Law: Extension of Greenhouse Gas Goals OK'd by Assembly," *The Mercury News*, August 23, 2016, www.mercurynews.com/2016/08/23/california-climate-change-law-extension-of-greenhouse-gas-goals-okd-by-assembly/ (accessed 9/24/16).

14. George Skelton, "Governor Hits Back at Big Oil," *Los Angeles Times*, August 25, 2016, p. B1.

15. James Fallows, "Jerry Brown's Political Reboot," *The Atlantic*, May 2013, www.theatlantic.com/magazine/archive/2013/06/the-fixer/309324/ (accessed 8/24/16).

16. Nicolas Riccardi, "Brown's 2011: Tall Hopes but Taller Hurdles," *Los Angeles Times*, December 27, 2011, p. A1.
17. Fallows, "Jerry Brown's Political Reboot." Egan, "Jerry Brown's Revenge." Lou Cannon, "Calif. Comeback: Jerry Brown Leads a Turnaround," *Real Clear Politics*, June 25, 2013, www.realclearpolitics.com/articles/2013/06/25/calif_comeback_jerry_brown_leads_a_turnaround_118943.html (accessed 8/24/16).
18. Fallows, "Jerry Brown's Political Reboot."
19. Dan Walters, "Could Anne Gust Brown Be the Next Governor," *Sacramento Bee*, March 8, 2015, www.sacbee.com/news/politics-government/politics-columns-blogs/dan-walters/article13044824.html (accessed 8/24/16).

Chapter 7

1. See *In re Sergio C. Garcia* on Admission, http://courts.ca.gov/documents/5202512 (accessed 10/3/16).
2. Court Statistics Report (2011), "Statewide Caseload Trends, 2000–2001 through 2009–2010," www.courts.ca.gov/documents/2011CourtStatisticsReport.pdf (accessed 9/22/14).
3. www.courts.ca.gov.
4. *Kleffman v. Vonage Holdings Corp.*, 232 P.3d 625 (2010), https://scholar.google.com/scholar_case?case=12406036530592040470&hl=en&as_sdt=6&as_vis=1&oi=scholarr (accessed 10/3/16).
5. *People v. Colvin*, 203 Cal.App.4th 1029 (2012).
6. *Unpublished* means that the memorandum may not be used for purposes of legal citation or precedent. http://gpo.gov/fdsys/pkg/USCOURTS-caed-2_11-cv-02939. The memorandum can be found here: U.S. Government Printing Office, *11-2939—Sacramento Nonprofit Collective et al v. Holder et al.*, http://cdn.ca9.uscourts.gov/datastore/memoranda/2014/01/15/12-15991.pdf (accessed 6/30/16).
7. "SB-643 Medical marijuana," California Legislative Information, https://leginfo.legislature.ca.gov/faces/billNavClient.xhtml?bill_id=201520160SB643 (accessed 10/3/16).
8. The Act can be found here: www.congress.gov/bill/113th-congress/house-bill/83/text (accessed 6/30/16).
9. Bob Egelko, "California Supreme Court Nomination a 'Statement' to U.S.," *SF Gate*, July 22, 2014, www.sfgate.com/politics/article/Brown-nominates-Stanford-professor-to-state-high-5638237.php (accessed 9/22/14).
10. David Siders, "Gov. Jerry Brown Names Obama Administration Lawyer to California Supreme Court," *Sacramento Bee*, November 24, 2014, www.sacbee.com/news/politics-government/capitol-alert/article4123447.html (accessed 12/3/14).
11. Prebloe Stolz, *Judging Judges: The Investigation of Rose Bird and the California Supreme Court* (New York: Free Press, 1981).
12. California Courts, "Judicial Council," www.courts.ca.gov/policyadmin-jc.htm?genpubtab (accessed 9/22/14).
13. Carmen Lo, Katie Londenberg, and David Nims, "Spending in Judicial Elections: State Trends in the Wake of *Citizens United*," http://gov.uchastings.edu/public-law/docs/judicial-elections-report-and-appendices-corrected.pdf (accessed 6/30/16).
14. 2008 Court Statistics Report.
15. Unlimited jurisdiction civil cases are disputes that involve more than $25,000. Limited jurisdiction civil cases are disputes that involve amounts from $10,000 to $25,000. See Court Statistics Report (2011), "Statewide Trends," 2014.
16. "California Courts Wrestle with Budget Cuts Old and New," *Los Angeles Times*, June 19, 2012, http://latimesblogs.latimes.com/california-politics/2012/06/california-court.html (accessed 9/22/14).
17. Maria Dinzeo, "IT Project Sinks in Sea of Criticism," *Courthouse News Service*, March 27, 2012, www.courthousenews.com/2012/03/27/45079.htm (accessed 9/22/14).
18. Cheryl Miller, "Judges Criticize Court Bureaucracy in Blistering Report," http://inlandpolitics.com/blog/2012/05/30/the-recorder-judges-criticize-court-bureaucracy-in-blistering-report/ (accessed 10/3/16).

Chapter 8

1. Legislative Analyst's Office, "2016–17 Budget: Higher Education Analysis," February 25, 2016, www.lao.ca.gov (accessed 8/2/16).
2. Rosanna Xia, "State Funding Cuts During the Recession Still Shortchanging Cal State Students, Officials Say," *Los Angeles Times*, July 21, 2016, www.latimes.com/local/lanow/la-me-cal-state-executive-compensation-20160719-snap-story.html (accessed 8/3/16).
3. Marla Dickerson, "State Fiscal Woes Threaten Cities' Budgets and a Leading Job Engine," *Los Angeles Times*, January 17, 2003, pp. C1+.
4. California Department of Finance, "History of Budgeting," February 24, 1998, www.dof.ca.gov (accessed 7/27/12).
5. California Department of Finance, "History of Budgeting."
6. George Skelton, "The 'Budget Nun' Earns Her Pay and Bipartisan Respect," *Los Angeles Times*, May 26, 2003, p. B5.
7. California Department of Finance, "California's Budget Process," www.dof.ca.gov/budget/Budget_Process/index.html (accessed 10/14/16).
8. Public Finance Division, "California's Current Credit Ratings," California State Treasurer, www.treasurer.ca.gov/ratings/current.asp (accessed 8/1/16). Dan Walters, "Moody's Raises California's Credit Rating," *Sacramento Bee*, June 25, 2014, http://blogs.sacbee.com/capitolalertlatest/2014/06/moodys-raises-californias-bond-credit-rating.html (accessed 8/1/14). Moody's Investors Service, "Moody's Fiscal Test of Most Populous States Show Texas Best Prepared for Next Recession, California Least Ready," www.moodys.com/research

/Moodys-Fiscal-test-of-most-populous-states-show-Texas
-best--PR_347649, April 21, 2016 (accessed 10/14/16).

9. William Chen, "Who Pays Taxes in California?" April 2015,
http://calbudgetcenter.org/wp-content/uploads/Who-Pays
-Taxes-in-CA_Issue-Brief_04.14.2015.pdf (accessed 8/1/16).
Justin Garosi and Jason Sisney, "'Top 1 Percent' Pays Half
of State Income Taxes," Legislative Analyst's Office, December 4, 2014, www.lao.ca.gov/LAOEconTax/Article/Detail/7
(accessed 10/14/16).

10. Katherine Barrett, Richard Greene, Michele Mariani, and
Anya Sostek, "The Way We Tax," *Governing*, February 2003,
p. 20.

11. Franchise Tax Board, State of California, "2012 Annual
Report," Table C-8, Corporation Tax, Tax Liability by
Net Income Class, Franchise Tax Board, 2011, www.ftb
.ca.gov/aboutFTB/Tax_Statistics/Reports/2012/2012_C-8
.pdf (accessed 10/14/16). See also Chen, "Who Pays Taxes
in California?"

12. Oliver Libaw, "Where Does Lottery Revenue Go?" ABC
News, August 26, 2001, http://abcnews.go.com/US/story
?id=92595&page=1 (accessed 8/5/16). See also Valerie
Strauss, "Mega Millions: Do Lotteries Really Benefit Public
Schools?" *Washington Post*, March 30, 2012, www.washington
post.com/blogs/answer-sheet/post/mega-millions-do
-lotteries-really-benefit-public-schools/2012/03/30/gIQAb
TUNlS_blog.html (accessed 10/14/16).

13. Barrett et al., "The Way We Tax."

14. Council on State Taxation, "The Best and Worst of State
Tax Administration," December 2013, www.cost.org (accessed 8/1/14).

15. See also Chen, "Who Pays Taxes in California?"

16. California Taxpayers Association, "Cal-Tax: Taxes Are a
Heavy Burden in California," http://digital.library.ucla.edu
/websites/2004_999_003/dynamic/downloads/individual
_download_file_link_1_english_10.pdf (accessed 10/10/16).

17. Tax Foundation, "State-Local Tax Burden Rankings FY
2012," http://taxfoundation.org/article/state-local-tax-burden
-rankings-fy-2012 (accessed 8/3/16).

18. See also Chen, "Who Pays Taxes in California?"

19. Betty T. Yee and the Controller's Council of Economic
Advisors on Tax Reform, "Comprehensive Tax Reform in
California: A Contextual Framework," June 2016, www
.sco.ca.gov/eo_cea_contextual_framework.html (accessed
8/4/16).

20. Carson Bruno, "California: CEOs Rate It Worst U.S. Business Climate for 8 Years Running," March 21, 2014, www
.realclearmarkets.com/articles/2014/03/21/california_ceos
_rate_it_worst_us_business_climate_for_8_years_running
_100963.html (accessed 8/1/14).

21. Institute for Taxation and Economic Policy, "'High Rate'
Income Tax States Are Outperforming No-Tax States,"
February 2012, www.itepnet.org (accessed 7/27/12).

22. Hans Johnson, "Defunding Higher Education" (San Francisco: Public Policy Institute of California, 2012), 4.

23. Phil Oliff, Vincent Palacios, Ingrid Johnson, and Michael
Leachman, "Recent Deep State Higher Education Cuts
May Harm Students and the Economy for Years to Come"
(Washington, DC: Center on Budget and Policy Priorities,
May 2013).

24. California's cap-and-trade program, according to the Center for Climate and Energy Solutions, "uses a market-based
mechanism to lower greenhouse gas emissions. Based on
the amount of emissions covered, California's program
is second in size only to the European Union's Emissions
Trading System. In addition to driving emission cuts in the
ninth largest economy in the world, California's program
will provide critical experience in how an economy-wide
cap-and-trade system can function in the United States. . . .
The cap-and-trade rules came into effect on January 1,
2013, and apply to large electric power plants and large
industrial plants. In 2015 they will extend to fuel distributors (including distributors of heating and transportation
fuels). At that stage, the program will encompass around
360 businesses throughout California and nearly 85 percent
of the state's total greenhouse gas emissions. As of January 1, 2014, California's program is linked to that of Qué-
bec. Under a cap-and-trade system, companies must hold
enough emission allowances to cover their emissions, and
they are free to buy and sell allowances on the open market.
California held its first auction of greenhouse gas allowances
on November 14, 2012." For more information, see www
.c2es.org/us-states-regions/key-legislation/california-cap
-trade (accessed 8/5/16).

25. James D. Savage, "California's Structural Deficit Crisis,"
Public Budgeting and Finance 12, no. 2 (Summer 1992):
82–97.

26. California Forward, "Curing Deficits and Creating Value:
Principles for Improving State Fiscal Decisions," s3.amazon
aws.com/zanran_storage/www.caforward.org/ContentPages
/1903423.pdf (accessed 12/3/12).

27. California Forward, "Curing Deficits and Creating Value."

28. Peter Nicholas and Virginia Ellis, "Budget Signals Narrowed
Ambitions," *Los Angeles Times*, February 18, 2004, p. A1.

Chapter 9

1. Bernard H. Ross and Myron A. Levine, *Urban Politics:
Power in Metropolitan America*, 6th ed. (Itasca, IL: F. E. Pea-
cock, 2001), p. 90.

2. Dale Krane, Platon N. Rigos, and Melvin B. Hill Jr., *Home
Rule in America: A Fifty-State Handbook* (Washington, DC:
CQ Press, 2001).

3. Daniel B. Rodriguez, "State Supremacy, Local Sovereignty:
Reconstructing State/Local Relations under the California
Constitution," in *Constitutional Reform in California: Making
State Government More Effective and Responsive*, ed. Bruce E.
Cain and Roger G. Noll (Berkeley: Institute of Gov-

ernmental Studies Press, University of California, 1995), pp. 401–29; Krane, Rigos, and Hill, *Home Rule in America*; Melvin B. Hill, *State Laws Governing Local Government Structure and Administration* (Washington, DC: U.S. Advisory Commission on Intergovernmental Relations [ACIR], 1993).

4. Ross and Levine, *Urban Politics*, p. 91.

5. John Taylor, "What Happened to Branciforte County?" in California State Association of Counties, *Introduction to California Counties*, www.counties.org/sites/main/files/file-attachments/tab_1_-_intro_to_california_counties.pdf (accessed 10/7/16).

6. County of Los Angeles, *2016–17 Recommended Budget, Volume 1*, April 2016, http://ceo.lacounty.gov/pdf/budget/2016-17/2016-17%20Recommended%20Budget%20Volume%20I%20-%20Online.pdf (accessed 5/24/16).

7. Aaron Claverie and David Downey, "Pechanga to Buy Quarry Site," *The Californian*, November 15, 2012, www.sandiegouniontribune.com/sdut-region-pechanga-to-buy-quarry-site-2012nov15-story.html (accessed 10/7/16).

8. For an excellent study of the 1963 Knox-Nisbet Act, which created LAFCos to impose order and control on the post–World War II explosion of new cities and annexations in California, see Tom Hogen-Esch, "Fragmentation, Fiscal Federalism, and the Ghost of Dillon's Rule: Municipal Incorporation in Southern California, 1950–2010," *California Journal of Politics & Policy* 3, no. 2 (2011): 1–22.

9. Voters in these elections may, of course, choose not to incorporate as a city and run their own show. The prospect of rapid growth and development, for example, scared many of the 57,000 residents of Castro Valley. In November 2002 they voted three to one against incorporation, opting to remain Northern California's largest unincorporated community and governed locally by the Alameda County Board of Supervisors.

10. U.S. Census Bureau, "2007 Census of Governments" (Washington, DC: Government Printing Office, 2007); California Association of Local Agency Formation Commissions, "California Cities by Incorporation Date," www.calafco.org/resources.htm#incorp (accessed 8/4/12).

11. See John H. Knox and Chris Hutchinson, "Municipal Disincorporation in California," *Public Law Journal* 32, no. 4 (Fall 2009), http://californiacityfinance.com/Disincorporation Knox2010.pdf (accessed 8/23/14).

12. Sandra Stokley, "Understanding the Disincorporation Issue," *The Press Enterprise*, September 18, 2013, www.pe.com/articles/-736166--.html (accessed 10/7/16). For more background on Jurupa Valley's tribulations, see Rick Rojas, "For Jurupa Valley, Cityhood Isn't What It Expected," *Los Angeles Times*, December 1, 2013, http://articles.latimes.com/2013/dec/01/local/la-me-jurupa-valley-20131202 (accessed 8/25/14); Sandra Stokley, "'Bitter' Announcement on Disincorporation," *The Press Enterprise*, December 18, 2013, www.pe.com/articles/city-682062-valley-jurupa.html

(accessed 8/21/14); Irvin Dawid, "Puff! There Goes California's Newest City," *Planetizen*, January 18, 2014, www.planetizen.com/node/66954 (accessed 10/7/16).

13. Sandra Stokley, "Jurupa Valley: City Says It Will Survive, After All," *The Press Enterprise*, September 29, 2015, www.pe.com/articles/county-781898-city-jurupa.html (accessed 10/12/15).

14. Zoltan L. Hajnal, Paul G. Lewis, and Hugh Louch, *Municipal Elections in California: Turnout, Timing, and Competition* (San Francisco: Public Policy Institute of California, 2002), pp. 23–24.

15. Ross and Levine, *Urban Politics*, pp. 165–78.

16. Amy Bridges, *Morning Glories: Municipal Reform in the Southwest* (Princeton, NJ: Princeton University Press, 1997).

17. International City/County Management Association (ICMA), "Officials in U.S. Municipalities 2,500 and Over in Population," in *The Municipal Year Book 2003* (Washington, DC: ICMA, 2003), pp. 195–200.

18. Bruce E. Cain, Megan Mullin, and Gillian Peele, "City Caesars? An Examination of Mayoral Power in California," presented at the 2001 annual meeting of the American Political Science Association, August 29–September 2, San Francisco.

19. Hajnal et al., *Municipal Elections in California*, p. 25.

20. Richard DeLeon, *Left Coast City: Progressive Politics in San Francisco, 1957–1991* (Lawrence, KS: University Press of Kansas, 1992). A recent study of over 7,000 U.S. cities found that district systems were better than at-large systems at achieving diverse city councils only in areas where underrepresented groups were highly concentrated geographically and constituted a sizable share of the population. See Jessica Trounstine and Melody Ellis Valdini, "The Context Matters: The Effects of Single-Member Versus At-Large Districts on City Council Diversity," *American Journal of Political Science* 52, no. 3 (July 2008): 554–69.

21. Jean Merl, "Voting Rights Act Leading California Cities to Dump At-Large Elections," *Los Angeles Times*, September 14, 2013, www.latimes.com/local/la-me-local-elections-20130915-story.html#axzz2tt5grBf9 (accessed 8/27/14).

22. Javier Panzar, "It's Official: Latinos Now Outnumber Whites in California," *Los Angeles Times*, July 8, 2015, www.latimes.com/local/california/la-me-census-latinos-20150708-story.html (accessed 5/4/16).

23. Teri Figueroa, "City Poised to Shake Up Voting System," *San Diego Union-Tribune*, June 21, 2016, www.sandiegouniontribune.com/news/2016/jun/21/san-marcos-considering-district-elections/ (accessed 6/30/16).

24. Austin Walsh, "Redwood City Elementary School District Looking at Shifting Election System," *San Mateo Daily Journal*, January 13, 2016, www.smdailyjournal.com/articles/lnews/2016-01-13/redwood-city-elementary-school-district-looking-at-shifting-election-system/1776425156687.html (accessed 6/30/16).

25. Spencer Woodman, "How California Is Solving Its Voting Rights Problem," *VICE Magazine*, May 26, 2016, www

.vice.com/read/how-california-is-solving-its-voting-rights -problem (accessed 6/30/16). For a critical perspective on the CVRA as a boondoggle for lawyers at taxpayers' expense, see Carolyn Schuk, "California Voting Rights Act: $14 Million Legal Bill for Taxpayers," *Santa Clara Weekly*, December 2, 2015, www.santaclaraweekly.com/2015/Issue -49/city-observer.html (accessed 6/30/16).

26. Hajnal et al., *Municipal Elections in California*, p. 26.

27. Matthew A. Melone and George A. Nation III, "'Standing' on Formality: *Hollingsworth v. Perry* and the Efficacy of Direct Democracy in the United States" (unpublished paper), March 2014, p. 289, http://works.bepress.com/matthew _melone/2/ (accessed 5/3/14).

28. Gregory Wallace and Robert Yoon, "Voter Turnout at 20-Year Low in 2016," *CNN*, November 12, 2016, www .cnn.com/2016/11/11/politics/popular-vote-turnout-2016/ (accessed 11/23/16).

29. Mark Baldassare, "California Is Different," Public Policy Institute of California, November 16, 2016, www.ppic .org/main/blog_detail.asp?i=2170 (accessed 11/23/16).

30. Hajnal et al., *Municipal Elections in California*, p. 3.

31. Hajnal et al., *Municipal Elections in California*, p. 64.

32. FairVote, a nonprofit advocacy group that promotes ranked-choice voting and other electoral reforms, provides useful background research and discussion of the pros and cons on its web site at www.fairvote.org.

33. For example, see Richard Briffault, "Home Rule and Local Political Innovation," *Journal of Law and Politics* 22 (Winter 2006): 1–32, which uses San Francisco's ranked-choice voting system as a case study exemplifying the idea that local government can act as "laboratories of democracy."

34. These are the unofficial results reported November 23, 2016. For more background on this measure and the outcome, see the Ballotpedia entry for "Local Measure N – Non-Citizen Voting in School Board Elections," https://ballot pedia.org/San_Francisco,_California,_Non-Citizen_Voting _in_School_Board_Elections_Amendment,_Proposition _N_(November_2016) (accessed 11/23/16).

35. For useful studies of these issues and initiatives, see Kathleen M. Coll, *Remaking Citizenship: Latina Immigrants and New American Politics* (Stanford, CA: Stanford University Press, 2010); Els de Graauw, "The Inclusive City: Public-Private Partnerships and Immigrant Rights in San Francisco," in *Remaking Urban Citizenship: Organizations, Institutions, and the Right to the City*, ed. Michael Peter Smith and Michael McQuarrie (New Brunswick, NJ: Transaction Publishers, 2012), pp. 135–50; Jennifer Ridgley, "Cities of Refuge: Immigration Enforcement, Police, and the Insurgent Genealogies of Citizens in U.S. Sanctuary Cities," *Urban Geography* 29, no. 2 (2008): 53–77; Joaquin Avila, "Political Apartheid in California: Consequences of Excluding a Growing Noncitizen Population," *Latino Policy & Issues Brief*, no. 9 (December 2003); Ron Hayduk, *Democracy for All: Restoring Immigrant Voting Rights in the United States* (New York: Routledge, 2006).

36. Senate Local Government Committee, *What's So Special about Special Districts? A Citizen's Guide to Special Districts in California*, 3rd ed. (Sacramento: California State Senate, 2002), p. 3.

37. California Department of Education, *Fingertip Facts on Education in California*, www.cde.ca.gov/ds/sd/cb/cef fingertipfacts.asp (accessed 8/2/12).

38. Chancellor's Office, California Community Colleges, www .cccco.edu/ (accessed 7/6/16).

39. California State Controller's Office, *Special Districts Annual Report 2009–2010*, p. vi, www.sco.ca.gov/Files-ARD -Local/LocRep/districts_reports_0910_specialdistricts.pdf (accessed 8/2/12).

40. California State Controller's Office, *Special Districts Annual Report 2011–2012*, p. vii, www.sco.ca.gov/Files-ARD-Local /LocRep/1112_special_districts.pdf (accessed 10/7/16).

41. California State Controller's Office, *Special Districts Annual Report 2009–2010*, www.sco.ca.gov/Files-ARD-Local/Loc Rep/districts_reports_0910_specialdistricts.pdf (accessed 12/9/16).

42. See, for example, California Special Districts Association, "What Is a Special District and What Do They Do?" www .csda.net/special-districts/ (accessed 8/22/14).

43. Brian P. Janiskee, "The Problem of Local Government in California," *Nexus* (Spring 2001): 219–33.

44. Gabriel Metcalf, "An Interview with Joe Bodovitz," SPUR report no. 378 (September 1999).

45. For a concise history of the birth, life, and death of California's redevelopment agencies, see Casey Blount et al., "Redevelopment Agencies in California: History, Benefits, Excesses, and Closure," working paper no. EMAD-2014-01, (Washington DC: U.S. Department of Housing and Urban Development, January 2014), www.huduser.gov/portal /publications/Redevelopment_WhitePaper.pdf (accessed 5/28/16).

46. For more background, see David Siders, "Jerry Brown Signs New Post-Redevelopment Bill," *Sacramento Bee*, September 22, 2015, www.sacbee.com/news/politics-government /capitol-alert/article36193152.html (accessed 5/28/16); and Allen Young, "Governor Signs Bill Creating Replacement for Redevelopment Agencies," *Sacramento Business Journal*, September 22, 2015, www.bizjournals.com /sacramento/news/2015/09/22/governor-signs-bill-creating -replacement.html (accessed 10/7/16).

47. Ryan Hagen, "San Bernardino Bankruptcy: Mediation, then Final Confirmation Scheduled," *The Sun*, November 16, 2016, www.sbsun.com/government-and-politics/20161116/san -bernardino-bankruptcy-mediation-then-final-confirmation -scheduled (accessed 11/23/16).

48. Harold Meyerson, "The Revolt of the Cities," *American Prospect*, April 22, 2014, http://prospect.org/article/revolt -cities (accessed 2/15/15).

49. James Nash and Esmé Deprez, "California's Democrats Are Ready for Political War," *Bloomberg Business Week*, November 18, 2016, www.bloomberg.com/news/articles

/2016-11-18/california-s-democrats-are-ready-for-political -war (accessed 11/23/16).

Chapter 10

1. Dan Barry, "Beside a Smoldering Dump, a Refuge of Sorts," *New York Times*, October 21, 2007, www.nytimes.com /2007/10/21/us/21land.html?_r=1 (accessed 7/10/12).

2. David Olson, "Duroville: Slum Mobile Home Park Finally Closes," *Riverside Press-Enterprise*, June 26, 2014, www .pe.com/articles/duroville-678572-park-mobile.html (accessed 8/1/14). See also Phil Willon, "Farmworkers' New Home Is Near Duroville, Yet a World Away," *Los Angeles Times*, March 25, 2013, www.latimes.com/news/local/la-me -duroville-20130325,0,5395710.story (accessed 8/1/14).

3. Paloma Esquivel, "Farmworkers Find a Bumper Crop of Squalor in Coachella Valley Trailer Parks," *Los Angeles Times*, October 5, 2015, www.latimes.com/local/california /la-me-farmworker-trailers-20151006-story.html (accessed 10/17/16).

4. California Budget Project, "School Finance Facts, a Decade of Disinvestment: California Education Spending Nears the Bottom," October 2011, www.cbp.org/pdfs/2011/111012 _Decade_of_Disinvestment_SFF.pdf (accessed 8/10/12). See also National Education Association, "Rankings and Estimates, Rankings of the States 2013 and Estimates of School Statistics 2014," NEA Research (March 2014), www.nea.org/home/rankings-and-estimates-2013-2014 .html (accessed 8/4/14).

5. "Quality Counts 2016: State Report Cards Map," *Education Week*, www.edweek.org/ew/qc/2016/2016-state-report -cards-map.html (accessed 10/17/16).

6. "State Schools Chief Torlakson Calls First Year of CAASPP Results California's Starting Point Toward Goal of Career and College Readiness," California Department of Education News Release, Release #15-69, September 29, 2015, www .cde.ca.gov/nr/ne/yr15/yr15rel69.asp (accessed 8/15/16).

7. Jeffrey Mount, Emma Freeman, and Jay Lund, "Just the Facts: Water Use in California," Public Policy Institute of California, July 2014, www.ppic.org (accessed 9/24/14).

8. Paul Rogers and Nicholas St. Fleur, "California Drought: Database Shows Big Difference Between Water Guzzlers and Sippers," *Mercury News*, February 7, 2014, www .mercurynews.com/2014/02/07/california-drought-database -shows-big-difference-between-water-guzzlers-and-sippers/ (accessed 10/17/16).

9. Matt Weiser, "California Allocates Vastly More Water Than Supplies Allow, Study Shows," *Sacramento Bee*, August 19, 2014, www.sacbee.com/news/local/article2607102.html (accessed 10/17/16).

10. Peter H. Gleick, "Solving California's Water Problems," *Huffington Post*, June 10, 2014, www.huffingtonpost.com /peter-h-gleick/solving-californias-water_b_5479569.html (accessed 9/3/14).

11. Gleick, "Solving California's Water Problems."

12. Caitrin Chappelle, Ellen Hanack, and Jeffrey Mount, "Just the Facts: Reforming California's Groundwater Management," Public Policy Institute of California, June 2014, www .ppic.org (accessed 9/3/14); Chappelle, Hanack, and Mount, "Just the Facts: California's Latest Drought," Public Policy Institute of California, February 2014, www.ppic.org (accessed 9/3/14).

13. "Covered California's Historic First Open Enrollment Finishes with Projections Exceeded," Covered California, April 17, 2014, news.coveredca.com/2014/04/covered -californias-historic-first-open.html (accessed 9/24/14).

14. Dan Walters, "Medi-Cal Expands to Cover 30 Percent of Californians," *Sacramento Bee*, May 20, 2014, http://inland politics.com/blog/2014/05/20/sacbee-dan-walters-medi-cal -expands-cover-30-percent-californians/ (accessed 10/17/16). For a more cautious view, see Laurel Beck and Shannon McConville, "Just the Facts: The Affordable Care Act in California," Public Policy Institute of California, May 2014, www.ppic.org/content/pubs/jtf/JTF_AffordableCareJTF .pdf (accessed 10/17/16).

15. For more information about Medi-Cal, see the many publications of the California HealthCare Foundation at their web site, www.chcf.org (accessed 8/17/12), or the Kaiser Family Foundation, www.kff.org (accessed 8/17/12).

16. California Healthcare Foundation, "California's Uninsured: By the Numbers (Charts)," www.chcf.org/chart-cart /presentations/uninsured (accessed 8/29/14).

17. Bruce E. Cain, "Searching for the Next Pat Brown: California Infrastructure in the Balance," in "California's Future in the Balance," *California Policy Issues Annual*, special edition, (Los Angeles: Edmund G. "Pat" Brown Institute of Public Affairs, November 2001).

18. Region 9, American Society for Civil Engineers, "California's Infrastructure Needs $65 Billion in Major Improvements, State's Infrastructure Earns an Overall Grade of 'C' from Local Civil Engineers," www.ascecareportcard.org (accessed 9/3/14).

19. Gary Stoller, "U.S. Roads, Bridges Are Decaying Despite Stimulus Influx," *USA Today*, July 29, 2013.

20. Daniel C. Vock, "Under Scrutiny, States Trim List of Bad Bridges," *Governing Magazine*, June 4, 2014.

21. C. Piller, "Bay Bridge's Troubled China Connection," *Sacramento Bee*, June 8, 2014.

22. Dan Walters, "California's Hefty Fuel Tax Buys Poor Roads," *Sacramento Bee*, July 2, 2013, www.sacbee.com /news/politics-government/politics-columns-blogs/dan -walters/article2577987.html (accessed 10/20/2016).

23. George Skelton, "On Road Repairs, Legislators Still in the Driveway," *Los Angeles Times*, August 22, 2016.

24. Stuart Leavenworth, "Logjam May Break on Mending Levees," *Sacramento Bee*, April 2, 2004.

25. Stuart Leavenworth, "Defenses Decayed: Neglected Levees Pushed Past Limits," *Sacramento Bee*, March 28, 2004.

26. Sara Lin and William Wan, "Crews Shore Up Levees as Concerns Rise over Upkeep," *Los Angeles Times*, June 10, 2004, pp. B1+.

27. Bettina Boxall, "A Delta Tunnel Project's Lofty Ambitions Have Been Scaled Back," *Los Angeles Times*, April 4, 2016, www.latimes.com/science/la-me-delta-pumps-2016 0404-story.html (accessed 8/31/16).

28. "State Supreme Court Rules in State's Favor on Delta Property Rights," *Sacramento Bee*, July 21, 2016, www.sac bee.com/news/state/california/water-and-drought/delta /article91048507.html (accessed 8/21/16).

29. 500 Nations, "500 Nations Indian Casinos SuperSite," http://500nations.com/Indian_Casinos.asp (accessed 9/24/14).

30. Steven Andrew Light and Kathryn R. L. Rand, *Indian Gaming and Tribal Sovereignty: The Casino Compromise* (Lawrence: University Press of Kansas, 2005), p. 67.

31. Howard Stutz, "Indian Casinos Set New Revenue Record, Topping $28.13 Billion," *Las Vegas Review-Journal*, March 26, 2014, www.reviewjournal.com/business/indian-casinos-set -new-revenue-record-topping-2813-billion (accessed 8/31/14).

32. See *Rincon Band v. Schwarzenegger*, 602 F.3d 1019 (2010).

33. Paul Pringle, "Players at Indian Slots Have No Clue on Payout," *Los Angeles Times*, February 10, 2003, p. B1. See also Fred Dickey, "Going, Going, Gone," *Los Angeles Times*, February 29, 2004, http://articles.latimes.com/2004/feb/29 /magazine/tm-gaming09 (accessed 10/20/16).

Photo Credits

Chapter 1

Pg. 4: AP Photo / Nick Ut. **Pg. 13:** Max Whittaker / Reuters / Newscom.

Chapter 2

Pg. 30: "The Curse of California." The Wasp. August 19. 1882. (Volume 9. Number 316. pp. 520-21.) Call No.: F850 .W18. Courtesy of the Bancroft Library, University of California, Berkeley. **Pg. 36:** AP Photo / Scott Applewhite.

Chapter 3

Pg. 54: Monte Wolverton / Cagle Cartoons / PoliticalCartoons .com. **Pg. 59:** AP Photo / Gregory Bull.

Chapter 4

Pg. 90: J.L. Sousa / Register / ZUMA Press / Newscom. **Pg. 107:** Kevork Djansezian / Getty Images.

Chapter 5

Pg. 125: AP Photo / Rich Pedroncelli. **Pg. 130:** Gary Coronado / Copyright © 2016. Los Angeles Times. Reprinted with Permission.

Chapter 6

Pg. 151: AP Photo / Rich Pedroncelli. **Pg. 161:** Robert Galbraith / Reuters / Newscom.

Chapter 7

Pg. 179: Max Whittaker / Reuters / Newscom. **Pg. 182:** Courtesy of the Supreme Court of California. Photo by Bob Knapik.

Chapter 8

Pg. 205: Ben Margot / AP Photo. **Pg. 210:** David Butow / Redux.

Chapter 9

Pg. 240: Michael Macor / San Francisco Chronicle / Polaris. **Pg. 243:** Terry Schmitt / UPI / Newscom.

Chapter 10

Pg. 259: Jim Wilson / The New York Times / Redux. **Pg. 264:** Monica Almeida / The New York Times / Redux.

Index

Page numbers followed by *b*, *f*, or *t* refer to boxes, tables, and figures respectively. Italic page numbers refer to photos.

access to courts, 178–79
accountability
  judicial, 184
  of legislature, 142
  in special districts, 239
Administrative Office of the Courts (AOC), 191
advisory regional governments, 240–41
affirmative action, 85
Affordable Care Act (ACA), 255–57
age
  of Californians, 5
  and political-party affiliation, 80, 81*f*
  of voters, 108, 109*t*, 110
agencies, state, 156, 168–70, 200
agricultural water use, 252
Aguilar-Curry, Cecilia, *90*
Allen, Ben, *125*
Allen, Doris, 38
Alliance of California Judges, 191
amendments, *See* constitutional amendments
American Independent Party, 79
appellate jurisdiction, 176
Applegate, Doug, 102
appointments, 155–56; *See also* court appointments
  by governor, 41, 154–55, 182
  by state Senate, 137–38
apportionment, 137
Assembly
  campaign fund-raising for, 56, 127
  committees of, 132*t*
  Democrats in, 129
  district size for, 127

leadership of, 129–30
  number of members in, 125
  term for members of, 126, 136
Assembly Bill 2 (AB 2), 242
Assembly Bill 83 (AB 83), 68
Assembly Bill 1725 (AB 1725), 237
Assembly Rules Committee, 130
Association of Bay Area Governments (ABAG), 241
Atkins, Toni, 129, 141
at-large council elections, 233–34
attorney general, 156, 166*b*, 167

Baldassare, Mark, 82, 235
ballot initiatives
  in 2010 election, 96
  in 2012 election, 98–99
  in 2014 election, 99–100
  in 2016 election, 92, 93, 102–3
  campaigns for, 91–93
  in city elections, 234
ballot(s)
  office block, 26, 77
  qualification for, 78, 91–92
  vote-by-mail, 112
Bass, Karen, 141
Bay Bridge project, 156, 259
BayVision 2020, 241
Beall, Jim, 259
Berryhill, Tom, 138–39
bicameralism, 121
big-box shopping centers, 204
bill of rights (California), 22, 24–26

Bill of Rights (United States), 24–25
bills, in legislature, 133–36, 135*f*
Bird, Rose, 184–85
Bismarck, Otto von, 120
Black, Marshall, 38
blanket primary system, 87–89, 126
Board of Equalization, 166, 166*b*, 168
boards, appointments to, 154, 155, 168–70
boards of supervisors, 225
bond funds, 201
bond ratings, 201
Boxer, Barbara, 95–96
bridges, 258–59
Brown, Anne Gust, *161*, 164
Brown, Cheryl, 129
Brown, Edmund G., 67
Brown, Jerry, *151*, *161*
  as attorney general, 167
  budgets of, 12, *13*, 190, 191, 199, 213–15
  campaign contributions for, 58
  court appointments by, 184, 187
  and current state of executive branch, 170
  elections of, 87, 95, 99
  exercise of formal powers by, 155, 157, 159, 160
  governing style of, 153
  gridlock under, 142
  gubernatorial term of, 160–64
  as head of state, 151
  leadership of, 145, 150
  mayoral campaign of, 232
  media coverage of, 67, 119
  policy on climate control, 143
  policy on water use, 253
  recent activities of, 149
  and redevelopment agencies, 242
  on state bureaucracy, 155
Brown, Pat, 160, 264
Brown, Willie, 11, 38, 136, 139
Brown Act, 235, 235*b*
budget, 195–217; *See also* budgetary process
  approving of, 10, 12–13
  governor's, 199
  governor's responsibility for, 157
  impact of, on court system, 190–91
  impact of, on residents, 195–97
  information contained in, 201–12
  initiatives impacting, 212–13
  propositions on, 96, 99–100
  recent, 213–14
  unified, 197, 199
budgetary process, 197–201, 198*b*
  current state of, 214–15
  executive proposal in, 197, 199
  gubernatorial action in, 200

implementation in, 200
  legislative adoption in, 199
  other groups involved in, 200–201
  in recent years, 213–14
Budget Conference Committee, 199
bureaucracy, 168–70
Burns, William J., 29
Burton, John, 131, 162
business climate, 15, 209
business expenditures, 211–12

cabinet, 154–55, 164, 166
Cain, Bruce, 258
Calderon, Ron, 61, 138
Calderon, Tom, 61
California Alliance of Child and Family Services, 49
California Applicants' Attorneys Association, 49
California Chamber of Commerce, 50
California Coastal Cleanup Day, *240*
California Coastal Commission (CCC), 156–57, 239, *240*
California Constitution, 11, 19–43
  of 1849, 21–23
  of 1879, 21, 23–26
  budget requirements in, 200*b*
  current concerns with, 40–41
  and direct democracy, 32–40, 138
  on governor's role, 153, 154, 157
  history of, 21–28
  preamble of, 5
  Progressive movement's influence on, 29–32
  role of, in government, 19–21
California Constitutional Revision Commission, 40–41
California Correctional Peace Officers Association (CCPOA), 56, 58, *59*, 168
California Courts of Appeal, 176, 177*f*, 181
California Democratic Party v. Jones (2000), 88
California dream, 2
California Fair Political Practices Commission, 63, 64
California Forward, 213
California Government Code, 229
California International Relations Foundation, 65
California Labor Federation, 49
California Medical Marijuana Regulation Safety Act (MMRSA), 181
Californians, demographics of, 5–9, 222, 225
California Political Reform Act of 1974 (PRA), 61, 62
California Postsecondary Education Commission, 158
California Public Utilities Commission (CPUC), 156
California State University, 195, 196
California Supreme Court
  ideological change on, 187
  judicial review by, 189
  in judicial system, 177–78
  members of, 178*t*

California Supreme Court (*cont.*)
  on same-sex marriage, 35, 36
  selection of judges for, 181
California Taxpayers Association, 208
California Voting Rights Act of 2001 (CVRA), 233–34
California WaterFix, 261
Caltrans, 156
campaign contributions
  by interest groups, 55–58
  for judicial campaigns, 185–87
  for legislative campaigns, 139
  limits on, 62*t*
  regulating, 61–65
campaign finance reform
  for judicial elections, 185–87
  for legislative elections, 106–7, 113
campaigns
  media attention in, 69, 70*t*
  for ballot initiatives, 91–93
  by governors, 160
  for legislature, 103–7
  and money in politics, 104–6
  public financing of, 14
Cantil-Sakauye, Tani Gorre, *182*, 191
capital gains, 10, 202
Carpenter, Paul, 60–61
caseload, for courts, 189–90
casework, of legislators, 122
Casey, Linda, 63
Central Pacific Railroad, 23
charter cities, 229
charter counties, 224
Chavez, Luis, 56
Chin, Ming W., *182*
Chinese immigrants, 23–24
cities
  charter, 229
  general-law, 229
  incorporation and dissolution of, 229–30
  powers of, 220
citizen lobbyists, 53
citizen's groups, 47
citizenship, 22
Citizens Redistricting Commission, 37, 96, 127
Citizens United v. Federal Elections Commission (2010), 63, 127, 186–87
city government, 229–36
  forms of, 231–36
  functions and responsibilities of, 230
  and incorporation and dissolution of cities, 229–30
  legal framework for, 229
  revenues and expenditures for, 230–31, 231*t*
civil courts
  caseloads of, 176, 190–91
  jurisdiction of, 178

Civil Justice Association of California (CJAC), 185
civil service, 27
Civil Service Act of 1913, 27
clean-money elections, 64
Clinton, Hillary
  2016 presidential race of, 87, 101, 111
  2016 primary race of, 76, 100
  oversight hearings on, 125
closed primary system, 87
Colvin, William Frank, 180–81
commander in chief, 155
Commission on Judicial Appointments, 181, 182
Commission on Judicial Nominees Evaluation, 182
commissions, appointments to, 154, 155, 168–70
committees; *See also specific committees by name*
  conference, 134
  independent expenditure, 63–64, 64*t*
  legislative, 131, 132*t*, 133–34
  political action, 55, 56, 58, 62–63
Common Core Standards, 251–52
community revitalization investment authorities, 242
companies, as interest groups, 47
Compassionate Use Act (CUA), 179, 180
Compromise of 1850, 23
conference committees, 134
conflict-of-interest laws, 64–65
consensus, 13–14
Consolidated and Further Continuing Appropriations Act of 2015, 181
constituency service, 122
constituents, 122
Constitution, *See* California Constitution
constitutional amendments
  from 1960 to present, 27
  to California vs. U.S. Constitution, 24–26
  process for making, 25*f*
  statutes vs., 36
contract lobbyists, 53
contribution limits, 64
controller, 166*b*, 167
corporation tax, 205
corrections and rehabilitation expenditures, 211
Corrigan, Carol A., *182*
council-manager plan, 232
Council of Economic Advisors on Tax Reform, 209
councils of government (COGs), 240–41
counties
  charter, 224
  general-law, 223–24
  locations of, 223*f*
  political-party affiliation in, 83*f*
  powers of, 220
  variability of, 222, 225
county government(s), 222–28
  associations of, 47

functions and responsibilities of, 226, 228
legal framework for, 223–24
and local agency formation commissions, 228
organization of, 224, 226*f*, 227*f*
court appointments
by Jerry Brown, 184, 187
by governors, 182
by Republicans, 183, 184
in U.S. Congress vs. California legislature, 137–38
Court Case Management System, 191
courts; *See also* judiciary; *specific courts*
access to, 178–79
caseload for, 189–90
current state of, 190–91
federalism and, 179–81
jurisdiction of, 178
criminal courts, caseloads of, 176, 191
criminal sentences, 100; *See also* Three Strikes law
Crocker, Charles, 23
Cronin, Tom, 152
Cuéllar, Mariano-Florentino, *182,* 184
cultural diversity
of Californians, 3
of California Supreme Court, 182
of legislature, 140–41
political culture and support for, 85–86
culture, political, 7, 84–87

Davis, Gray
consensus after recall of, 13–14
media coverage of, 67, 69
recall of, 38–39, 94, 161
support of tribal casinos by, 263
death penalty
California Supreme Court cases on, 184–85
propositions on, 86, 92, 98–99, 102–3
Declaration of Rights, 24–26
de Léon, Kevin, *125*
democracy, direct, *See* direct democracy
Democratic Party
demographics of, 80, 81*f*, 82
geographic areas voting for, 7, 82, 83*f*
in legislature, 128–29
in recent elections, 95, 102
strength of, 77–78
supermajority for, 98
voter affiliation with, 79, 80*f*
Department of Finance, 197, 200
Department of Motor Vehicles, 107–8
Desert Mobile Home Park, 249; *See also* Duroville
Deukmejian, George, 67, 182, 184–85
devolution revolution, 221
Dickson, Edward, 30
Dillon, John F., 220

Dillon's Rule, 220, 222
direct democracy, 32–40
in city government, 234–35
criticisms of, 93
defined, 31
initiatives as, 32–37, 91
and judicial review, 188–89
merits of, 39–40
in Progressive movement, 26–27
recalls in, 38–39
referenda in, 37–38
reforms for, 113
Disaster Preparedness and Flood Prevention Act, 261
discretion, judicial, 177
dispensaries, marijuana, 180–81
disposable bags, 11, 37–38, 103
dissolution of cities, 229–30
district council elections, 233–34
districts
determining, 28; *See also* redistricting
enterprise, 237–38
independent, 238
legislators' offices in, 125–26
school and community college, 237
size of, 27, 137
special, 220, 237–39
swing, 89
Draper, Tim, 68
driver's licenses, for undocumented immigrants, 8, 9
drought of 2013-14, 253, 254
Duffy, Laura, *179*
Duro, Harvey, Sr., 249
Duroville, 249, 264, *264*
Dutton, Bob, 142

early voting, 112
economy of California, 3, 209
education funding, 86, 98, 210; *See also* Proposition 30 (2012)
education level
of Californians, 5
and political-party affiliation, 80, 81*f*
of voters, 108, 109*t*
Eighteenth Amendment (U.S.), 24
elected administrative offices, 166–68
elections; *See also* general elections; primary elections
at-large vs. district council, 233–34
clean-money, 64
gubernatorial, 87, 88, 94, 95, 104, 105*t*, 113, 161
judicial, 184–87
legislative, 97–98, 102, 126–29
of past decade, 87–103
presidential, 75–76, 87, 89–91, 94–95, 97, 100–101
retention, 182, 184–85
runoff, 236

electoral politics, 75–116
    in California and United States, 75–76
    campaigning in, 103–7
    in past decade, 87–103
    and political cultures in California, 84–87
    political parties in, 76–83
    and public financing of campaigns, 14
    reforms for, 113
    special interest groups in, 55–58
    and voting, 107–12
elitism, 48–49
employer-sponsored insurance (ESI), 256
English-only education, 102
enterprise districts, 237–38
ethnicity, *See* race and ethnicity
Evans, Jodie, 142
executive branch, 149–72
    in 1849 Constitution, 22
    appointments to, 41
    current state of, 170
    formal powers of governor, 153–60
    governor's influence over, 152–53
    lobbying of, 54–55
    members of, 165*f*
    organizing and managing, 155–57
    recent activities of, 149–50
    and role of governor vs. president, 150–53
    structure of, 164–70
    unique features of, 21
executive budget proposal, 197, 199
expenditures
    for city government, 230–31, 231*t*
    in state budget, 209–12, 211*f*
experience of legislators, 139–41

Facebook, 67
Fahey, Scott, 95
fair housing initiatives, 34
Fair Political Practices Commission, 106
federal funds, 201, 214*b*
federalism, 179–81
filibusters, 138
Fiorina, Carly, 95–96
First Amendment (U.S.), 25
fiscalization of land use, 204
Fitch Ratings, 201
Fix California Challenge, 68
foreign-born residents, 5
formal powers of governor, 152–60
    as commander in chief, 155
    defined, 152
    independent executive actions, 154–55
    informal vs., 153–54, 154*b*
    judicial, 159
    legislative, 158–59

making appointments, 154–55
    over executive branch, 155–57
    preparing budgets, 157
    and public roles of governor, 159–60
    veto, 157–58
Fourteenth Amendment (U.S), 188, 189
Frazier, Jim, 259
fund-raising, in legislative campaigns, 56, 127

Gann, Paul, 34
Garcia, Sergio, 175–76
Gatto, Mike, 68
gender
    political-party affiliation and, 80, 81*f*
    of voters, 110
general elections
    of 2008, 94–95
    of 2010, 95–96
    of 2012, 12–13, 97–99
    of 2014, 99–100
    of 2016, 92, 93, 100–103
    defined, 77
    for legislators, 126–27
general fund, 201
general-law cities, 229
general-law counties, 223–24
general-purpose governments, 219
genetically engineered foods, 99
Genovese, Michael, 152
George, Ronald M., 186
Gerber, Elizabeth, 60
Gerry, Elbridge, 127
gerrymandering, 127
get-out-the-vote (GOTV) operations, 59
Goldwater, Barry, 78
Gonzalez v. Raich (2005), 179, 180
governor, 166*b*
    in budgetary process, 197, 199, 200
    court appointments by, 182
    election of, 41
    executive branch appointees of, 41
    formal powers of, 152–60, 154*b*
    informal powers of, 153, 154, 154*b*
    line-item vetoes by, 136, 153, 157–58, 200
    Progressive era, 31
    recall of, 38–39, 94, 161
    role of U.S. president vs., 150–53
governor's budget, 199
Grant, Edwin, 38
grassroots mobilization, 58–60
Great Recession, local governments since, 242–44
gridlock, 136, 141–43
Grodin, Joseph, 184–85
groundwater management, 253, 255

gubernatorial elections
    of 2010, 95, 105*t*, 161
    of 2014, 87, 88
    campaign contributions in, 113
    recall election of 2003, 94
    spending in, 104, 105*t*
"gut and amend" tactic, 134

Hansen, Steve, 68
Harris, Kamala, 88, 100–102, 149, 167
Hasen, Richard, 234
head of government, 150–51
head of state, 150–51
health and human services (HHS) expenditures, 209, 210
health insurance, 255–58
Healthy Families, 210, 258
Hernandez, Roger, 139
higher education
    budget and cost of, 195–97, 196*f*
    expenditures on, 210, 211
    funding for, 252
high-speed rail project, 149, *161*, 211–12, 262
highways, 258–60
Hill, Elizabeth, 199
Hispanic residents, *See* Latinos
Hollingsworth v. Perry (2013), 36, *36*, 189
home rule, 220, 221*b*
Hopkins, Mark, *30*
Horcher, Paul, 38
household water use, 252–53
housing
    expenditures on, 211–12
    fair housing initiatives, 34
    and population growth, 7
    public housing projects, 249–50

immigrants; *See also* undocumented immigrants
    and 1879 California Constitution, 23–24
    countries of origin for, 8*t*
    political-party affiliation of, 80, 81*f*
    voter turnout for, 109*t*
immigration
    and 1879 Constitution, 23
    court cases involving, 175–76
    population growth due to, 8–9
immunity, sovereign, 263
impeachment, of judges, 187
income inequality, 5, 7
income tax, 202, 208
incorporation of cities, 229–30
incumbents, 56, 127–28
independence, judicial, 184
independent districts, 238
independent executive actions, 155
independent expenditure committees, 63–64, 64*t*

Indian Gambling Regulatory Act (IGRA), 262
Indian gaming
    public policy on, 262–64
    referenda on, 37
    as revenue source, 205
individual health insurance marketplace, 256
informal powers of governor, 153, 154, 154*b*
infrastructure
    defined, 258
    future of, 262
    highways, 258–60
    levees, 261, 262
    and methods of transportation, 260
    and public policy, 258–62
in-house lobbyists, 53
initiatives, 32–37; *See also* ballot initiatives
    budget-impacting, 212–13, 215
    California Constitution on, 19–20
    campaigning for, 160
    contributors to ballot committees for, 35*f*
    ease of passing, 11
    frequency of use for, 21, 33–37, 33*f*
    from grassroots mobilization, 59–60
    and judicial review, 188–89
    and legislature, 143
    process for creating, 14, 32–33
    public opinion on, 39, 40*f*
    reforms related to, 14
    in U.S. Congress vs. California legislature, 138
Innovate Your State, 68
instant runoff voting, 236
insurance commissioner, 166*b*, 168
interest groups, 47–72
    in California politics, 21
    character of, 48–53
    current role of, 70–71
    defined, 47–48
    diversity of, 49–51
    influence on politics of, 3, 47–48, 71
    legislative influence of, 60–65
    media on, 65–70
    proliferation of, 51–53
    public, 53
    strategies used by, 53–60
    and term limits for legislators, 140
Internet media, 67–69, 70*t*
Issa, Darrell, 38–39, 94, 102
issue networks, 131

Jackson, Clay, 60–61
Jarvis, Howard, 34
Johnson, Hiram
    budgetary process of, 197, 199
    in Progressive Party, 31, 32
    and strength of political parties, 105

Johnson, Lyndon, 78
judges, 181–87
    demographics of, 182, 183
    elections for, 184–87
    ideologies of, 182, 184
    qualifications of, 181
    removing, 187
Judicial Campaign Task Force for Impartial Courts, 186
judiciary, 175–93
    in 1849 Constitution, 23
    accountability of, 184
    in budgetary process, 200–201
    contemporary issues in, 187–90
    current state of, 190–91
    discretion of, 177
    function and importance of, 175–76
    independence of, 184
    review of, 188–89
    selection of judges for, 181–87
    structure of, 176–81, 177f
jurisdiction of courts, 178
Jurupa Valley, 229–30

Kashkari, Neel, 87, 99
Katami, Paul, 36
Kelly, Walt, 145
Kleffman v. Vonage Holdings Corp. (2010), 177
Kruger, Leondra R., 182, 184

lack of accountability, for legislature, 142
LAFCos (local agency formation commissions), 228–30
land use, fiscalization of, 204
land-use policy, 226, 227
Latinos, 5
    in city government, 233–34
    and growth of Democratic Party, 78
    political-party affiliation of, 80, 81f, 82
    and Proposition 30, 107
    voter turnout for, 101, 108–11
League of Lincoln-Roosevelt Republican Clubs, 30–31
legal framework
    for city government, 229
    for county government, 223–24
    for government in special districts, 238
    for local government, 220–22
Legislative Analyst's Office, 133, 199
legislative candidates
    campaign contributions for, 55, 55t
    elections for, 126–29
    expenditures by, 104
Legislative Council, 133
legislative elections
    of 2012, 97–98

of 2016, 102
    characteristics of, 126–29
legislative powers of governor, 158–59
legislative recommendations, 159
legislative referenda, 37
legislature, 119–47
    in 1849 Constitution, 22
    amendment of initiatives by, 39
    in budgetary process, 199
    calendar for, 37
    challenges facing, 138–43
    citizens' attitudes about, 119–21
    contacting members of, 124b
    current state of, 144–45
    districts in, 125–26, 27
    elections to, 126–29
    functions of, 121–25
    and the governor, 158–59, 170
    initiative reform bills in, 93
    interest groups' influence on, 60–65
    lobbying of, 54
    organization of, 129–33
    policy-making process of, 133–36
    reforming calendar for, 14
    tax reform acts in, 204, 209
    term limits for members of, 11–12
    U.S. Congress vs., 136–38
levees, 261, 262
Levine, Peter, 97
Liberty Quarry controversy, 228
lieutenant governor, 41, 166b, 167
limited-purpose governments, 219
Lincoln-Roosevelt League, 30–31
Linda (town), 261
line agencies, 164, 166
line-item veto, 136, 153, 157–58, 200
liquor control initiatives, 34
Liu, Goodwin H., 182, 184
lobbying
    of executive branch, 54–55
    expenditures on, 51, 52t
    by interest groups, 49–51
    of legislature, 54
    as strategy, 53–55
    types of, 50t
lobbyists, 54
    citizen, 53
    contract, 53
    employers of, 49–51, 51t
    in-house, 53
    legislative scandals involving, 60–61
    professional, 53
    strategies used by, 53–55
local agency formation commissions (LAFCos), 228–30

local government, 219–47
  at city level, 229–36
  at county level, 222–28
  current conditions for, 242–44
  function and importance of, 219–20
  legal framework for, 220–22
  lobbying by, 50–51
  during Progressive movement, 29–30
  recalls in, 38
  redevelopment agencies in, 241–42
  at regional level, 239–41
  in special districts, 237–39
  unique features of, 21
local television, 65–66
logrolling, 134
Los Angeles City Council, 233
Los Angeles County
  infrastructure problems in, 259–60
  organizational chart for, 227f
  political culture of, 84–87, 84t
  in Progressive era, 29
  voter turnout in, 75
Los Angeles County Superior Court, 185
lower courts, 176
Lucas, Malcolm, 185

majoritarian government, 3–4
management of executive branch, 155–56
marijuana
  legalization of, 86, 103; See also Proposition 64
    (2016)
  medical, 179–81
marriage, same-sex, See same-sex marriage
Matthews, Joe, 24
mayor-council systems, 232
May revise, 197
McCain, John, 94
McClintock, Tom, 112
media, 65–70
  influence on political campaigns, 104
  Internet, 67–69
  newspapers, 66–67
  television, 65–66
media markets, 104
media visibility
  of governor, 150, 159–60
  of political campaigns, 69, 70t
  of U.S. Congress vs. California legislature, 137
Medicaid, 256, 257
Medi-Cal, 209, 210, 255–57
medical marijuana, 179–81
Medical Marijuana Program Act (MMPA),
  179–81
Medicare, 256, 257

Melone, Matthew, 234
Meyerson, Harold, 244
minimum wage, 244
minority rule, 142–43
mobility, of Californians, 5
modified closed primary system, 88
money
  in California politics, 57, 104–6
  clean-money elections, 64
  and influence over legislature, 139
monopoly, 29
Moody's ratings, 201
Motor Voter Act, 107–8
Mountain View Estates, 250
Munger, Charles, 134
municipal incorporation, 229–30
Muratsuchi, Al, 130
Murray, Conrad, 190

Nation, George, III, 234
National Guard, 155
National Voter Registration Act of 1993, 107–8
Neustadt, Richard, 152
New Politics movement, 53
Newsom, Gavin, 167
newspapers, 66–67
Nixon, Richard, 78
noncitizens, political representation of, 236
Non-Partisan Committee of One Hundred, 29
nonpartisanship, 26, 77, 232–33
no party preference, 79, 80, 80f, 81f
Nussbaum, Harris, 90

Oakland, 232
Obama, Barack, 94–97, 101, 151
Obergefell v. Hodges (2015), 188–89
Occupy Movement, 242, 243
O'Connor, Sandra Day, 185
office block ballots, 26, 77
Official California Voter Information Guide, 93
Olin, Spencer, 76–77
O'Neill, Tip, 125
online voter registration, 97, 108
open meetings law, 235
open primary system, 87
Orange County, 101, 224
ordinances, 224
organizing executive branch, 155–56
oversight hearings, 124–25
overtaxation, 208–9
Owen, James, 38

Pacifica, 234
PACs, See political action committees

Palmdale, 233
Pan, Richard, *125*
partisanship, 141
Paul, Mark, 24
People v. Colvin (2009), 180–81
Pérez, John, 141
Perry, Kristin, *36*
Perry v. Brown (2010), 36
Perry v. Schwarzenegger (2010), 36
personal income tax, 202, 208
personal staff, 154, 164
Phelan, James D., 29
Placer County, 226*f*
plea bargaining, 190
pluralism, 48–49
policy-making process, 124–25, 133–36
political action committees (PACs)
    campaign contributions by, 55, 56, 58
    Super PACs, 62–63
political consultants, 104, 105
political cultures, 7, 84–87
political ideology, 84
political parties, 76–83
    campaign spending and strength of, 105
    interest groups and strength of, 51, 52
    political culture and registration in, 84
    Progressive movement's impact on, 76–77
    strength of Democratic and Republican, 77–78
    third parties, 78–79
political party affiliation
    of legislators, 123
    on primary ballots, 89
    of voters, 79–82, 83*f*, 102–6
political protest, 85
Political Reform Act of 1974, 106
Political Reform Division, 106
politics in California, 1–17; *See also* electoral politics
    and the California dream, 2
    content and character of, 4–9
    and government in daily life, 1–2
    interest groups' influence on, 47–48, 71
    money in, 57, 104–6
    Progressive movement's influence on, 29–32
    and recurring government crises, 9–15
popular referenda, 37
population growth, 3, 6–9
    in counties, 222
    and Progressive-era reforms, 32
Populist movement, 29
prescription drug prices, 102
president, role of governor vs., 150–53
presidential elections
    of 2008, 94–95
    of 2012, 97

of 2016, 87, 100–101
    primaries, 75–76, 89–91, 100
president pro tempore, 130–31
primary elections
    of 2012, 96–97
    of 2016, 100
    date of, 89–91
    defined, 77
    for legislative candidates, 126, 128–29
    presidential, 75–76, 89–91, 100
    in Progressive movement, 26
primary systems
    blanket, 87–89, 126
    closed, 87
    controversy over, 87–89
    modified closed, 88
    open, 87
    top-two, 10, 26, 88, 126, 128–29
principal acts, 238
problem-solving justice, 191
Progressive movement, 29–32
    and California Constitution, 21, 26–27
    and county governments, 231–36
    decline of, 31–32
    defined, 21
    ideals of, 19
    in local politics, 29–30
    in state politics, 30–32
    and strength of political parties, 51, 52,
        76–77
progressive policies, support for, 85–86
progressive tax, 202
property taxes; *See also* Proposition 13 (1978)
    initiatives related to, 34–35
    as revenue source, 204, 205
Proposition 1 (2014), 99–100, 160
Proposition 1A (2000), 263
Proposition 2 (2014), 99–100, 160
Proposition 5 (1998), 262–63
Proposition 8 (2008), 36, *36*
    campaigning for, 92
    get-out-the-vote operations on, 59
    judicial review of, 189
    political culture and support for, 85–86
Proposition 11 (2008), 10, 96, 128, 144, 170
Proposition 13 (1978), 34–35
    effects of, 206*b*–207*b*
    impact on budget of, 170, 197, 212
    and infrastructure improvements, 259
    interest groups supporting, 50, 51
    and political culture, 85
    and property tax revenues, 204, 205, *205*
    weakening of legislature by, 143
Proposition 14 (1964), 34

Proposition 14 (2010)
  campaigning for, 160
  influence on legislature of, 170
  and primary system, 88, 126, 144
  redistricting initiatives and impact of, 128
Proposition 15 (1982), 11
Proposition 20 (2010), 96, 128, 144
Proposition 22 (2000), 35–36
Proposition 23 (2010), 160
Proposition 25 (2010), 12, 96, 141, 144–45, 199
Proposition 27 (2010), 96, 144
Proposition 28 (2012)
  effect of, on current legislature, 144–45
  and knowledge/experience of legislators, 140
  and leadership of legislature, 131
  and term limits, 12, 121, 136
Proposition 29 (2000), 37
Proposition 30 (2012), 98
  and 2012 election turnout, 97
  and Jerry Brown's gubernatorial term, 162
  campaigning for, 160
  legislative adoption of budget after, 199
  and minority rule/gridlock, 142, 143, 145
  and personal income tax, 202
  political culture and support for, 86
  tax increases in, 12, 157, 251
Proposition 32 (2012), 69
Proposition 33 (2012), 11
Proposition 34 (2000), 62, 64, 106, 113
Proposition 34 (2012), 92, 98–99
Proposition 36 (2012), 99
Proposition 37 (2012), 99
Proposition 38 (2012), 98
Proposition 47 (2014), 86, 100
Proposition 49 (2002), 212
Proposition 50 (2016), 61, 139
Proposition 53 (2016), 160
Proposition 54 (2016), 134
Proposition 55 (2016), 142, 145, 162, 202
Proposition 58 (2016), 102
Proposition 61 (2016), 102
Proposition 62 (2016), *4*, 86, 102–3
Proposition 63 (1993), 64
Proposition 63 (2016), 103
Proposition 64 (2016), 86, 103, 179, *179*
Proposition 65 (2014), 103
Proposition 66 (2016), *4*, 102–3
Proposition 67 (2016), 103
Proposition 71 (2004), 212
Proposition 73 (1988), 106
Proposition 78 (1993), 64
Proposition 87 (2006), 20, 92
Proposition 94 (2008), 37
Proposition 95 (2008), 37

Proposition 96 (2008), 37
Proposition 97 (2008), 37
Proposition 98 (1988), 143, 212, 251
Proposition 99 (1988), 212
Proposition 103 (1988), 168
Proposition 111 (1990), 212
Proposition 140 (1990)
  and knowledge/experience of legislators, 139–40
  staff reductions related to, 131, 133
  and term limits, 11, 121, 136
  weakening of legislature by, 143
Proposition 187 (1994), 38, 59, 85
Proposition 198 (1996), 88
Proposition 208 (1996), 64, 106
Proposition 209 (1996), 85, 92–93
Proposition 215 (1996), 179
public financing, 14
public housing projects, 249–50
public interest groups, 53
public policy, 249–67
  defined, 251
  on health insurance, 255–58
  on Indian gaming, 262–64
  influence of government via, 249–52
  and infrastructure, 258–62
  timeline for enacting, 264–65
  on water use, 252–55
public roles of governor, 159–60

qualification process
  for initiatives, 91–92
  for third parties, 78
Quimby, John P., Sr., 50, 51

race and ethnicity
  of Californians, 5
  and political-party affiliation, 80, 81*f*
  of voters, 108, 109*t*, 110
racial and ethnic diversity, 5
Rainy Day Budget Stabilization Fund Act, *See* Proposition 2 (2014)
Ralph M. Brown Act of 1953, 235, 235*b*
ranked-choice voting, 236
Reagan, Ronald, 38, 67, 78, 153
recalls, 38–39
  for city officials, 234
  defined, 3
  frequency of use, 38–39
  for governors, 38–39, 94, 161
  for judges, 187
  process for, 38
redevelopment agencies, 241–42
redistricting
  as 2010 election issue, 96
  court cases on, 187–88

redistricting (*cont.*)
  defined, 10
  impact on legislature of, 127–28
  referenda on, 37
  responsibility for, 28
Redlawsk, David, 93
referenda, 37–38
reform governments, 231
Regents of the University of California, 156
regional governments, 239–41
  advisory, 240–41
  function of, 219
  regulatory, 239–40
regional planning, 239
registration method, for qualifying third parties, 78
regressive tax, 204, 208
regulatory commission investigations, 187
regulatory regional governments, 239–40
Rendon, Anthony, 129, *130*, 137
representation
  by legislature, 121–24
  and voter turnout, 235–36
representative government, 234, 235
republican government, 3–4
Republican Party
  demographics for, 80, 81*f*, 82
  geographic areas voting for, 7, 82, 83*f*
  strength of, 77–78
  voter affiliation with, 79, 80*f*
rescissions, 256
retention elections, 182, 184–85
Reuf, Abraham, 29
revenues, 201–7
  for city government, 230–31, 231*t*
  defined, 201
  and Proposition 13, 206*b*–207*b*
  sources of, 202–5, 202*f*
  variation in, 207
Reynoso, Cruz, 184–85
right to vote, 22
Riverside County, 228, 249–50
Robbins, Alan, 60–61
Roberti, David, 38
Romney, Mitt, 96, 97
Roosevelt, Theodore, 29, 31, 32
Roth, Richard, 230
Rowell, Chester, 30
Rumford Fair Housing Act, 34
runoff elections, 236
Ryan, Paul, 137

Sacramento
  legislators time in districts vs., 125, 126
  strong-mayor system in, 232
Sacramento Nonprofit Collective v. Holder (2014), 181

Sacramento River levees, 261
safety net programs, 7
sales tax, 202, 204, 208
same-sex marriage; *See also* Proposition 8 (2008)
  court cases involving, 188–89
  initiatives on, 35–36
Samish, Arthur, 60
Sanchez, Loretta, 89, 100–102
Sanders, Bernie, 76, 100
San Diego
  political culture of, 84–87, 84*t*
  strong-mayor system in, 232
San Francisco
  county government in, 224
  current conditions in, 243
  district council elections in, 233
  home-rule powers in, 221*b*
  political culture of, 84–87, 84*t*
  in Progressive era, 29
  representation of noncitizens in, 236
San Francisco Bay Conservation and Development Commission (BCDC), 240
San Marcos, 234
Schaupp, Charlie, *90*
Scheer, Peter, 235
school and community college districts, 237
schools
  and population growth, 7
  and property tax, 204, *205*
  and public policy, 251–52
Schrag, Peter, 142
Schwarzenegger, Arnold
  ballot initiative campaigning by, 160
  budgets of, 213, 214
  on California dream, 2
  campaign spending by, 104
  candidacy and election of, 39, 94
  governorship of, 161–62
  as head of state, 151
  media coverage of, 67, 69, 119, 159
  popularity of, 153
  redistricting initiative of, 188
  revenue from Indian casinos under, 205
  vetoes by, 157
secession, 228
secretary of state, 166*b*, 167
Senate (state)
  appointments by, 137–38
  campaign fund-raising by candidates for, 56, 127
  committees of, 132*t*
  conflicts of interest at, 65
  Democrats in, 128–29
  district size for, 127
  leadership of, 130–31
  members of, 125

scandals involving, 60–61, 138–39
term for members of, 126, 136
Senate Bill 270 (SB 270), 103
Senate Bill 420 (SB 420), 179
Senate Bill 1253 (SB 1253), 143
Senate Rules Committee, 61
seniority, in legislature, 138
separation of powers, 22
sick leave, 244
65th Assembly District, 127
Skelton, George, 98, 142, 159, 259
South Coast Air Quality Management District (SCAQMD), 239, 240
Southern California Association of Governments (SCAG), 241
Southern Pacific Railroad, 29–31, *30*
Southwest Voter Registration Project, 233–34
sovereign immunity, 263
speaker, 129, 130
special acts, 238
special districts, 220, 237–39
special funds, 201, 215
special interests, 11, 37; *See also* interest groups
spending lobby, 50, 51
staff
legislative, 131–33
personal, of governor, 154, 164
staff advisory agencies, 166
Standard & Poor's ratings, 201
Stanford, Leland, *30*
Starr, Kevin, 23
state agencies, 156, 168–70, 200
State Auditor's Office, 133
state employees, number of, 169*b*
state government
growth of, 52
during Progressive movement, 30–32
recalls in, 38
state lottery, 205
State of the State, 159
statutes, 36
Stier, Sandra, 36
Strauss v. Horton (2009), 36
strong-mayor systems, 232
student organizations, 47
superagencies, 154–55
superintendent of public instruction, 166*b*, 168
superior courts, 176
caseloads for, 189–90
in judicial system, 176, 177*f*
selection of judges for, 182
supermajority, 12–13
in legislature, 98
for passing budgets, 157
reforms involving, 14

Super PACs, 62–63
Sustainable Groundwater Management Act (SGMA), 255
swing district, 89

tax administration agencies, 41
taxation, level of, 208–9
taxes
raising, 12–14, 199
revenue from, 202, 204, 205, 208
and state budgets, 10–11
tax-increment financing (TIF), 241
tax rates, lowering, 15
tax structure, 14
tax system, 207–8
Taylor, Mac, 199
Taylor, Zachary, 22
Tea Party, 14
television, 65–66
term limits; *See also* Proposition 28 (2012); Proposition 140 (1990)
in California Constitution, 41
and knowledge/experience of legislators, 139–41
and proliferation of interest groups, 52–53
propositions involving, 11–12, 121, 136
for U.S. Congress vs. California legislature, 136
Tesla, *210*
third house, 48, 52–53
third parties, 78–79
Three Strikes law, 86, 99, 189
top-two primary
Constitutional revisions related to, 27
defined, 10
impact on legislature of, 126, 128–29
other primary systems vs., 87–89
Torlakson, Tom, 251–52
trade associations, 47, 50
transportation
expenditures on, 211–12
methods of, 259, 260
population growth and, 7
treasurer, 166*b*, 168
tribal casinos, 263
TRICARE, 257
Trump, Donald
in 2016 elections, 87, 100–101
anti-immigrant campaign of, 111
health insurance reform under, 255–56
and local governments, 244
trustee style of representation, 122
Twitter, 67
two-thirds vote, 10, 12–13, 142

undocumented immigrants, 8–9; *See also* Proposition 187 (1994)
court cases involving, 175–76
driver's licenses for, 8, 9

undocumented immigrants (*cont.*)
    initiatives involving, 85
    states with top populations of, 9*t*
unified budget, 197, 199
uninsured residents, 257–58
Union Pacific Railroad, 23
unions
    as interest groups, 47, 56, 58
    Internet media campaigns by, 69
University of California, 156, 195, 196
Unruh, Jesse, 56, 121, 139
urban-based political movement, 243–44
U.S. Congress
    2010 elections to, 95–96
    2012 elections to, 97–98
    2016 elections to, 101–2
    California legislature vs., 136–38
    power of, 120–21
U.S. Constitution, 24–26
U.S. Court of Appeals, Ninth Circuit, 181,
    263
user fees, 237–38

Ventura County, 89
vetoes
    defined, 128
    line-item, 136, 153, 157–58, 200
Vidak, James, 56
vote
    early, 112
    by mail, 111–12
    right to, 22
    two-thirds, 10, 12–13, 142
voter registration, 107–8

voters
    demographics of, 108–12
    political party affiliations of, 79–82, 83*f*
voter turnout, 3
    in 2012 election, 97
    in 2016 election, 101, 109, 111
    election-specific differences in, 75–76, 111*f*
    for local elections, 235–36
    and political culture, 85
    in primary elections, 90–91

Walters, Dan, 13, 259
Warren, Earl, 60
water bond, 99–100
water policy, 252–55, 265
water supply, 253
water use, 252, 254
weak political parties
    and campaign spending, 105
    Progressive movement's influence on, 76–77
    and proliferation of interest groups, 51, 52
Werdegar, Kathyrn M., *182*, 184
Whitman, Meg, 95, 161
Wikibills web site, 68
Wilson, Pete, 38, 58, 67, 262
winner-take-all systems, 76, 126
Workingmen's Party, 23–24
Wright, Rod, 61, 138

Yee, Betty, 209
Yee, Leland, 61, 75, 138
Yuba River levee, 261

Zarrillo, Jeffrey, *36*